RAND ARROYO CENTER

TURKEY'S NATIONALIST COURSE

Implications for the U.S.-Turkish Strategic Partnership and the U.S. Army

Stephen J. Flanagan, F. Stephen Larrabee,
Anika Binnendijk, Katherine Costello,
Shira Efron, James Hoobler,
Magdalena Kirchner, Jeffrey Martini,
Alireza Nader, Peter A. Wilson

Prepared for the United States Army

Approved for public release; distribution unlimited

For more information on this publication, visit www.rand.org/t/RR2589

Library of Congress Cataloging-in-Publication Data is available for this publication.
ISBN: 978-1-9774-0141-0

Cover: Rouhani, Putin, and Erdogan: Tolga Bozoglu/AP.
Erdogan Stoltenberg: AP. Istanbul: Kivanc Turkalp/Getty Images/iStockphoto.

Cover design by Rick Penn-Kraus

Support RAND
Make a tax-deductible charitable contribution at
www.rand.org/giving/contribute

www.rand.org

Preface

This report documents research and analysis conducted as part of a project entitled *Turkey's Volatile Dynamics—Implications for the U.S.-Turkish Strategic Partnership and the U.S. Army*, sponsored by the Office of the Deputy Chief of Staff, G-3/5/7, U.S. Army. The purpose of the project was to analyze trends in Turkish internal, foreign, and defense policies and assess their implications for U.S. defense strategy and force planning.

This research was conducted within RAND Arroyo Center's Strategy, Doctrine, and Resources Program. RAND Arroyo Center, part of the RAND Corporation, is a federally funded research and development center (FFRDC) sponsored by the United States Army.

RAND operates under a "Federal-Wide Assurance" (FWA00003425) and complies with the *Code of Federal Regulations for the Protection of Human Subjects Under United States Law* (45 CFR 46), also known as "the Common Rule," as well as with the implementation guidance set forth in U.S. Department of Defense (DoD) Instruction 3216.02. As applicable, this compliance includes reviews and approvals by RAND's Institutional Review Board (the Human Subjects Protection Committee) and by the U.S. Army. The views of sources utilized in this study are solely their own and do not represent the official policy or position of DoD or the U.S. Government.

Contents

Figures, Tables, and Boxes

Figures

Tables

Boxes

Summary

A strategic partnership with the Republic of Turkey has been a central element of U.S. strategy in the Mediterranean region and the Middle East for more than six decades. Turkey remains a powerful North Atlantic Treaty Organization (NATO) ally at the nexus of three regions that have become increasingly important to U.S. security since the end of the Cold War: the Levant, the wider Middle East and Persian Gulf, and the Caucasus and Central Asia. In all three areas, Turkey is seeking to play a larger role and has significant capacity to influence events. It controls (in accordance with international conventions) the straits of the Bosporus and the Dardanelles, which link the Black Sea with the Mediterranean Sea. The United States and Turkey have long cooperated on a range of global issues, including countering terrorism and violent extremism, preventing the proliferation of weapons of mass destruction, enhancing energy security, and promoting prosperity and development.

Turkey's Nationalist Course

Strains in a Longtime Partnership

The partnership between the United States and Turkey has become strained in recent years because U.S. and Turkish interests and assessments of various challenges are not as aligned as they once were, and significant disagreements have emerged on policies to address several of these challenges. Differences over dealing with Syria and the Kurdish question, tensions concerning Turkey's relations with its neighbors, an escalating terrorism threat, and U.S. concerns about the authoritarian drift in Turkish politics under President Recep Tayyip Erdoğan have combined to constrain cooperation and undermine mutual confidence. Compounding tensions are several thorny bilateral problems, including

- the continued presence in the United States of Fethullah Gülen, a self-exiled leader of a Sufi Islamic movement that Turkish authorities contend is a terrorist organization that masterminded a failed July 2016 military coup d'état
- Ankara's purchase of Russian-made S-400 air and missile defense systems

- Turkey's arrests of American and European nationals on questionable terrorism charges
- the U.S. trial of a gold trader accused of orchestrating a large money-laundering scheme designed to circumvent sanctions against Iran in coordination with senior officials in the Turkish government.

Anti-American sentiment in Turkey has deepened, as have doubts in Turkey about the reliability of the U.S. commitment to Turkey's stability and security—both exacerbated by inflammatory statements by Erdoğan and other Turkish leaders.

Domestic Polarization, Nationalism, and Authoritarian Rule

Turkey remains a highly polarized country as President Erdoğan and the governing Justice and Development Party (Adalet ve Kalkınma Partisi [AKP]) move to implement fundamental changes in governance and society, which have accelerated since the failed July 2016 coup. In the aftermath of the coup attempt, and through the state of emergency invoked shortly thereafter and extended multiple times through July 2018, the AKP government accelerated its massive crackdown and systematic purges of alleged members of the Gülenists movement from government institutions, closed civil society outlets, and seized assets of companies linked to the movement and its followers. As constitutional changes narrowly approved in a 2017 referendum are being fully realized through decrees in the wake of the presidential and parliamentary elections on June 24, 2018, those changes are consolidating the establishment of an authoritarian state with political power centralized in a strong executive president and the dominant party. Erdoğan has embraced ethnic Turkish nationalism as his guiding ideology while taking steps to enlarge the role of religion in public life and to marginalize his opponents and a large segment of the population that still supports the long-standing parliamentary system and secular order. Erdoğan will be president through at least 2023 and is eligible for a third, five-year term thereafter, having already led the country since 2003. The main opposition parties have been marginalized by the government's domination of the media and legal challenges, and parliamentary oversight of the presidential administration is even more limited under the new system. Nevertheless, the three leading opposition parties garnered 46 percent of the 2018 presidential vote and 44 percent of the parliamentary vote, thereby forcing the AKP to maintain a tacit coalition with its ultranationalist Nationalist Movement Party (Milliyetçi Hareket Partisi [MHP]) to advance key legislation. These results, as well as the 2019 election of Republican People's Party (Cumhuriyet Halk Partisi) candidates to be mayors in six of Turkey's ten largest cities—particularly the decisive victory of Ekrem İmamoğlu in Istanbul—illustrate that Erdoğan and the AKP are not invincible.

Turkey's internal security situation will remain fraught in the absence of a sustained effort to address the concerns of the Kurds and other national minorities and the continuation of harsher measures to combat the continuing transnational insurgency being waged by the Kurdistan Workers Party (Partiya Karkerên Kurdistanê [PKK]) and other violent Kurdish groups. There is little prospect that Erdoğan will revive the peace talks with the PKK, pursued between 2008 and 2015, in the foreseeable future.

Foreign and Defense Policy: From "Zero Problems" to "Precious Loneliness"

The AKP has moved away from the strategy of its first years in power, which gave priority to European integration and leveraging Turkey's economic strength and Ottoman heritage to build good relations with all its neighbors, a policy that was dubbed "zero problems." Erdoğan is now pursuing a more assertive balancing strategy in foreign affairs, seeking to leave open options that will best advance his consolidation of power and Turkish national interests. Erdoğan is more focused on building the country's stature in the Islamic world and forging new ties with Russia and China. He has not given up on the West but appears to hope that his balancing efforts will elicit favorable policy changes. Turkish leaders have tried to forge wary partnerships with historic rivals Russia and Iran, particularly as these two governments gained control over the end game in the Syrian civil war since 2015. Differences with Iraq, many Gulf states, and Egypt over the AKP's ties to the Muslim Brotherhood, policies in the wake of the Arab Spring, and stance on Qatar have diminished Turkey's stature in the Arab world. As policy differences with nearly all of Turkey's neighbors, the United States, and other allies have mounted, Turkish leaders have argued that the country must be more self-reliant in protecting its interests and accept a "precious loneliness" in taking principled stands to defend its values and national interests.

Over the next five to ten years, Erdoğan, with the urgings of his MHP partners, is likely to pursue assertive foreign and defense policies that are contrary, in varying degrees, to the interests of the United States and other NATO allies and that undermine long-standing aspects of defense and security cooperation. If a viable coalition were to emerge in Turkey during this period and dislodge Erdoğan and the AKP from power after 2023, one could expect a more conciliatory approach, as the three leading opposition parties in the 2018 elections ran on platforms calling for revitalizing relations with NATO allies and the European Union (EU). Nevertheless, deep public suspicion of the United States and Europe would constrain the pace and scope of a rapprochement. This situation warrants a considered reassessment of U.S. and European strategy toward Turkey, preparations for disruptive developments in some aspects of relations, and initiatives that could maintain cooperation on abiding mutual interests over the next decade and help restore long-standing ties if these negative trends are reversed.

Impact on the Turkish Armed Forces

Erdoğan and the AKP have systematically strengthened civilian authority over the military since 2008 by gaining a decisive hand in the promotion and selection process, overseeing purges of military personnel, and increasing legal authorities for command and control. Reforms implemented since the 2016 coup attempt and constitutional changes approved in 2017 further reinforced presidential and civilian control over the Turkish Armed Forces (Türk Silahlı Kuvvetleri [TSK]), muddied the chain of command, increased interservice rivalry, and led to a politicization of the officer corps. Parliamentary oversight of the military budget and posture has diminished under the constitutional changes. Recent leadership changes make clear that Erdoğan wants the armed forces to focus on succeeding at operations in Syria, combating terrorism, and rooting out Gülenists, with priority being given to the Turkish Land Forces and the Gendarmerie.

The TSK leadership ranks have been significantly reduced by post-coup purges. In particular, 46 percent of general and flag officers in the Army, Navy, and Air Force have either been cashiered or involuntarily retired. As of December 2018, 15,154 members of the TSK, including 7,595 officers (about 23 percent of early 2016 totals), had been dismissed, and another 1,386 personnel were purged by April 2019. The government has plans to recruit about 43,000 new personnel to fill its depleted ranks and reform all levels of professional military education, with the goals of breaking down the TSK's insular culture as guardians of secularism and ensuring that more-diverse recruits are being enlisted. The purges and military reforms have also adversely affected the TSK's strategic and tactical capacity, readiness, and morale. The purges have been most damaging to the Air Force and may slow defense transformation efforts. Mid-level officers are reported to be extremely frustrated with the military leadership and concerned about being removed in the continuing post-coup purges. This discontent could even lead to another coup attempt at some point, and Erdoğan appears to take the threat seriously. Public trust in the military, previously seen as the guardian of order and the secular state, eroded but has been restored somewhat following the success of the TSK's operations in 2018 against Kurdish forces in Syria's Afrin province.

Relations with Neighbors

The Levant and the Middle East: Problems in All Directions

As Turkish leaders survey the country's regional environment, wherever they look, they are faced with upheaval and changes that complicate their strategic choices. Within Turkey's own backyard, the situation looks particularly gloomy.

Despite lingering mutual suspicions and deep religious and political differences, Turkey and Iran have pursued a pragmatic cooperation over the past 20 years when certain interests converge. The Syrian war and growing Iranian influence in Iraq have strained relations between Tehran and Ankara, but shared concerns about the possible development of independent Kurdish states in Syria and Iraq have led to wary cooperation. Mutual interests in economic cooperation, energy trade, and border security, as well as limiting the influence of extra-regional powers in their neighborhood constitute a base for future cooperation that has been institutionalized for several years up to the cabinet level. The two countries have exchanged visits by top military officials and have spoken of jointly fighting regional threats. Turkish-Iranian ties will, however, remain tense well into the future. Sectarian sentiments continue to influence political practice, and no mechanism to overcome this has been established so far.

Turkey's relations with the Iraqi central government are likely to remain tense. While Baghdad and Ankara came together in 2017 to thwart the independence referendum by the Kurdistan Regional Government (KRG), they remain wary of each other's long-term intentions. In addition, there remains potential for conflict over the enduring Turkish military presence near Mosul, the role of the Shi'a Popular Mobilization Units, and the PKK presence in Sinjar in northwestern Iraq. Turkey's leverage over the KRG has increased since the fall of Kirkuk, but it remains to be seen whether this will bolster their cooperation in countering the PKK in the post–Masoud Barzani era. Washington expects Turkish policy toward both Iran and Iraq to often be at odds with U.S. interests.

The Arab states to Turkey's south have long looked to Ankara as a highly capable Sunni partner in blunting the Iranian challenge to the regional order, a desire that has become more acute with the growth of Iranian influence in Iraq and Syria. Ankara's more-pragmatic policies toward Iran and Syria have disappointed the Arab world, but maintaining Turkey as a key partner remains a priority among Arab states. The AKP's embrace of the forces of change, particularly support for the Muslim Brotherhood, disrupted Turkey's relationships with Egypt and the United Arab Emirates. In contrast, Qatar and Turkey are building a genuine strategic partnership, based on a deepening economic and military cooperation and a shared vision that political Islam play a crucial role in the region's development. The complex relationships between Turkey and the Arab states could improve or deteriorate under various scenarios but will constrain what can be achieved in advancing U.S. foreign policy and security interests.

The overarching challenge for the United States is that the differing priorities of Turkey and Arab states are likely to continue to create obstacles for Washington in gaining partner support for regional initiatives, as happened in the efforts to assemble the coalition to counter the Islamic State of Iraq and Syria (ISIS). The second major challenge for the United States stemming from intraregional competition is the impact of Turkish involvement in the rift among the Gulf Cooperation Council (GCC) states (Bahrain, Kuwait, Oman, Qatar, Saudi Arabia, and the United Arab Emirates) concerning Qatar. On the one hand, this involvement might have been beneficial insofar as it helped deter the Saudi-led bloc from taking military action against its neighbor. But on the other hand, Turkey's involvement has prolonged the dispute among GCC and other states because its support for Doha puts Qatar on closer parity with its GCC challengers—allowing Doha to avoid concessions that might otherwise resolve the dispute. U.S. leaders have been anxious to resolve these issues in order to restore unity among Gulf Arab states and present a united front against Iran. Erdoğan is likely to remain assertive in Arab Gulf affairs over the next five years.

Israeli-Turkish relations have always been linked to developments on the Arab-Israeli and Israeli-Palestinian fronts. After a long period of close economic, diplomatic, and military ties, bilateral relations between Israel and Turkey soured during the 2000s. The second Palestinian uprising, the AKP's more confrontational stance toward Israel, the Second Lebanon War, and clashes over Israel's Gaza policies exacerbated tensions, culminating in a six-year rift between the countries from 2011 to 2016. Their partial reconciliation in mid-2016 encouraged stakeholders in each country eager to resume aspects of collaboration, but little progress has been made, and the prospects for the next few years remain dim. Improved Israeli-Turkish relations face formidable obstacles, primarily deep mistrust between the current political leadership in each country and fundamental divergences on the Palestinian issue and the status of Jerusalem. Palestinians celebrated Erdoğan's 2018 reelection, rightly anticipating continued Turkish activism on their behalf. Israel's efforts to expand energy and defense cooperation with Cyprus and Greece as a counterweight to Turkey and support for Kurdish independence reflect further differences with Ankara. Given this volatility, Washington could use its leverage to encourage Israel and Turkey to insulate pragmatic cooperation on mutual interests from ideological differences; encourage both countries to avoid escalatory rhetoric on sensitive issues; and enlist both countries' complementary efforts to stabilize the Middle East in the aftermath of the war in Syria, counter Iran's regional aspirations, and combat terrorism. Israel's new association with NATO is another avenue for U.S.-Turkish-Israeli cooperation that is in Washington's interest and hinges on continued Turkish consent. The United States has geostrategic and economic interests in realizing an Israeli-Cypriot-Greek gas deal and in avoiding a conflict among allies in the Eastern Mediterranean. Turkey's ties with Hamas could, at some point, be helpful to the United States and its other allies in the region in advancing an Israeli-Palestinian peace process.

Russia, the Caucasus, and Central Asia

Turkish-Russian relations historically have been defined by competition for influence and power across the Black Sea region. A circumspect warming in relations since the end of the Cold War has been driven in large measure by mutual interests in expanded economic and energy ties. Today, the two governments claim to be pursuing a strategic partnership but are pulled between elements of cooperation and potential for conflict.

Examination of five key elements of the Turkish-Russian relationship—economic and energy ties, Western institutions, authoritarian domestic politics, Black Sea issues, and Middle East ambitions—indicates that, although some convergent interests may continue to draw the two countries together in the coming years, there are also significant points of friction and divergent interests. Deepening energy and economic ties, including a new TurkStream gas pipeline under the Black Sea; close personal ties between Erdoğan and Russian President Vladimir Putin; recent bilateral diplomatic and military coordination in Syria; and Turkey's purchase of Russian S-400 air and missile defense systems represent tangible manifestations of improved relations. The surge in Russian ambitions and relative military power in the Black Sea region, enduring differences between each country's policies and goals in the Middle East (especially in Syria), and the tension between Turkey's enduring interest in retaining a NATO security guarantee and Russia's efforts to lure Ankara away from the Alliance and diminish its unity present sizable impediments to a deep bilateral partnership.

The crisis of 2015–2016, which came after Turkey shot down a Russian bomber that violated Turkish airspace, demonstrated that economic and leadership ties, while currently strong, have failed to prevent volatile shifts in bilateral relations. Whether Russia and Turkey are able to reach a new modus vivendi or will continue to muddle through in a mix of cooperation and conflict by managing important differences will likely depend on Russia's stance on Kurdish autonomy and military presence in Syria and on Turkish willingness to acquiesce to expanding Russian ambitions and accept growing energy dependence. Even if Turkey is willing to accommodate Russia on many issues, unintended conflict in any one of the five areas could well derail a long-term rapprochement. Nevertheless, U.S. policymakers should expect Turkey to remain an unpredictable ally that is more willing to work with Russia at cross purposes to NATO when its shifting national interests dictate.

Turkey's aspirations to become a more influential force in the Caucasus and Central Asia and a hub for regional energy and trade routes are likely to continue to be constrained by resource limitations, domestic turmoil, and other priorities. Turkey remains committed to advancing integration in the South Caucasus through its cooperation with Georgia and Azerbaijan to strengthen and protect the east-west economic and energy transit corridor and limited bilateral and trilateral security cooperation. Turkey's efforts help bolster the sovereignty and independence of these states, thereby supporting U.S. and European interests in the region. Ankara's appeal to Georgia and Azerbaijan as a bridge to Euro-Atlantic political and security frameworks has, however, been diminished by Turkey's strained ties with the EU and its NATO allies, as well as its cooperation with Russia. Tbilisi and Baku still look to Ankara as a partial counterbalance to Moscow's power in the region, but Ankara will continue to approach regional security with some circumspection, aware that it cannot afford to be too confrontational with its powerful neighbor.

Ankara's early 1990s vision of reviving cultural and economic links among Turkic peoples in Central Asia and the Caspian to form a Turkic Union that would enhance regional development and expand Turkey's influence has not been realized. Nevertheless, the Turkish government and various nongovernmental organizations have provided considerable development and educational assistance to Central Asian countries, and commercial trade, investment, and construction projects have grown considerably over the past decade. Turkey has also supported modest bilateral security and defense cooperation efforts with several Central Asian governments, as well as NATO Partnership for Peace exercises in Central Asia and training for regional forces. Governments in the region value Turkey's engagement with them but also have to balance relations with Moscow, which retains and has not hesitated to exercise significant leverage over those governments and their relations with Turkey. A moderately increased level of Turkish outreach to the region is likely in the coming years, characterized by constrained resources, limited commitment, and uneven appetite for new engagement.

Turkey's Ties with Europe, the European Union, and NATO

Turkey's relations with the EU have reached an acrimonious, 30-year low point that threatens the collapse of membership accession talks, stalled since 2005 and effectively frozen since the April 2017 constitutional referendum. How successful Turkey and the EU are at managing differences on migration, travel, counterterrorism policies, NATO and EU cooperation, and Cyprus will determine the longevity of the accession process and the development of alternative futures for the relationship. The two sides have sparred over implementation of the 2012 deal in which Turkey agreed to slow the number of refugees coming from Syria and provide temporary relief to them in return for EU humanitarian assistance and visa liberalization for Turkish citizens. Turkey has taken a strident stance since the failed July 2016 coup, as Europe's concerns about Erdoğan's authoritarian rule, restrictions on civil and political rights, and various foreign policy moves have deepened. Although Ankara made gestures in early 2018 that suggest that it may be seeking a reset of relations in the midst of its of growing isolation, a broad reconciliation is improbable. EU-Turkish relations are likely to become even more transactional and focused narrowly on free trade, immigration, and counterterrorism, but even this model will be hard to establish in the near future given lingering differences on these issues.

If the EU refuses to implement visa liberalization for Turkish citizens because Turkey fails to meet EU benchmarks on domestic reforms, Erdoğan may threaten to break off accession talks, but he is unlikely to risk the domestic downsides of pursuing this course. Concern about the authoritarian developments in Turkey could push a majority of EU member governments to suspend the talks as well. A full collapse of Turkey's EU membership negotiations would have profound economic and political costs to both sides and would be detrimental to U.S. interests. It would mark a significant failure of the EU's ability to bolster policy reforms in third countries (i.e., non-EU countries) as a means of projecting stability and would make it both more urgent and more difficult for Washington to engage Turkey directly on several sensitive issues.

The enduring stalemate on Cyprus between the Greek and Turkish communities (which have suspended United Nations negotiations since July 2017) and Ankara's hard line on security issues, both of which are likely to persist, make resolution of the Cyprus dispute elusive for the foreseeable future. In addition, Turkey's disputes with Cyprus and Greece over maritime and energy development claims in the Aegean and Eastern Mediterranean regions, as well as Turkey's concern about its neighbors' growing military cooperation with Israel, are adding to regional tensions. Given this context,

Ankara is unlikely to support further institutionalization of EU-NATO cooperation, and Turkish leaders are also less inclined to join EU missions as a way of anchoring their country to the West. These positions will not only reduce Ankara's engagement with the EU but also continue to drag bilateral conflicts into NATO, thus undermining Alliance cohesion.

At the same time, there are many elements of continuity in Turkey's engagement in NATO. For example, the Alliance still plays a central role in Turkey's national security strategy and plans for defense against high-intensity threats. NATO membership provides Turkey a seat at the North Atlantic Council, where key policy decisions on Euro-Atlantic security are developed. Turkey remains actively engaged in other Alliance political institutions, the integrated military structure, and exercise programs and continues to make substantial contributions to current operations, standing forces, and the NATO Response Force. Turkey hosts forces from other NATO countries at its İncirlik and Konya air bases, forces from the NATO Allied Land Command in Izmir, and the U.S. early-warning radar in Kürecik that is part of the European Phased Adaptive Approach to missile defense. When regional tensions have risen in recent years, Turkey has promptly turned to the United States and other NATO allies for military support.

However, doubts among the Turkish public and political elite about the reliability of NATO's collective defense commitment and the Alliance's relevance in addressing the country's most-immediate security threats—countering terrorism and separatism at home and in Turkey's neighborhood—have grown in recent years. Most Turks also see the policies that the United States and other allies have been pursuing in Syria as inimical to Turkey's security. The *Eurasian vision*—that is, disengaging from NATO and pursuing deeper cooperation with Russia, Iran, and other major powers to address Turkey's security challenges more effectively—has gained resonance in political and academic circles, particularly following the U.S. decision in May 2017 to provide heavy weapons to Syria's People's Protection Units (Yekîneyên Parastina Gel [YPG]). Advocates of this reorientation have reportedly gained bureaucratic influence as they have assumed some positions in the foreign ministry and armed forces vacated by Atlanticists purged in the wake of the coup.

Moscow has been adept at exploiting and amplifying these fissures within Turkey and among allies—including through an active media influence campaign—to cast itself as a more reliable political and security partner. At the same time, Moscow has made clear to Ankara that its military buildup in the Black Sea region and upper hand in the Syrian conflict give it considerable leverage. Lingering unease in Ankara about Moscow's long-term intentions and growing military capabilities have limited the effectiveness of this appeal. Turkey has reacted to geopolitical realities and the duality of Russian strategy by trying to balance relations with its longtime allies and newfound partner.

Allied governments have also been increasingly dismayed by some of Ankara's confrontational rhetoric and periodic brinkmanship, as well as the fact that it regularly requires top-level political intervention with President Erdoğan to gain Ankara's assent to important NATO operational and policy decisions. The acrimony between Berlin and Ankara led Germany to redeploy its military personnel and aircraft supporting the counter-ISIS coalition from İncirlik to Jordan in 2017, when the Turks barred German lawmakers for the second time from visiting their forces. The United States and other allies are not without significant leverage over Ankara and should not be reluctant to use it in seeking to manage policy differences. Turkish leaders know that NATO remains the most reliable framework for maintaining their security. U.S. and allied leaders will need strategic patience and steady engagement to manage those differences as Turks seek to sort out their internal political differences and cope with their deteriorating security situation. This engagement could, over time, lead future Turkish governments to pursue more-convergent foreign and security policies. Given Turkey's geostrategic position and regional influence, it is far better to have Turkey inside NATO than actively seeking to thwart allied efforts from the outside.

Implications for U.S. Foreign Policy, Defense Planning, and the U.S. Army

Table S.1 provides a summary of our assessment of where Turkish interests are convergent, divergent, or in conflict with those of its key neighbors, the United States, and other allies. Turkey, the United States, and other NATO allies still have many convergent strategic interests, including countering terrorism, promoting peace in the Middle East, constraining the growth of Russian and Iranian power, and expanding energy transit corridors. However, differences over the policies to best advance these interests have become more pronounced and exacerbated by deepening mutual suspicions. The trends described in this report suggest the following four potential futures for Turkey:

1. *Difficult ally*: Turkey continues to be a difficult and sometimes wavering U.S. and NATO ally but remains committed to NATO missions and reliant on the Alliance's collective security guarantees.
2. *Resurgent democracy*: An opposition leader or coalition is able to defeat Erdoğan after 2023, walk back some of the constitutional changes approved in the 2017 referendum, and resume a more Western-oriented foreign and security policy.
3. *Strategic balancer*: Turkey moves to more openly balance its ties with its NATO allies and those with its emerging partners in Eurasia (particularly, Russia, Iran, and China), sometimes supporting Western positions but often forming shifting coalitions.
4. *Eurasian power*: As tensions with Europe and the United States reach a breaking point, Turkey moves to formally leave NATO and pursue closer cooperation and various alignments with partners in Eurasia and the Middle East.

Table S.1
Alignment of Turkish Interests with Neighbor and Partner Interests

Neighbor or Partner	Converging Interests	Diverging Interests	Conflicting Interests
Iran	• Expanded trade in goods and energy; economic cooperation • Opposition to the development of Kurdish mini-states in Iraq and Syria • Limited influence of outside actors • Border security • Caution toward Russia • Turkish facilitation of Iranian sanctions avoidance • Turkish support for Qatar in disputes with GCC and other Arab states	• Iran's political and military ties to Baghdad • Approach to Kurdish separatism • Settlement in Syria (Turkey wants to limit Iranian influence) • Relations with the United States and Europe • Counterterrorism • Iranian regional activities and influence	• In Syria: Iranian cooperation with the PKK to achieve an energy transit corridor • Religious differences between the Sunni and Shi'a denominations • Turkey's NATO membership • Iran's nuclear program • Resettlement of depopulated areas in Syria and Iraq • Turkish support to Sunni Islamist and jihadist groups
Iraq	• Opposition to the development of Kurdish mini-states in Iraq and Syria • Trade and energy transit	• Influence of Iran and Shi'a militias in Iraq • Relations with the KRG, particularly on energy flows	• Turkish military presence in northern Iraq • Turkish ties to Sunni separatist Turkmen in Iraq
Arab Middle East	• Opposition to Iranian regional influence, although the Arab Gulf states question Turkey's commitment • Opposition to Syria's Bashar al-Assad regime, although the Arab states were concerned that Turkey has been more focused on countering the YPG than aiding the Sunni-Arab opposition; the states were also concerned with Turkey's support to jihadis and the Free Syrian Army	• The endgame and settlement terms in Syria, which are affected by Turkey's dealings with Iran and jihadi groups • Palestine: Turkey has ties to Hamas and the Muslim Brotherhood; others have ties to the Palestinian Authority • Turkey's cross-border operations against the PKK and the YPG, which raise sovereignty concerns	• Muslim Brotherhood: Turkey and Qatar support the group; others oppose • Turkish support of other Islamist groups in Syria and Libya, as well as its enabling of some jihadist groups • Turkey's deepening ties to Qatar • Rift with Egypt over Muslim Brotherhood and Palestinian issues • Management of shared water resources
Israel	• Trade • Possible development of the Leviathan natural gas field as a driver of reconciliation • Humanitarian relief in the Gaza Strip • Limited Iranian influence	• Political, economic, and security relations with countries in the wider Middle East • Israeli facilitation of U.S. regional presence and involvement	• Palestine: statehood, East Jerusalem, Gaza closure, and Hamas • Israel's support for Kurdish autonomy • Israeli cooperation with Egypt's Abdel Fattah al-Sisi government • Growing Israeli partnership with Cyprus and Greece

Table S.1—Continued

Neighbor or Partner	Converging Interests	Diverging Interests	Conflicting Interests
Russia	• Trade expansion • Energy cooperation (Russian gas supplies; nuclear plant) • Tensions with the EU and West • Arms trade • Illiberalism and authoritarian governance	• Energy transit corridors • Counterterrorism issues • Russian role in the Middle East, the Caucasus, and Central Asia • Relations with the United States	• Endgame and Russian presence in Syria • Russian engagement with Syria's Democratic Union Party (Partiya Yekitiya Demokrat [PYD]) and the YPG • Russian military buildup in the Black Sea • Turkey's NATO membership, especially its missile defense site and other deployments
Caucasus	• Development of connectivity and infrastructure for trade and energy • Facilitation of wider economic links with Europe • Turkey's alignment with Azerbaijan on the Nagorno-Karabakh conflict	• Baku's and Tbilisi's efforts for closer political and security ties with Europe • Georgia's desire for stronger support against Russia • Turkish deference to Russia in the Black Sea region	• Differences between Turkey and Armenia on the Nagorno-Karabakh conflict and whether to refer to Turkey's actions in 1915 as genocide • Armenian provision of military basing to Russia
Central Asia	• Some trade and development ties • Minor security cooperation	• Alignment with Russia • Turkic integration limited by Central Asian nations' quest to deepen national identity	• Official secularism versus Islamism
EU	• Trade and energy • Economic ties	• Migration crisis • Counterterrorism and the flow of foreign fighters • EU visa liberalization	• Democratic backsliding in Turkey • Turkish diasporas in Europe • Syria policy • European asylum to Gülenists and coup suspects • Irregular detention of EU citizens in Turkey • Turkey's competing maritime claims with Greece and Cyprus in the Mediterranean and Aegean Seas
NATO	• Solidarity against threats to Turkish territorial integrity • Turkish role in Afghanistan • Denial of Russian dominance in and power projection from the Black Sea	• Democratic backsliding in Turkey • Approach to Russia • Restrictions on Incirlik Air Base, which affect U.S. and German operations	• Acquisition of non-NATO defense systems • Aggressive Turkish challenges to Greek and Cypriot maritime claims, which risk conflict

Table S.1—Continued

Neighbor or Partner	Converging Interests	Diverging Interests	Conflicting Interests
United States	• Solidarity against threats to Turkish territorial integrity • Turkish role as energy supplier to Europe • Turkish role in Afghanistan • Concerns about Russian efforts to dominate and project power from the Black Sea	• Democratic backsliding • Approach to Russia • Iran sanctions • Approach to foreign fighters and Islamist groups in Syria • Restrictions on Incirlik, which affect U.S. operations • Wider Turkish role in the region and Muslim world • Turkish desire for increased defense industrial self-sufficiency	• Syria policy • U.S. tactical engagement with the YPG, the PYD, and Syrian Democratic Forces • Extradition of Gülen • U.S. court case against gold trader Reza Zarrab, who implicated Erdogan in criminal activity • Anti-U.S. propaganda in Turkish government rhetoric and in official and semi-official press • Turkey's acquisition of non-NATO defense systems, particularly Russia's S-400 system • Turkey's detention of U.S. citizens

Either continuation of current trends (the difficult ally possible future) or the emergence of one of the third or fourth futures (strategic balancer or Eurasian power) will lead to Turkish foreign and defense policies that are contrary, in varying degrees, to the interests of the United States and other NATO allies and that further undermine long-standing aspects of defense and security cooperation. This volatile situation warrants a considered reassessment of U.S. and European strategy toward Turkey, preparations for disruptive developments in all aspects of relations, and initiatives that could maintain and restore long-standing ties if current trends are reversed.

The developments in Turkey's domestic politics, foreign and defense policies, and military posture have significant implications for U.S. defense planning and the U.S. Army, particularly with respect to three of the most-pressing regional security challenges: stabilizing post-ISIS Syria and the evolving counterterrorism struggle in the Middle East, containing Iranian influence in the Middle East and the Persian Gulf, and counterbalancing Russian influence and military activities in the Black Sea region and beyond.

State of Bilateral Military-to-Military and Defense Industrial Relations

The U.S. and Turkish militaries have a long history of close cooperation, which has evolved in light of shifting priorities. Relations suffered a major setback after 2003, when the Turkish Parliament denied the U.S. request for the 4th Infantry Division to use Turkish territory to launch operations into Iraq, and the United States subsequently declined the Turkish government's offer to send 10,000 troops to Iraq as members of the coalition. Differences over U.S. policies in Iraq after the fall of Saddam Hussein led to further strains and limited senior contacts. Relations improved after 2007, as cooperation on countering the PKK improved, and they have continued to function fairly well in recent years, with a few bumps in the road.

The TSK has demonstrated that it wants to work effectively with U.S. forces; however, our interlocutors confirm that the relationship has retained a transactional character. Turkey's minister of defense and chief of the Turkish General Staff (TGS) have met regularly with their U.S. counterparts in recent years. The pace and nature of the TSK's engagement with U.S. counterparts had been improving before the 2016 coup, and although the pace slowed somewhat in the immediate months after the coup, most planned operations and activities with United States Army Europe forces are continuing. The depth of U.S. military-to-military interactions with the TSK has varied by service. Cooperation with the Turkish Air Force has been consistently strong over the years, including continuing operations at İncirlik and regular exercises. Considerable interaction between the two navies takes place in NATO operations and exercises, as well as regular staff talks. For many years, there was very little interaction between the U.S. Army and the Turkish Land Forces. The first-ever talks between the U.S. Army Staff and the TGS took place in January 2009 and led to a plan of exercises and unit-level exchanges. Cooperation among special operations forces also saw marked improvement after 2008 and has continued for operations in Afghanistan and Syria.

In addition, the United States and Turkey maintain a long-standing defense trade relationship. This has included a consortium between U.S. and Turkish aerospace firms to coproduce most of Turkey's 240 F-16s in Turkey during the 1980s and 1990s and a similar $3.5 billion deal finalized in 2014 to produce 109 Turkish-version Black Hawk helicopters in Turkey. Turkey was also a level-3 partner in the Joint Strike Fighter program, committed to purchasing 116 F-35A Lightning aircraft. However, the Department of Defense suspended Ankara from the program following the delivery of Russian S-400 air defense units to Turkey in July 2019, and Russia-related U.S. sanctions are likely to be imposed on Turkey—barring a presidential waiver. Turkey entered into negotiations with the United States in 2011 and 2012 to purchase and coproduce the Phased Array Tracking Radar to Intercept of Target (PATRIOT) Advanced Capability (PAC)-3 air and missile defense system, but the talks collapsed at that time because of costs and disagreements over technology transfers.[1] This was an important factor in Turkey's decision to seek alternatives. Despite these efforts to achieve diversification of supply and self-reliance, the TSK will remain heavily dependent on U.S.-origin military equipment for at least the next decade, which is another positive factor in sustaining the military-to-military relationship.

Stabilization of Syria and Future Counterterrorism Efforts

Differences between the United States and Turkey over the goals, strategy, and tactics for ending the Syrian civil war have grown more pronounced. Ankara's top priority has been to prevent the Syrian PYD and its YPG militias, which Ankara views as integral elements of the outlawed PKK, from gaining control of the entire length of Turkey's 500-mile-long southern border with Syria. The Turks have viewed the 2015 U.S. decision to train and equip the YPG, and then to supply them with heavy weapons and equipment two years later in advance of the assault on ISIS in Raqqa, as the equivalent of an ally arming an enemy. Discontent with U.S. policy led Erdoğan to launch Operation Olive Branch against YPG forces in Afrin in early 2018. The Turkish move into Afrin brought into stark relief the contradictions and limitations of U.S. policy in Syria. U.S. forces advising and assisting YPG forces near Manbij and other places east of the Euphrates River were at risk of being attacked by their Turkish treaty allies. The June 2018 agreement between Washington and Ankara on a Manbij roadmap avoided a crisis but created new demands on the Army to maintain security in northern Syria, and the risk of clashes between Turkish and YPG forces elsewhere remains. Defusing the current and future confrontations over Syria will require agile U.S. dip-

---

[1]   Discussions between the United States and Turkey on the purchase of the PAC-3 system were revived in 2018 and 2019, but their outcome was uncertain at the time of publication.

lomatic engagement with its Turkish allies and Kurdish partners and likely further policy adjustments.

In conducting operations to prevent the reemergence of ISIS and stabilize Syria and Iraq, the U.S. Army will need to remain mindful of the tensions with Ankara concerning the Kurds and other elements of U.S. policy. As diplomatic and civilian stabilization initiatives in Syria and Iraq unfold, Army training efforts and operations could support a sustainable end state by

- ensuring that security force training programs are as inclusive as possible so that areas with mixed Kurdish and Arab residents develop a more diverse force, as has happened in Manbij
- working with the TSK to mitigate tensions along east-west lines of control in northern Syria between those dominated by the YPG and those under control of the Turkish-backed Free Syrian Army
- providing security and support to U.S. State Department and Agency for International Development personnel working in northern Syria with the United Nations, partners in the Global Coalition to Defeat ISIS, and various nongovernmental organizations to help local and regional authorities restore essential services in liberated areas and establish an environment conducive to resettlement of refugees
- taking steps to enhance U.S. Army cooperation with the Turkish Land Forces and special operations forces, which are likely to also be operating in Syria to protect safe zones and monitor border areas
- initiating a focused dialogue with TSK counterparts—in addition to whatever efforts are taken to sustain the Global Coalition—on how regional efforts to combat terrorism should unfold following the defeat of ISIS.

The Black Sea and the Eastern Mediterranean

Both Russia and Turkey have long sought to limit maritime operations by nonlittoral powers in the Black Sea and develop a cooperative approach to regional security. Russian aggression against Georgia and Ukraine, as well as efforts to strengthen Russia's position in the Black Sea and ability to project maritime power, have strained this cooperative approach. The deployment of new reconnaissance assets, submarines with Kalibr cruise missiles, new aircraft, and the Bastion coastal defense missile system have given Moscow an even more robust anti-access/area denial capability against NATO navies and air forces and have strengthened Russia's ability to project power into the Eastern Mediterranean and Middle East regions. Russia's improvements in the size and readiness of ground forces in its Southern Military District, continuing patronage of the breakaway Georgian province of Abkhazia, and enhancements of its military presence in Armenia have strengthened Russian ground and air power in the Black Sea region.

Turkish perceptions have shifted with the recognition that Russia has again become Turkey's most formidable military threat, and there remains a deep wariness about Russia's military capabilities and intentions. Nevertheless, because of Turkey's vulnerability to Russian military and economic pressure, its balancing strategy between NATO and Russia is likely to continue. A future contingency in which Russia uses its military might to intimidate Turkey or undermine its security interests in the Black Sea or the Middle East would likely be the true test of how this shifting regional military balance will affect the future course of Turkey's relations with its NATO allies and Russia. This balancing strategy has the following implications for U.S. defense and security cooperation plans:

- The U.S. Army and other services should continue to deepen their engagement with Turkish counterparts in the development of NATO's tailored forward presence in southeastern Europe and in U.S. European Command's Black Sea exercise program, particularly the Saber Guardian and the Sea Breeze series.
- Given uncertainty about how the TSK might respond in a period of heightened tensions with Russia, the U.S. Army should design and deploy flexible logistic options to support any NATO peacetime deterrent or crisis flexible deterrent options for Bulgaria and Romania.
- If Turkey proceeds with deployment of Russian S-400s, the U.S. Army, as the owner and operator of the PATRIOT and Terminal High Altitude Area Defense surface-to-air missile systems, will have to evaluate the risk and manage any integration of those systems with non-NATO surface-to-air missile systems.
- Turkish cooperation with the Russian Navy, as well as the fact that Turkey's navy is not a top priority of the Turkish political leadership, may have an adverse effect on cooperation with the United States and NATO in Black Sea maritime operations. However, U.S. and NATO forces' continued engagement with Turkish naval and marine forces can help counterbalance these influences.

Other Force Planning and Regional Issues

Turkey will continue to seek to balance concerns about Iran's expanding influence in the Middle East and improving military capabilities, including a nuclear breakout capability, with Turkish interests in deepening economic and energy cooperation and in finding ways to defuse volatile elements of Sunni-Shi'a tensions. The Turkish government does not assess Iran's nuclear program and testing of long-range ballistic missiles as an imminent threat. Erdoğan and other officials have repeatedly defended Iran's right to develop a nuclear-fuel cycle, accepted that the program is peaceful, continued to support the 2015 Joint Comprehensive Plan of Action, circumvented sanctions against Iran, and vowed to ignore 2018 U.S. sanctions on Tehran for its regional aggression. That said, Iran's prospective acquisition of nuclear weapons is inimical to Turkey's security and is another reason that Turkey has continued to support NATO

European Phased Adaptive Approach missile defense programs and efforts of the nuclear dimension of Alliance deterrent capabilities. An Iranian move to break out of the Joint Comprehensive Plan of Action could bring Turkey closer to the United States and NATO on countering this threat.

Turkey's political and military support to Qatar in the dispute with GCC and other countries is likely to remain strong, potentially inviting a situation in which the United States is forced to choose between competing constellations of Middle East partners. In a worst-case scenario, perceived U.S. favoritism toward one of those camps could lead to denial of U.S. military access in the nations of the other camp, complicating response to a military contingency in the U.S. Central Command's area of responsibility, such as a naval escalation with Iran in the Persian Gulf. Given the U.S. Army's major role in the military's forward presence (and rapid reinforcement) in the Persian Gulf region south of Iraq (to hedge against Iranian regional aggression and to assure Israel and other regional partners), Army planners will need to be cognizant of these tensions that could disrupt current contingency plans.

Given the volatility of relations with Turkey, U.S. defense planners need be prepared to deal with the loss of access to İncirlik Air Base and other U.S. and NATO facilities in Turkey. The implications of this loss to sustain Operation Inherent Resolve (to counter ISIS) and other operations in Southwest Asia would be enormous, and alternative facilities in the region have substantial limitations.

With respect to military-to-military relations, further efforts should be taken to deepen dialogues between U.S. military and TGS leaders and to revitalize the U.S.-Turkish High-Level Defense Group, taking into account the increased importance of the Turkish minister of defense. Finally, the U.S. Army and other services could seek to assist Turkey with the development of curricula at its new National Defense University and could encourage the TSK to continue to send officers to schools in the United States. These steps could help improve civil-military relations in Turkey and influence the future course of the TSK in ways that could strengthen bilateral and NATO cooperation with Turkey over the long term.

Acknowledgments

We would like to thank the many U.S., Turkish, and other foreign officials, military officers, experts, and journalists who shared their insights on Turkey's internal political and social dynamics, developments in civil-military relations, defense strategy, and shifting foreign relations. We are grateful to MG William Hix, director of Strategy, Plans, and Policy, G-3/5/7, which sponsored this project, and to COL Mark E. Solomons, chief of the Strategic Assessments Division, G-3/5/7, for his continuing interest and engagement throughout the course of our work. The final report benefited from insightful peer reviews by Bryan Frederick of the RAND Corporation and by Gönül Tol, founding director of the Middle East Institute's Center for Turkish Studies.

Within RAND, we greatly appreciate the support of Sally Sleeper, director of RAND Arroyo Center and previously of the Center's Strategy, Doctrine, and Resources Program, who took a deep interest in the project from the outset. We also value the encouragement and good counsel we received from Dalia Dassa Kaye, director of the Center for Middle East Public Policy. This report also benefited from program reviews by Michael Hansen, associate director of RAND Arroyo Center, and Jennifer Kavanagh, associate director of RAND Arroyo Center's Strategy, Doctrine, and Resources Program.

In addition, Ali Scotten provided helpful research on Iran, and MAJ Bret Williams, a U.S. Army Fellow at RAND, was helpful on several military issues. We are also very grateful to Kysha Barnes for her support during the planning and execution of the research, Julia Brackup for her superb efforts in compiling and assembling the project report, Allison Kerns for her meticulous and insightful editing of the final manuscript, and Francisco Walter for his most helpful advice on many aspects of the project.

Abbreviations

AKP	Adalet ve Kalkınma Partisi (Justice and Development Party, Turkey)
BSEC	Organization of the Black Sea Economic Cooperation
CHP	Cumhuriyet Halk Partisi (Republican People's Party, Turkey)
CSDP	Common Security and Defense Policy
CSTO	Collective Security Treaty Organization
EU	European Union
GCC	Gulf Cooperation Council
HDP	Halkların Demokratik Partisi (Peoples' Democratic Party, Turkey)
HTS	Hayat Tahrir al-Sham
IDF	Israel Defense Forces
İHH	Humanitarian Relief Foundation (İnsani Yardım Vakfım, Turkey)
İP	İYİ Parti (Good Party, Turkey)
ISIS	Islamic State of Iraq and Syria
KDP	Partiya Demokrat a Kurdistanê (Kurdish Democratic Party, Iraq)
KDPI	Hîzbî Dêmukratî Kurdistanî Êran (Kurdish Democratic Party of Iran)
KRG	Kurdistan Regional Government
MİT	Millî İstihbarat Teşkilatı (National Intelligence Organization, Turkey)
MHP	Milliyetçi Hareket Partisi (Nationalist Movement Party, Turkey)
MOU	memorandum of understanding
NATO	North Atlantic Treaty Organization
PATRIOT	Phased Array Tracking Radar to Intercept of Target
PJAK	Partiya Jiyana Azad a Kurdistanê (Kurdistan Free Life Party, Iran)
PKK	Partiya Karkerên Kurdistanê (Kurdistan Workers Party)
PUK	Yekêtiy Niştîmaniy Kurdistan (Patriotic Union of Kurdistan, Iraq)
PYD	Partiya Yekîtiya Demokrat (Democratic Union Party, Syria)
SDF	Syrian Democratic Forces

TİKA	Türk İşbirliği ve Koordinasyon İdaresi Başkanlığı (Turkish Cooperation and Coordination Agency)
TGS	Turkish General Staff
TSK	Türk Silahlı Kuvvetleri (Turkish Armed Forces)
YAŞ	Yüksek Askerî Şûra (Supreme Military Council, Turkey)
YPG	Yekîneyên Parastina Gel (People's Protection Units, Syria)
UAE	United Arab Emirates
USSR	Union of Soviet Socialist Republics

CHAPTER ONE

Introduction

Stephen J. Flanagan

A strategic partnership with the Republic of Turkey has been a central element of U.S. strategy toward Eurasia and the Middle East for more than six decades. This partnership was forged in the early years of the Cold War in response to Soviet territorial demands on Turkey. Turkish leaders turned to the United States for economic, political, and military assistance, which formally began with the enunciation of the Truman Doctrine in 1947. The expansion of U.S. defense ties with Turkey paved the way for Turkey's eventual incorporation into the North Atlantic Treaty Organization (NATO) in 1952. Turkey served as a critical bulwark against the expansion of Soviet power into the Mediterranean and the Middle East throughout the Cold War.[1]

The end of the Cold War did not diminish Turkey's strategic importance to the United States. Turkey remains a powerful NATO ally at the nexus of three regions that have become increasingly important to U.S. security since the end of the Cold War: the Levant, the wider Middle East and Persian Gulf, and the Caucasus and Central Asia. In all three areas, Turkey is seeking to play a larger role and has significant capacity to influence events. It controls (in accordance with international conventions) the straits of the Bosporus and the Dardanelles, which link the Black Sea with the Mediterranean. The United States and Turkey have long cooperated on a range of global issues, including countering terrorism and violent extremism, preventing the proliferation of weapons of mass destruction, enhancing energy security, and promoting prosperity and development.

Managing a Troubled Partnership

This partnership has become strained in recent years because U.S. and Turkish interests and assessments of various challenges are not as aligned as they once were, and significant disagreements have emerged on policies to address many of these chal-

---

[1] For a discussion of the development of the partnership, see F. Stephen Larrabee, *Troubled Partnership: U.S.-Turkish Relations in an Era of Global Geopolitical Change,* Santa Monica, Calif.: RAND Corporation, MG-899-AF, 2010, pp. 3–7.

lenges. U.S.-Turkish relations have gone through cycles of close cooperation and deep mistrust.[2] Differences over dealing with Syria and the Kurdish question, tensions in Turkey's relations with its neighbors, an escalating terrorism threat, and deepening U.S. concerns about the authoritarian drift in Turkish politics under President Recep Tayyip Erdoğan have combined in recent years to constrain cooperation and undermine mutual confidence. Anti-American sentiment has deepened, as have doubts about the reliability of the U.S. commitment to Turkey's stability and security—both exacerbated by inflammatory statements by Erdoğan and other Turkish leaders. Internal strife over the past decade had largely been confined to poorer southeastern provinces but has spread to the western parts of Turkey, including Istanbul and Ankara. Turkey's regional security situation has also deteriorated as a consequence of the Syrian civil war, the growth of the Islamic State of Iraq and Syria (ISIS), the failure of the Arab Spring, and Sunni-Shi'a frictions.

Methodology

In light of these developments, we (the authors of the various chapters of this report) assess the key challenges confronting the U.S.-Turkish strategic partnership over the coming decade and recommend possible courses of action to sustain it during what is likely to be a turbulent period. With our combined expertise on Turkey, the Middle East, Europe, Russia, Eurasia, and defense policy, we undertook a systematic assessment in 2017 and 2018 of trends in Turkey's domestic situation, external relations, and defense policy and strategy. We drew insights from an extensive literature review, including a substantial body of previous RAND Corporation reports on Turkey and its neighbors; semi-structured dialogues with more than 100 civilian officials, military leaders, scholars, and journalists in Turkey, Europe, Israel, and the United States; international conferences; and several seminars at RAND's Arlington, Virginia, office.

To provide a long-term, strategic perspective, we used an analytic framework of comparative national interests. The research focused first on the political, social, and economic trends that are changing Turkey's internal dynamics and global interests. We then assessed how the leaders of Turkey's neighbors and two institutions—the European Union (EU) and NATO—perceive Turkey's evolving international role and policies in relation to their own major interests. Next, we compared how Turkey's evolving interests and those of these neighbors and institutions converge, diverge, or are in conflict, which helps identify the forces that will likely shape the course of these bilateral and multilateral relations over the coming decade. Summaries of how these interests

---

[2]   For a review, see Stephen J. Flanagan, Samuel J. Brannen, Bulent Aliriza, Edward C. Chow, Andrew C. Kuchins, Haim Malka, Julianne Smith, Ian Lesser, Eric Palomaa, and Alexandros Petersen, *Turkey's Evolving Dynamics: Strategic Choices for U.S.-Turkey Relations*, Washington, D.C.: Center for Strategic and International Studies, March 2009.

compare are provided at the end of each regional chapter (Chapters Three through Eight), and they are aggregated as Table 9.1 in the final chapter (Chapter Nine). The final chapter also advances four potential Turkish futures—that is, plausible geostrategic orientations for Turkey over the coming decade based on a simplified scenario-axes analysis of the most-significant driving forces in Turkish domestic and external affairs.

Organization of This Report

The report begins with an analysis of Turkey's volatile internal situation (Chapter Two), including deep political divisions, growing nationalism, the development of authoritarian rule under the Justice and Development Party (Adalet ve Kalkınma Partisi [AKP]) government, the aftermath of the July 2016 attempted military coup, the revived Kurdish insurgency, and escalating terrorism problems.

We then explore Turkey's changing relations with key neighbors, including Iran and Iraq (Chapter Three), the Arab world (Chapter Four), Israel (Chapter Five), and Russia (Chapter Six), as well as Turkey's ambitions in the Caucasus and Central Asia (Chapter Seven) and interactions with the EU and NATO (Chapter Eight). We project that Turkey's relations with most of its neighbors in Eurasia and the Middle East will remain uncertain or strained, with limited alignment of national interests and some in sharp conflict. We argue that Turkey's strategic interests and those of the United States and its other NATO allies still converge in several areas, including countering terrorism, promoting peace in the Middle East, preventing the emergence of Russian or Iranian regional hegemony, and expanding energy transit corridors. Differences over the policies to best advance these interests have, however, become more pronounced and exacerbated by deepening mutual suspicions. We conclude that domestic political and social upheaval and fundamental shifts in Turkey's governance, together with regional turmoil, will lead to Turkish foreign and defense policies that are contrary, in varying degrees, to the interests of the United States and other NATO allies and that undermine long-standing aspects of defense and security cooperation.

In Chapter Nine, we assess the implications of these trends for U.S. foreign policy, defense planning and the U.S. Army, given Turkey's enduring geostrategic importance. We identify initiatives to prepare for disruptive developments in the partnership with Turkey and restore its previous scope if and when there are favorable changes in Turkish policies. Finally, we suggest steps to manage differences with Turkey in addressing three critical regional security challenges: stabilizing post-ISIS Syria and the evolving counterterrorism campaign; containing hostile Iranian influence in the Middle East; and deterring Russian aggression in the Black Sea region and beyond.

CHAPTER TWO

Turkey at a Crossroads

Stephen J. Flanagan, Magdalena Kirchner, and F. Stephen Larrabee

Turkey is undergoing profound political and social upheaval and fundamental shifts in governance. The likely continuation of current trends will lead to Turkish foreign and defense policies that are contrary, in varying degrees, to the interests of the United States and other NATO allies and that undermine long-standing aspects of defense and security cooperation. This situation warrants a considered reassessment of U.S. and European strategy toward Turkey, preparations for disruptive developments in all aspects of relations, and initiatives that could maintain and restore long-standing ties if these trends are reversed.

Deepening Authoritarianism and Instability

Under the leadership of Erdoğan and his AKP, democratic and civil rights have steadily declined since 2012, a trend dramatically accelerated by emergency rule, ongoing since July 2016. Through constitutional change, Turkey is being transformed from a parliamentarian system with strong checks and balances into an authoritarian state in which political power is fully concentrated in the hands of an executive president and the dominant party. These constitutional amendments, approved in an April 16, 2017, national referendum and implemented following the June 24, 2018, general elections, substantially removed powers from legislative and judiciary bodies. Executive decisions have diminished political pluralism, democratic institutions, and civil society and are expected to go further. The closeness of the voting on both the referendum (51.4 percent for and 48.5 against, with an 87.4 percent turnout) and the presidential election (52.6 percent for Erdoğan and 46.3 percent for the three main opposition parties, with 86.2 percent turnout), even with the government's manipulation of the processes and domination of the media, are indicative of the deep polarization of Turkish society.[1]

In this chapter, we examine Turkey's volatile internal dynamics. We begin with a review of Turkey's domestic political development since 2002 under AKP govern-

---

[1] "The Latest: Turkey Releases Official Referendum Results," *U.S. News and World Report*, April 27, 2017; and "Turkey's Supreme Election Board Announces Final Results in June 24 Elections," *Daily Sabah*, July 4, 2018.

ments, the drift toward an authoritarian political system, growing nationalism, and the aftermath of the July 2016 attempted military coup. We then examine tensions between the government and the Kurdish population, the failed peace process with the Kurdistan Workers Party (Partiya Karkerên Kurdistanê [PKK]), the revived insurgency, and the uptick in other terrorist activity. Next, we assess the implications of these dynamics for Turkey's foreign policy decisionmaking, civil-military relations, and likely future course. Subsequent chapters explore major trends and driving forces in Turkey's relations with its neighbors, the EU, and NATO and the implications for U.S. national security and defense planning.

An Enduring Battle of Two Visions

Traditionally, fissures in Turkish politics reflected deep and enduring tensions between two contending ideologies or visions of Turkish identity: Kemalist secularism and political Islam. In recent years, however, this division has been at least partially overshadowed by the AKP's efforts to form a new nativist-nationalist alliance against both liberal forces challenging the country's drift into authoritarianism and those perceived as outsiders—including Kurds and other minorities, as well as Syrians. The merger of those two once-opposed visions was manifested on March 10, 2018, in the southern Turkish city of Mersin, when President Erdoğan first saluted attendees at a rally with the ultranationalist "Bozkurt" gesture and only minutes later with the four-fingered with thumb bent "Rabia" gesture, aligning himself with the Muslim Brotherhood.

Given the fact that the AKP's domination of political life in Turkey since 2002 coincided with Erdoğan's accumulation of power within the party, these fundamental cleavages have sharpened into an irreconcilable division between his supporters—a coalition of conservative, center-right, Islamist, some right-wing nationalist, and nativist forces—and his opponents—secular liberals and leftists, many nationalists, followers of Fethullah Gülen, and the majority of Kurds.[2] This polarization has been exacerbated by a deteriorating internal security situation and tensions with most neighboring states.

Kemalism, named after the first President of the Republic Mustafa Kemal Atatürk, had been the dominant ideology since the founding of the Turkish Republic in 1923. It is based on six main pillars as articulated in the constitution since 1937: republicanism, statism (envisioning a strong state role in developing industry, regulating the economy, and supporting social welfare), populism, rigid secularism, nationalism (emphasizing

---

[2]   Soner Cagaptay, *The New Sultan: Erdoğan and the Crisis of Modern Turkey*, London: I.B. Tauris, 2017, Chapter 1.

domestic assimilation and nonaggression; "Peace at home, peace in the world"), and modernizing reformism to adapt Western practices to Turkish conditions.[3]

Atatürk extolled these principles as the pathway to assure the transformation of the multireligious, multi-ethnic, but—as he saw it—backward Ottoman Empire into the secular, modern, unitary Turkish Republic that would be competitive in every field with the most-advanced nations in the world. Although modeled on the French concept of *laïcité* (secularism), which is also designed to keep religion out of governmental and political affairs, Kemalist secularism went further by creating (1) strict rules regulating religious expression in the public sphere and (2) a Directorate of Religious Affairs (Diyanet İşleri Başkanlığı) to provide firm state supervision and regulation of religious practice and teaching. Kemalists also rejected the concept of multiculturalism in favor of deepening Turkishness.

Since the early days of the republic, the Turkish military has played a major role as the self-proclaimed guardian of the Kemalist system. After a military coup in 1961 and a subsequent constitutional change, the Turkish General Staff (TGS) assumed a persistent role in politics through the newly formed National Security Council. Further coups in 1971 and 1980, as well as constitutional amendments under respective periods of military rule, expanded this system of "military tutelage," which also included sweeping autonomy with respect to promotions, appointments, military education, and reform.[4]

While the military, government bureaucracy, and urban elites embraced the Kemalist path, the citizens in the Anatolian heartland clung to old traditions and the Kurds resisted assimilation, which left enduring cultural and ethnic gaps that have grown over time to undermine the Kemalist construct.[5] In the 1970s and 1980s, various Islamist parties struggled to gain a footing, such as the National Salvation Party (Millî Selâmet Partisi), which reflected the pan-Islamist and anti-Western ideology

---

[3] Sina Akşin, "The Nature of the Kemalist Revolution," *PAGES of the United Nations Association of Turkey*, Vol. 2, No. 2, October 1999.

[4] The 1961 constitution made the TGS answerable directly to the prime minister, rather than through the Defense Ministry. It also established the National Security Council, which included leading members of the civilian government and the TGS, to serve as an advisory body (later a more directive one) to the Council of Ministers. The Turkish Armed Forces Internal Service Law No. 211 of January 1961, Article 35, states, "The duty of the Turkish Armed Forces is to protect and preserve the Turkish homeland and the Turkish Republic as defined in the constitution." This article has been cited as granting the military the right to remove civilian governments that violate the constitution. See Gareth Jenkins, "Continuity and Change: Prospects for Civil–Military Relations in Turkey," *International Affairs*, Vol. 83, No. 2, 2007, pp. 341–342; Koray Caliskan, "Explaining the End of Military Tutelary Regime and the July 15 Coup Attempt in Turkey," *Journal of Cultural Economy*, Vol. 10, No. 1, 2017; and Giacomo Fantini, "The Coup and the Referendum: Ascent and Decline of Military Influence on Turkish Constitutionalism," Lista Dei Working Paper, March 2017.

[5] M. Hakan Yavuz, *Islamic Political Identity in Turkey*, Oxford, United Kingdom: Oxford University Press, 2003, pp. 265–274; and Philip H. Gordon and Ömer Taşpınar, *Winning Turkey: How America, Europe, and Turkey Can Revive a Fading Partnership*, Washington, D.C.: Brookings Institution Press, 2008, pp. 11–15.

espoused by its founder Necmettin Erbakan and the National Outlook (Milli Görüş) movement. Aligned with Egypt's Muslim Brotherhood, these Islamist parties advocated strengthening Islamic values at home and turning away from the negative influences of the Western world in favor of closer relations with Muslim countries.

The political, social, and economic reforms begun under former Prime Minister and President Turgut Özal after 1983 led to the emergence of a prosperous, middle class of entrepreneurs in the Anatolian heartland. These "Anatolian tigers" are actively engaged in the global economy but are conservative in social and religious practices.[6] With the backing of this new middle class, the Islamist Welfare Party (Refah Partisi), led by Erbakan, came to power as the senior partner in a 1996–1997 coalition government. After Erbakan was forced to step down as prime minister in a bloodless military coup in 1997 and the Welfare Party was banned in 1998, Turkey's Islamist forces split into two wings. In contrast to the traditionalist Felicity Party (Saadet Partisi)—which was established and led by Erbakan—Erdoğan, Abdullah Gül, and others concluded that retaining power and challenging the strictures of Kemalist secularism would require a new form of political mobilization. Hence, they formed the AKP, a Muslim version of a European Christian democratic party, embraced certain market and social reforms, support for small and medium-sized enterprises, and a commitment to EU and NATO membership. Subsequently, Erdoğan, the charismatic former mayor of Istanbul, who was briefly jailed in 1999 and thus banned from political office, led the AKP in winning nearly two-thirds of the seats in the Grand National Assembly (hereafter referred to as Parliament) in the November 2002 general elections. He then became prime minister in March 2003—after his ban was lifted by Parliament—of the first single-party government in a decade. The AKP held this majority in Parliament for 13 years, lost it in June 2015, and regained it in the snap election of November 2015. Erdoğan stepped down as prime minister when he won the first direct elections for president in 2014 with about 52 percent of the vote for a five-year, renewable term.

Coming to power after a succession of weak coalition governments, war with the Kurds, religious controversy, and economic turmoil during the 1990s (known as the "lost decade"), the AKP focused initially on sustaining an economic recovery and trying to initiate accession negotiations with the EU. This agenda enabled the AKP to widen its appeal across the political spectrum, including liberal elements of society. In addition, the party has benefited from the weakness of the main opposition parties: the center-left Republican People's Party (Cumhuriyet Halk Partisi [CHP]); the ultranationalist Nationalist Movement Party (Milliyetçi Hareket Partisi [MHP]); and, in recent years, the pro-Kurdish Peoples' Democratic Party (Halkların Demokratik Partisi [HDP]).

---

[6] Henri J. Barkey, "Turkey's Moment of Inflection," *Survival*, Vol. 52, No. 3, June–July 2010b, pp. 40–41.

The AKP and the "New Turkey"

Four main cleavages have dominated Turkey's domestic political landscape since 2002, at times mutually reinforcing each other: long-standing divisions over the role of religion and the secularist nature of Turkish society and the public sphere; the transformation of the political system from a parliamentarian one into an executive presidency, securing ultimate power to Erdoğan; the ongoing marginalization of the Kurdish minority and the related armed insurgency by the PKK; and the power rivalry within the "pious" camp (Erdoğan's term) between the AKP leadership and the Gülen movement.

Suspicion in the Kemalist establishment that conservative and especially religious parties pose a threat to the state principle of secularism, and hence to modernism and orientation toward the West, remains widespread. This has been especially the case since 2012, when Erdoğan declared that his political ambition was "to raise devout generations."[7] He elevated the status of the Directorate of Religious Affairs and has reportedly used it for political patronage and to encourage government-friendly sermons in mosques. At the same time, the aforementioned cultural and political marginalization of Turkey's religious communities has instilled a constant fear of violent overthrow among the AKP leadership under the pretext of securing the secular order.[8] In the early years of AKP rule, this concern focused on state institutions, especially the military and judiciary. However, since widespread anti-government protests in summer 2013, the concern has shifted to criticism from the media and civil society, which have often been accused of being agents of hostile external forces.[9] From 2007 to 2011, there was substantial escalation in the power struggles between (1) the AKP and (2) Fethullah Gülen and the followers of his Islamic Hizmet (service) movement (the AKP's then-key ally), as well as between (1) the AKP and (2) the military and state bureaucracy.[10]

Gülen, a Sufi imam who has resided in northeastern Pennsylvania since 1999 because he feared arrest after the 1997 military coup, was an early supporter of Erdoğan and the AKP. Gülen and the AKP leadership are both mainstream Sunni Muslims, and they shared a vision of Islamic modernism and many common goals, particularly promoting a more pious society and protecting it from shared political enemies.[11] They differed, however, in their approach. The AKP, just as the Welfare Party and other Islamist party predecessors, engaged directly in the political process and achieved

---

[7]   Burak Bekdil, "Erdogan Raising 'Devout Generations,'" Gatestone Institute, April 1, 2015a.

[8]   Howard Eissenstat, *Uneasy Rests the Crown: Erdoğan and "Revolutionary Security" in Turkey*, Washington, D.C.: Project on Middle East Democracy, December 2017, p. 2.

[9]   Semih Idiz, "Erdogan Blames International Conspiracy for Protests," *Al-Monitor*, June 14, 2013; and Svante E. Cornell, "Erdoğan's Looming Downfall," *Middle East Quarterly*, Vol. 21, No. 2, Spring 2014.

[10]   David Capezza, "Turkey's Military Is a Catalyst for Reform: The Military in Politics," *Middle East Quarterly*, Vol. 16, No. 3, Summer 2009.

[11]   Eissenstat, 2017, p. 2.

electoral success. Gülen and his followers emerged from the Nursi movement, which emphasizes faith and shied away from political Islam.[12] Gülen has sought to increase his influence in Turkey and abroad by enlisting followers in overtly and covertly affiliated businesses and nongovernmental organizations, particularly schools in Turkey, Central Asia, and Africa. Gülen denied having a political agenda, but on the eve of his departure from Turkey, ostensibly for medical treatment, he advised his followers to "move in the arteries of the system, without anyone noticing your existence, until you reach all the power centers."[13] Gülen's followers did exactly that and gained significant influence in the police force, the judicial system, the education sector, and the media. They also amassed significant financial resources.

In April 2007, many secularists took issue with the AKP's nomination of then–Foreign Minister Abdullah Gül as successor to Turkey's staunch secularist President Ahmet Sezer, especially because Gül's wife was publicly wearing a headscarf. Moreover, his election would also allow the AKP to hold three key levers of political power in Turkey: the posts of prime minister, president, and the speaker of Parliament. The nomination sparked large-scale public demonstrations and a blunt warning posted on the website of the Turkish Armed Forces (Türk Silahlı Kuvvetleri [TSK])— referred to as the *e-memorandum*—declaring that the military was the "absolute defender of secularism" and that the TSK "maintain their sound determination to carry out their duties stemming from laws to protect the unchangeable characteristics of the Republic of Turkey."[14] The TSK message was viewed by many Turks as a veiled threat of a military coup, yet it backfired when the AKP refused to back down and won an overwhelming victory in early elections in July 2007, gaining 46.6 percent of the vote—12 percent more than in 2002. Gül's subsequent election marked a watershed in Turkish politics but did not end the secularist-religious confrontation.[15]

Erdoğan's decision in late autumn 2007 to lift the ban on women wearing the headscarf in universities was seen by the secular establishment as a direct assault on core principles and a step toward the Islamization of Turkish society. Under growing

---

[12] Gülen and his followers claimed that promotion of faith, tolerance, peace, and intercultural and interreligious dialogue in Turkey and abroad was their goal. See Bayram Balci, "What Are the Consequences of the Split Between Erdoğan and Gülen on Turkey's Foreign Policy?" *Foreign Policy Journal*, January 17, 2014; and Çınar Oskay, "Government Supported 'Ergenekon' Case, Says Turkey's Former Military Chief," *Hürriyet Daily News*, April 24, 2016.

[13] This quote is taken from sermons that Gülen delivered to supporters, footage of which was aired on Turkish television and posted for a time on YouTube but subsequently removed. See "Profile: Fethullah Gulen's Hizmet Movement," BBC News, December 18, 2013.

[14] "Excerpts of Turkish Army Statement," BBC News, April 28, 2007.

[15] Bulent Aliriza, "Turkey's Changing Dynamics," in Stephen J. Flanagan, Samuel J. Brannen, Bulent Aliriza, Edward C. Chow, Andrew C. Kuchins, Haim Malka, Julianne Smith, Ian Lesser, Eric Palomaa, and Alexandros Petersen, *Turkey's Evolving Dynamics: Strategic Choices for U.S.-Turkey Relations*, Washington, D.C.: Center for Strategic and International Studies, March 2009a, pp. 2–3.

pressure from the military and secular elements, the chief prosecutor initiated legal proceedings in the Constitutional Court in March 2008 to ban the AKP. The indictment called for the closure of the AKP and political bans of 71 party members, including Erdoğan and Gül, for violating the principles of secularism under Article 2 of the Turkish constitution.[16] The motion was eventually rejected but deprived the AKP of significant state party funding and forced it to put key governmental priorities on the back burner for five months.[17]

Having survived what they deemed first a military and then a judicial coup, AKP leaders, in collaboration with prosecutors and police who were members of the Gülen movement, struck against their common enemies. A police raid in 2007 that discovered an illegal weapon stockpile led to a series of investigations and trials between 2008 and 2013 of hundreds of civilians and military personnel—including a former chief of the TGS—on charges of being members of a purported ultra-nationalist group called *Ergenekon* that planned to precipitate a military coup by fomenting unrest and widespread violence throughout the country.[18] In early 2010, prosecutors initiated a related investigation into an alleged 2003 military plan, known as *Balyoz* (sledgehammer), to undertake violent acts that would serve as a pretext for a coup d'état against the AKP government. *Balyoz* resulted in lengthy prison sentences for 230 officers, including 11 four-star generals, in September 2012—all of which were annulled in 2015.[19] During this period, Erdoğan also gradually eroded the TGS's bureaucratic autonomy and started an unprecedented—and unchallenged—interference in the military's promotions, retirements, and internal discipline. In the face of these challenges and in the wake of the arrest of two top generals in the *Balyoz* case in February 2011, the commanders of the Ground Forces, Navy, and Air Force resigned in protest en masse hoping to engender public support to stop the process. This gambit failed badly. The

---

[16] See Larrabee, 2010, pp. 98–109.

[17] See Günter Seufert, *Is the Fethullah Gülen Movement Overstretching Itself? A Turkish Religious Community as a National and International Player*, Berlin: German Institute for International and Security Affairs, January 2014, p. 16.

[18] *Ergenekon* (named for a mythical Central Asian valley) became a watchword for efforts by a secular "deep state" to end the AKP's rule. The investigations led to the arrest and trial of criminals and militant nationalists (whom the military allegedly planned to use for covert domestic operations), citizens and journalists close to the military, and former and active military officers. See Seufert, 2014. The Supreme Court of Appeals ruled in 2016 that the organization did not exist and dismissed most convictions due to lack of evidence and investigation irregularities. See Metin Gurcan, "What Turkey Can Learn from Coup Plot Case Dismissal," *Al-Monitor*, April 25, 2016a.

[19] In the *Balyoz* investigation, 365 suspects, including top commanders, were found guilty in 2012. An appeals court dismissed charges against 88 defendants in 2013, and the Turkish Constitutional Court granted the remaining defendants a retrial in June 2014. The second trial in 2015, coming as the AKP's efforts to root out Gülenists deepened, resulted in a mass acquittal. The evidence in the case was seen as flimsy from the outset, and Erdoğan asserted in 2015 that the government had been misled by (Gülenist) prosecutors. See Cagri Ozdemir, "Analysis: Turkey's Former Generals Walk Free on 'Coup' Verdict," *Middle East Eye*, April 5, 2015.

military's reputation was already tarnished, and the resignations allowed Erdoğan to appoint a new, more compliant chief of the TGS and other military leaders and to further strengthen civilian control of the TSK. *Milliyet* columnist Asli Aydıntaşbaş declared these events "the symbolic moment where the first Turkish republic ends and the second republic begins."[20]

On the judicial front of this power struggle, Erdoğan was able to secure strong support (58 percent of the vote) in a 2010 referendum for a package of constitutional amendments—including several progressive measures—that the AKP billed as democratizing the civilian courts and curbing the power of the military courts. The goal (and the net effect) of the measures, however, was to upend the secular establishment's domination of the civilian courts and give the government greater political control over the entire judicial system.[21]

The Authoritarian Drift Deepens Under Growing Nationalism

As it has moved to consolidate power, the AKP government has also restricted media freedom and forcefully repressed several flare-ups of dissent from civil society. The AKP's initial support for enhanced freedom of expression has stalled and steadily declined with the prosecution of more than 250 journalists, publishers, and activists since 2007. The Committee to Protect Journalists regularly names Turkey the world's leading jailer of journalists—73 in 2017—and Freedom House had declared the status of Turkey's press as "not free" since 2014, especially due to a crackdown on media outlets during and after the Gezi Park protests.[22] In summer 2013, authorities brutally evicted a group of environmental activists who were protesting the loss of green space as the result of government plans, backed personally by Erdoğan, to construct a shopping center in a section of Taksim Gezi Park in central Istanbul. The actions against the protesters triggered anti-government demonstrations by more than 3 million people across Turkey that were also forcefully repressed by police. By the end of August, eight people died, at least four as a result of police action, and about 8,000 were injured.[23] Although the government agreed to halt the construction, many of those who had sup-

---

[20] Gul Tuysuz and Sabrina Tavernise, "Top Generals Quit in Group, Stunning Turks," *New York Times,* July 29, 2011.

[21] Cornell, 2014.

[22] Elana Beiser, "Record Number of Journalists Jailed as Turkey, China, Egypt Pay Scant Price for Repression," Committee to Protect Journalists, December 13, 2017; and Freedom House, "Freedom of the Press 2014: Turkey," webpage, 2014.

[23] These figures were compiled by Turkish medical organizations. See Amnesty International, *Gezi Park Protests: Brutal Denial of the Right to Peaceful Assembly in Turkey,* London, October 2, 2013; and "Timeline of Gezi Park Protests," *Hürriyet Daily News,* June 6, 2013.

ported the protests lost their jobs, and some faced criminal charges.[24] Though unprecedented in scale, the protests neither galvanized Turkish and Kurdish critics of the AKP to form a unified opposition nor turned into a sustainable political power.[25]

Since the Gezi Park protests, authorities have broken up numerous demonstrations, and the police have been granted more legal powers to use force against protesters.[26] The AKP also undertook an intense campaign to undermine critical media outlets and establish new, more-pliant ones that would echo the party line. The AKP continued its polarizing efforts to transform Turkish society, and its commitment to political and economic reforms diminished markedly. As we discuss in Chapter Eight, the lack of progress in accession negotiations with the EU further diminished the incentives to pursue reforms.[27] As with corruption charges that surfaced in late 2013, the Gezi Park protests focused not on the AKP and the government as an institution but on Erdoğan personally. Some interlocutors have suggested that Erdoğan has since begun to see his power position as essential to his physical survival.[28] When the AKP failed to gain a supermajority in the June 2015 general elections, which would have allowed Erdoğan to consolidate presidential power through constitutional changes, it underlined that he could not count on the party's ongoing success at the ballot box to achieve this key goal. This set the stage for another turning point in Turkish politics.

Beyond Turkey's drift toward authoritarianism, the June 2015 parliamentary elections coincided with a new strategy by Erdoğan to secure his political survival. As the HDP was running on its own and on a platform explicitly against Erdoğan's presidential ambitions, polls indicated even before the general elections that a liberal stance toward the PKK would lose him more votes in the Turkish nationalist camp than could be gained in the Kurdish and liberal one.[29] Erdoğan had previously played the nationalist card prior to the June 2011 elections, ordering the destruction of the Statue of Humanity on the Turkish-Armenian border, which local authorities had commissioned as a symbol of dialogue and reconciliation.

---

[24] Constanze Letsch, "A Year After the Protests, Gezi Park Nurtures the Seeds of a New Turkey," *The Guardian*, May 29, 2014.

[25] See Ezgi Başaran, *Frontline Turkey: The Conflict at the Heart of the Middle East*, London: I.B. Tauris, 2017, pp. 94–97.

[26] Freedom House "Freedom in the World 2017: Turkey," webpage, 2017.

[27] See Larrabee, 2010, pp. 98–109.

[28] Several interlocutors noted a personal component to this, implying that Erdoğan was also concerned about possible legal persecution once out of office, given his own previous experiences in prison, the 2013 Egyptian coup against democratically elected President Mohamed Morsi, and the corruption charges against Erdoğan's family in late 2013.

[29] Cagaptay, 2017, p. 139; and Başaran, 2017, pp. 144–145.

Voting patterns in the 2015 election reflected the deepening political polarization. The AKP and the MHP dominated in the provinces of the conservative, nationalist Anatolian heartland; the CHP held on to its base along the Aegean and parts of the Mediterranean coast and urban areas; and the HDP won most provinces in the Kurdish southeast. One of the big winners of the June 2015 elections had been the MHP, which won more than 1.1 million votes away from the AKP.[30] The party's leader, Devlet Bahçeli, had announced in March 2015 that he would not recognize Erdoğan, whom he accused of "constitutional crimes" and corruption as the president of Turkey and resisted joining a coalition with the AKP after the June 2015 vote.[31] But by shelving the peace process with the PKK and siding with Bahçeli when he came under attack from MHP dissidents challenging his leadership in 2016, the AKP secured Bahçeli and his followers as important allies for the 2017 referendum proposing a new constitution (discussed later) and the 2018 presidential and parliamentary elections. Although the army's position as a guardian of the political republican status quo eroded, especially after the July 15, 2016, military coup attempt, it has regained public support as a source of national pride in Turkey's military operations in northern Syria and Iraq, indicating closer coordination between the political and military leadership.[32]

Erdoğan's nationalistic stance not only is an outcome of political alignment with the MHP but also reflects an outlook that is growing among other political leaders and the public. In January 2018, Erdoğan called on Turkish youths to learn "what we once were" by studying the life of Abdul Hamid II, the Pan-Islamist 34th Ottoman Sultan. Also named the "Red Sultan," Abdul Hamid II ordered the massacre of thousands of Armenians in the late 19th century, suspended the constitution in 1878, and cracked down on press freedom and political dissent under the pretext of keeping the empire intact.[33] Invocations of Abdul Hamid II's era in AKP and MHP rhetoric and popular culture also emphasize the threats stemming from foreign powers—and the West in particular, often laced with anti-Semitic conspiracy theories—to Turkey's integrity and survival.[34] In 2018 polls, 84 percent of Turks surveyed agreed that "global eco-

---

[30] Sezgin Tüzün, *Lost and Regained AKP Votes and the Ways for Plebiscite Constructed Through the State of Emergency*, London: Research Turkey, 2017.

[31] "'I Do Not Recognize Erdoğan as President,' MHP Head Says," *Hürriyet Daily News*, May 22, 2015.

[32] Gönül Tol and Omer Taşpınar, "Erdogan's Turn to the Kemalists: How It Will Shape Turkish Foreign Policy," *Foreign Affairs*, October 27, 2016.

[33] Igor Torbakov, "Royal Role Models: Historical Revisionism in Russia and Turkey," *Eurasianet*, January 16, 2018. The MHP 2018 election manifesto, entitled "National Revival, Blessed Uprising," said more obliquely that the nation will need to embrace its historical values in order to overcome its problems and to stand up against global challenges. See Sibel Uğurlu, "Turkey's Opposition MHP Unveils Election Manifesto," Anadolu Agency, May 5, 2018.

[34] Aykan Erdemir and Oren Kessler, "A Turkish TV Blockbuster Reveals Erdogan's Conspiratorial, Anti-Semitic Worldview," *Washington Post*, May 15, 2017.

nomic and political elites have too much power over Turkey and should be resisted."[35] While AKP and MHP leaders continuously stress that Turkey is a country under siege, they also strive to link contemporary policy and military successes to the "Golden Age" of the late Ottoman Empire.[36]

The resumed escalation of Ankara's counterinsurgency efforts in southeastern Turkey, northeastern Syria, and northwestern Iraq; the marginalization and outright persecution of the HDP and other dissidents; and the state of emergency declared following the failed July 2016 coup have increased nationalist sentiments, polarization, and citizens' tolerance for restrictions on the political freedoms of others.[37] The AKP's failure or abandonment of its earlier emphasis on religious kinship over ethnic cleavages has been accompanied by growing nativist and anti-Syrian sentiment. In nationwide polls in late 2017, more than two-thirds of respondents saw Turkey's "moral values and traditions" under threat as a result of Syrian immigration, more than 70 percent would not want to have a Syrian refugee as a neighbor, and 86 percent agreed that all Syrians should go back once the war is over.[38] This became a contentious issue in the 2018 elections, with opposition parties criticizing that the enormous resources spent on refugees could be better applied to other domestic priorities and urging prompt repatriation to Syria.[39]

The Gülen Movement and the Impact of the July 15, 2016, Coup Attempt

On July 15, 2016, a renegade faction of the TSK launched a relatively well-planned, but hastily implemented, coup attempt, including synchronized air and ground attacks in Istanbul and Ankara, as well as a commando raid to capture or assassinate Erdoğan, who was on vacation in the resort city of Marmaris. The plotters planned to run the country through a "Peace at Home Movement."[40] Putschist-operated aircraft attacked and damaged the Turkish Parliament and the headquarters of the Turkish National Intelligence Organization (Millî İstihbarat Teşkilatı [MİT]), while land forces closed the Bosporus bridges in Istanbul and fired on civilians who had been encouraged by

---

[35] John Halpin, Michael Werz, Alan Makovsky, and Max Hoffman, "Is Turkey Experiencing a New Nationalism? An Examination of Public Attitudes on Turkish Self-Perception," Center for American Progress, February 11, 2018, p. 18.

[36] They do this, for example, by likening the TSK's capture of the Syrian city of Afrin from forces of the Kurdish People's Protection Units (Yekîneyên Parastina Gel [YPG]) in 2018 to the Turkish defeat of the British and French navies at Çanakkale in 1915. See Nigar Göksel, "Turkey's Siege Mentality," International Crisis Group, March 23, 2018.

[37] Emre Erdoğan and Pınar Uyan Semerci, "Attitudes Towards Syrians in Turkey—2017," presentation slides, Ankara, March 12, 2018; and Halpin et al., 2018, p. 14.

[38] Erdoğan and Semerci, 2018.

[39] Barçın Yinanç, "What Will Happen to Syrian Refugees After Turkey's Election?" *Hürriyet Daily News*, June 21, 2018.

[40] Aaron Stein, "Inside a Failed Coup and Turkey's Fragmented Military," *War on the Rocks*, July 20, 2016.

Erdoğan to protest the blockade. The decision of top military leaders to remain loyal to the government and the rapid mobilization of the AKP's societal base, among other factors, led to a quick faltering of the coup attempt, which nevertheless cost the lives of up to 290 people—among them more than 100 alleged coup plotters—and left more than 1,400 others injured.[41] While investigations are still underway, there are credible reports that the coup attempt was mounted so haphazardly because the plotters became aware of government plans for imminent mass arrests of suspected Gülenists within the TSK in connection with an ongoing espionage investigation. These reports indicate that Erdoğan had approved the prosecutor's plan to make the arrests before the August 1–4 meeting of the Supreme Military Council (Yüksek Askerî Şûra [YAŞ]) and to possibly launch a massive purge of the ranks during the Council.[42]

The coup attempt came as a profound shock to the Turkish public, which believed that the days of periodic military intervention in politics were over, and appears to have also caught Erdoğan and the AKP leadership by surprise.[43] Most Turks had assumed that the reforms undertaken in the previous decade had established a solid barrier against the intervention of the military in Turkish politics. Hours after the failed coup, Erdoğan and AKP leaders blamed Gülen and the followers of his movement in the military, security forces, and civil service for orchestrating the coup.

The AKP-Gülen alliance dominating Turkish politics since 2002 had begun to fray when Erdoğan, seeking to prevent the Gülen movement from becoming a rival power center, refused to include dozens of Gülenists in AKP electoral lists for the June 2011 parliamentary elections.[44] There were also growing policy differences. Gülen opposed the government's negotiations with the PKK during confidential talks in Oslo and efforts to normalize relations with Iran. He also criticized Erdoğan's handling of the Turkish-Israeli flotilla crisis (see Chapter Five) and the Gezi Park protests. In early 2012, leaks proved that the Oslo talks had been illegally taped, and when prosecutors linked to the movement sought to question the head of MİT, Hakan Fidan (who was a close confidant of Erdoğan), about his role in the talks, tensions between the two camps escalated further. Relations reached a breaking point in November 2013 as Erdoğan announced government plans to close Gülenist education centers. In turn, followers of Gülen in the judiciary and police force pursued investigations of alleged widespread corruption within the AKP involving the sons of several ministers (who subsequently resigned), as well as an inquiry into the business activities of Erdoğan's

---

[41] Patrick Kingsley, "Turkey Detains 6,000 over Coup Attempt as Erdoğan Vows to 'Clean State of Virus,'" *The Guardian,* July 17, 2016.

[42] Metin Gurcan, "Why Turkey's Coup Didn't Stand a Chance," *Al-Monitor,* July 17, 2016b.

[43] Henri J. Barkey, "One Year Later, the Turkish Coup Attempt Remains Shrouded in Mystery," *Washington Post,* July 14, 2017.

[44] M. Kemal Kaya and Svante E. Cornell, "The Big Split: The Differences That Led Erdogan and the Gulen Movement to Part Ways," *Turkey Analyst,* Vol. 5, No. 5, March 5, 2012.

sons Bilal and Burak, which was reportedly thwarted. In the wake of this episode, Erdoğan publicly accused Gülen and his followers of operating a parallel state; dismissed alleged members from government positions, especially from the police and judiciary; closed Gülenist preparatory schools and media outlets; and seized companies owned by Gülen supporters.[45] On May 26, 2016, Turkey's National Security Council designated the Gülen movement as a terrorist organization—calling it the Fethullah Terrorist Organization (known as FETO).[46]

In the aftermath of the July 2016 coup attempt, and through the state of emergency invoked shortly thereafter and extended seven times at three-month intervals, the AKP government closed civil society outlets; accelerated its massive crackdown and systematic purges of alleged Gülenists from government institutions; and seized, as of July 2017, assets worth $11 billion of some 1,000 companies linked to the movement and its followers.[47] More than 150,000 people were dismissed from their jobs between July 2016 and January 2018. This figure includes about 110,000 civilian government officials, military personnel, university academics, teachers in state schools (40,000 of whom Turkish authorities claim have since been reinstated), and teachers in private schools whose licenses were revoked. Ministries where the Gülenists were alleged to have gained strong footholds experienced the biggest purges; these included civil servants in the Ministry of Education (33,629, many of whom were teachers), Ministry of Justice (6,168, plus 4,463 judges and prosecutors), Security General Directorate (24,419), Ministry of Interior (5,210), and Ministry of Foreign Affairs (813).[48] As of January 2018, more than 78,000 people had been arrested, with 54,000 released pending trial and 24,660 still in pre-trial detention. In the year following the attempted coup, the Turkish Ministry of Justice reported that more than 169,000 people were the subject of legal proceedings.[49] Approximately 1,500 civil society institutions, including associations, private schools, universities, and research institutions, have been closed. More than 319 journalists have been arrested, at least 150 of whom remain in prison,

---

[45] Jillian Kestler-D'Amours, "Analysis: Dissecting Turkey's Gulen-Erdogan Relationship," *Middle East Eye*, July 21, 2016.

[46] Zülfikar Doğan, "Erdogan Expected to Put Anti-Gulen Movement in High Gear," *Al-Monitor*, June 17, 2016b; and Mark Lowen, "Turkey's Erdogan Battles 'Parallel State,'" BBC News, December 17, 2014. Once the Turkish government officially designated the movement as the Fethullah Terrorist Organization, it sought to have others in the international community do likewise, including the Gulf Cooperation Council (GCC) in October 2016 and the Asian Parliamentary Assembly (APA) in December 2016 at its Ninth Plenary Session.

[47] Mehul Srivastava, "Assets Worth $11bn Seized in Turkey Crackdown," *Financial Times*, July 7, 2017. All dollar values in this report are in U.S. dollars.

[48] These figures were collected by the independent website Turkey Purge, whose numbers include data from the Official Gazette of the Republic of Turkey, as of July 1, 2018 (see Turkey Purge, homepage, undated). See also European Commission, *Turkey 2018 Report*, Strasbourg, April 17, 2018a, pp. 3–8.

[49] European Commission, 2018a.

and 189 media outlets have been shuttered. The purges continue to threaten to reach the higher echelons of the AKP, which had been closely aligned with Gülen for years.[50]

Public support for the initial anti-Gülen purges was strong: According to one poll, 65 percent of Turks surveyed believed Gülen was behind the coup.[51] Many people in the private and public sector—including interlocutors in the Turkish Foreign Ministry—claim to have directly or indirectly experienced Gülen affiliates being promoted faster or favored over various colleagues.[52] Many secular Turks resented the Gülenists for the unwarranted turmoil they caused in orchestrating the *Ergenekon* conspiracy trials, and these Turks feared that a successful coup might have led to the establishment of an Islamist state with even more purges. In the coup's aftermath, many Turks saw Erdoğan as a stabilizing figure who prevents mob violence, among other things, against the Alevi religious minority, and many were also relieved that the economy proved resilient.[53] As the purges turned increasingly into a systematic crackdown on any form of opposition, however, popular support declined. Many Turks across the political spectrum have been alarmed with how the state of emergency accelerated trends toward centralization of power and how AKP officials bluntly used the coup attempt to bully potential rivals to embrace its domestic agenda—above all, the transformation of the political system.

The 2017 Referendum and the Path to the Executive Presidency

Since 2012, the overarching political goals of President Erdoğan and the AKP have been to enact constitutional changes that would transform Turkey's governance from a parliamentary system into a strong executive presidency and to achieve a cultural orientation that reflects the values of the AKP's religiously conservative constituencies.[54] There has been broad political consensus in Turkey that the 1982 constitution imposed by the military should be replaced with one oriented toward civilians and

---

[50] Ulrich von Schwerin, "Is Turkey's AKP Showing Goodwill Towards Gulen Sympathizers Within the Party?" *Deutsche Welle*, June 16, 2017.

[51] The poll was taken by the Andy-Ar organization, which is linked to the AKP. See Daren Butler, "Turks Believe Cleric Gülen Was Behind Coup Attempt: Survey," Reuters, July 26, 2016.

[52] Turkish Foreign Ministry officials, discussion with the authors, Ankara, November 2016 and July 2017; and Turkish Foreign Ministry official, discussion with the authors, Washington, D.C., October 2017.

[53] Alevism is a branch of Islam practiced by ethnic Turks and Kurds that incorporates Shi'a, Sufi, Sunni, and local traditions. It is distinct from Alawism in Syria. Alevis constitute an estimated 10–20 percent of Turkey's population, making them the largest religious minority. See Religious Literacy Project, "Alevism," Harvard Divinity School, webpage, undated.

[54] This agenda is ironically the maturation of the "Turkish-Islamic synthesis" that the military supported in the 1980s to help stabilize the country after a decade of political violence and to counter the spread of Communist groups. General Kenan Evren, who assumed office following the 1980 coup, was a strong, but nonexecutive, president from 1982–1989; he pushed through various constitutional reforms, including restrictions on civil liberties. Evren also made religious education mandatory to counter the appeal of leftist radicalism and stabilize the political violence of the 1970s, under a policy that came to be known as the Turkish-Islamic synthesis. See Banu

democratic principles. Erdoğan declared his interest in a presidential, yet constitutionally amended, system in 2010.[55] After the 2011 general election, parties agreed to form a constitutional commission and to a partial draft, but the commission was dissolved in 2016 after the CHP flatly rejected the AKP's push for a presidential system. The AKP set out to draft a constitution on its own but lacked the requisite two-thirds majority in Parliament to approve it. The AKP then sought a parliamentary vote to present the draft constitution to a national referendum, which stalled until after the July 2016 coup attempt, when MHP leader Bahçeli announced his support for a strong executive presidency on the condition that the first four articles of the existing constitution (which reaffirm secularism and Kemalist nationalism) remain intact.[56]

The April 16, 2017, referendum, held under emergency rule and the AKP's domination of the media, was heavily weighted to ensure passage of the government's proposed constitutional amendments.[57] The closeness of the vote despite these advantages reflects deep divisions along political, class, and ethnic lines and confirmed the predictions of many political observers that it would be difficult for Erdoğan to gain sufficient public support for the constitutional changes, given the sluggish economic conditions at the time. As Figure 2.1 illustrates, conservative voters in the AKP's stronghold in the Anatolian heartland voted for the referendum, while areas where the secular opposition remains strong—Istanbul, Ankara, and along the Aegean coast—and the predominantly Kurdish provinces in the southeast voted against. Because of irregularities in the voting process, the CHP and the HDP called for annulment of the referendum, without success.[58]

AKP Rifts Widen, Opposition Is Diminished in and Outside of Parliament

Erdoğan's growing centralization of power and authoritarianism have also affected the AKP itself. The 2007 presidential election led to destruction of the political equilibrium within the AKP leadership. As Gül assumed the nonpartisan presidency, his fellow AKP co-founder Bülent Arınç simultaneously ended his term as the speaker of Parliament. The duo had acted as balancing and moderating influences on Erdoğan

---

Eligür, *The Mobilization of Political Islam in Turkey*, Cambridge, United Kingdom: Cambridge University Press, 2010, pp. 85–96.

[55] Halil Karaveli, "Referendum Victory Opens the Way for Erdogan's Presidency," *Turkey Analyst*, September 15, 2010.

[56] Berk Esen and Şebnem Gümüşçü, "A Small Yes for Presidentialism: The Turkish Constitutional Referendum of April 2017," *South European Society and Politics*, Vol. 22, No. 3, October 2017.

[57] Organization for Security and Co-operation in Europe, *Turkey, Constitutional Referendum, 16 April 2017: Final Report*, Warsaw, June 22, 2017.

[58] Patrick Kingsley, "Videos Fuel Charges of Fraud in Erdogan's Win in Turkey Referendum," *New York Times*, April 18, 2017b.

Figure 2.1
Results of the April 18, 2017, Constitutional Referendum

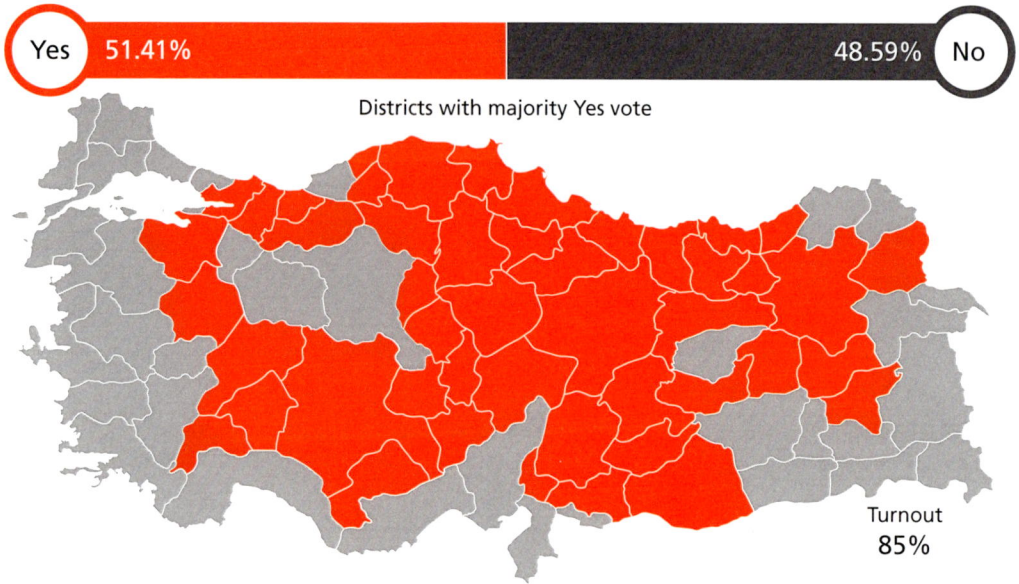

SOURCE: "Turkey Referendum: The Numbers That Tell the Story," BBC News, April 17, 2017. Used with permission.

within the party.[59] A heavily personalist style of party and government leadership emerged, accompanied by purges first of allies of Gül and Arınç and, in 2013, of Gül himself and later Foreign Minister Ahmet Davutoğlu, through reshuffles in the cabinet and party ranks.[60] Specifically, the 2013 corruption scandal was a stress test for the AKP's cohesion, and it resulted in the dismissal of several cabinet members yet no formal investigation. Gül began to distance himself from Erdoğan during the Gezi Park protests, by publicly defending the right of protest and later by expressing his preference for a reform of the existing parliamentary system. He was denied a formal return to politics when his term ended the same year.[61]

In August 2014, Erdoğan, who "appears to regard himself as the embodiment of the national will,"[62] assumed the officially nonpartisan position of president and was thus forced to pass official party leadership to the prime minister. However, Erdoğan continued to heavily and effectively influence cabinet and party politics by, among

---

[59] Cornell, 2014.

[60] Cornell, 2014.

[61] Maximilian Popp, "Turkish Power Struggle: Brotherly Love Begins to Fray in Ankara," *Spiegel Online*, June 25, 2013; and Lauren Williams, "Turkey's AKP Power Struggle Comes to a Boil," *Al Jazeera*, August 26, 2014.

[62] Gareth Jenkins, "Erdoğan's Volatile Authoritarianism: Tactical Ploy or Strategic Vision?" *Turkey Analyst*, Vol. 5, No. 23, December 5, 2012, p. 19.

other things, enhancing societal polarization and mobilizing conservative nationalists against Kurds, Alevis, and secular intellectuals.[63] Erdoğan's personal dominance of political life has intensified and has diminished the independence of state institutions, pluralism, and intraparty democracy. This has weakened the functioning of political and economic institutions to the point where even formally independent bodies, such as the Central Bank, refrain from making important decisions without the president's consent. Moreover, because the 2017 constitutional amendments allow the president to remain affiliated with a political party, Erdoğan resumed the position of AKP chair during an extraordinary party congress in May of that year and started shifting personnel and reshaping electoral lists.[64]

Despite these rifts within the AKP, the aftermath of the 2016 coup attempt has put the party in a much more comfortable position over any opposition, including legally and politically. Parliament is no longer functioning as an effective overseer of the government, and opposition parties have been largely neutralized. The secular, social-democratic CHP, the second-largest party in Parliament, had been marginalized in the political discourse in recent years, in large measure by a nearly constant media presence of government officials and the president. Representatives of both the CHP and the HDP have come under legal attack, particularly since the AKP won approval of constitutional amendments in 2016 to lift immunity for more than one-third of the members of Parliament.[65]

Despite the fact that the MHP won only 11.9 percent of the vote in the 2015 parliamentary elections and endured substantial intraparty strife, the party and Bahçeli turned out to be big winners in the coup attempt, the subsequent *Yenikapı* consensus, and the 2018 elections.[66] Prior to the 2017 referendum, Bahçeli had been seen by many as Erdoğan's "kingmaker," and the MHP had functioned as an informal coalition partner since it helped assure the AKP's control of government in 2015.[67] Although many

---

[63] M. K. Kaya, "Candidate Lists for the Election to Parliament Display Worrying Fault Lines," *Turkey Analyst*, Vol. 8, No. 8, April 22, 2015; and Turkish analysts, discussion with the authors, Ankara, November 2016.

[64] The April 2017 referendum failed in 17 of Turkey's 30 largest cities, and Erdoğan has attributed this fact to a "metal fatigue" in the AKP's ranks (Serkan Demirtaş, "Is Only President Erdoğan Immune to 'Metal Fatigue'?" *Hürriyet Daily News*, October 25, 2017). He has since pushed out several high-level party officials, including some mayors of major cities. See Carlotta Gall, "Erdogan Trains His Broom on a Sweep of Turkey's Governing Party," *New York Times*, December 23, 2017b.

[65] Mehul Srivastava and Stefan Wagstyl, "Turkey's Parliament Votes to Strip Immunity from a Third of MPs," *Financial Times*, May 20, 2016. The amendment was carefully crafted to apply only to charges that prosecutors sought to file while the bill was being drafted. It is not retroactive, thereby exempting AKP legislators implicated in the 2013 corruption scandal.

[66] Named after a pro-government rally attended by up to 5 million people in Istanbul's Yenikapı district on August 7, 2016, the *Yenikapı* consensus describes an informal multi-party agreement among the AKP, the MHP, and the CHP to set political differences aside in favor of national unity and protecting democracy from common threats. See "Millions Stand for Democracy in Turkey," *Hürriyet Daily News*, August 5, 2016.

[67] Sukru Kucuksahin, "This Woman May Be the Biggest Opposition to Erdoğan," *Al-Monitor*, May 26, 2016.

prominent members of the MHP split from the party to form a new center-right party opposing the executive presidency in October 2017, Bahçeli maintained his position as party leader.[68] The government announced plans to fill some 60,000 new positions in the state bureaucracy in 2017, most of them in the Ministries of Defense, Health, and Interior, as well as in the police forces. According to one interlocutor, one-third of these positions likely will be staffed with MHP cadres in return for the party's support for introducing the presidential system.[69] The MHP also has helped mobilize pro-AKP demonstrators through its ties to the Islamist National Outlook (Milli Goruş) and ultra-nationalist Grey Wolves organizations.

Representatives of international nongovernmental organizations report that civil society has been demobilized and silenced in a situation where system conformity to new social norms is no longer a guarantee of security. Especially the state of emergency empowered the government to ban or restrict any form of gathering and rallies and to declare certain public and private areas off limits—especially in the Kurdish areas in Turkey's southeast.[70]

A Short-Lived Opening to the Kurds

The AKP's historic anti-secularist stance and the decline of political and civil liberties in the past decade have shaped its policies toward Turkey's largest minority, the Kurds. Close to 20 percent of the population identifies themselves as Kurdish, and although these Turks are heavily concentrated in southeastern provinces, significant numbers now live in cities across the country. Many Kurds had resisted Atatürk's concept of assimilation from the outset and staged major uprisings in the 1920s and 1930s that were forcibly suppressed. Violence flared again in 1984 when PKK founder Abdullah Öcalan launched a terrorist insurgency, focused on southeastern Turkey and supported from safe havens in Iraq and Syria, to establish a separate Kurdish state. The terrorist campaign and government countermeasures have continued over the past three decades with several ceasefires, resulting in an estimated 30,000–45,000 fatalities, including 6,000 Turkish military and police forces and many Kurdish civilians. Thousands of Kurdish villages have been destroyed, and hundreds of thousands of Kurds have been displaced from their homes.[71] After his capture in 1999, Öcalan proposed to

---

[68] Umut Uras, "Ex-Turkish Minister Meral Aksener Launches New Party," *Al Jazeera*, October 26, 2017.

[69] Turkish analyst, discussion with the authors, Ankara, November 2016. Another interlocutor reported five additional cabinet posts that were promised to the MHP.

[70] Freedom House, 2017.

[71] The totals of fatalities, wounded, and displaced persons estimated by Turkish authorities and the PKK have a wide range. The Turkish government reports that "more than 40 thousand people lost their lives because of PKK terrorism" (Republic of Turkey Ministry of Foreign Affairs, "PKK," webpage, undated-b; see also Berkay Mandıracı, "Turkey's PKK Conflict: The Death Toll," International Crisis Group, July 20, 2016b). Since the col-

help the Turkish government settle the conflict. He directed that PKK militants implement a ceasefire and committed to using political means to gain cultural rights, constitutional changes, and freedom of expression. Turkey's designation as a candidate for membership in the EU that same year led to the elimination of laws restricting teaching and broadcasts in the Kurdish language and of the death penalty—which saved Öcalan's life. After the fall of Saddam Hussein in 2003, the PKK took advantage of the changed situation to renew its campaign in southeastern Turkey from safe havens in Iraq's Qandil Mountains. The Turkish military responded forcefully, including after a further uptick in 2007, with air attacks and a major ground operation into northern Iraq.[72] In the second half of that decade, Turkey's security establishment recognized that a purely military solution was impossible. In light of this assessment, the National Security Council authorized secret contacts with the PKK in 2007, accelerating internationally supported mediation efforts since 2005, the so-called "Oslo talks."[73]

By 2009, the AKP declared openly that it was pursuing a process with the goal of resolving the Kurdish question. The AKP's initial strategy was to achieve disarmament of the PKK in return for democratic reforms and recognition of the Kurds' cultural and political rights.[74] The AKP resorted to a more nationalist stance, however, after suffering a setback in the 2009 municipal elections and after several incidents between the PKK and security forces undermined public support for the process.[75] While the MHP argued that such a process would lead to the partition of the country, the CHP issued mixed messages and demanded that the National Assembly, rather than the government, lead the process. HDP and PKK leaders voiced support for the process as a chance to deepen democracy in Turkey but cast the government's actions as inadequate and wavering. The PKK committed to several ceasefires and sought to use the process to transform from an internationally outlawed terrorist organization to a legitimate political power within Turkey. The reconciliation process faced many challenges from the start and faltered amid the June 2011 general elections, after which the negotiations broke down again.[76]

---

lapse of the two-and-a-half-year ceasefire in July 2015, the International Crisis Group has maintained an interactive website with the latest tallies of the human cost (see International Crisis Group, "Turkey's PKK Conflict: A Visual Explainer," as updated April 5, 2019).

[72] Aliriza, 2009a, p. 8.

[73] Başaran, 2017, pp. 73–74; and F. Stephen Larrabee and Gönül Tol, "Turkey's Kurdish Challenge," *Survival*, Vol. 53, No. 4, August/September 2011, p. 145.

[74] As part of the effort to recognize Kurdish culture, the public broadcasting agency, TRT, launched a 24-hour Kurdish-language channel, and the Council of Higher Education took steps to establish Kurdish-language and literature departments in universities. See Mesut Yeğen, *The Kurdish Peace Process in Turkey: Genesis, Evolution and Prospects*, Istanbul: Stiftung Mercator, Istituto Affari Internazionali, and Istanbul Policy Center, Global Turkey in Europe Working Paper 11, May 2015, pp. 5–11.

[75] Aliriza, 2009a, pp. 1–3.

[76] Başaran, 2017, pp. 76, 87–88.

Following another cycle of conflict that ended in stalemate, a further round of talks between the Turkish government and the PKK took place between early 2013 and summer 2015, during which both sides declared that a framework accord was in reach. While the AKP was assuming a sustained ceasefire would be beneficial in critical elections in 2014 and 2015, especially amid deteriorating relations with the Gülen movement, the PKK's military attention had moved southward when the Syrian civil war appeared to provide a historic opportunity to establish an autonomous Kurdish state in northern Syria.[77]

Even prior to their collapse in 2015, the talks failed to produce substantial results for a variety of reasons.[78] Ankara's hostile policy toward the PKK's Syrian offshoot, the Democratic Union Party (Partiya Yekîtiya Demokrat [PYD]) and its militias, created additional discontent among the Kurdish public. This was particularly true when the conflict between Syrian Kurds and Islamist anti-Assad rebels, many of them assumed to be backed by Turkey and its allies, escalated and peaked with ISIS's October 2014 siege of the Kurdish border town Kobanî.[79] More than 50 people died in protests against the government's unwillingness to assist Kobanî and other areas in southeast Turkey where subsequent clashes broke out. The crisis demonstrated not only Ankara's disregard for Turkish Kurds' concerns regarding their Syrian kin but also the perpetual failure of the AKP to develop a comprehensive Kurdish policy at home and in the region.[80]

Despite the failings of the government's strategy, nearly two-thirds of Kurdish voters in Turkey (about 16 percent of the electorate) supported the AKP in national elections in 2002, 2007, and 2011, as well as in the municipal elections in 2004 and 2009.[81] Although this electoral dominance in the Kurdish region had been substantially challenged by the HDP's success in the June 2015 general elections, the AKP managed to regain 1 million Kurdish votes in the November 2015 snap elections through a massive campaign against resumed PKK violence in the southeast and mass arrests of

---

[77] Some argued that a positive outcome of the peace process could have also ended Öcalan's imprisonment. See Başaran, 2017, p. 82.

[78] The problems included a lack of parliamentary oversight or a credible independent commission; the government's arbitrary position on the success of talks; its vetoing of critical voices from the Kurdish delegation; and disagreements over the conditions of the PKK's withdrawal to northern Iraq (which partially was implemented from May 8 to September 9, 2013), disarmament, and amnesty to former fighters. See Başaran, 2017, pp. 90–103.

[79] Analysts close to the government argued that Turkish security forces did not intervene on behalf of Kobanî's residents because ISIS was then holding hostage 46 members of the Turkish consulate staff in Mosul, who were released one week after the siege started. See Yeğen, 2015, pp. 8–11; Chris Johnston, "Isis Militants Release 49 Hostages Taken at Turkish Consulate in Mosul," *The Guardian*, September 20, 2014; and Başaran, 2017, p. 110.

[80] See Başaran, 2017, p. 115.

[81] Şener Aktürk, *Regimes of Ethnicity and Nationhood in Germany, Russia, and Turkey*, Cambridge, United Kingdom: Cambridge University Press, 2012, p. 180.

HDP officials.[82] While this strategy proved to be successful for the AKP also regaining the parliamentary majority that it had lost in the June national elections, Erdoğan's personal campaign against the HDP continued. According to HDP sources, 8,711 of its members and supporters were detained and 2,705 arrested between July 2015 and early 2017.[83] In November 2016, the party's then co-chairs, Selahattin Demirtaş and Figen Yüksekdağ, and 11 other members of Parliament were arrested, and they remained in jail as of mid-2019.[84] Although the government made no move to actually ban the party, the sweeping disenfranchisement of the HDP's leadership and voter base destroyed most of its political leverage.[85] Surprisingly, the party was able to garner 11.7 percent of the vote in the 2018 election, crossing the 10-percent threshold required to be seated in Parliament. Nevertheless, the HDP remains marginalized in a chamber with diminished authority, where two-thirds of parliamentary colleagues are from nationalist parties. The HDP's seating in Parliament also allows the AKP to argue with international critics that Kurds are not denied a voice in politics.[86]

Implications for Civil-Military Relations and Military Capabilities

Because of mutual suspicions, Erdoğan's relations with the TSK were tense during the first five years of his tenure.[87] The AKP was able to build support among a broad political coalition to implement several reforms that brought civil-military relations more in line with democratic norms, particularly by linking them with other domestic reforms required to enhance the country's candidacy for EU accession negotiations. The aforementioned 2007 *e-memorandum* crisis gave Erdoğan a stronger hand in dealing with the military and led to a new modus vivendi with the TSK.[88] Since 2010, the government has strengthened its authority over the YAŞ substantially—for example, vetoing the appointment of officers detained in the *Ergenekon* and *Balyoz* cases and imposing

---

[82] Gönül Tol, "Turkey's Kurds Split by AKP Policies," *Cairo Review of Global Affairs*, December 10, 2015.

[83] "Prosecutor Seeks Life Sentence for HDP Co-Chair," *Rudaw,* December 1, 2017.

[84] Demirtaş, who is facing 142 years in prison for, among other things, "establishing a terrorist organization" and "spreading terror group propaganda," ran for president from prison in June 2018. Yüksekdağ served as co-leader of the HDP for seven years, until her parliamentary membership and later her party membership were revoked by the courts following a six-year prison sentence for allegedly distributing terrorist propaganda. See Daren Butler, "Pro-Kurdish Opposition Leader's Trial Opens in Turkey," *Reuters,* December 7, 2017.

[85] Ayla Jean Yackley, "One Year into Crackdown, Turkey's Pro-Kurdish Opposition Battered but Defiant," *Al-Monitor*, November 6, 2017a; and Ayla Jean Yackley, "Trial of Turkey's Opposition Leader Starts Without Him in Court," *Al-Monitor*, December 8, 2017b.

[86] Yavuz Baydar, "Questions and Bitter Truths in a Hazy Post-Election Landscape," *Ahval News*, June 28, 2018.

[87] Caliskan, 2017, p. 103.

[88] Acar Kutay, "From Guardianship to Civilian Control: How Did the Turkish Military Get Here?" *Outlines of Global Transformations*, Vol. 10, No. 3, 2017.

its own list of promotions and retirements.[89] Following the resignation of the top military leadership in July 2011, Erdoğan appointed a new, more compliant military leadership.[90] Since then, and especially after the Gülen-AKP conflict erupted and the collapse of the peace process with the PKK, relations between the top commanders of the TSK and AKP leadership have improved substantially under a more compliant TSK leadership and following the success of the 2018 military campaign in Afrin, Syria.

The TSK ranks have been significantly reduced by post-coup purges. Eleven high-ranking officers from the Army, Navy, Air Force, Gendarmerie, and Coast Guard were discharged in the immediate aftermath of the failed coup. Of 325 general and flag officers in the Army, Navy, and Air Force, 150 (46 percent) have either been cashiered or involuntarily retired.[91] In the seven months after the attempted coup, there was also approximately a 20-percent reduction in commissioned officers, from 32,451 to 25,728; an elimination of 1,400 staff officers (77 percent of the total); and the abolition of the staff officer system in August 2016.[92] A total of 16,409 cadets at all levels of professional military education were also dismissed by the end of 2017.[93] The reformed military academies and officer schools have produced students to replace those purged, but in early 2018, the number of officers (27,000) and the number of noncommissioned officers (67,000) who had graduated were insufficient to restore the TSK's pre-coup force levels.[94] In January 2018, the TSK announced plans to recruit 42,938 personnel, including 3,755 officers, 5,375 noncommissioned officers, 13,213 specialized sergeants, and 20,595 contracted rank and file personnel.[95] Defense Minister Aker stated in December 2018 that 15,154 personnel, including 7,595 officers—of whom

---

[89] Erdoğan also subsequently refused to sign YAŞ decisions in military headquarters, and, for the first time ever, several generals and admirals were suspended by civilian ministers in November 2010 because of alleged involvement in coup cases. See Tuba Eldem, *Guardians Entrapped: The Demise of the Turkish Armed Forces as a Veto-Player*, doctoral thesis, Toronto: University of Toronto, 2013, p. 298; Saban Kardas, "Turkish Civilian-Military Relations Overhauled," *Eurasia Daily Monitor*, Vol. 7, No. 156, August 12, 2010; and Mehmet Bardakçi, "Coup Plots and the Transformation of Civil–Military Relations in Turkey Under AKP Rule," *Turkish Studies*, Vol. 14, No. 3, 2013, p. 419.

[90] Steven A. Cook, "Tarnished Brass," *Foreign Policy*, August 2, 2011.

[91] Metin Gurcan, "Turkish Military Purges Decimate Career Officer, Pilot Ranks," *Al-Monitor*, May 29, 2018.

[92] Gurcan, 2018.

[93] The 16,409 cadets included 4,090 from military high schools, 6,140 from noncommissioned officers' colleges, and 6,179 from university-level military schools. These figures are from Turkey Purge (undated) as of December 2017.

[94] Gurcan, 2018.

[95] "Turkish General Staff to Recruit over 40,000 Personnel as Compensation for Post-Coup Attempt Dismissals," *Hürriyet Daily News*, January 2, 2018.

150 were generals or admirals—had been dismissed from the TSK over their links to the Gülen movement since 2016.[96]

Because the military purges were focused on senior leadership and on officers involved in staff positions and personnel management, the Turkish government likely assessed that the Gülenists first sought to gain influence over recruitment and promotions, as has been alleged in the Foreign Ministry and other civilian agencies. The government case appears to be that, once that goal was accomplished, the Gülenists were able to infiltrate sympathizers into headquarters staffs and military specialties that could prove decisive operationally, as well as the military intelligence, judicial, and health systems, to advance their hidden agenda.[97] This assessment undoubtedly influenced the significant post-coup reforms and restructuring that gave the president and the ministers of defense and interior new authorities over the TSK. An emergency decree-law promulgated on July 31, 2016, initiated a historical overhaul in Turkish civil military relations.[98]

First, under the decree-law, the Land Forces, Naval Forces, and Air Force commanders have come under the immediate control of the civilian minister of defense, reducing the authority of the chief of the TGS. Under the new constitution, the president can receive information from and issue orders directly to service commanders. The Gendarmerie General Command and Coast Guard Command had earlier been brought under the control of the Interior Ministry. The Parliament's role in oversight of the TSK has not figured in public discussions of the reforms.

Second, the government established a National Defense University, which should serve as "an umbrella body encompassing all educational institutions of the Turkish Army"; at the same time, the government closed all existing military academies, which had been "crucial incubators of the armed forces' distinctive culture."[99] In October 2016, without consulting the military, Erdoğan appointed a head of the National Defense University; he selected Erhan Afyoncu, a historian without prior military—or relevant academic—experience.[100] In addition, under the decree-law, the number of

---

[96] "Turkey Remands in Custody 118 Soldiers over Suspected FETÖ Links," *Hürriyet Daily News*, December 18, 2018. The total number of military personnel dismissed grew to 16,540 by April 2019 ("Turkish Military Dismissed 16,540 Personnel Since Coup Attempt," *Hürriyet Daily News*, April 29, 2019).

[97] Gurcan, 2018; Turkish analysts, discussion with the authors, Ankara, June 2017; and Turkish analyst, discussion with the authors, Washington, D.C., October 2017.

[98] "Turkish Gov't Introduces New Decree Law to Overhaul Army," *Hürriyet Daily News*, July 31, 2016.

[99] Mark Galeotti, "What Turkey Can Learn from Russia About Coup-Proofing the Military," *War on the Rocks*, August 2, 2016.

[100] Metin Gurcan, "Turkey Seeks to Replenish Severely Depleted Military," *Al-Monitor*, May 10, 2017b.

contract officers, who graduate from civilian universities instead of military academies, has increased substantially.[101]

Third, the structure of the YAŞ, the forum for all decisions regarding military promotions, retirement, and disciplinary measures, is now subject to greater civilian influence. Prior to 2016, the prime minister headed the YAŞ, and the only other civilian joining all 15 four-star generals and admirals had been the minister of defense.[102] The YAŞ's new composition includes the deputy prime minister and the foreign, justice, and interior ministers. At the same time, the number of generals and admirals had been significantly reduced—to just the chief of the TGS and the service commanders. Most prominently, the Gendarmerie commander will no longer be a member of the YAŞ, and the defense minister assumed the role of YAŞ secretary-general from the deputy chief of the TGS.[103] At the August 2, 2017, YAŞ meeting, Erdoğan approved new commanders for the Land, Naval, and Air Forces while retaining the chief of the TGS. These leadership changes reflect the increasing politicization of military promotions and Erdoğan's desire that the armed forces focus on succeeding in Syria, combating terrorism, and rooting out Gülenists. This was the first meeting of the YAŞ since it was restructured following the failed July 2016 military coup, and both the president and prime minister appear to have played major roles in developing and finalizing the promotion lists; these lists had previously been shaped in secrecy by the senior military leadership before the YAŞ and routinely approved as presented.[104] There was a major shake-up in the leadership of the Turkish Navy, which left the service with a commander who has the lowest seniority among his fellow chiefs. The YAŞ also extended the terms of an unusual number of senior officers who qualified for retirement, and others were promoted to one-star rank. These actions may be designed to help deal with the effects of purges after the coup, which created a significant gap between the number of four-star and one-star generals and flag officers and has likely diminished the readiness of some units.

The purges and military reforms appear to have adversely affected the TSK's readiness, capability, and morale, as well as civil-military relations. Informed observers report that the organizational reforms, driven by political considerations, have clouded the chain of command, increased inter-service rivalry, reduced the TSK's tactical and strategic capacity, and led to a politicization of the officer corps. The purges have been

---

[101] The National Defense University was tasked to educate staff officers; provide graduate-level education; and operate service schools, noncommissioned officer colleges, and noncommissioned officer vocational schools for higher education. The Ministry of Defense will execute all administrative tasks of the university, especially the recruitment of academic and administrative personnel ("Turkish Gov't Introduces New Decree Law to Overhaul Army," 2016; Gurcan, 2017b).

[102] See Eldem, 2013, p. 297.

[103] "Turkish Gov't Introduces New Decree Law to Overhaul Army," 2016.

[104] "Army, Navy, Air Force Commanders Reshuffled in Turkey's Supreme Military Council," *Daily Sabah*, August 2, 2017.

most damaging to the Air Force and have led to a substantial shortage of trained pilots (see Chapter Nine). The TSK has attempted to reactivate some retired officers, but only a small number appear to have returned to active military service thus far. More than 200 mid-level officers, many of whom had received advanced education in the United States and were involved in work on military transformation projects, were purged in 2016, which could slow modernization efforts.[105]

Unusual political activity by the military leadership and a general decline in professionalism have alienated lower ranks of the TSK. Mid-level officers are reported to be extremely frustrated with the military leadership. Some observers believe that this discontent might even lead to another coup attempt at some point. Public trust in the military, previously seen as the guardian of order and the secular state, has eroded, but it has been restored somewhat following the success of the TSK's operations in 2018 against Kurdish forces in Syria's Afrin province.[106]

Throughout this turmoil, Hulusi Akar has remained a key interlocutor for the U.S. and other foreign militaries. His retention of his position as TGS chief in 2017 and subsequent appointment as Minister of Defense in July 2018 in the first presidential decree under the new executive presidential system suggest that he will continue to be the leading figure in Turkish defense affairs for some time.[107]

Gendarmerie

The security-sector reforms after the coup attempt also included transferring control of Turkey's paramilitary police force, the Gendarmerie, from the TSK to the Ministry of Interior.[108] Until March 2015, the TGS had decided promotions and dismissals inside the formally Ministry of Interior–controlled Gendarmerie General Command.[109] The European Commission's *Turkey 2015 Report* commended the transfer "of authority to

---

[105] Metin Gurcan, "Why U.S.-Educated Turkish Officers Could Soon Be out of Their Jobs," *Al-Monitor*, October 18, 2016d.

[106] According to a poll conducted by Kadir Has University in December 2016, the military had lost its decades-long status as the most trusted institution as a result of the coup attempt on July 15 of that year. In late 2015, 62.4 percent had named the armed forces as the most trusted institution, but in late 2016, only 47.4 percent agreed to this. As the presidency rose from 46.9 percent to 49.4 percent in the poll, the military came in second. See "Public Trust in Military Plunges After Turkey's Failed Coup: Poll," *Hürriyet Daily News*, January 19, 2017.

[107] "Turkey's New Top Soldier Appointed by First Presidential Decree," *Hürriyet Daily News*, July 10, 2018. In that same decree, Erdoğan appointed the then–Commander of the Turkish Land Forces, General Yaşar Güler, to be chief of the TGS, reflecting his enhanced control over military appointments.

[108] In November 2014, the Gendarmerie had about 190,000 personnel (31 generals, 28,000 officers and non-commissioned officers, 40,000 professional specialist sergeants, 3,500 civilian workers and clerks, and 117,000 conscripts) and served as Turkey's paramilitary rural police force responsible for 80 percent of the country's territory. With the Gendarmerie General Command having its own "commando brigades, air elements, special forces battalions and van-based corps," columnist Metin Gurcan called it a "fully-fledged military machine" (Metin Gurcan, "Splitting Gendarmerie from Turkish Army: Reform or Bad Timing?" *Al-Monitor*, November 3, 2014).

[109] Ali Ünal, "Turkey Ends Tutelage by Military with Gendarmerie Reform," *Daily Sabah*, March 10, 2015.

appoint, suspend and supervise gendarmerie personnel in the provinces" to the Ministry of Interior, because it "widened civilian oversight of the law enforcement duties of the gendarmerie."[110] Those opposing the reform, however, anticipate (1) an AKP plan to fill Gendarmerie ranks with AKP partisans and to create a force loyal only to the party and (2) an expected $7 billion in additional costs if civil servants would replace unpaid conscripts.[111] From a security perspective, increased political influence could reduce discipline and professionalism in the Gendarmerie, as well as the morale of personnel. In the fight against terrorism, where the Gendarmerie and the TSK have cooperated closely in the past, command and control problems could occur at the operational level, and the military would be deprived of the experience and networks of the Gendarmerie and, in case of a war, would have 150,000 fewer troops readily available.[112] Although new legislation after the coup attempt transferred procurement and logistics authorities and especially education from the TSK to the Ministry of Interior, the "civilianization" of the Gendarmerie remains incomplete: It continues to be commanded by a four-star general, and the staff at General Command headquarters largely hail from military backgrounds.[113]

National Intelligence Organization

Despite the apparent infiltration of MİT by Gülenists, the organization and its chief, Hakan Fidan, appear to remain highly influential in security policy.[114] In early November 2016, an executive decree created two new MİT departments—one charged with coordination among state institutions and one for special operations (a paramilitary operations unit with military functions)—in addition to the existing strategic intelligence department in charge of foreign intelligence-gathering and analysis.[115] These reforms indicate that MİT is moving more toward external operations in the context of the new security concept, discussed later in this chapter, and that it will have less involvement in domestic politics; these shifting responsibilities point toward Turkey founding a new domestic intelligence agency.[116]

---

[110] European Commission, *Turkey 2015 Report*, Brussels, November 10, 2015b, p. 11.

[111] Gurcan, 2014.

[112] Gurcan, 2014.

[113] Metin Gurcan and Megan Gisclon "Turkey's Security Sector After July 15: Democratizing Security or Securitizing the State?" *Turkish Policy Quarterly*, Winter 2017, p. 76.

[114] In response to the coup attempt and the overall changes in the security sector, MİT had discharged some 10 percent of its 3,000 staff members in February 2017, mostly from the electronic and signal intelligence departments (Gurcan and Gisclon, 2017, p. 74).

[115] Pinar Tremblay, "Post-Coup Shake-Up at Turkey's Intelligence Agency," *Al-Monitor*, November 6, 2016a.

[116] Tremblay, 2016a.

Police, Neighborhood Guards, and Private Security Companies

Assumed to be also heavily infiltrated by Gülenists, the police force had been subject to nearly constant purges for years, and, in response to the 2013 protests, it was heavily militarized and granted extensive authorities to suppress domestic and particularly urban dissent.[117] The arrests of at least 40,000 personnel, expanded counterterrorism operations, and several targeted attacks on its cadres added to the pressures on remaining police forces.[118] The uptick in domestic terrorism in 2015 and 2016 made security of cities a major issue.[119] During the re-escalation of tensions with the PKK in the southeast, provincial governors started to hire more than 2,300 "neighborhood guards" (sometimes called "city guards"), who work with local police forces. After the coup attempt, the guards also appeared in Turkey's western cities.[120] A decree in October 2016 broadened these guards' authority, announcing that they would be issued heavy weapons and equipment, would be paid a minimum salary, and would have social security benefits.[121] By March 2017, the number of guards had reportedly increased to 5,400 men in 20 provincial centers, and they were mostly armed with pistols and AK-47 rifles and paid a monthly salary of up to $700.[122] The Ministry of Interior had also announced plans to boost the number of these guards to 12,500 in Istanbul alone in 2017.[123]

Finally, private security firms have become increasingly important in Turkey, with up to 350,000 personnel and revenue of $300 million in 2015.[124] In early 2017, several executive decrees authorized private security guards to use guns while on duty and local administrators to outsource security to such guards (e.g., for nuclear facilities, airports, or conference and sports venues). The decrees stipulate that, if the administrators feel that the state authorities are overstretched by counterterrorism and other tasks, the administrators must declare the facilities to be of strategic importance before authorizing the private security guards.[125]

Since 2016, Turkey's security sector has experienced fragmentation, and purges and shuffles have further strengthened nonmilitary forces. Given an urgent need to fill thou-

---

[117] Eissenstat, 2017, p. 3.

[118] Gurcan and Gisclon, 2017, p. 75.

[119] Metin Gurcan, "Turkish Government Outsources Urban Security," *Al-Monitor*, March 6, 2017a.

[120] Nurcan Baysal, "Why Turkey Is Posting Paramilitary Forces to Its Own Cities," *Ahval News*, November 13, 2017.

[121] Baysal, 2017.

[122] Gurcan, 2017a.

[123] Gurcan, 2017a.

[124] Gurcan and Gisclon, 2017, p. 77.

[125] Local administrators are not allowed to hire private security guards to secure schools, health facilities, private meetings and demonstrations, game halls, and alcoholic entertainment venues (Gurcan and Gisclon, 2017, p. 78).

sands of vacant positions in this sector quickly and insufficient recruits from the AKP base, the government turned to secularist and ultranationalist forces—among them, military officers convicted in the *Ergenekon* and *Balyoz* trials, as well as the Eurasianist and socialist Perincek Group. Because this alignment is based on shared hostility toward the Gülen organization, Turkish nationalism, and anti-Western sentiment, the medium- and long-term political reliability of police and military forces remains a headache for the government and could put the AKP leadership at odds with its religious base.[126]

A prominent indication of the growing importance of informal security providers is the August 2016 appointment of Adnan Tanrıverdi—head of the military consulting and training firm SADAT and a former one-star general expelled from the Army in 1996 because of concerns over his religiosity—as military adviser to the president.[127] But on the heels of recent espionage claims, including by German authorities, that MİT has targeted Gülenists and PKK affiliates abroad, SADAT's pan-Islamist outlook (which, according to some observers, is even sympathetic to Salafi-Jihadism) and command of well-trained and experienced personnel has raised concerns about possible extrajudicial targeting of the AKP's political enemies in Turkey—and abroad.[128]

Old and New Security Threats at Home

The growth of the AKP's domestic strength has been accompanied by a serious deterioration of Turkey's internal security environment because of increased political violence and instability. Initially, the violence was mainly confined to the less developed parts of southeastern Turkey. It has, however, spread to the more modern, Westernized parts of Turkey, particularly Istanbul and Ankara, and has included increasingly frequent suicide bombings. This situation has created growing anxiety among the Turkish public about the ability of the government and security forces to counter diverse threats.

Several factors have contributed to this situation. The first is the growing strength of the PKK as the Syrian civil war unfolded.[129] The Syrian Kurds initially refrained

---

[126] Eissenstat, 2017, pp. 4–5; and Metin Gurcan, "Power Struggle Erupts in Turkey's Security Structure," *Al-Monitor*, October 12, 2016c.

[127] Reportedly, armed SADAT staff fought against coup plotters on July 15, 2016, which prompted claims that the president had enlisted Tanrıverdi to help install loyalists in the Army or to mobilize a paramilitary counter-guerrilla force (Michael Rubin, "The Showdown for Control of Turkey's Military," American Enterprise Institute, November 29, 2016; Patrick Kingsley, "Turkey in Turmoil and Chaos Since Purge Aimed at Dissenters," *New York Times*, April 12, 2017a; and Leela Jacinto, "Turkey's Post-Coup Purge and Erdogan's Private Army," *Foreign Policy*, July 13, 2017.

[128] Amberin Zaman, "Are Hit Squads About to Take Aim at Turkey's Dissidents Abroad?" *Al-Monitor*, December 20, 2017; and Eissenstat, 2017, pp. 5–6.

[129] See F. Stephen Larrabee, "Turkey and the Changing Dynamics of the Kurdish Issue," *Survival*, Vol. 58, No. 2, April–May 2016.

from joining the insurgency in Syria when the unrest first broke out in March 2011. When the Syrian government troops withdrew from the Kurdish-inhabited areas in mid-2012, the PYD took over the administration of these towns and prevented any armed Kurdish presence other than that of its own YPG. Given the high number of Syrian Kurds who had joined the PKK—especially throughout the 1990s, when they had made up some 30 percent of the group's fighters—and the dramatic decline in Syrian border security measures, alarm bells rang in Ankara that these developments could provide the PKK with an unprecedented level of strategic depth in northern Syria.[130] It is well established that the PKK and the PYD regularly provide each other with personnel and weapons across borders and that the PKK military command provides strategic direction to the YPG, so the latter's growing strength has been a grave concern for Ankara.[131] While challenged politically and military by the PKK along three red lines (nation state, national unity, and territorial integrity), Ankara found itself in the uncomfortable situation of confronting this situation without traditional allies in Damascus, Tehran, and Baghdad. In the past year, however, Ankara responded with a more assertive policy, pressing the PKK on three fronts—in southeastern Turkey, northern Syria, and northern Iraq—and restoring working relations with regional states on containing Kurdish nationalism.

In the fight against ISIS in northern Syria and northern Iraq since mid-2014, transnational sentiments and links among Kurdish communities in the region, as well as the international standing of their militias as highly capable ground forces of the Global Coalition to Defeat ISIS, grew stronger. Turkey's fears have been exacerbated by the growing cooperation between the United States and the YPG in efforts to defeat ISIS in northern Syria. Turkish officials vehemently objected to the U.S. decision to provide additional arms and equipment to the YPG for the assault on the then–ISIS capital of Raqqa, and Erdoğan made a personal plea to U.S. President Donald Trump to reverse the decision during their May 2017 meeting, arguing that the action was inconsistent with bilateral strategic cooperation. Erdoğan was not appeased by reported assurances by the United States that it would provide the YPG just enough weapons and ammunition to take Raqqa and would prevent the YPG from remaining in control of Raqqa once ISIS was expelled. Turkey's most important security objective in Syria is to prevent the YPG militias from gaining control of the territory west of the Euphrates River, which would give the Kurds control of nearly all of Syrian territory along its southern border. Although Trump, according to Turkish officials, assured Erdoğan in November 2017 that the United States would stop arming YPG once ISIS was defeated, there was little trust among Turkish policymakers that "pending adjust-

---

[130] Magdalena Kirchner, *Why States Rebel: Understanding State Sponsorship of Terrorism*, Opladen, Germany: Barbara Budrich, 2016, pp.179–180.

[131] Kim Bode and Alessandria Masi, "Expert View: The YPG, PKK and Turkey's Options in Syria," *Syria Deeply*, May 15, 2017.

ments to the military support provided to our partners on the ground in Syria" would completely cease cooperation between Washington and the YPG.[132]

The second crucial factor contributing to the upsurge of violence and instability in Turkey was the collapse of the peace negotiations between the AKP and the PKK in July 2015 and the resurgence of attacks by the PKK on the Turkish military and security forces. The PKK and its offshoot group the Kurdistan Freedom Falcons (Teyrêbazên Azadiya Kurdistan) are deemed responsible for some 450 incidents in Turkey and Western Europe between mid-2015 and late 2016; these attacks left more than 570 security forces and civilians dead and nearly 2,000 injured.[133] Two car bombings, in central Ankara in February and March 2016, claimed the lives of nearly 70 civilians and security personnel. On December 10, 2016, twin bombings near the football stadium in Istanbul's Beşiktaş neighborhood killed 48, mostly police officers, and injured 166 more. The Kurdistan Freedom Falcons later claimed responsibility for these and several other attacks.[134] At the same time, a looser chain of command in the Kurdish insurgency transferred the battle from the mountains and countryside to larger cities through the PKK's youth wing, the Patriotic Revolutionary Youth Movement (Yurtsever Devrimci Gençlik Hareket), presenting the TSK with urban warfare challenges.[135] Between 2015 and mid-2017, the International Crisis Group estimated that the ongoing cycle of violence had killed three times as many people as the 2011–2012 escalation did.[136] The military escalation in southeastern Turkey, including curfews and dragnet security operations, is reminiscent of operations conducted during the civil war in the 1990s.

The 2016 coup attempt, which galvanized the conservative-nationalist AKP-MHP alliance, led to a hardening and further militarization of Ankara's Kurdish policy. The government has also initiated a campaign to rejuvenate the "village guard" system, planning to equip loyalist Kurds with machine guns, rocket-propelled grenades, and armored vehicles and increase their number from about 67,000 to 90,000.[137] At the same time, executive decrees ended the temporary status of the guard system and made the village guard force a "permanent entity within the Turkish security apparatus" under the

---

[132] "US to Stop Arming Anti-IS Syrian Kurdish YPG Militia—Turkey," BBC News, November 25, 2017.

[133] National Consortium for the Study of Terrorism and Responses to Terrorism, Global Terrorism Database, undated.

[134] "Istanbul Stadium Attacks: Kurdish TAK Group Claim Attacks," BBC News, December 11, 2017; and Constanze Letsch, "Ankara Bombing: Kurdish Militants Claim Responsibility," *The Guardian*, March 17, 2016.

[135] See Başaran, 2017, pp. 154–155; and "A New Generation of Kurdish Militants Takes Fight to Turkey's Cities," Reuters, September 15, 2016.

[136] Berkay Mandıracı, "Turkey's PKK Conflict Kills Almost 3,000 in Two Years," International Crisis Group, July 20, 2017a.

[137] Gurcan, 2017a. Village guards are separate from the neighborhood guards noted earlier. Village guards, which "assist in the fight against the PKK," should be "the largest armed paramilitary body in the country, followed by the neighborhood guards."

control of the Ministry of Interior.[138] By February 2017, village guards made up more than 20 percent of pro-government armed forces in the Kurdish regions, increasing the risk of casualties, exposing civilians to PKK counterattacks and human rights violations committed by unprofessional guards that continue to be met with impunity, and thus creating new societal problems in the area.[139] Besides the PKK's frustration over the standstill in the peace process and the government's Syria policy, it was Ankara's inability to address the threat of jihadist terrorism, particularly targeting secular Kurds in Turkey, that contributed to the PKK's decision to de facto end the ceasefire in 2015.

Since 2012, reports about Turkish support for the armed opposition in Syria, as well as its open border policy, coincided with the growing importance of Salafist and even jihadist insurgents in northern Syria and with the influx of foreign fighters through Kilis and other border crossings from Turkey.[140] In September 2013, the liberal-leftist Turkish newspaper *Radikal* pointed out several cases of Turkish ISIS fighters and authorities' inaction after reports from families.[141] In January 2014, the Gendarmerie stopped four trucks in Hatay and Adana that were reportedly escorted by MİT officers; the trucks contained ammunition and arms, including missiles, mortars, and anti-aircraft ammunition, which the Gendarmerie confiscated.[142] Erdoğan and Interior Minister Efkan Ala claimed that the prosecutors who ordered the search were Gülenists and then had them and the officers conducting the investigation arrested on suspicion of espionage, thus portraying the search as part of the Gülenist attempt to overthrow the government.[143]

In the run-up to the June 2015 general elections and amid the YPG's successful campaign to oust of ISIS from the strategically important town Tel Abyad in northern Syria, ISIS launched several mass casualty attacks in Turkey.[144] Throughout 2016, ISIS

---

[138] Gurcan and Gisclon, 2017, p. 77.

[139] Gurcan and Gisclon, 2017, p. 76

[140] Charles Levinson, "Leadership Rifts Hobble Syrian Rebels," *Wall Street Journal*, September 10, 2012.

[141] See Başaran, 2017, p. 120.

[142] Fehim Taştekin, "Turkish Military Says MİT Shipped Weapons to al-Qaeda," *Al-Monitor*, January 15, 2015.

[143] After Turkey's oldest newspaper, *Cumhuriyet*, published the story the following May, the paper's editor-in-chief, Can Dündar, and Ankara bureau chief, Erdem Gül, were arrested and sentenced to five years in prison for revealing state secrets. Initially, they were also charged with aiding a terrorist organization—the Gülen movement. On June 15, 2017, CHP lawmaker Enis Berberoğlu was sentenced by a local court to 25 years in jail for providing *Cumhuriyet* with information about the Adana incident. See Başaran, 2017, pp. 117–118, 122.

[144] Five people were killed by a bomb attack during an HDP campaign rally in Diyarbakır just a week before the election; 34 young Kurdish activists lost their lives in a suicide bombing in Suruç near the Syrian border the following month; and on October 10, 2015, a twin bombing killed 107 participants of a peace rally in Ankara, injuring more than 500. All perpetrators grew up and were radicalized in the same Turkish town, and authorities had been aware of their affiliation with ISIS for years. The PKK accused the government of being complicit in the murder of Kurds by ISIS, and two policemen in Suruç were shot and killed in their beds; the government responded with an aerial bombing raid against PKK bases in the Qandil Mountains. See Başaran, 2017, pp. 120–122.

conducted attacks against the wider Turkish public and international targets, reflecting a substantial ISIS presence in the country, the lack of a comprehensive framework of dealing with foreign or local ISIS fighters, and a growing ISIS hostility toward Turkey since it joined the anti-ISIS coalition in July 2015.[145] Although there were no major terrorist incidents in Turkish cities between January 2017 and the writing of this report in mid-2018, the staggering number of terrorism-related incidents in 2017 (19,759 by the PKK, and 4,522 by ISIS) highlights that terrorism remains a key security issue and major challenge for Turkey's police forces and judiciary.[146]

Foreign and Defense Policy: From "Zero Problems" to "Precious Loneliness"

During its early years in office, the AKP government actively pursued a course toward European integration that was shaped by Abdullah Gül, who served as foreign minister from 2003 to 2007. AKP strategists, particularly Ahmet Davutoğlu, who was an adviser to Erdoğan and later himself foreign and prime minister, advanced the argument that Turkey's Western ties should be complemented by deeper engagement with partners elsewhere, particularly in the Middle East and the wider Islamic world. Davutoğlu contended that Turkey possesses "strategic depth" because of its geographic location and positive elements of the Ottoman legacy that could be leveraged to form a new synthesis in foreign and domestic policy. He envisioned Turkey as a central hub in regions of the Sunni Muslim world where Ottoman culture and influence were once strong—the Middle East, Central Asia and the Caucasus, and the Balkans. Davutoğlu forecasted that Turkey could emerge as a leader of the Islamic world and a bridge to other regions. To advance this concept, he articulated the policy of "zero

---

[145] See Natasha Bertrand, "ISIS Is Exploiting a Crucial Weakness in Turkey That Lets Them Walk 'Free,'" *Business Insider*, August 1, 2015; and Constanze Letsch, Kareem Shaheen, and Spencer Ackerman "Turkey Carries Out First Ever Strikes Against Isis in Syria," *The Guardian*, July 24, 2015. Rockets fired from ISIS-held territory killed more than 20 Syrian and Turkish civilians between March and May 2016 in the Turkish border town Kilis (Selin Girit, "Syria Conflict: Kilis, the Turkish Town Enduring IS Bombardment," BBC News, May 9, 2016). ISIS-suicide bombings targeted tourists in separate incidents in Istanbul on January 12 and March 19, 2016. Two of the 17 victims were of dual Israel-U.S. nationality (Nick Tattersall and Ayla Jean Yackley, "Suicide Bomber Kills Four, Wounds 36 in Istanbul Shopping District," Reuters, March 16, 2016).

On June 28, 2016, three armed gunmen—who were later identified as ISIS members stemming from the Russian North Caucasus region, Uzbekistan, and Kyrgyzstan and who entered Turkey a month earlier from Syria—attacked Istanbul's Atatürk airport with automatic weapons and explosive belts, killing 45 people and injuring more than 230 others ("Timeline: The Worst Airport Shootings in the Last 15 Years," Fox News, January 6, 2017). ISIS did not claim responsibility for the attack, in contrast to a shooting perpetrated by another Uzbekistan-born ISIS member on New Year's Eve 2016 at Istanbul's famous Reina nightclub, killing 39 people and injuring 70 others, among them a U.S. citizen (Huseyin Kulaoglu and Burcu Arik, "Turkish Court Remands 44 in Nightclub Attack Trial," Anadolu Agency, December 16, 2017).

[146] "Turkey 'Neutralized' over 2,000 Terrorists in One Year," *Yeni Şafak*, December 27, 2017.

problems" that would seek to build good relations with all neighbors through active engagement, leveraging Turkey's economic strength and Islamic heritage. Although Davutoğlu's thinking was often-dubbed "neo-Ottoman," one analyst who studied his writings closely has argued that his thinking was actually pan-Islamist.[147]

The AKP's foreign policy continues to reflect a wariness of globalization and a resurgent nationalism that sprung from the widespread beliefs that Turkey had paid too high a price economically and politically for supporting the United States in the Gulf War and that Europe, despite declaring Turkey a candidate for membership in the EU in 1999, continues to hold it at arm's length and is not serious about integration.[148] As policy differences with nearly all of Turkey's neighbors and allies have mounted in the wake of the Arab Spring and the Syria crisis, leaders of the AKP and the MHP have argued that Turkey must be more self-reliant in protecting its interests. Presidential adviser Ibrahim Kalın has commented that Turkey needs to be prepared to accept a "precious loneliness" in taking principled stands to defend its values and national interests.[149]

Institutional Shifts in Foreign Policymaking

The Foreign Ministry is widely assessed to have lost influence in policy formulation since Mevlüt Cavuşoğlu took over the position as minister in 2014 from Ahmet Davutoğlu. Under Davutoğlu's tenure as prime minister (2014–2016), his office became the center of gravity of Turkish foreign policy. Since Davutoğlu was pushed out of office by AKP leadership in May 2016 in a power struggle with Erdoğan and succeeded by then–Minister of Transport, Maritime and Communication Binali Yıldırım, the epicenter of foreign policymaking has been the president's office, steered by his closest and most loyal advisers—İbrahim Kalın and Berat Albayrak. Albayrak, Erdoğan's son-in-law who currently serves as minister of treasury and finance and previously served as energy minister, has been a rising figure in the cabinet since 2015 and was one of the candidates for prime minister after the ousting of Davutoğlu. Kalın, the president's chief adviser and spokesman, is reported to have played a leading role in the new national security concept, has assumed a higher profile in articulating and defend-

---

[147] The concept was articulated in Davutoğlu's 2001 book, *Stratejik Derinlik, Turkiye'nin Uluslararası Konumu* (*Strategic Depth, Turkey's International Position*), which has not been translated into English. Davutoğlu wrote an article reflecting on the concept's application during the first five years of the AKP's tenure (Ahmet Davutoğlu, "Turkey's Foreign Policy Vision: An Assessment of 2007," *Insight Turkey*, Vol. 10, No. 1, Winter 2008). One of his former students has reviewed most of Davutoğlu's scholarly articles and makes a case that Davutoğlu envisioned Turkey developing a sphere of influence in the Islamic hinterland in order to become a global power (see Behlül Ozkan, "Turkey, Davutoglu and the Idea of Pan-Islamism," *Survival*, Vol. 56, No. 4, August–September 2014).

[148] F. Stephen Larrabee and Ian O. Lesser, *Turkish Foreign Policy in an Age of Uncertainty*, Santa Monica, Calif.: RAND Corporation, MR-1612-CMEPP, 2003, pp. 10–11.

[149] "Turkey Not 'Lonely' but Dares to Do So for Its Values and Principles, Says PM Adviser," *Hürriyet Daily News*, August 26, 2013.

ing the president's policies, and is a possible future foreign minister. Turkey's highly regarded career foreign service has also experienced diminished influence, with 10 percent of ambassador-level posts now held by those who are not career diplomats.[150]

Impact of the AKP-Gülen Conflict on Foreign Policy

In addition to its relative decline in the decisionmaking process, the Foreign Ministry has also experienced significant purges of alleged Gülenists, with possible impact on the ministry's orientation and operations. As of December 2017, between 394 and 671 career diplomats and between 96 and 200 technical and administrative personnel in the ministry had been fired. The 394 figure represents almost one-third of the career diplomatic cadre, and this situation has reportedly led to a major overstretch in embassies abroad. Three prominent former ambassadors were also detained: One had been a senior adviser to President Gül and to Davutoğlu, while two others were in charge of personnel management.[151]

The internal conflict with the Gülen movement has had an impact on aspects of Turkey's external relations. The European Commission and European governments expressed concern that the state of emergency and the nature and scope of the purges and arrests are inconsistent with due process of law and European human rights norms, which added another strain to accession talks.[152] On the other hand, Turkish officials criticized the United States and Europe for what they perceived as belated and circumspect denunciations of the coup. Ankara pressed officials in Pakistan, Central Asia, and Africa to allow the Maarif Foundation, established by the Turkish government in 2016 with funding from Saudi Arabia and the Islamic Development Bank, to take over administration of educational institutions operated by the Gülen movement in those areas.[153] The breach with Gülen may have had a positive effect on Turkish-Iranian relations because the Gülen organization was unable to establish a substantial presence in Iran and had strongly denounced the AKP's rapprochement with the Iranian government.

It remains unclear whether Gülen and his followers' positive stance toward the West has been genuine or instrumental in achieving the movement's political goals. Nevertheless, the removal of alleged Gülenists from the Foreign Ministry since 2013 has led to recruitment of MHP loyalists and more Eurasianists, who are skeptical of

---

[150] Turkish analysts, discussion with the authors, Ankara, November 2016 and June 2017; and Sinan Ulgen, "Get Ready for a More Aggressive Turkey," *Foreign Policy*, July 2, 2018.

[151] The lower figures (394 and 96) come from a February 2017 Foreign Ministry statement (Abdullah Bozkurt, "Turkey's Foreign Ministry Labels 394 Turkish Diplomats as Terrorists," Stockholm Center for Freedom, May 22, 2017). The higher figures are from Turkey Purge (undated), as of December 2017.

[152] European Commission, *Turkey 2016 Report*, Brussels, September 11, 2016a, pp. 8–9.

[153] Inamullah Khattak, "Pak-Turk Schools to Be Taken Over by Turkey's Maarif Foundation," *Dawn*, February 14, 2017; and Safure Cantürk, "Students Educated by Maarif Foundation Exceed 10,000," *Daily Sabah*, November 6, 2017.

Ankara's reliance on the United States and NATO and support a closer relationship with Russia and Middle Eastern neighbors. This trend has been accelerated by the coup and subsequent purges.[154] With regard to the overall direction of foreign policy, there is growing convergence between the MHP and the AKP especially. The MHP remains critical of support for Islamist parties abroad, skeptical toward the Kurdistan Regional Government (KRG) in Iraq, and cautious in its assessment of Iran. But it favors the recent rapprochements with Russia and Israel, as well as the commitment to protect Turkmens in Iraq.

New Security Concept

In 2016, Turkish officials announced a new security concept that they contend will better address the complex challenges the country confronts and neutralize emerging threats beyond the country's borders. The concept, which puts emphasis on prevention and preemption, was developed in 2015 and 2016 by presidential staff and military leaders. As Erdoğan stated in a speech in January 2016, "Instead of playing defense, as Turkey had been doing up until very recently, in the future, Turkey will take preemptive and preventive measures designed to forestall threats before they can get underway."[155] The concept calls for restructuring the military to improve foreign operational capabilities and establishing new military bases abroad. Indeed, in April and September 2016, Turkey established new military bases in Qatar and Somalia, respectively.[156] These come in addition to the controversial Bashiqa base in northern Iraq, established in late 2015, and the Cyprus Turkish Peace Force Command, present in the Turkish Republic of Northern Cyprus since 1974. The strategic concept also mandates reconfiguring the MİT to concentrate on foreign intelligence and to support the domestic defense industry; however, the organization's covert operations are expected to remain an important national security tool.[157]

The 2018 and 2019 Elections and Turkey's Future Course

On April 18, 2018, following a meeting with MHP leader Bahçeli, Erdoğan surprised the nation by calling for snap parliamentary and presidential elections on June 24, 2018—17 months before they were due. Erdoğan said that the shift to the new system

---

[154] Turkish analysts, discussion with the authors, Ankara, November 2016.

[155] Metin Gurcan, "Turkey's New 'Erdogan Doctrine,'" *Al-Monitor*, November 4, 2016e.

[156] On September 30, 2017, Turkey opened its Mogadishu military training base as its largest forward base in the world, with the initial goal of training more than 10,000 soldiers (Pınar Akpınar, *From Benign Donor to Self-Assured Security Provider: Turkey's Policy in Somalia*, Istanbul: Istanbul Policy Center, Sabanci University, December 2017).

[157] Burhanettin Duran, "Turkey's New Security Concept," *Daily Sabah*, October 26, 2016.

of government had become more urgent in order to address regional security threats—a thinly veiled reference to the Kurdish question—with strength.[158] It was an apparent effort to limit the ability of opposition parties to organize and to have voting completed before the projected economic downturn deepened or any adverse developments in Syria materialized.[159] There were indications in the months right up to election day that Erdoğan was vulnerable or could at least be forced into a second-round runoff.

A Flawed but Participatory Democratic Process

During summer 2017, CHP leader Kemal Kılıçdaroğlu led a peaceful "justice march" from Ankara to Istanbul over 25 days, protesting the post-coup government crackdown. Tens of thousands of citizens walked for miles, and 100,000 attended the closing mass meeting in Istanbul. These were the largest anti-government demonstrations in Turkey since the ones triggered by the repression of the Gezi Park protests in 2013.[160] When the snap elections were announced, Kılıçdaroğlu took himself out of the running for president and designated Muharrem İnce, a member of Parliament since 2002 who twice challenged Kılıçdaroğlu for party leadership, as the CHP candidate.[161] İnce, a compelling orator with an affable demeanor, emerged as an inspirational campaigner who energized the CHP base and reached out to pious conservatives and Kurds, avowing that he would be an inclusive and impartial president who would struggle for democracy and fight against terrorism and corruption—a message that resonated with a wide range of voters, including many women and young people.[162] HDP leader Demirtaş was ruled eligible to be on the ballot but was forced to campaign from prison to diminish his impact on the race.

Meral Akşener, a dissident former MHP member who campaigned against the constitutional referendum in the face of intimidation by the AKP, formed the new Good Party (İYİ Parti [İP]) in late 2017. Akşener, a charismatic politician and former interior minister with appeal to conservatives and secularists, was seen as a formidable

---

[158] Susan Fraser, "Erdogan Catches Turkey Off Guard by Calling Early Elections," PBS NewsHour, April 18, 2018.

[159] Bulent Aliriza, "Erdogan Wins a Fresh Mandate in Turkey's New Presidential System," Commentary, Center for Strategic and International Studies, June 25, 2018; and Henri J. Barkey, "For Erdogan and His Cronies, Losing Was Never an Option," *The National*, June 26, 2018.

[160] Carlotta Gall, "'March for Justice' Ends in Istanbul with a Pointed Challenge to Erdogan," *New York Times*, July 9, 2017a.

[161] Kılıçdaroğlu's public position was that political party leaders should not run in presidential elections because the position (under the previous constitution) requires political impartiality. But there were other factors. If he had run for president, he could not have participated in parliamentary elections, and if he had lost his presidential bid, he would have also lost his chairmanship of the CHP. Finally, he was not perceived as an effective challenger to Erdoğan because of his personal style and status as a minority Alevi.

[162] "CHP Presidential Candidate İnce Vows to Be 'Everyone's President,'" *Hürriyet Daily News*, May 4, 2018; and Murat Yetkin, "İnce Brings a New Style to Turkish Politics," *Hürriyet Daily News*, June 30, 2018.

threat to Erdoğan running as a right-of-center, nationalist, rule-of-law candidate.[163] Former President Gül also briefly explored the possibility of running for the presidency as a consensus candidate of those tired of one-man rule, but he withdrew.[164]

In March 2018, the AKP-controlled Parliament passed legislation implementing controversial changes in election procedures; for example, parties had been required to receive 10 percent of the votes in national elections in order to take seats in Parliament, and under the new legislation, the 10-percent threshold applies to the sum of the votes received by all parties in an alliance.[165] At the time the legislation was passed, AKP and MHP leaders announced the formation of a "People's Alliance," out of concern that the latter party might fail to cross the 10-percent threshold to enter Parliament after supporting Erdoğan's re-election, thereby jeopardizing the AKP's control of the legislature. In early May, the CHP joined with the İP, the right-wing Democrat Party (Demokrat Parti), and the small Islamist Felicity Party in forming the "Nation Alliance," pledging to defeat the People's Alliance, dilute the AKP's parliamentary majority, and support several common principles.[166]

With İnce, Akşener, Demirtaş, and several other candidates in the presidential race, it seemed unlikely that Erdoğan could earn the requisite 51 percent of votes to win in the first round—even if there were substantial cheating. The key question at the time was whether the Nation Alliance parties would back a single candidate in the second round. In the end, despite vigorous campaigns by opposition parties, Erdoğan and the AKP proved unstoppable, given their domination of the media and a distorted electoral process under a state of emergency that offered them every advantage. Erdoğan won a decisive first-round victory with 52.59 percent of the vote; however, the AKP parliamentary totals fell from 49 percent to 42.56 percent, forcing the party into an informal coalition with the MHP. İnce had a stronger-than-expected showing with 30.64 percent, and his tally might have been higher if the announcement of his candidacy had not been delayed 16 days into the two-month campaign. The CHP fared less well in Parliament, winning 22.65 percent of the vote, with polling indicating that the party lost seats to İP candidates. Demirtaş received 8.40 percent of the presidential vote, and the HDP won 11.70 percent of the seats in Parliament, a 1-percent gain. Akşener ran a strong campaign and won 7.29 percent of the presidential poll, while her

---

[163] "She-Wolf v Sultan: A Challenge to Turkey's Erdogan," *The Economist*, November 17, 2017.

[164] Gül was seen as a candidate who could attract conservative voters disillusioned with Erdoğan's rule, as well as liberals and some Kurdish voters. Kılıçdaroğlu even indicated his willingness to support Gül to save the country from one-man rule. Gül decided not to run in the face of pressure from former AKP colleagues, resistance on the part of CHP regulars, and Akşener's refusal to step aside (Ayla Jean Yackley, "Former Turkish President Rules Himself Out of Election," *Financial Times*, April 28, 2018).

[165] "Turkish Parliament Passes Controversial Law on Election Alliances amid Brawl," *Hürriyet Daily News*, March 13, 2018.

[166] "Four-Party Opposition Bloc Set Up for Turkey's Snap Parliamentary Election," *Hürriyet Daily News*, May 2, 2018.

İP achieved 9.96 percent of the parliamentary vote, which was an impressive achievement for a first-time party.[167]

The preliminary report of the Organization for Security and Co-operation in Europe's International Election Observation Mission concluded that the elections afforded voters "a genuine choice despite the lack of conditions for contestants to compete on an equal basis." The report cited several factors that made the elections far from fair, including the skewed media coverage of Erdoğan and the AKP; restrictions on freedoms of assembly, association, and expression; and hastily adopted changes to the election legislation that removed safeguards for election day procedures. Nevertheless, Turks demonstrated their commitment to democracy by participating in large numbers in campaign rallies and by an 86-percent turnout of eligible voters.[168] Despite clear irregularities, none of the opposition parties felt that they were significant enough to contest the results.

The vote reflected the continuing polarization of the country along ethnic and social lines. Voting patterns were very similar to the June 2015 general elections. Figure 2.2. illustrates that, in the presidential election, Erdoğan dominated in the provinces of the conservative, nationalist Anatolian heartland; İnce held on to the CHP base along the Aegean and European Istanbul; and Demirtaş won most provinces in the Kurdish southeast. The fact that the three leading opposition parties garnered 46 percent of the 2018 presidential vote and 44 percent of the parliamentary vote illustrates that Erdoğan and the AKP are not invincible.

One of the key political developments to watch is whether the Nation Alliance, which İP leaders decided was no longer needed after the elections, can be reunited in a future election or whether another political leader or party can emerge that would bring together a coalition of pious conservatives, liberals, and Kurds, along the lines that Özal did with the Motherland Party in the 1980s.[169] İnce attempted to open the door to such a coalition in 2018 but did not have sufficient time, and the CHP remains divided over its future leadership and strategy. Deeper cooperation between the CHP and the HDP, based on common social-democratic, liberal values, has sometimes been discussed but would likely encounter strong resistance from CHP traditionalists and suspicion among Kurds about the CHP's Kemalist-nationalist legacy. However, by cultivating cross-party support, including from the HDP, CHP candidates were elected to

---

[167] Republic of Turkey, Supreme Election Council, "C) Parliamentarian Election Results Including Domestic, Overseas and Customs," election notice, July 5, 2018a; and Republic of Turkey, Supreme Election Council, "D) Presidency Election Results Including Domestic, Overseas and Customs Ballot Boxes," election notice, July 5, 2015b.

[168] International Election Observation Mission, *Republic of Turkey—Early Presidential and Parliamentary Elections—24 June 2018: Statement of Preliminary Findings and Conclusions*, Ankara: Organization for Security and Co-operation in Europe, June 25, 2018.

[169] Muhittin Ataman, "Özal Leadership and Restructuring of Turkish Ethnic Policy in the 1980s," *Middle Eastern Studies*, Vol. 38, No. 4, October 2002.

Figure 2.2
Results of the 2018 Presidential Election

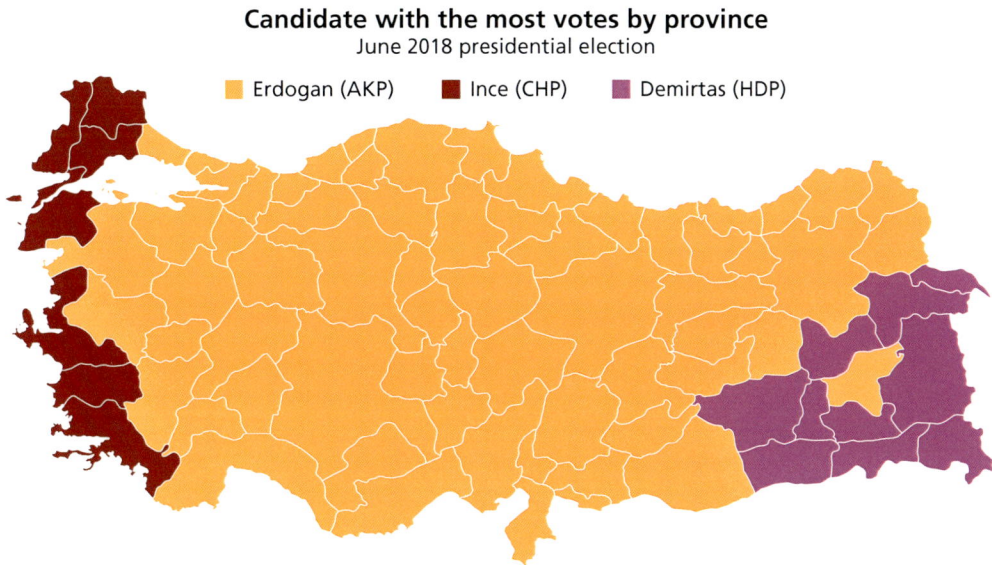

Candidate with the most votes by province
June 2018 presidential election

Erdogan (AKP)   Ince (CHP)   Demirtas (HDP)

SOURCE: "Turkey's Elections Explained in 100 and 500 Words," BBC News, June 25, 2018. Used with permission.

be mayors in six of Turkey's ten largest cities in 2019. Ekrem İmamoğlu's inclusive politics and decisive victory as mayor of Istanbul have led to his emergence as Erdoğan's most formidable challenger in the 2023 national elections.[170]

Domestic Implications

Erdoğan will be president through 2023 and is eligible for a third, five-year term thereafter, having led the country since 2003. The new constitution, which went into effect after the 2018 elections, created an authoritarian system with a powerful executive presidency and eliminated most checks and balances. The prime minister's office was abolished, and two vice president positions were created. Elections for president and Parliament will happen on the same day every five years, instead of the current four-year term of the Parliament. The president became the head of the executive branch and is allowed to retain leadership of the dominant political party. The president can appoint and dismiss ministers and the chief of the TGS directly—as Erdoğan did in July 2018—and has broad authority over the appointment of the high council of judges and prosecutors. Under the new constitution, military commissions and mili-

---

[170] Carlotta Gall, "Istanbul's New Mayor Quickly Emerges as a Rival to Erdogan," *New York Times*, July 3, 2019; and Cengiz Çandar, "A Generational Change Is Looming in Turkish Politics," *Al-Monitor*, September 13, 2019.

tary courts will be abolished. In addition, Parliament lost its right to interpellation of government actions, limiting oversight of the presidential administration.[171]

Turkey's internal political, security, and economic situations will likely remain volatile for some time. President Erdoğan is likely to double down on his efforts to consolidate power, reign in the military and security services, and step up the counter-insurgency and counterterrorism campaigns.

The state of emergency declared after the failed July 2016 coup, which was subsequently extended with Parliament's consent seven times for three-month intervals, remained in place through the 2018 elections. Erdoğan pledged during the campaign to lift the state of emergency, and a few days after the elections, he and the MHP's Bahçeli reached agreement to do so. Bahçeli reportedly extracted a major concession, however, in that the AKP and the MHP introduced new antiterrorism and internal security legislation, quickly approved by Parliament, which opposition parties said effectively extends emergency rule for three years.[172] The two leaders also agreed to establish a commission on national consensus to coordinate legislative and electoral strategies, but the potential for policy differences remains.[173] Erdoğan, the AKP, and the MHP ran in the 2018 election on a platform focused on eliminating both the PKK and the YPG militias in Syria. Harsher measures to combat the PKK, the YPG, and other terrorist groups are certain, and there is little prospect that Erdoğan will revive the peace talks with the PKK, pursued between 2008 and 2015, in the foreseeable future.

Erdoğan's project to raise "pious generations"—more in a loyalist than religious sense—through substantial changes in the educational sector is creating further social and political tensions. Religious indoctrination even at an early age is spreading, academic standards are deteriorating, and both civic inaction and brain drain effects are rising.[174] These developments are eroding civil society and could, over time, stifle growth and innovation.

The Turkish economy had been hampered by slower growth and remains vulnerable to a steep decline in foreign direct investment, as well as the flight of *hot money*—that is, short-term investments in treasury bonds and stock shares. Turkish capital flight has not yet reached a significant level. Economic experts assess that the Turkish economy is stuck in the middle-income trap, particularly given the lack of

---

[171] Alan Makovsky, "Erdoğan's Proposal for an Empowered Presidency," Center for American Progress, March 22, 2017; and "Turkish Parliament Debates Controversial New Constitution," *The Guardian,* January 9, 2017.

[172] "Erdoğan, Bahçeli Agree Not to Extend State of Emergency in First Meeting After Elections," *Daily Sabah,* June 27, 2018; and Gulsen Solaker, Daren Butler, and Ali Kucukgocmen, "Turkish Parliament Passes Security Law to Replace Emergency Rule," Reuters, July 25, 2018.

[173] Ayla Ganioglu, "How Long Can Erdogan's Alliance Survive?" *Al-Monitor,* July 2, 2018.

[174] Pinar Tremblay, "Erdogan's 'Pious Generation' Curriculum Gets Failing Grade," *Al-Monitor,* November 17, 2017.

substantial institutional reform since 2007.[175] The Turkish growth rate declined from an unsustainable 8 percent in 2014 to 3.2 percent in 2016—which was close the average annual rate over the previous decade. It bounced back to 7.1 percent in 2017 as a result of increased government spending and expanded exports. The Organisation for Economic Co-operation and Development forecasted growth of about 5 percent in 2018 and 2019. The exchange rate remains highly volatile, and in the first five months of 2018, the lira depreciated 20 percent and inflation grew by 11 percent.[176] Increased youth unemployment, high private-sector debt, a persistently high current account deficit, and a reliance on speculative foreign capital flows all point to continuing economic volatility, which could be affected negatively or positively by domestic and regional geopolitical developments.[177]

Implications for Foreign and Defense Policy

As Turkish leaders survey the country's regional environment, wherever they look, they are faced with upheaval and change that complicate their strategic choices. Within Turkey's own backyard, the situation looks particularly gloomy. Iraq and Syria are failed states, to varying degrees, with continuing dangers of spillover of unrest and terrorist attacks on Turkish territory. Relations with Europe and the United States are at historic low points. Erdoğan's combative diplomacy toward allies reflects his assessment that the West has growing enmity toward Islam and that the United States and Europe are actively seeking to undermine Turkey's security. Erdoğan has been more openly embracing conservative nationalism as his guiding ideology, with a foreign policy and defense posture focused on securing national interests and sovereignty from the "reactionary and exclusionary actions of states."[178] He is also seeking, with mixed success, to

---

[175] The *middle-income trap* is an economic development theory wherein a country that attains a certain income level remains stuck at that level. Economists assess that some newly industrialized countries lose their competitive edge in the export of manufactured goods because of rising domestic wages and are unable to compete with economically more-developed countries in the high-value-added market. The result is that these countries remain in what the World Bank defines as the *middle-income range* because their per capita gross national product has remained between $1,000 to $12,000 at constant (2011) prices. These countries suffer from low investment, slow growth in the secondary industry, limited industrial diversification, and poor labor market conditions. See Mehmet Simsek, "Proposal—Escaping the Middle Income Trap: Turkey's Strategy," Global Economic Symposium, 2014; and "The Middle-Income Trap Has Little Evidence Going for It," *The Economist*, Special Report: Emerging Markets, October 7, 2017.

[176] Organisation for Economic Co-operation and Development, "Turkey," *OECD Economic Outlook*, Vol. 2018, No. 2, December 2018; and "Turkey's Economy Is One of the World's Fastest Growing; But for How Long?" *The Economist*, January 4, 2018.

[177] Organisation for Economic Co-operation and Development, "Turkey," *OECD Economic Outlook*, Vol. 2017, No. 2, November 2017.

[178] The quote is from Erdoğan's 2018 election manifesto. See Semih Idiz, "After Erdogan's Win, What's Next for Turkey's Foreign Policy?" *Al-Monitor*, July 3, 2018; and Ulgen, 2018.

build Turkey's stature in the Islamic world and Eurasia. This strategy reflects the realist, hard side of "precious loneliness"—a worldview shared by Bahçeli.

Erdoğan, with the urgings of his MHP partners, is likely to pursue even more-assertive foreign and defense policies. Turkey will continue to press the United States to help it clear YPG militias from the Syrian border. The Turkish government declared that it would not support the additional sanctions the United States imposed on Iran in May 2018 to press Tehran for further constraints on its nuclear program and to end its regional interventions. Further afield, Erdoğan is intent on continuing his activism on the Palestinian issue and using Turkey's military presence in Qatar and Djibouti, as well as an agreement with Sudan, to expand Turkey's regional influence. Despite allied concerns and threats of U.S. legislation that would block the transfer of F-35 aircraft to the TSK, Ankara shows no signs of backing off its deal to purchase Russian S-400 air defense systems. These issues are discussed in more detail in subsequent chapters.

If a viable opposition leader or coalition were to emerge in Turkey and dislodge Erdoğan and the AKP from power after 2023, one could expect a more conciliatory approach from Turkey, based on the fact that the three leading opposition parties in the 2018 elections ran on platforms calling for revitalizing relations with NATO allies and the EU. Nevertheless, deep public suspicion of the United States and Europe would constrain the pace and scope of a future rapprochement. In an October 2017 survey conducted by Istanbul Economics, 68 percent of Turks expressed certainty that Turkey's Western alliance with Europe and the United States was breaking; more than 71 percent were in favor of Turkey entering a political, economic, and security alliance with Russia.[179]

As we will illustrate in subsequent chapters, although Turkey and its long-standing allies still have many convergent strategic interests, including countering terrorism, promoting peace in the Middle East, constraining the growth of Russian and Iranian power, and expanding energy transit corridors, differences over the policies to best advance these interests have become more pronounced and exacerbated by deepening mutual suspicions. The trends outlined in the analysis in this chapter suggest four potential futures for Turkey:

1. *Difficult ally*: Turkey continues to be a difficult and sometimes wavering U.S. and NATO ally but remains committed to NATO missions and reliant on the Alliance's collective security guarantees.
2. *Resurgent democracy*: An opposition political leader or coalition is able to defeat Erdoğan after 2023, walk back some of the constitutional changes approved in the 2017 referendum, and resume a more Western-oriented foreign and security policy.

---

[179] Marc Champion, "Conspiracy or Not, Turkey's Ties to West Are at Risk," *Bloomberg*, December 5, 2017.

3. *Strategic balancer*: Turkey moves to more openly balance its ties with its NATO allies and those with emerging partners in Eurasia (particularly Russia, Iran, and China), sometimes supporting Western positions but often forming shifting coalitions.

4. *Eurasian power*: As tensions with Europe and the United States reach a breaking point, Turkey moves to formally leave NATO and pursue closer cooperation and various alignments with partners in Eurasia and the Middle East.

Either continuation of current trends (the difficult ally potential future) or the emergence of one of the third or fourth futures (strategic balancer or Eurasian power) will lead to Turkish foreign and defense policies that are contrary, in varying degrees, to the interests of the United States and other NATO allies and that further undermine long-standing aspects of defense and security cooperation. This volatile situation warrants a considered reassessment of U.S. and European strategy toward Turkey, preparations for disruptive developments in all aspects of relations, and initiatives that could maintain and restore long-standing ties if current trends are reversed. These plans and options are addressed in Chapter Nine, following the analysis in the next six chapters of how Turkey's relations with its key neighbors and allies are likely to develop over the coming decade.

CHAPTER THREE

Turkey's Relations with Iran and Iraq: Enduring Rivals or a New Modus Vivendi?

Alireza Nader

The Turkish-Iranian relationship is unique in the Middle East. The two countries are historic nation-state rivals dating back five centuries to conflicts between the Ottoman and Safavid empires over Mesopotamia and the South Caucasus. Despite lingering mutual suspicions and deep religious and political differences, the two governments have demonstrated over the past 20 years an openness to a more pragmatic engagement if mutual national interests are at stake. The Syrian war has created a wide gulf between Tehran and Ankara, but the apparent near-total victory of the Assad regime over its foes and the rising threat to Turkey of the PKK and an autonomous Kurdish region in northern Syria (Rojava[1]) have translated into a warmer relationship. In a nearly unprecedented move, the two countries have exchanged visits by top military officials and have spoken of jointly fighting regional threats. The defeat of ISIS has opened Iraq and the Levant to additional Iranian influence—a fact of enduring concern to the Erdoğan government as it attempts to restore security on Turkey's borders. An expanding Iranian economy and Turkey's interests in its neighbor's energy reserves are helpful to better ties. But Turkish-Iranian ties will be defined by tensions well into the future. Turkey views itself as the protector of the Turkmen (many of them Shi'a) and resents Iranian influence in northern Iraq.

Turkey also had much better relations with the KRG than with the Iraqi central government until then–Kurdish President Masoud Barzani called the September 2017 independence referendum. A future conflict between Baghdad and the KRG could draw in Iran and Turkey on opposite sides. And although Turkey has accepted the existence of the Assad regime without precondition, it is wary of Iranian influence in Syria and the Levant. It would not be surprising to see Turkey and Iran both clash and cooperate with each other on various issues in such places as Iraq. But Washington can count on Turkey to, at times, pursue relations with Iran and Iraq in ways that may not suit U.S. interests. Cooperation among Turkey, Iran, and Iraq in crushing the KRG's

---

[1] Rojava is a de facto autonomous region of northern Syria composed of three cantons: Afrin in the west, Kobanî in the center, and Cizre in the east.

bid for independence demonstrates that these countries can overcome mutual distrust when it suits their individual interests.

Iranian Interests Fueling Rivalry and Cooperation with Turkey

Turkey's main objectives with regard to the unrest in Iraq and Syria are to maintain security on its borders, counter the PKK, and staunch Iranian influence in the region.[2] Ankara's approach to the conflicts is influenced by its belief that Iran, in encroaching toward the Mediterranean, is attempting to revive the Persian Empire.[3]

For its part, Iran seeks to prevent a strong Iraq from emerging that could act as a counterweight to its regional ambitions. It also wants to ensure that parts of Iraqi and Syrian territory can serve as a land corridor to Hezbollah, as well as the Mediterranean coast. Iran sees Turkey's activities as attempts to recreate the Ottoman Empire.[4]

Iranian Influence over Baghdad

Since the U.S. overthrow of Saddam Hussein, Iran has amassed great influence over the Iraqi government—a power that was enhanced following the fall of Mosul to ISIS in 2014. To achieve its objectives, Iran has, since 2003, pursued a strategy of propping up Shi'a political organizations while simultaneously creating multiple Shi'a militant groups that can pressure politicians and prevent the Baghdad government from becoming too stable and independent.[5]

Often playing a role in creating crises, Tehran then steps in as an indispensable actor in resolving them. Islamic Revolutionary Guard Corps Qods Force Commander Qassem Soleimani, who has emerged as the implementer of Iran's Iraq policy, has been at the center of many of the Baghdad government's major decisions.[6] In 2006, for example, Soleimani sneaked into Baghdad's Green Zone to help achieve the deal that made Nouri al-Maliki Iraq's first post-Saddam prime minister. Two years later, Soleimani brokered a ceasefire between Iraqi forces and Moqtada al-Sadr's Jaish al-Mahdi forces, which were engaged in fighting that threatened to tear the country apart. And in 2012, Soleimani helped resolve tensions between Baghdad and the KRG by convincing Maliki to stand down in his dispute with Erbil, the capital city of Iraqi Kurdistan, following Erdoğan's historic March 2011 visit there. And when the ill-prepared Iraqi

---

[2]   Aaron Stein, "A Collapsing Regional Order: Turkey's Troubles in Iraq and Syria," *War On the Rocks*, March 12, 2015.

[3]   Ali Vaez, "Turkey and Iran's Dangerous Collision Course," *New York Times*, December 18, 2016.

[4]   Vaez, 2016.

[5]   Alireza Nader, *Iran's Role in Iraq: Room for U.S.-Iran Cooperation?* Santa Monica, Calif.: RAND Corporation, PE-151-OSD, 2015.

[6]   Nader, 2015.

forces melted away in the face of the ISIS takeover of Mosul in 2014, Iran immediately stepped in to fill the vacuum—assistance that was highlighted by Iraqi Prime Minister Haider al-Abadi while also noting that U.S. military assistance was slower to arrive.[7]

Years of building up multiple militant organizations also has paid off for Tehran, as groups loyal to Iran's supreme leader, such as the Badr Organization, Asaib Ahl al-Haq, and Kataib Hezbollah, have played prominent roles in the anti-ISIS campaign.[8] Iran-allied groups, assisted by the Islamic Revolutionary Guard Corps, were instrumental in early and high-profile victories, taking back eastern Iraqi cities, such as Tuz Khurmatu and Jurf al-Sakhar, in 2014.

However, as the battlefront moved west, Turkey became increasingly sensitive to Iran's prominent role in the anti-ISIS fight. The city of Tal Afar in Nineveh province provides one example. The area has a Shiʻa Turkmen–majority population, and Turkey and Iran competed over who should be considered the area's protector.[9] In October 2016, Erdoğan said that the "Turkmen city of Tal Afar is a matter of great sensitivity to us."[10] Badr Organization leader Hadi al-Amiri replied that "Tal Afar will be the cemetery of Turkish soldiers should Turkey attempt to take part in the battle" to liberate it.[11] In February 2017, as fighting in Mosul was underway, the Turkish foreign minister warned that "Iran wants to turn Syria and Iraq into Shiʻite" areas, prompting Iran to summon the Turkish ambassador to Tehran.[12]

Meanwhile, Turkish-Iranian tensions have not interfered with the Baghdad government's military cooperation with Tehran. In December 2016, Iran and Iraq conducted a joint naval exercise in the Shatt Al-Arab waterway, which was overseen by the Islamic Revolutionary Guard Corps.[13] The exercise marked the first such activity since the 2003 U.S. invasion. At the exercise, Iranian Border Guard Commander Brigadier General Qassem Razayee announced, "These maneuvers confirm that the two countries will not allow any third party to intervene in the security affairs of the region, to sow the seeds of discord and division between our countries."[14]

In addition to strengthening military ties, Iran and Iraq are continuing to deepen their economic and energy relations. The two governments signed a memorandum of understanding (MOU) in February 2017 to explore the construction of an oil pipeline

---

[7]   Nader, 2015.

[8]   Nader, 2015.

[9]   Mustafa Saadoun, "Iran, Turkey Fight over Tal Afar," *Al-Monitor*, November 18, 2016.

[10]   Saadoun, 2016.

[11]   Saadoun, 2016.

[12]   Babak Dehghanpisheh, Tulay Karadeniz, Tuvan Gumrukcu, and Parisa Hafezi, "Iran Summons Turkish Envoy over Comments by President, Foreign Minister," Reuters, February 20, 2017.

[13]   Sara al-Qaher, "Iran, Iraq Seek to Send a Message with Joint Naval Exercises," *Al-Monitor*, January 9, 2017a.

[14]   al-Qaher, 2017a.

from Kirkuk to Iran, and they agreed to commission a feasibility study the following July.[15] The latter announcement, coming weeks before the independence referendum in Kurdistan, was denounced by the KRG as a ploy to deny it revenue and increase the Iraqi central government's leverage in preventing secession. After the fall of Kirkuk to Iraqi forces in October, however, the KRG lost control of the disputed oil fields, which accounted for 70 percent of the KRG's daily oil production and a major source of its revenue.[16] Iran and Iraq have also discussed the feasibility of shipping Iraqi oil to a refinery in Abadan, Iran, with Iran returning byproducts to Iraq, and reached an initial agreement in July 2017 to settle a dispute over joint oil fields that straddle their border—a dispute in which Iranian extraction from the shared fields had cost Iraq billions of dollars.[17] After a four-year delay resulting from the security situation in Iraq, Iran started exporting natural gas to Iraq in June 2017 under two contracts—one for Baghdad power plants and the other to Basra. Iran already supplies electricity to Iraq.[18]

Iran does, however, face challenges in Iraq. First, Iran's backing of Shi'a militias and its support for the Assad regime in Syria have decimated support for Iran among Iraqi Sunnis. Meanwhile, Iran's form of governance is not popular, even among Iraqi Shi'as.[19] Moreover, Iraqis in general have bristled from Iran's interference in their domestic politics.

Iranian Overtures to the Kurds

Iran's strategy with regard to the Iraqi Kurds is shaped largely by its competition with Turkey for influence in Iraqi Kurdistan. Tehran's major objectives are to prevent the rise of a Kurdish state on its border that would spawn separatism among Iranian Kurds and be under the orbit of NATO ally Turkey. (See Figure 3.1 for a map of the Kurdish areas in the region.) This concern is not unfounded: During the 1990s, Turkey provided weaponry to the Kurdish Democratic Party of Iran (Hîzbî Dêmukratî Kurdistanî Êran [KDPI]), a dissident group based in Iraqi Kurdistan.[20] Also, in the event that

---

[15] "Iran, Iraq Initialize Plans for Oil Sector Cooperation," *Radio Free Europe/Radio Liberty*, February 20, 2017; and Tsvetana Paraskova, "Iran, Iraq Plan Pipeline to Export Kirkuk Crude Oil," *OilPrice*, July 31, 2017. Iraq's central government and the KRG both pump oil from different wells at the field, which spans their respective areas of control.

[16] David Zucchino, "Iraqi Forces Retake All Oil Fields in Disputed Areas as Kurds Retreat," *New York Times*, October 17, 2017.

[17] Sara al-Qaher, "Iraq and Iran Agree to Resolve Dispute on Joint Oil Fields," *Al-Monitor*, March 5, 2017b; and "Iran, Iraq Agree to Build Kirkuk Pipeline," *Iraq Business News*, July 31, 2017.

[18] According to an Iranian deputy oil minister, the exports started at a daily rate of 7 million m^3 but may reach 35 million m^3 in the future (Irina Slav, "Iran Starts Exporting Nat Gas to Iraq," *OilPrice*, June 22, 2017).

[19] Nader, 2015.

[20] Of course, Iran was, at the same time, providing safe haven to the anti-Turkey PKK. In 2004, as part of a thaw in Ankara-Tehran tensions following the rise of Erdoğan's AKP, Iran labeled the PKK a terrorist organization. See Alireza Nader, Larry Hanauer, Brenna Allen, and Ali G. Scotten, *Regional Implications of an Independent Kurdistan,* Santa Monica, Calif: RAND Corporation, RR-1452-RC, 2016.

Figure 3.1
Map of Kurdish Areas of Iraq, Syria, Turkey, and Iran

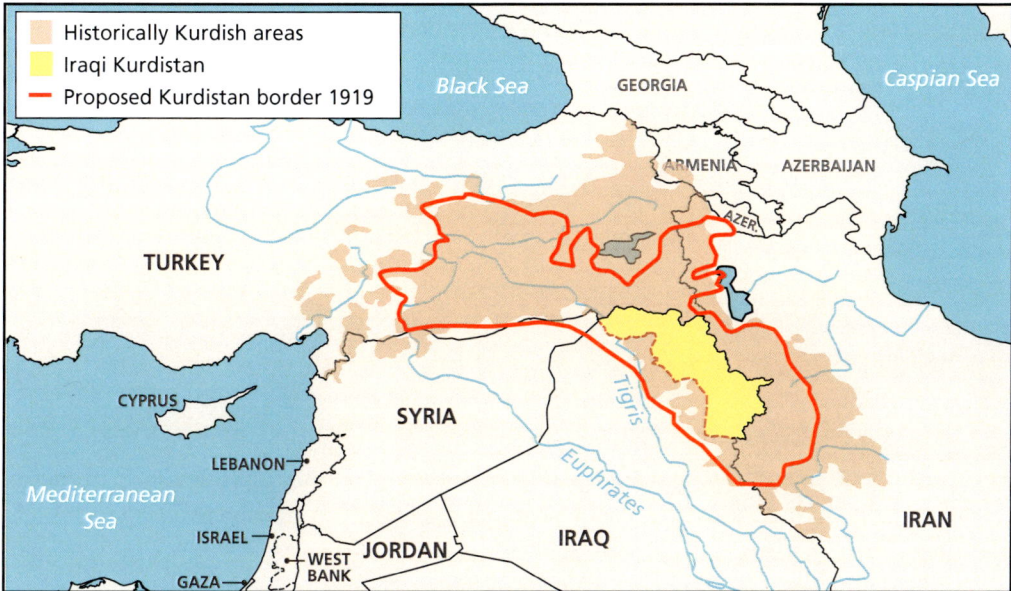

NOTE: Iraqi Kurdistan is an autonomous region within Iraq.

the Iraqi government breaks free from Iran's hold, the Iranians would want influence over the KRG in order to counterbalance Baghdad.[21] Therefore, Tehran has sought to gain a political and economic foothold in Iraqi Kurdistan.

Just as it has with the Baghdad government, Iran has tried to play the various Kurdish parties off of each other and ultimately serve as a mediator of intra-Kurdish disputes.[22] Since the Islamic Revolution, Iran has maintained close ties to the Patriotic Union of Kurdistan (Yekêtiy Niştîmaniy Kurdistan [PUK]), an Iraqi Kurdish party that rivals the Kurdish Democratic Party (Partiya Demokrat a Kurdistanê [KDP]), which dominates the KRG. Iran still provides the PUK with weapons that are not being adequately supplied to it by the KRG.[23] Moreover, in 2013, Iran was instrumental in deciding the successor to PUK leader Jalal Talabani.

But Iran also has improved its ties with the KDP in recent years. Qasem Soleimani is rumored to get along well with KRG Prime Minister Nechirvan Barzani, who is the nephew of KDP head and former Kurdish President Masoud Barzani.[24] The KDP also has been keen to improve relations with Tehran in order to convince it to back away

---

[21] Nader et al., 2016.

[22] Nader et al., 2016.

[23] Nader et al., 2016.

[24] Amberin Zaman, "The Iraqi Kurds' Waning Love Affair with Turkey," *Al-Monitor*, September 1, 2015.

from the PUK and the PKK.[25] In January 2014, KDP and PUK leaders asked Iran to intervene to help resolve a deadlock in the formation of the KRG. And in April 2017, Soleimani traveled back and forth between Baghdad, Erbil, and Kirkuk to resolve a dispute over the Kirkuk provincial council's raising of the Kurdish flag alongside the Iraqi flag.[26] Ultimately, Soleimani proved to be pivotal in convincing the PUK to withdraw its troops from Kirkuk, allowing Baghdad to recapture Kirkuk and all of the disputed territories.

In addition, Iran is seeking to compete with Turkish businesses in Iraqi Kurdistan—especially in the fields of energy and construction—in order to increase its leverage over the KRG. Iran has been known to close the border between Iran and Iraqi Kurdistan, slowing commercial traffic, as a means of political pressure.[27] It has also threatened the KRG that, if the Kurds act against Iranian interests, Tehran could build a Kirkuk-Iran pipeline that would bypass KDP-controlled areas.[28] At the same time, Iran has pursued economic opportunities with the KRG that have upset Baghdad. In 2014, Tehran and Erbil reportedly signed an agreement to build an oil and gas pipeline from Iraqi Kurdistan into Iran.[29] However, Iran faces an uphill battle in its competition with Turkey. As of 2015, Iranian-Kurdish trade was $6 billion, which amounted to only half of Turkey's trade with Iraqi Kurdistan.[30]

Several other factors also could improve Turkey's hand over Iran with regard to the KRG. Following the completion of the anti-ISIS campaign, the Kurds and Shiʻa militias could come into conflict over territory, which would complicate Tehran's relations with the KRG. Erbil, and especially the KDP, likely supports the Turkish troop presence in Bashiqa as a hedge against future Shiʻa militia attempts to push Peshmerga forces out of Nineveh.[31] Also, the Kurdish populace is frequently angered by Tehran's attacks on Kurdish groups in Kurdish territory. For instance, Iran was

---

[25] Nader et al., 2016.

[26] Kurdish provincial councilors had voted for raising the Kurdish flag, angering their Arab and Turkmen colleagues (Tallah Abdulrazaq, "Iranian General Is Iraq's Kingmaker and Arbiter," *Arab Weekly*, April 30, 2017).

[27] David Pollock, "To Kurdistan and Back: Iran's Forgotten Front," Fikra Forum, Washington Institute for Near East Policy, March 3, 2017.

[28] Pollock, 2017.

[29] See "Iran-Erbil Agree on Energy Deals and Boosting Trade," *Rudaw*, April 24, 2014; and Pollock, 2017. The KRG-Iran oil pipeline had not progressed past the signing stage when the Iraqi central government took control of the fields in 2017 after the failed Kurdistan independence referendum ("Iraq to Stop Kirkuk Oil Exports to Iran, Deal in Works to Use KRG Pipeline: Report," *Rudaw*, October 26, 2018).

[30] Nader et al., 2016.

[31] Amberin Zaman, "Iraqi Kurds Step into Ankara-Baghdad Row," *Al-Monitor*, October 6, 2016a; and Semih Idiz, "Why KRG Will Remain Turkey's Main Ally in Iraq," *Al-Monitor*, October 25, 2016b. The Peshmerga are the military forces of Iraqi Kurdistan.

accused of planting improvised explosive devices at the KDPI headquarters in Koya in December 2016.[32]

Iran has also played a double game in countering Kurdish terrorist groups. The PKK and its Iranian affiliate, the Kurdistan Free Life Party (Partiya Jiyana Azad a Kurdistanê [PJAK]), have long used the rugged Qandil Mountains region in northern Iraq as a base for launching their attacks into Turkey and Iran, respectively. As the Iraq War wound down, Turkey was frustrated that U.S. forces had not taken more-effective actions in combating the PKK. Although the PJAK is not as big a threat to Iran as the PKK is to Turkey, Iran was interested in developing a partnership with Turkey and saw countering Kurdish terrorism as an opening. In 2008, Ankara and Tehran signed an MOU on security cooperation, subsequently shared tactical intelligence about ongoing operations, and conducted coordinated air strikes against Kurdish insurgents.[33] However, recent contacts between Tehran and the PKK are a concern for Turkey. In December 2016, Turkish pro-Erdoğan media outlets accused Iran of hosting three PKK camps inside its territory and claimed that Soleimani was meeting with PKK leaders in Baghdad and Halabja.[34] Tehran would have several reasons for collaborating with the PKK. First, the PKK could help rein in anti-Iranian Kurdish groups, including the PJAK. In 2015, PKK fighters may have even stopped some KDPI fighters from entering Iran.[35] Iran may also want the PKK and its affiliated Syrian Kurdish group, the YPG, to secure a land bridge through Iraq and Syria to the Mediterranean. Ankara is also worried that Tehran seeks PKK control over Iraq's oil route to Turkey.[36] The PKK has a history of disrupting the flow of energy resources into Turkey. In July 2015, in response to Ankara's killing of PKK-affiliated fighters in Syria and Iraq, the PKK attacked a pipeline in Turkey that brought natural gas from Iran.[37]

Given this checkered history, it seems likely that policy related to Kurdish groups and territory will remain contentious in Turkish-Iranian relations. For now, Turkey and Iran have coordinated their policies on the KRG, but each country has had a long history of using various Kurdish groups to protect its own interests. For more on the Syrian civil war, see Box 3.1.

---

[32] Franc Milburn, "Iranian Kurdish Militias: Terrorist-Insurgents, Ethno Freedom Fighters, or Knights on the Regional Chessboard?" *CTC Sentinel*, Vol. 10, No. 5, May 2017.

[33] See Haim Malka, "Turkey and the Middle East: Rebalancing Interests," in Stephen J. Flanagan, Samuel J. Brannen, Bulent Aliriza, Edward C. Chow, Andrew C. Kuchins, Haim Malka, Julianne Smith, Ian Lesser, Eric Palomaa, and Alexandros Petersen, *Turkey's Evolving Dynamics: Strategic Choices for U.S.-Turkey Relations*, Washington, D.C.: Center for Strategic and International Studies, March 2009, pp. 46–47.

[34] Pinar Tremblay, "Iranian-Turkish Tug-of-War over Kurds." *Al-Monitor*, December 13, 2016b.

[35] Nader et al., 2016.

[36] Semih Idiz, "Turks Blame US, Iran for Encouraging Baghdad Against Ankara," *Al-Monitor*, October 11, 2016a.

[37] Keith Johnson, "Striking Pipeline, Kurdish Militants Deal Blow to Fellow Kurds," *Foreign Policy*, July 30, 2015.

Box 3.1
The Syrian Crucible

Jeffrey Martini

The Syrian civil war is a particularly destructive microcosm of broader regional power competition. This one conflict encompasses Arab-Iranian rivalry; Turkish-Kurdish posturing; jihadism; and U.S., Russian, and Iranian plays for influence. The result is more than eight years of fighting that has killed hundreds of thousands of Syrians and displaced half of the remaining population.

In early 2018, it appeared that the Syrian civil war was winding down as the regime consolidated its control over the majority of the country's more densely populated western spine, and the PYD exercised de facto authority in sections of the country's north and east. As for the Syrian opposition, it has been relegated to a series of noncontiguous enclaves in the south, Idlib governorate, and suburbs east of Damascus. ISIS holds no major population centers. By mid-February, fighting spiked in several areas as the regime sought to expand its control and leading powers intensified military actions to advance their competing regional interests.

Stakeholders have been moving to make accommodations with the perceived winners (the regime and its backers) while laying out their minimum conditions for supporting an eventual settlement. The actors that have shown the most flexibility and that have the leverage for Damascus to seek their accommodations are Turkey, the PYD, and the United States.

The basic quid pro quo that could generate Turkish support for a political settlement to the conflict has been clear since Turkey became a sponsor of the Astana process and guarantor of one of the de-escalation zones it produced—namely, that Turkey could support a settlement on Damascus's terms as long as Ankara's interest in blunting Kurdish autonomy is protected. And because Turkey is critical to cutting off the supply routes (particularly Bab al-Hawa) and foreign sanctuary that was sustaining the insurgency, there is reason for Damascus to seek Turkish buy-in.

The PYD has the opposite calculus of Turkey, but it also has the interest alignment and leverage to cut a deal with the regime. The PYD seeks what Turkey fears—sanctuary in northern Syria that will allow the PYD to continue its experiment in self-government via the so-called Autonomous Administration while also having room to advance Kurdish aspirations inside Turkey via the PKK. Although the Syrian regime is unlikely to grant the entirety of this ask, the PYD holds enough territory, including strategic areas that contain a share of the country's water and energy resources, that it may have the leverage to secure a measure of autonomy in Kurdish-majority areas while still recognizing the state and deferring to it on sovereign portfolios (e.g., defense and foreign affairs).

As for the United States, its core objective, the defeat of ISIS's physical caliphate, has already been achieved. Its remaining interests are to prevent the conditions that would give birth to ISIS 2.0 and to keep Iran from exercising control over a swath of territory stretching from Tehran to Beirut that passes through Syria. To accommodate those interests, the Syrian regime would need to show some commitment to reconciliation with Sunni Arabs or decentralization in opposition-held areas. Damascus would also need to be willing to rely on Russia—rather than Iran—as its main external security provider and to keep residual Iranian forces away from the so-called land bridge and the Israeli border. Damascus should care about these interests because the United States could choose to empower the PYD to pursue more-maximalist objectives or could regularly intervene in eastern

Syria (likely via air strikes) to target men or material bound for Hezbollah. This would pose an escalation risk for the regime and would become an embarrassing roadblock to Damascus recovering its sovereignty.

Should the Syrian regime and its patrons be willing to accommodate a share of these demands, it appears that there could be a settlement in the offing that would effectively recognize the regime's victory and table discussion of a genuine political transition. This would not satisfy the "revolution" or provide a measure of justice for those killed or displaced in the war. But what it might do is end the fighting so that the country's humanitarian needs can finally be addressed.

Views from Baghdad and Erbil on Relations with Turkey

Although Turkey's strategy in the past decade has been to play Baghdad and Erbil off of each other, in the end, Turkey has clear incentives to tilt in favor of the Kurds.[38] Turkey's position as the main trade partner with the KRG provides it with powerful leverage. Ankara used its economic power to kill the KRG's bid for independence and is now more influential than before, given the KRG's loss of Kirkuk's abundant oil resources.[39]

Moreover, Turkey's Ottoman legacy makes Iraqi Arabs—especially Shi'as—sensitive to Ankara's political activities in their country. Before the Sunni-dominated Baghdad government was put in place by the British in 1921, the Ottomans had been marginalizing Iraqi Shi'as for centuries.[40] Iraq was part of the Ottoman Empire from the 16th century until the end of World War I and was divided into the *vilayets* of Mosul, Baghdad, and Basra.[41] Turkish nationalists claim that the British cheated the Turks out of Mosul. They hang on to the argument in the Turkish National Pact—the final decisions made by the Ottoman Parliament in 1920—that all land still held by the Ottomans at the time they signed the 1918 armistice with the Allies should belong to Turkey.[42] This would include Mosul. Furthermore, in 2016, Erdoğan complained that the Treaty of Lausanne, signed between Mustafa Kemal Atatürk and the British in 1923, had left Turkey too small.[43] Erdoğan's rhetoric has been a mix of

---

[38] Hoshnag Ose, "Relationship Issues: Feud Between Turkey and Iraq Is All Syria's Fault," *Niqash*, February 9, 2012.

[39] Nader et al., 2016.

[40] Adweed Dawisha, *Iraq: A Political History from Independence to Occupation*, Princeton, N.J.: Princeton University Press, 2009.

[41] Carl L. Brown, *Imperial Legacy: The Ottoman Imprint on the Balkans and the Middle East,* New York: Columbia University Press, 1996.

[42] "Erdoğan Not Backing Down on Turkish Role in Mosul," *Al-Monitor*, October 16, 2016.

[43] Nicholas Danforth, "Turkey's New Maps Are Reclaiming the Ottoman Empire," *Foreign Policy*, October 23, 2016.

nationalism and sectarianism, also speaking about protecting Turkey's "Sunni Arab brothers" in Mosul.[44]

Baghdad-Ankara Relations Post-Saddam

Since the overthrow of Saddam, relations between Iraq and Turkey have been uneven, wavering from tense to cooperative. Shortly after the 2003 U.S. invasion of Iraq, the Turks became involved in Iraqi politics by forging close ties among the Iraqi Turkmen population.[45] Although Turkish leaders claimed that these closer ties were to protect their Turkish brethren, some suspected that this was simply an excuse to meddle in Iraqi affairs—especially to prevent the Kurds from taking over Kirkuk.[46] By 2007, Turkey was seen as so influential over Turkmen and some Sunni politicians that Prime Minister Maliki reached out to Ankara to help resolve a parliamentary dispute that had Sunni members threatening to resign (the Sunni-dominated Iraqiya Party is especially close to Turkey).[47] That same year, Baghdad and Ankara signed an MOU allowing Turkish troops to enter Iraq to pursue PKK insurgents.[48] This greatly angered the KRG, which argued that the MOU gave Turkey an excuse to invade Kurdish territory at will. However, by 2012, relations were on a downward trajectory, with Erdoğan accusing Maliki's government of stoking sectarianism.[49] Specifically, Maliki's issuance of an arrest warrant against the Sunni Vice President Tariq al-Hashimi and Turkey's subsequently providing him with a safe haven damaged relations.[50] In December 2015, Turkey established a military base in Bashiqa, Nineveh province, sending in 1,000 Turkish soldiers and 20 tanks without Iraqi permission.[51] Turkey claimed that it was invited into the area by the KRG, which requested that Turkish forces train the Peshmerga in preparation for fighting in Mosul.[52] For its part, the KRG claimed that it had facilitated only the troop transfer and that it had been conducted with Baghdad's consent.[53] The Iraqi Parliament disagreed and, in October 2016, demanded that

---

[44] Danforth, 2016.

[45] Danforth, 2016.

[46] Turkey's lowering of vocal support for the Turkmen following its rapprochement with the KRG lends credence to this argument (Nader et al., 2016).

[47] Ose, 2012.

[48] Klaas Glenewinkel, "Kurds Condemn Security Agreement Between Turkey and Iraq," *Niqash*, October 1, 2007.

[49] Ose, 2012.

[50] Zeynep Kosereisoglu, "Turkey and Iraq: How Identity and Interests Mix in Foreign Policy," *Muftah*, January 23, 2014.

[51] Fehim Taştekin, "Turkey's Brash Behavior Riles Iraq," *Al-Monitor*, October 7, 2016.

[52] Zaman, 2016a.

[53] Zaman, 2016a.

the Turkish troops leave Bashiqa.[54] Baghdad also called for an emergency session of the United Nations Security Council to discuss the situation.[55] The rapprochement between Baghdad and Ankara following mutual actions to quash the September 2017 Kurdish independence referendum has diminished Iraqi concerns. In late 2017, the two governments agreed to undertake combined military actions against terrorist organizations in the Qandil and Sinjar areas of Iraq (long-standing PKK safe havens), and officials indicated that the campaign could begin in mid-May 2018.[56]

Turkey's close ties with the Sunni Nujaifi family in Nineveh is also a concern for Baghdad. Osama al-Nujaifi is Turkey's main ally in Baghdad.[57] As one of three vice presidents, he is pushing for a Sunni autonomous region similar to that of the Kurds. Baghdad fears that this would bring Nineveh province under Turkey's orbit.[58] Meanwhile, Nineveh province's former governor, Atheel al-Nujaifi, has created his own Sunni militia, the Hashd al-Watani, which is being trained by Turkey.[59]

Despite periods of tension, economic interests have helped stabilize bilateral relations. By 2012, Iraq had become Turkey's second-most-valuable national destination for exports after Germany, reaching $10.8 billion (7 percent of total Turkish exports).[60] Turkish goods had a larger presence in Baghdad's markets than Iranian goods did. In January 2015, a session of the Iraqi-Turkish Joint Economic Commission was held for the first time since 2006.[61] The Turkish energy minister and the Iraqi oil minister agreed at the meeting that the Kirkuk-Ceyhan pipeline would be the only oil export route from Iraq to Turkey. This was a welcome gesture to Baghdad, which had been angered by previous oil shipment agreements between Ankara and the KRG that had been made without Baghdad's consent.

---

[54] Idiz, 2016a.

[55] Zaman, 2016a.

[56] Zülfikar Doğan, "Turkey Poised to Open a Military Front in Iraq," *Al-Monitor*, March 12, 2018. However, analysts doubt that the campaign will materialize (Paul Iddon, "Coordinated Iraqi-Turkish Action Against PKK Unlikely," *Rudaw*, March 11, 2018).

[57] Stein, 2015.

[58] Kirk H. Sowell, "The Regional and Domestic Political Context of the Mosul Offensive," *Sada*, October 18, 2016.

[59] Wilson Fache, "What Is Turkish Army Really Doing In Iraq?" *Al-Monitor*, September 6, 2016.

[60] Daniel Dombey and Funja Guler, "Turkey Emerges as True Iraq War Victor," *Financial Times*, March 12, 2013. In 2016, Iraq slipped to third place, with $7.6 billion (5.4 percent of total Turkish exports), behind Germany ($14 billion; 9.8 percent) and the United Kingdom ($11.7 billion; 8.2 percent). See World Integrated Trade Solution, "Turkey Exports, Imports and Trade Balance by Country and Region 2012," web tool, undated. Iraq was Turkey's leading trading partner before the 1991 Gulf War.

[61] Zülfikar Doğan, "Iraq, Turkey Strengthen Energy Relationship," *Al-Monitor*, January 23, 2015.

Turkey's Opening to the Kurdistan Regional Government

In the mid-2000s, relations between Turkey and the Iraqi Kurds, long strained over Ankara's concerns that the KRG might push for independence and was not taking sufficient actions to restrict PKK terrorist operations in Turkey from bases in Iraqi Kurdistan, began to improve. What eventually became a "180-degree turn" in Ankara's policy toward the KRG was driven by various factors.[62] Turkey realized that it needed to shift strategy in preparation for the eventual withdrawal of U.S. troops from Iraq; forging close ties with the KRG could serve as a balance against what would likely be Iran's increased influence over Baghdad. Furthermore, closer ties with the resource-rich Iraqi Kurds would allow Turkey to diversify its energy sources away from Iran and Russia.[63] Helping the KRG gain greater autonomy from Baghdad would allow the Kurds to sell oil and gas directly to Turkey without any challenges from Baghdad or, by extension, Iran. Finally, a KRG under Turkey's orbit could be pressured to take proactive steps to prevent the PKK from operating inside Iraq and could undermine the PYD's influence in Syria. As of 2008, the KRG was reining in PKK activities in Iraq in an effort to improve ties with Ankara. The next year, when President Abdullah Gül visited Iraq—marking the first visit to the country by a Turkish leader in 30 years—he met with KRG Prime Minister Nechirvan Barzani in Baghdad.[64]

Turkey has been willing to put its ties with the Baghdad government at risk in order to pursue this strategy. Since 2008, Ankara has helped mitigate Baghdad's withholding of payments to the KRG by occasionally paying KRG employee salaries and providing loans to the Kurds.[65] In 2009, the KRG began trucking its oil directly into Turkey.[66] This was contrary to Iraq's wishes: Baghdad claims that it is illegal for Kurdistan to export oil through any entity other than the State Organization for Marketing of Oil.[67] In 2011, Iraqi Prime Minister Maliki called Turkey a "hostile state" because of its direct connections to the Kurds and Arab Sunni politicians.[68] This did not deter the Turks, who in May 2012 signed a deal with the KRG to construct two oil pipelines and one gas pipeline from Iraqi Kurdistan to Turkey.[69] The next year, KRG Prime Minister Nechirvan Barzani announced that the KRG had signed a secret agreement

---

[62] Henri J. Barkey, *Turkey's New Engagement in Iraq: Embracing Iraqi Kurdistan*, Washington, D.C.: United States Institute of Peace, 2010a, p. 2.

[63] Nader et al., 2016.

[64] Nader et al., 2016.

[65] Nader et al., 2016.

[66] Barkey, 2010a.

[67] Nader et al., 2016.

[68] Dombey and Guler, 2013.

[69] Nader et al., 2016.

with Ankara that involved cooperation for 50 years on a variety of issues.[70] The agreement apparently calls for the KRG to help bring a peaceful resolution to the Ankara-PKK dispute. It also seeks to boost the direct sale of Kurdish oil to Turkey. There may also have been a section pledging Turkish support to the KRG in the event of a future conflict between the Kurds and Baghdad, although Turkey later supported Baghdad's recapture of Kirkuk. By 2014, the KRG was piping its oil directly to Turkey.[71] In January 2016, the KRG announced plans to export natural gas to Turkey as early as 2019.[72] And in January 2017, Iraqi Prime Minister al-Abadi accused the KRG of secretly shipping oil to Turkey.[73] The Iraqis also accused a KRG minister of offering Turkey several oil fields for $5 billion.

Between Baghdad and the KRG, the latter has served as the more lucrative trade partner for Turkey. As of 2013, there were 1,500 Turkish companies operating in Iraqi Kurdistan, constituting three-fifths of all foreign companies there.[74] In 2014, the $8 billion in trade between Turkey and Iraqi Kurdistan constituted two-thirds of Turkey's overall trade with Iraq.[75] The Kurds have benefited greatly from direct oil sales to the Turks. In 2015, the KRG earned $630 million per month from such sales to Turkey, covering almost 75 percent of its budgetary needs.[76] It had been predicted that Turkey-KRG trade would reach $20 billion by 2023, but the KRG's loss of the oil fields in Kirkuk will no doubt diminish this prospect.[77]

The KRG's increasing reliance on the Turkish economy has dragged it into the Turkey-PKK dispute. In December 2016, Prime Minister Nechirvan Barzani called for the PKK to resume its ceasefire with Ankara.[78] However, this has also made the KRG vulnerable to retaliation. In July 2015, the PKK attacked an oil pipeline in Turkey that brought in oil from Iraqi Kurdistan.[79] Although the attack was claimed to be a response to Turkish targeting of PKK forces in Syria and Iraq, according to one

---

[70] "Matter of National Security? The Turkish-Kurdish 'Secret Agreement,'" *Niqash*, April 23, 2015.

[71] In 2015, Baghdad and the KRG agreed that the Kurds could pump their oil directly to Turkey as long as they shared the proceeds with Baghdad; in addition, Baghdad could ship some of its oil through the Kurdish pipeline and be reimbursed by the KRG (Nader et al., 2016).

[72] Nader et al., 2016; Johnson, 2015.

[73] Ali Mamouri, "Iraqi Kurdistan Oil a Slippery Issue," *Al-Monitor*, January 6, 2017.

[74] Nader et al., 2016.

[75] Nader et al., 2016.

[76] Keith Johnson, "A Mysterious Pipeline Closure Is Bankrupting Iraqi Kurds," *Foreign Policy*, March 2, 2016.

[77] Nader et al., 2016.

[78] Amberin Zaman, "KRG PM: Talk of Iraqi Kurdish Independence Red Line for Iran, but Not Turkey," *Al-Monitor*, December 23, 2016b.

[79] Johnson, 2015.

analyst, it was "directed as much toward fellow Kurds as it was against Turkish President Recep Tayyip Erdoğan."[80]

Turkey's Future Relations with Iran and Iraq

Relations with Iraq Following the Campaign to Retake Mosul

There is the potential for a flare-up between Ankara and Baghdad following the liberation of Mosul and its surrounding areas from ISIS. In October 2016, Erdoğan said, "After liberating Mosul from [ISIS], only Sunni Arabs, Turkmens and Sunni Kurds should stay there."[81] However, in a January 2017 meeting between Iraqi and Turkish officials, Turkish Prime Minister Binali Yıldırım hinted that Turkey would withdraw its troops from Bashiqa once Mosul is liberated.[82] This may hinge on whether Shi'a militias loyal to Iran stay out of the area. Keeping troops in the area could hurt Turkey's bottom line; in October 2016, amid the dispute with Iraq over Turkish troops in Bashiqa, several Iraqi provincial councils threatened to boycott Turkish companies. It has been estimated that such a boycott would cost Turkey $11 billion in trade.[83]

Relations with Iran Following the Syrian War

Although Turkey's agreement to the so-called Moscow Declaration in December 2016 suggests that Ankara will no longer push for Assad to step down, this means that Turkey will focus heavily on what it sees as the Kurdish threat on its southern border, as discussed in Chapter Two.[84] Meanwhile, Iran's desire to create a military supply and oil pipeline corridor through parts of Iraq and Syria to the Mediterranean is a concern for Turkey because this corridor would run along its border.[85] Specific areas of contention along this route would be Sinjar and Tal Afar in Iraq, as well as Kobanî and Qamishli in Syria.[86] This objective could bring Tehran and the PKK closer together because the PKK wants to maintain control over Sinjar in order to smuggle goods to the PYD in Syria.[87] Moreover, Iran may be concerned that a PYD-controlled region in

---

[80] Johnson, 2015.

[81] "Erdoğan Not Backing Down on Turkish Role in Mosul," 2016.

[82] "Baghdad 'Reaches Deal' on Turkish Forces in Northern Iraq," *Middle East Eye*, January 7, 2017.

[83] This would, however, also lead to massive price increases for Iraqi consumers (Adnan Abu Zeed, "Will Iraq Boycott Turkey?" *Al-Monitor*, October 19, 2016).

[84] Ben Hubbard and David E. Sanger, "Russia, Iran and Turkey Meet for Syria Talks, Excluding U.S.," *New York Times*, December 20, 2016.

[85] Joost Hiltermann, "Syria: The Hidden Power of Iran," *New York Review of Books*, April 13, 2017.

[86] Hiltermann, 2017; Tremblay, 2016b.

[87] Hiltermann, 2017.

Syria outside of Iran's orbit could become a base for Western military and intelligence.[88] A potential Iran-PKK corridor would cut across Iraq's north-south pipeline to Turkey. As one respected analyst noted, "A disruption of the pipeline by Iran or the PKK would have consequences for Iraqi Kurds, for Turkey, and for European consumers—leverage that could potentially be a strategic asset for Iran in time of war."[89]

Furthermore, with closer ties to the PKK, Iran could convince the organization to rein in the activities of PJAK.[90] This is especially critical for Iran because PJAK fighters received valuable combat experience fighting alongside the PKK and the YPG against ISIS.[91] A potential uptick in Iranian Kurdish attacks on Iranian forces would make this all the more imperative; in March 2017, the resistance group Komala announced that it was joining with five other Iranian Kurdish groups to cooperate over "joint military activities."[92] One of the groups, the Kurdistan Freedom Party (Parti Azadi Kurdistan), claims to have received military training from U.S. forces in 2015 as part of the anti-ISIS campaign.[93] For now, the PJAK has not joined that coalition.

Finally, Russia's recent cooperation with Turkey in Syria could cause tension between Tehran and Ankara. In December 2016, the Russians provided air support to Turkish ground troops, rather than the YPG, in the battle to take back al-Bab.[94]

Relations with the Kurds

Ankara and the KRG are mostly aligned over their desire to weaken the PKK's influence in Iraq and Syria. In December 2016, Kurdish Prime Minister Nechirvan Barzani warned that the KRG was willing to use force to remove the PKK from Sinjar.[95] The KRG has also trained around 5,000 Syrian Kurdish fighters, generally referred to as the Rojava Peshmerga, to counterbalance the strength of the PYD.[96] In early 2017, the KRG deployed 500 of these fighters to the KRG-Syrian border area near Sinjar. In March 2017, the Rojava Peshmerga attacked a PKK base in Khanasur.[97] Several fighters on both sides were killed.

---

[88] Tremblay, 2016b.

[89] Hiltermann, 2017.

[90] Milburn, 2017.

[91] Milburn, 2017.

[92] Milburn, 2017, p. 29.

[93] Milburn, 2017.

[94] David Hearst, "Can Turkey and Russia Push Back Iran in Syria?" *Middle East Eye*, January 3, 2017.

[95] Zaman, 2016b.

[96] These new fighters are close to the KDP; the Iraqi PUK has a history of ties to the PKK ("Rojava Peshmerga Deployed to Syrian Border, No Plans to Enter Rojava," *Rudaw*, March 2, 2017; and Hiltermann, 2017).

[97] Hiltermann, 2017.

However, if Turkey were to step up its attacks on the PKK in the Kurdish region, it could lead to a backlash from the local population. In August 2015, there was public outrage over civilian deaths caused by a Turkish air strike on what Turkey believed were PKK positions in the Qandil Mountains.[98] Increased attacks on the PKK could also lead to fissures within the KRG, because the PUK has a history of relations with the PKK.[99] Already, in January 2017, Najmaldin Karim, the Kirkuk governor who is part of the PUK, suggested creating a new province (including Sulaimaniyeh, Halabja, Kirkuk, and Khanaqin) that would weaken the KDP's control over all Kurds.[100] All of this could push the PUK closer to Iran. Karim also has proposed construction of an oil pipeline from Kirkuk to Iran that would go through PUK-controlled Sulaimaniyeh.[101]

The KDP held an independence referendum on September 25, 2017.[102] Turkey's reaction was harsh, and Erdoğan contended that Barzani had "betrayed" Turkey. The Kurds may have counted on their special relationship with Ankara to buttress their independence bid, but Turkey's shared interests with Iran and Iraq to prevent Kurdish independence and preserve other elements of their cooperation, coupled with the threat of combined military action, ensured that the KRG goals were thwarted.[103]

Table 3.1 provides a summary assessment of where Turkish interests are convergent, divergent, or in conflict with those of Iran and Iraq.

Conclusion and Implications for the United States

Turkey and Iran appear to have become closer over two important regional issues: the Syrian civil war and the KRG's independence drive. Ankara has realized that Assad will remain Syria's ruler and has worked with Iran and Russia to de-escalate the war. Turkey and Iran also worked together to thwart Kurdish independence in northern Iraq. This does not mean that Ankara and Tehran are friends. Rather, Turkey and Iran can be expected to cooperate on specific issues when it suits their respective interests, and perhaps at times to the detriment of U.S. interests. But Turkey may have helped expand Iranian power in both Syria—through its engagement with Iran in the Astana process to resolve the Syrian conflict—and northern Iraq—by collaborat-

---

[98] Zaman, 2015.

[99] Hiltermann, 2017.

[100] Mamouri, 2017.

[101] Mamouri, 2017.

[102] Hamdi Malik, "Can Iran Stop Iraqi Kurdistan Independence?" *Al-Monitor*, April 20, 2017.

[103] Malik, 2017.

Table 3.1
Alignment of Turkish Interests with Iranian and Iraqi Interests

Neighbor or Partner	Converging Interests	Diverging Interests	Conflicting Interests
Iran	• Expanded trade in goods and energy; economic cooperation • Opposition to the development of Kurdish mini-states in Iraq and Syria • Limited influence of outside actors • Border security • Caution toward Russia • Turkish facilitation of Iranian sanctions avoidance • Turkish support for Qatar in disputes with GCC and other Arab states	• Iran's political and military ties to Baghdad • Approach to Kurdish separatism • Settlement in Syria (Turkey wants to limit Iranian influence) • Relations with the United States and Europe • Counterterrorism • Iranian regional activities and influence	• In Syria: Iranian cooperation with the PKK to achieve an energy transit corridor • Religious differences between the Sunni and Shi'a denominations • Turkey's NATO membership • Iran's nuclear program • Resettlement of depopulated areas in Syria and Iraq • Turkish support to Sunni Islamist and jihadist groups
Iraq	• Opposition to the development of Kurdish mini-states in Iraq and Syria • Trade and energy transit	• Influence of Iran and Shi'a militias in Iraq • Relations with the KRG, particularly on energy flows	• Turkish military presence in northern Iraq • Turkish ties to Sunni separatist Turkmen in Iraq

ing with Tehran to prevent the KRG independence referendum.[104] The United States appears to be a relatively minor player in both places; even an enduring presence of some U.S. troops in liberated areas of Syria is unlikely to serve as an effective buffer against Iran, given the confluence of interests and policies among Syria, Turkey, Iran, and Iraq. All four countries, in addition to Russia, aim to eradicate ISIS and prevent the re-emergence of a similar Sunni Jihadi group. For now, Turkey and Iran see a need to cooperate. However, the future is likely to bring new sources of tension.

Turkey confronts some enduring challenges in Iraq. The Kurds have noted that, when ISIS fighters approached Erbil, it was Iran and not Turkey that came to their aid.[105] Furthermore, the faction within the Iraqi Parliament that is close to Ankara is not very large; as of October 2016, the alliance between Masoud Barzani and Iraqi Vice President Osama al-Nujaifi had only 35 of the 328 parliamentary seats.[106] Meanwhile, some Arabs in Nineveh have been angered over the Nujaifi alliance with the Kurds, putting such a coalition on shaky ground.[107] Finally, because at least 50 per-

---

[104] The *Astana process*—named for the neutral site of Astana, Kazakhstan—is an effort led by Russia, Turkey, and Iran to foster a peace settlement between the Syrian government and various rebel groups, particularly by formalizing security arrangements and de-escalating tensions in various regions.

[105] Zaman, 2015.

[106] Sowell, 2016.

[107] Sowell, 2016.

cent of Iraqi Turkmen are Shiʿa, there does not appear to be an overwhelming desire to come under Ankara's control.[108] In fact, some Turkmen are wary that Erdoğan's feuding with Baghdad puts them in a bad light.[109] While Baghdad and Ankara came together in thwarting Kurdish independence, they remain wary of each other's intentions, and the potential for conflict over the enduring Turkish military presence near Mosul persists. These tensions between Ankara and Baghdad could complicate U.S. efforts to enhance security, Sunni-Shiʿa reconciliation, and economic development in Iraq after the defeat of ISIS. Turkey's leverage over the KRG has increased since the fall of Kirkuk, but it remains to be seen whether this will bolster their cooperation in countering the PKK in the post–Masoud Barzani era and whether Ankara will push the KRG closer to Baghdad or continue to deepen Turkey and the KRG's mutually beneficial economic and political ties. If Ankara overplays its hand in strikes against the PKK, it could be counterproductive and exacerbate fissures within the KRG that could be detrimental to Turkish interests.

Turkey will continue to welcome U.S. efforts to counter Iran's drive for regional hegemony, but specific Turkish policies toward Iran, Iraq, and Syria will often be at odds with U.S. approaches. For example, Ankara supports the unity of Iraq but has lingering impulses to intervene in Iraqi politics and harbors territorial claims. Ankara also shares U.S. support for maintaining the territorial integrity of Syria, but its priority there is to prevent the emergence of a Kurdish mini-state along Turkey's southern border, which it sees as being fostered by U.S. support for the YPG. Ankara also shares U.S. and European concerns that Iran plans to develop a military supply and oil pipeline corridor through parts of Iraq and Syria to the Mediterranean that would run along that same border. And Turkey shares the U.S. and European interest of limiting Russian influence in Syria and the Eastern Mediterranean, even as Turkey has been forced to deal with both Moscow and Tehran in trying to end the conflict.

The biggest arena for future tensions and cooperation will likely continue to be Syria. Iran and Turkey have cooperated on Syria since 2017, especially because they are both concerned about Kurdish irredentism. For example, both countries coordinated their joint pressure campaign against the KRG after its independence referendum. But the entry of pro-Syrian forces into the Afrin fight may complicate the up and down nature of Turkish-Iranian relations. Tehran and Ankara cooperate when convenient for both, and although their strategic interests may be aligned currently, any tensions or even armed conflict between their respective camps may end what appears to be increasing strategic cooperation.

---

[108] Barkey, 2010a.

[109] Taştekin, 2016.

CHAPTER FOUR

Turkey and the Arab World: Mixed Views and Interests

Jeffrey Martini

This chapter examines the perspectives of key Arab states toward Turkey, focusing on the extent to which the interests of these states and Turkey's align and diverge. From the Arab state side, the research focuses on Egypt, Jordan, Qatar, Saudi Arabia, and the United Arab Emirates (UAE). The choice of these countries is based on their importance to the regional security architecture, which is undergirded by strong security cooperation with the United States. Interest alignment is used both to explain the recent pattern of state relationships between these Arab countries and Turkey and to set plausible bounds for the evolution of these relationships over the next ten years. The analysis is intended to help the U.S. national security community factor intraregional alliances and competition into U.S. Central Command activities, ranging from reassurance of partners to defense planning for military contingencies.

Arab State Perspectives of Turkey

Although the United States' key Arab partners do not possess a uniform view of Ankara, there are clear patterns among them. For Saudi Arabia, the UAE, and Jordan, Turkey represents both an opportunity and a threat. The opportunity is that this large and militarily capable Sunni-Muslim state will assist its fellow Sunni-Arab states in containing Iranian influence. The threat is that Turkey will serve as a champion of the Muslim Brotherhood and its affiliated political parties, backing what these Arab capitals see as the strongest challenger to their legitimacy and internal stability.

The two other Arab partners considered in this chapter are outliers. The first, Egypt, generally aligns with the Riyadh–Abu Dhabi–Amman perspective, but with a calculus tinged by Egypt's recent upheavals. Given Cairo's distance and relative security from Iranian threats and the fact that the *ancien régime* in Cairo was overturned by a Muslim Brotherhood–led government that Turkey backed, Egypt's current order places less value on Turkey as a partner in Iranian containment and instead focuses on Turkey as a threat to the regime's security based on Turkey's support for internal opposition. Added to the fear and frustration with Ankara is Egypt's clinging to an underlying order—military control—which President Erdoğan upended in Turkey over the past decade as he achieved tight civilian control of the military (see Chapter Two).

The other outlier in the Arab state perspective of Turkey is Qatar. Doha is the regional partner that possesses the strongest relationship with Turkey and does not share Egypt's view of the threat posed by the Muslim Brotherhood. Turkey and Qatar do share common ideological backgrounds (e.g., support for political Islam), have taken similar stances on key issues (e.g., backing the Islamist opposition in the Syrian civil war), and have stood side by side when their positions have been challenged in the post–Arab Spring backlash that has targeted these two countries. The most recent crisis—the GCC-Qatari rift—has deepened Qatar's dependence on Turkey and increased the military dimension of their partnership.

Interest Convergence Between Turkey and the Arab States

Several factors tend to draw Turkey together with its Arab neighbors to the south. Since the Iranian Revolution in 1979, the most important factor is the Arab states' hope that Sunni solidarity will translate to Turkey blunting Iranian influence and fighting for the preservation of the existing regional order that Iran challenges. This is not to say that the Turkish state is as Sunni-sectarian in its identity as several of the GCC states or that Ankara is committed to the containment of Iran as comprehensively as the Saudi-led bloc is.[1] But in Ankara, U.S.-aligned Arab partners see the potential for a Sunni check on the political and security threats posed by their adversary. Like Iran, Turkey is populous, rooted in a coherent nation-state, technologically advanced, and militarily capable. As a result, Arab states see Turkey as potentially contributing to the Sunni balance of Iran, a need that has become more acute since the overturning of the Sunni-led regime in Baghdad and the growth of Iranian influence in Iraq and Syria.

Turkey has not always lived up to Arab aspirations in this regard. Ankara's expressions of the shared threat posed by Iran, such as President Erdoğan's rebuke of "Persian expansionism,"[2] are the embodiment of the hope. But because those statements are often belied by a more pragmatic foreign policy in which Turkey attempts to stake out a middle ground and preserve political and economic relations with Iran,[3] most GCC states question the depth of Turkey's commitment to roll back Iranian influence. However, from the Arab state perspective, Iran is too much of a threat, and Turkey

---

[1]   The GCC member states are Bahrain, Kuwait, Oman, Qatar, Saudi Arabia, and the UAE.

[2]   "Erdoğan: Listu Radian 'an At-Tawasu' Al-Farasi" ["Erdoğan: I Am Not Content with Persian Expansionism"], *Asharq al-Awsat*, June 17, 2017; and "Turkey Disapproves of Iran's 'Persian Expansionism': Erdoğan," *Hürriyet Daily News*, June 16, 2017. Erdoğan has also used the phrase in the past, specifically to critique Iranian influence exerted through the Popular Mobilization Units in Iraq.

[3]   Mohamed Talib Hamid, *Al-Siyasa Al-Kharijiya Al-Turkiya wa Athriha 'ala Al-Amn Al-'Arabi* [*Turkish Foreign Policy and Its Impact on Arab Security*], Cairo: Al-Arabi Publishing, 2016.

too important a regional partner, to give up on Ankara playing this role. One attempt to more closely bind Turkey to the Sunni-Arab states was Saudi Arabia's initiative in January 2016 to form a "strategic cooperation council" to better enable the two powers to address "negative Iranian interventions in the affairs of the region."[4] Like many initiatives before it, the strategic cooperation council has not led to greater coordination between the two capitals, but it does signal Saudi effort in cultivating Turkish support, even if that cooperation has not always been forthcoming.

The Arab hope that Turkey's Sunni identity makes it a potential partner is manifested not only in the Iran issue but also in the related issue of the Syrian civil war. On Syria, Turkey was seen in Arab capitals as the tip of the spear in the battle to overthrow the Assad regime and, with it, break a critical node of Iranian influence in the Levant. From the Arab state perspective, Syria's relationship with Iran provides Tehran the key enablers it needs to project regional influence. Namely, it offers supply routes for equipping Hezbollah and a site from which to provide material support and grow its relationship to Hamas. For this reason, Riyadh saw the initial uprising in Syria as an opportunity to cleave the Damascus-Tehran axis and coax a post-Assad Syria back into the Arab fold.[5]

Thus, in the early years of Syria's civil war, the Saudi-led bloc was pleased to see Turkey challenge the Assad regime, rhetorically by calling for its removal and practically by opening Turkey's border with Syria to oppositionists of all stripes. This was advantageous to Jordan, which was relieved from having to use its border as a haven for the insurgency, mitigating the risk of regime retaliation against Amman or blowback in the form of Syrian armed groups turning against their patron. It was also advantageous to the Arab Gulf states, which had a clear channel for backing the opposition. Even more appealing to those states, it was Ankara, and not themselves, that was the main recipient of U.S criticism over enabling foreign fighters to reach the battlefield.[6]

But like in the Iran case, in which Arab states see the execution of Turkish foreign policy as falling short of the ideal, there have been Arab critiques of Turkey's implementation of its Syria strategy. Reflecting the evolution of the Arabs states' views of the conflict, there are internal contradictions within their three main critiques. The first concern is Turkey's dubious commitment to champion Sunni-Arab oppositionists rather than protect Turkey's narrower interest in preventing an autonomous and contiguous Kurdish region led by the PYD along Turkey's 500-mile-long southern border with Syria. Specifically, in the Astana process, which grew out of a Russian-

---

[4]   The description was from Saudi Foreign Minister Adel al-Jubeir. See Raghia Dargham, "At-Ta'awun Al-Istratiji bayn As-Sa'udiya wa Turkiya fi Wajh At-Tahidiyat" ["Strategic Cooperation Between Saudi Arabia and Turkey in the Face of Challenges"], *Al Hayat*, January 1, 2016.

[5]   Guido Steinberg, *Leading the Counter-Revolution: Saudi Arabia and the Arab Spring*, Berlin: German Institute for International and Security Affairs, June 2014.

[6]   Tim Arango and Eric Schmitt, "A Path to ISIS, Through a Porous Turkish Border," *New York Times*, March 9, 2015.

Turkish-Iranian initiative, some Arab capitals fear that Turkey will concede Sunni-Arab demands in return for checks on PYD gains. A second, and somewhat contradictory, concern is that Turkey is enabling the growth of jihadi groups inside Syria, including Hayat Tahrir al-Sham (HTS) (an umbrella group that includes the former Nusra Front). This fear is most commonly expressed by Egypt and the UAE, which are concerned about genuine jihadi groups (e.g., HTS), as well as Turkish championing of the Free Syrian Army, which they see as dominated by the Muslim Brotherhood. The third concern is in direct contradiction to the first: It is frustration that Turkey is prolonging the Syrian civil war, placing pressure on such refugee hosts as Jordan and Lebanon, when the former champions of the Syrian opposition have all but given up on the war and are looking for an off ramp that trades the benefit of regional stability for the perceived cost of reinforcing Russian and Iranian influence inside Syria.

Interest Divergence Between Turkey and the Arab States

Although Turkey is seen by most Arab states as a potential Sunni bulwark against Iranian influence, this interest convergence is partially offset by areas of interest divergence between Ankara and its Arab counterparts. The most glaring is a perception in Arab capitals that Erdoğan and the AKP share the same political project as the Muslim Brotherhood, which has been designated a terrorist organization by Saudi Arabia, the UAE, and Egypt. This leads all three states—but the UAE and Egypt in particular—to accuse Turkey of backing a movement that they view as a threat to their own security and the broader political status quo in the region.

Although these Arab states are prone to exaggerating the case against Ankara, it is true that Turkey has supported the Muslim Brotherhood in its post–Arab Spring moment and subsequent struggles. Riyadh, Abu Dhabi, and Cairo accuse Turkey of backing Mohamed Morsi and the Freedom and Justice Party during the heady days after the January 25 Revolution in Egypt that brought the Muslim Brotherhood to power in 2011. During the July 2013 rollback that occurred in Egypt, it was Turkey (and Qatar) that provided refuge for Muslim Brotherhood leaders. And it was President Erdoğan who expressed strong opposition to the incarceration of President Morsi after his removal by the Egyptian military.[7] For the Arab states opposed to the Muslim Brotherhood, Egypt was the most serious case of Turkish meddling, but it was not the only one. Arab states also accuse Ankara of arming Islamist groups in Misrata and Benghazi, Libya. And in Turkey's efforts to break the blockade of Gaza, Arab states see Ankara legitimizing Hamas (a Muslim Brotherhood affiliate) and outbidding Arab leaders on one of the issues that has historically resonated most in the Arab street.

---

[7] "Erdoğan Won't Restore Egyptian Ties 'Until Morsi Freed,'" *Al Jazeera*, April 9, 2015.

One example that illustrates Turkish involvement in the Israeli-Palestinian dispute raising the ire of the traditional frontline states in the conflict (e.g., Egypt and Jordan) is the 2017 Temple Mount crisis. In that incident, discussed in detail in Chapter Five, Ankara was aligned with Hamas and the Egyptian Muslim Brotherhood and was opposed by Jordan, Egypt, and the Palestinian Authority. Turkey's attempt to insert itself into the situation was seen by regional players as a neo-Ottoman attempt to assert Turkish prerogatives and challenge the core stakeholders' leadership.[8]

In addition to diverging perspectives on the Arab Spring and views of the Muslim Brotherhood, there are more-enduring tensions that manifest themselves in Arab states' relationships with Turkey. The first is the management of shared water resources: Turkey has a geographic advantage in capturing these resources before they reach Turkey's neighbors. Because both the Tigris and Euphrates rivers originate in Turkey before flowing to Syria and Iraq, Turkey has a strong incentive to dam the rivers, both for agricultural and hydroelectrical use. Conversely, Syria and Iraq are heavily dependent on these same waters and would obviously prefer Turkey to allow the resources from the two rivers to reach them in an unimpeded fashion to support agriculture and electricity generation.

Not surprisingly, Turkey has pursued a self-interested approach, extensively damming the rivers at their head waters.[9] Turkey's approach to riparian management has created tensions between Ankara and its Arab neighbors, but, thus far, it has not led to direct military conflict.[10] This is partly because Turkey's military is stronger than Iraq's and Syria's; its advantage particularly strengthened after 1991, when the impact of the Gulf War and no-fly zones greatly limited Iraq's military capabilities. A second explanation is that, despite Turkey's attempts to exploit the water resources, most of the Tigris's flow still reaches Iraq, mitigating Baghdad's concerns. And the third reason is that Syria has aggressively dammed the Euphrates River before it reaches Iraq's western border, dividing Baghdad's attention over which neighbor is most responsible for eating into what Baghdad perceives as Iraq's share of these resources.

A second enduring issue that creates chronic tensions between these same states is Turkey's counterinsurgency campaign against the PKK, which raises sovereignty concerns. Turkey not only has reserved the right to pursue PKK fighters that retreat within Turkey's borders but also has unilaterally gone after PKK sanctuaries in neighboring territory. In the first decade of the 2000s, these actions were focused in Iraqi Kurdistan, and more specifically the Qandil Mountains, which are viewed by Turkey as a

---

[8] Israeli National Security Council official, discussion with the authors, Jerusalem, January 24, 2017.

[9] Joel Whitaker and Anand Varghese, "The Tigris-Euphrates River Basin: A Science Diplomacy Opportunity," Washington, D.C.: United States Institute of Peace, Peace Brief 20, April 22, 2010.

[10] Turkey did come close to armed conflict with both Syria and Iraq in 1990 when Ankara curtailed the flow of the Euphrates River with the construction of a dam for a reservoir (Joost Jongerden, "Dams and Politics in Turkey: Utilizing Water, Developing Conflict," *Middle East Policy Council Journal*, Vol. 17, No. 1, Spring 2010).

PKK sanctuary and thus have been a frequent target of Turkish military operations. More recently, Turkey has focused on the gains made by the Syrian PYD in the context of that country's civil war. As a result, Turkey has expanded its objectives beyond limiting sanctuary to ensuring that the PYD cannot control the Azaz corridor (an area west of the Euphrates) that would link the PYD's cantons into a Kurdish-dominated contiguous zone on the Turkish border.

Over the long term, Syria's Assad regime shares Ankara's objective of limiting PYD influence.[11] However, Damascus sees itself as the authority responsible for realizing this objective, and Turkey's efforts to overthrow the Assad regime in the preceding years will not soon be forgotten. The Syrian regime is also pursuing short-term objectives—defeating the Sunni-Arab insurgency—for which PYD cooperation is arguably useful. For those reasons, Syria opposed Turkey's incursion in Jarabulus and al-Bab (Operation Euphrates Shield), particularly because the local surrogate that Turkey is working through to cut off Afrin from Kobanî is the very Sunni-Arab opposition that the regime has prioritized defeating. This poses an escalation risk because Turkish-backed opposition groups are operating in proximity to regime forces, each of which is seeking to consolidate territory east of Aleppo that was previously held by ISIS.[12]

Special Cases of Egypt and Qatar

Although this chapter of the report primarily addresses Turkey's relationships with five Arab states (Egypt, Jordan, Qatar, Saudi Arabia, and the UAE), two of the five require additional treatment. This is because Egypt and Qatar are outliers in their relationships with Ankara. Cairo and Doha fall on opposite ends of the spectrum: Egypt's relationship with Turkey is nearly uniformly negative, whereas Qatar has embarked on a genuine strategic partnership with Turkey.

Today's relations between Egypt and Turkey are defined by the events of July 2013, when the Egyptian military removed then-President Mohamed Morsi from power after large-scale protests against his rule. What followed, however, was not the deposing of a single figure but a broad-based, state-led crackdown on the Muslim Brotherhood, which included incarcerating its leadership, outlawing its political wing (the Freedom and Justice Party), shuttering its social welfare activities, declaring it a terrorist organization, and criminalizing membership in it. Not content with stamp-

---

[11] Syrian Foreign Minister Walid Muallem's comments on this topic are instructive. At the time of Operation Euphrates Shield, he first criticized proposals for Kurdish autonomy as an infringement of Syrian sovereignty. But he also noted that the regime considers the Turkish incursion to be an invasion. See "Al-Mu'alim: Fikra Idara Dhatiya fi Sharq Halab Marfuda Jamlatan wa Tafsilan" ["Muallem: The Idea of Self-Administration East of Aleppo Is Rejected Part and Parcel"], *ChamTimes*, November 20, 2016.

[12] Tom Perry and Humeyra Pamuk, "Turkey-Backed Syrian Rebels Clash with Army in North," Reuters, February 27, 2017.

ing out the Brotherhood at home, the new regime also looked to stop its momentum elsewhere and deny its leadership refuge abroad. To that end, Cairo has backed an anti-Islamist offensive in neighboring Libya led by General Khalifa Haftar. And it has coordinated with like-minded GCC states—most notably, the UAE—to pressure the Brotherhood in the Persian Gulf and deny it sanctuary in Qatar.

In 2014, Egypt and several of the GCC states succeeded in forcing Doha to expel some Egyptian Muslim Brotherhood leaders, who quietly left for Istanbul. Another demand from the anti–Muslim Brotherhood bloc was that Doha shut down its broadcasting of Al Jazeera Mubasher, an Egypt-based television station operated by Qatar that Cairo accused of providing a platform for the Brotherhood to incite efforts against the military-led order. Although Doha largely capitulated to the anti-Brotherhood demands, Turkey was undeterred and continued to host Muslim Brotherhood leaders and direct criticism at the conduct of the Egyptian security forces on the heels of the revolution.[13]

Relations between the two countries regressed to the point that Egypt expelled the Turkish ambassador from Cairo in November 2013. In the absence of bilateral diplomacy, Egypt and Turkey found myriad issues to squabble over. For example, Cairo has been a strident critic of Turkey's approach to Syria, accusing it of undermining a regional military that, if added to the removal of the former Iraqi regime, would leave the Arab world bereft of its traditional military powers (except for Egypt). In addition, Turkey saw Egypt as rooting on the attempted military coup against Erdoğan in 2016.[14] And relations were dealt a further setback when the Egyptian Parliament proposed a measure in 2016 to recognize the Armenian genocide, a step seen by Turkey as a deliberate provocation.[15] Egypt has previously also opposed Turkish construction of a Gaza port because it would be considered a symbol of sovereignty over Gaza and an ultimate prize for Hamas. In addition, Egypt opposes any other Turkish political involvement in the Palestinian sphere, including in the Gaza Strip. From Cairo's perspective, Erdoğan's and the AKP's deep ties with the Muslim Brotherhood disqualify them from any political role in the region.[16] The intra-GCC dispute over Qatar—in which Turkey sided with Doha in defiance of the so-called Arab Quartet of Bahrain, Saudi Arabia, the UAE, and Egypt—further cemented the recent trend of Egyptian-Turkish hostility.

---

[13] Gregg Carlstrom, "Why Egypt Hates Al Jazeera," *Foreign Policy*, February 19, 2014.

[14] Egypt, which at the time of the failed coup had a rotating seat on the 15-member United Nations Security Council, vetoed draft language that called on all parties to "respect the democratically elected government of Turkey" (Michelle Nichols, "Egypt Blocks U.N. Call to Respect 'Democratically Elected' Government in Turkey," Reuters, July 16, 2016).

[15] Safa Joudeh, "Why Turkey and Egypt Won't Reconcile Anytime Soon," *Al-Monitor*, August 2, 2016.

[16] Expert on Turkey, discussion with the authors, Tel Aviv, January 25, 2017.

On the other end of the spectrum is Doha, the Arab state that has developed the strongest partnership with Turkey and a relationship that appears to be gaining further momentum, given Qatar's threat perceptions of its Arab neighbors. Warm ties between Qatar and Turkey are not new, but the relationship has progressed considerably in the post–Arab Spring period. In the early days of the transitions, Turkey and Qatar shared a similar vision in which political Islam would serve as a crucial part of the region's political development. To that end, Doha and Ankara celebrated the victories of Islamists in early elections in Egypt and Tunisia that brought the Muslim Brotherhood and its affiliate Al-Nahda, respectively, to power. Qatar was a major financial benefactor of the Muslim Brotherhood–led government in Egypt, while Erdoğan and the AKP postured to take credit for what they characterized as the movement's moderate impulses.

The Islamist star faded quickly, and, by 2013–2014, the Muslim Brotherhood was in retreat in Egypt, Tunisia, and Libya. Despite the Brotherhood's declining popularity, Turkey and Qatar continued to bet on this political current. For example, Qatar backed Islamist fighters in Syria—most notably, Ahrar al-Sham,[17] whose political office is based in Doha. Turkey backed similar groups, offering its border as a crucial node to arm and supply insurgents of all persuasions. And helping to relieve pressure on Qatar, Turkey took in Muslim Brotherhood leaders when Qatar was forced to expel them to placate Egyptian and GCC pressure.

Turkish-Qatari relations received a further boost in summer 2017, when Ankara came to the defense of Doha after it was politically and economically isolated by its GCC neighbors. Declaring that Qatar was in breach of the 2014 Riyadh agreement, a Saudi-led bloc cut off diplomatic relations and moved to close Saudi Arabia's border with Qatar. This action threatened to strangle Qatar's economy, given that the country's only land border abuts Saudi Arabia. In this moment of Qatari vulnerability, Turkey offered support that effectively broke the siege. Specifically, Turkey provided Qatar with food exports to replace its reliance on its neighbors. Turkey also increased flights in and out of Doha, providing an important window for Qataris to be able to travel abroad. And most importantly, in a strong signal of commitment to Sheikh Tamim bin Hamad Al Thani and his ruling family, Turkey launched joint exercises with the Qatari Armed Forces and bolstered its military presence in the country.

A 2014 defense cooperation agreement between Doha and Ankara allowed Turkey to establish military bases in Qatar.[18] As the intra-GCC crisis deepened, the Turkish parliament approved the deployment of several hundred forces to Qatar in sev-

---

[17] Ahrar al-Sham does not necessarily subscribe to the Muslim Brotherhood's approach. It includes a strong Salafi current.

[18] Tom Finn, "Turkish Troops Hold Exercises in Qatar," Reuters, August 7, 2017.

eral tranches during 2017 to augment an existing presence of 150 soldiers.[19] In terms of equipment, Turkey has deployed armored vehicles (ACV-15) and artillery (T-155 Fırtına).[20] Turkey has announced its intentions to deploy as many as 3,000 ground forces in Qatar in a show of support for its Arab ally. Ankara and Doha have also agreed on the deployment of Turkish naval and air forces in Qatar. Turkey intervened on behalf of Qatar in the face of strong resistance by the anti-Qatar Arab Quartet. Indeed, one of the 13 demands issued by the boycotting states was that Qatar expel Turkish forces from military bases in the country.[21] Rather than comply with this demand, Turkey added to its forces inside Qatar and announced plans with Doha for future increases.

Future Outlook for the Arab States' Relationships with Turkey

Although core interests endure, the Middle East regional system is rife with examples of states cultivating relationships, falling out with partners, and even flipping sides in their basic orientations toward regional and extra-regional powers.[22] With that as background, it is not prudent to assume a straight-line trajectory in which the current relationships between key Arab partners and Turkey will mirror those relationships over the next decade. There are two main mechanisms by which the character of relations could change. First, Arab states and Turkey could regress to the norm in areas in which their traditionally strong interest alignment might have been temporarily lost during the upheavals and crises in the region. This would lead to some improvement in relations between the countries. The other mechanism for change is the prioritization of state interests, which will evolve based on shifts in the structure of regional economics, politics, or security and thus change how these states see one another. This second mechanism could lead to either an improvement or a deterioration in relations depending on the shift in underlying conditions.

In the first instance, there is reason to believe that the shock of the 2011 uprisings threw Turkey's relationships with its Arab neighbors into disarray, and if the regional system settles into a more stable political condition, that will lead to a mellowing of relations between Turkey and the Arab states currently most wary of it (i.e., Egypt and the UAE). The idea is that, as Arab states feel less threatened by the Muslim Brother-

---

[19] As of summer 2019, the troops were still there, and on August 14, 2019, the Turkish government announced that it is building a second base in Qatar and will expand its military presence significantly (Hande Fırat, "New Military Base in Qatar to Inaugurate in Autumn," *Hürriyet Daily News*, August 14, 2019).

[20] Jeremy Binnie, "Turkey Deploys Artillery to Qatar," *Jane's Defense Weekly*, July 19, 2017.

[21] "Hadhahi Matalib al-Duwal al-Muqati'a li Qatar wa Mahla 10 Ayam li Tanfidhiha" ["These Are the Demands of the Boycotting States and the 10 Day Deadline to Implement Them"], al-Arabiya, June 23, 2017.

[22] Jeffrey Martini, Becca Wasser, Dalia Dassa Kaye, Daniel Egel, and Cordaye Ogletree, *The Outlook for Arab Gulf Cooperation*, Santa Monica, Calif.: RAND Corporation, RR-1429-RC, 2016.

hood and as Turkey is forced to accept that movement's declining influence, Turkey and the anti-Brotherhood bloc will be better able to bracket this disagreement and focus on areas of mutually beneficial cooperation. One path by which this could occur is if Ankara pursued confidence-building measures designed to placate its Arab neighbors. Hypothetical examples include Turkey expelling Muslim Brotherhood leaders from Istanbul or pressuring Qatar to accede to a portion of the Quartet's demands.

A rapprochement could also occur around a symbolic issue involving Iran, which is the issue of greatest importance to the Saudi-led bloc. For instance, the 2016 arson attacks on Saudi diplomatic facilities in Iran were followed by condemnation of the events at the subsequent meeting of the Organisation of Islamic Cooperation in Jidda, Saudi Arabia. The meeting was used by Saudi Arabia to isolate Iran and to test the solidarity of Muslim-majority countries. Countries that were viewed by Saudi Arabia as insufficiently pro-Saudi in their reaction to the event, such as Lebanon and Iraq, were labeled suspect and had fallouts in their relationships with the Saudis.[23] In contrast, the countries that enthusiastically condemned Iran and ignored the Saudi actions that precipitated the attacks were recognized for their solidarity. In a future moment like this, Turkey could show Saudi Arabia that it prioritizes their relationship over a more neutral foreign policy that seeks cooperation with all regional players—including Iran.

In the second instance of potential change mechanisms, a shift in underlying structural conditions could lead to either an improvement or deterioration in relations between Turkey and Sunni-Arab states. One possible change in the underlying security structure would be the development of Saudi Arabia and the UAE into more-self-reliant security actors in the Persian Gulf. This trend line is already underway as those two states lead the military campaign in Yemen and intervene elsewhere in an independent fashion (e.g., UAE air strikes in Libya via bases in Egypt, without prior U.S. coordination). Should Saudi Arabia and the UAE continue down this path, they will need to overcome manpower shortages, given their small populations. This is a particularly limiting factor for the UAE, which has a population of roughly 1.5 million native Emirati citizens. The UAE has partially offset this limitation by adopting national service (i.e., conscription) and by relying on defense cooperation with populous Arab countries, including Egypt and the Sudan.

Turkey is attractive as a potential partner in defense cooperation because it possesses a large armed force—albeit with a background in defending its borders and combating an internal insurgency but not a strong background in external operations. However, over time, states with smaller population bases but high-end military capabilities (e.g., the UAE) could see Turkey as a partner that provides (1) access to the Levant and Iranian land border and (2) a complementary force in the sense of compensating for the smaller country's manpower limitations. The increasingly assertive national-

---

[23] Ben Hubbard, "Saudis Cut Off Funding for Military Aid to Lebanon," *New York Times*, February 19, 2016.

ism of the Arab Gulf states could also bring these states into greater alignment with Turkey in terms of political culture, feeding a drive for Middle East ownership over the regional security structure rather than reliance on an external security guarantor.

Conversely, changes in structural conditions could also lead to greater divergence between Turkey and the Arab states. For example, an acceleration of the trend away from fossil fuels would further erode the influence of the GCC states and leave more-diversified economies in a stronger position relative to their extractive counterparts. Under such conditions, Turkey may see little value in deepening cooperation with the Arab Gulf states. Moreover, when balancing relations between these states on the one hand and Iran on the other, Turkey may come to see the latter as a better long-term bet, given that Iran's natural-resource economy is better supplemented by a stronger base in science and technology. And in this case, unlike in the former example in which the political culture of the Gulf sheikhdoms trends toward Turkey, it may be that Turkey and Iran view each other as more aligned because they have non-Arab ethnic identity, republican forms of government, and coherent national identities. This could lead Turkey to deprioritize relations with the Arab states and opt to explore greater alignment with Iran in an outside-in approach to the Middle East.

Table 4.1 provides a summary assessment of where Turkish interests are convergent, divergent, or in conflict with those of the Arab Gulf states and Egypt.

Table 4.1
Alignment of Turkish Interests with Key Arab State Interests

Neighbor or Partner	Converging Interests	Diverging Interests	Conflicting Interests
Arab Middle East	• Opposition to Iranian regional influence, although the Arab Gulf states question Turkey's commitment • Opposition to Syria's Assad regime, although the Arab states were concerned that Turkey has been more focused on countering the YPG than aiding Sunni-Arab opposition; the states were also concerned with Turkey's support to jihadis and the Free Syrian Army	• The endgame and settlement terms in Syria, which are affected by Turkey's dealings with Iran and jihadi groups • Palestine: Turkey has ties to Hamas and the Muslim Brotherhood; others have ties to the Palestinian Authority • Turkey's cross-border operations against the PKK and the YPG, which raise sovereignty concerns	• Muslim Brotherhood: Turkey and Qatar support the group; others oppose • Turkish support of other Islamist groups in Syria and Libya, as well as its enabling of some jihadist groups • Turkey's deepening ties to Qatar • Rift with Egypt over Muslim Brotherhood and Palestinian issues • Management of shared water resources

Conclusion and Implications for the United States

As U.S. policymakers and defense planners engage with the Middle East, the complex relationships between Arab partners and Turkey will constrain what can be achieved to advance U.S. foreign policy and security interests. The overarching challenge is that the differing priorities of Ankara and Arab capitals create obstacles for the United States in gaining partner support for regional initiatives. Indeed, this dynamic—disagreements among Ankara, Abu Dhabi, Amman, Cairo, Doha, and Riyadh—is holding back U.S. efforts today, and there is every reason to expect this situation to continue.

The most obvious example of this was the U.S. effort to assemble and lead a counter-ISIS coalition to address common threats to partner security and the U.S. and European homelands. At first blush, this issue seemed ripe for cooperation because all the states that are the subject of this chapter agreed that ISIS posed a threat to their security. But although the members of the coalition agreed that ISIS was a threat, their perceptions of how ISIS fit within their overall threat environments differed dramatically. Ankara has prioritized containment of Kurdish autonomy over ISIS rollback, whereas the United States has prioritized the rollback of ISIS even at the risk of abetting Kurdish ambitions. Turkey has attempted to peel off HTS fighters judged by Ankara as Syria-focused—rather than transnational jihadists—to use as a force in confronting Kurdish control of Afrin. Egypt quietly roots for the preservation of the Syrian state, not wishing to lend momentum to the impulse for regime change that only recently targeted Cairo. Riyadh initially saw an opportunity to weaken Iran, whereas Doha saw an opportunity to back Islamists. Amman is understandably anxious about being inundated by refugees, given the delicate balance there, in which those of Palestinian descent already have a numeric advantage over East Bankers. The result is that, although these countries have been nominally part of the U.S.-led coalition to counter ISIS, each pursues its own strategy, and those strategies often operate at cross purposes.

This challenge will continue to cast a shadow over post-ISIS caliphate counterterrorism efforts. For instance, the United States will confront a transnational jihadist threat in Syria in the form of HTS after the defeat of ISIS's caliphate. Just as in the preceding example, Turkey and key Arab partners differ in the prioritization of that threat relative to other national interests. Qatar may also be tempted to back elements of HTS to maintain a viable Syrian opposition force that Doha can influence. Other regional states that are ideologically opposed to Islamists (Egypt and the UAE, most notably) will staunchly oppose any support to HTS or inclusion of the group in a negotiated settlement. And Saudi Arabia, as the leading Arab Gulf power, is likely to want any residual opposition force to have its loyalties rest with Riyadh, for which Ghouta-based Jaysh al-Islam is the obvious candidate. This leaves the United States with counterterrorism partners that are conflicted in their views of HTS and that see the group as a mechanism for advancing their parochial interests, complicating any future counterterrorism campaign against them.

The second challenge for the United States stemming from intraregional competition is the impact of Turkish involvement in the intra-GCC rift. On the one hand, Turkey's role is beneficial insofar as it may deter the Saudi-led bloc from military action against Qatar. On the other hand, it will almost certainly prolong the dispute because Turkey's support for Doha puts Qatar on closer parity with its GCC challengers, allowing it to avoid concessions that might otherwise resolve the dispute, albeit on the Saudi-led bloc's terms. The stakes of that conflict are likely to further bind Qatar and Turkey, potentially inviting a situation in which the United States is forced to choose between competing constellations of Middle East partners. In a worst-case scenario, perceived U.S. favoritism toward one of those camps could lead to denial of U.S. military access in the nations of the other camp, which could complicate response to a military contingency in the U.S. Central Command area of responsibility, such as a naval escalation with Iran in the Persian Gulf.

The potential opportunity for the United States in the current alignment is that intraregional competition will limit the risk of *chain-ganging*—a scenario in which one country drags an ally into war—because fissures among the Sunni-Arab states prevent the emergence of a coalition strong enough to mount an offensive against Iran that would fuel a larger regional war that the United States would feel compelled to enter. The logic here is that the more unified the Sunni states are, the more likely they would calculate that they could win an offensive against Iran that would defang Tehran militarily or even lead to a change in the country's regime. And although the United States does have an interest in Sunni support for Iranian containment, Washington does not have an interest in a Sunni offensive against Iran that is not coordinated with Washington. Although, given the current military balance, such an offensive is unlikely, it would force the United States to enter the conflict.

CHAPTER FIVE

Wary Partners: The Future of Israeli-Turkish Relations

Shira Efron

Turkey and Israel have long been considered natural allies. For decades, they have collaborated episodically at different levels to advance some shared interests and counter common regional enemies. However, since their initiation in 1949, bilateral relations have been volatile and extremely sensitive to developments on the Arab-Israeli front. Turkey has downgraded its diplomatic relations with Israel three times. After a period of close economic, diplomatic, and military cooperation in the 1990s, bilateral relations soured during the 2000s. The second intifada (Palestinian uprising), the AKP's rise to power, the Second Lebanon War, and clashes over Israel's Gaza policies exacerbated tensions, culminating in a six-year rift between the countries from 2011 to 2016.

Turkey and Israel partially reconciled in mid-2016, based on a realpolitik assessment by stakeholders in both countries that certain economic and geostrategic interests might allow resumption of elements of their decades-old, multilayered collaboration. But the incentives that brought the two countries together in 2016 have, for the most part, dissipated. The two countries remain deeply divided on central issues—most notably, the status of Palestine and its people, independence for Iraqi Kurdistan, and the composition of a post-war Syria. Turkey's divisions with the United States and its Arab-Sunni allies, with which Israel shares important objectives, have only compounded these differences. In addition, Israeli and Turkish leaders, particularly Prime Minister Benjamin Netanyahu and President Recep Tayyip Erdoğan, deeply mistrust each other. This and a spate of mutual recriminations continue to make it hard to put differences aside and focus on some shared interests.

In May 2018, another diplomatic crisis between Israel and Turkey ensued when Israel Defense Forces (IDF) killed dozens of Palestinians and injured more than 2,000 in violent protests in Gaza. Turkey recalled its ambassador to Israel; Israel followed suit and expelled the Turkish consul in Jerusalem, who represents Turkey to the Palestinian Authority. The expulsions were accompanied by public humiliations of diplomatic staff on each side.[1]

---

[1] Michael Bachner, "Turkey, Israel Humiliate Each Others' Envoys in Escalating Diplomatic Tiff," *Times of Israel*, May 16, 2018.

This chapter examines Israeli-Turkish relations, with special insights on official and expert Israeli thinking drawn from extensive discussions in Israel; the prospects for those relations over the next decade; and the implication for U.S. interests. It briefly reviews the history of Israeli-Turkish relations and the six-year reconciliation process. It then discusses the status of bilateral relations covering key dimensions—economy and trade, energy, security cooperation, and political and diplomatic ties. The last dimension is inseparable from the Palestinian issue, and thus Turkish-Palestinian relations are explored in detail. Finally, the chapter concludes with an assessment of possible challenges and opportunities for future Israeli-Turkish relations and their implications for U.S. interests in the Middle East.

A History of Ups and Downs in Bilateral Relations

Turkey and Israel, two non-Arab Middle Eastern powers, have long been considered natural allies and have collaborated at various times on shared interests. Despite this longtime cooperation, their relationship was transformed into strategic partnership only in the 1990s.

1949–1990: Limited and Covert Ties

Turkey was one of the first countries, and the first Muslim-majority country, to recognize the state of Israel in 1949.[2] It subsequently followed a more cautious approach, keeping its engagement with Israel mostly secretive for fear of Arab backlash.[3]

In 1958, then–Israeli Prime Minister David Ben-Gurion and then–Turkish Prime Minister Adnan Menderes met secretly to form the basis for their countries' partnership, agreeing on the "peripheral pact," which would involve intelligence-sharing, joint public-relations campaigns to influence their constituencies at home, and mutual support to strengthen their respective militaries.[4] After the Six-Day War in 1967, Turkey joined the Arab countries in calling Israel to withdraw from the lands it occupied in the war; however, Ankara refrained from joining the other countries in referring to Israel as an "aggressor state." Nevertheless, in 1979, Palestinian leader Yasser Arafat traveled to Ankara to open an office for the Palestine Liberation Organization (PLO), which was then considered a terrorist organization by Israel, the United States, and

---

[2]   Brock Dahl and Danielle Slutzky, "Timeline of Turkish-Israeli Relations, 1949–2006," Washington Institute for Near East Policy, 2006.

[3]   Ofra Bengio, *Turkish-Israeli Relationship: Changing Ties of the Middle Eastern Outsiders*, London: Palgrave Macmillan, 2004. Ankara's sensitivity to Arab opinion became apparent when, in 1956, after Israel invaded Egypt's Sinai Peninsula as part of the Suez Operation, Turkey downgraded its diplomatic ties with Israel to the level of *chargé d'affaires* (a diplomat at a level lower than an ambassador or minister).

[4]   Dahl and Slutzky, 2006.

other countries.[5] In 1980, Turkey downgraded its diplomatic relations with Israel to a symbolic level, citing Israel's annexation of East Jerusalem.[6] Throughout the 1980s, Turkey showed no intention of repairing relations. It was only after the Madrid peace process in 1991 that Turkey reengaged with Israel at the ambassadorial level, and it concurrently elevated its diplomatic ties with the Palestinian Authority to the same level.[7]

1990s: Marriage of Convenience Transforms into Strategic Ties

In the 1990s, capitalizing on the post–Cold War environment and regional developments—including the Madrid peace conference, the first Gulf War, and the Oslo Accords[8]—ties between Turkey and Israel deepened quickly, transforming from primarily economic relations to a strong security partnership.[9] The basis for the strategic Turkish-Israeli alliance in the 1990s was "a marriage of convenience for both sides, sustained partly by the mutual perception of Syria as a security threat."[10]

Seeking to modernize its military to better address multiple security challenges, Turkey benefited from Israeli willingness to supply it with weapons that were otherwise unavailable. Israel, in turn, gained as Turkey became a lucrative market for its defense industry.[11] Simultaneously, tourism and trade grew between the nations, and Turkey was considered one of Israel's closest friends on multiple levels. After a massive earthquake hit Turkey in 1999, Israel quickly offered official and private assistance that reportedly saved many Turkish lives and engendered goodwill in Turkey.[12] In 2000, Israel and Turkey signed an agreement that allowed Israel to purchase water from Turkey, as well as a first MOU for promoting scientific cooperation.[13] Overall, what began as a marriage of convenience between Israel and Turkey in earlier decades was celebrated as a honeymoon from 1992 to 2000.

---

[5] Dahl and Slutzky, 2006.

[6] Ufuk Ulutaş, *Turkey-Israel: A Fluctuating Alliance*, Ankara: Foundation for Political, Economic, and Social Research, Policy Brief No. 42, January 4, 2010.

[7] Meliha Altunışık, "The Turkish-Israeli Rapprochement in the Post-Cold War Era," *Middle Eastern Studies*, Vol. 36, No. 2, 2000.

[8] Oğuz Çelikkol, *Turkish-Israeli Relations: Crises and Cooperation*, Istanbul: Global Political Trends Center and Mitvim Institute, November 2016.

[9] Mahmut Bali Aykan, "The Turkey-U.S.-Israel Triangle: Continuity, Change, and Implications for Turkey's Post-Cold War Middle East Policy," *Journal of South Asian and Middle Eastern Studies*, Vol. 22, No. 4, Summer 1999.

[10] Kilic Bugra Kanat, "Turkish-Israeli Reset: Business as Usual?" *Middle East Policy Council*, Vol. 20, No. 2, Summer 2013.

[11] Alon Liel, *Turkey and Israel: A Chronicle of Bilateral Relations*, Ramat Gan, Israel: Mitvim Institute and Friedrich-Ebert-Stiftung, February 2017.

[12] Liel, 2017.

[13] Dahl and Slutzky, 2006.

2000s: The End of the Israeli-Turkish Honeymoon

The outbreak of the second intifada in late 2000 and the images of Israeli soldiers suppressing violence by Palestinian youth had a negative influence on Turkish public opinion toward Israel.[14] Still, substantial military and civilian cooperation was maintained.[15] The AKP's 2002 election victory shook this alliance as then–Prime Minister Erdoğan became more vocal about his anti-Israel sentiment. Relations were not strained until 2004, when, after Israel assassinated Hamas leader Sheikh Ahmed Yassin, Erdoğan denounced the killing as a "terror act"[16] and said more generally that Israel conducts "state terror" in Gaza.[17] Nevertheless, diplomatic ties were sustained, as were civil and military cooperation.

Considering Israeli plans to withdraw from Gaza, Erdoğan even visited Israel in May 2005—his first and only visit—and invited then–Israeli Prime Minister Ariel Sharon to visit Ankara. In September, Turkey brokered the first public, official talks between Israel and Pakistan, an effort seen as part of Turkey's overall pursuit of a regional mediator role. The continued multilevel Israeli-Turkish partnership illustrated that, although Erdoğan did not sympathize with Israel, he was pragmatic.[18]

However, Hamas's victory in the Palestinian legislative elections in 2006, and the subsequent meeting between Hamas leaders and Turkish government officials at AKP headquarters, upset the Israeli-Turkish balance. Escalation of violence in Gaza and the Second Lebanon War led to anti-Israel rhetoric and widespread protests in Turkish cities. Still, even during these times, Israeli-Turkish ties were sustained, and in 2007–2008, Turkey officially mediated highly sensitive and secretive talks between Israel and Syria, which reportedly were on the verge of being fruitful.[19]

A watershed moment in Israeli-Turkish ties came in December 2008. Only three days after then–Israeli Prime Minister Ehud Olmert visited Ankara to discuss Turkish mediation efforts with Syria, Israel launched Operation Cast Lead in Gaza. The

---

[14] Liel, 2017.

[15] In 2001, there was a bilateral exercise between Israel and Turkey and combined exercises among Israel, Turkey, and the United States. In early 2002, despite harsh anti-Israel statements by Turkish politicians, Turkey signed a secret agreement with Israeli military industries to upgrade 170 M-60A1 Turkish tanks, and the two countries signed an agreement to import Turkish water to Israel. Israel withdrew from the deal, opting for desalination instead. See Dahl and Slutzky, 2006.

[16] "Turkish-Israeli Relations: An Axial Shift?" *Stratfor*, March 25, 2004. In 2004, there were high-level visits by heads of the Turkish Air Force and Naval Forces and by the IDF chief of staff. The Turkish military bought three unmanned aerial vehicle systems from Israeli industries at $183 million, and the IDF agreed to supply Turkey with surveillance equipment to better protect its border with Iraq.

[17] Jean-Christophe Peuch, "Turkey: Prime Minister's Criticism of Israel Does Not Mark Shift in Policy," Radio Free Europe/Radio Liberty, June 10, 2004.

[18] For example, Erdoğan and the AKP made an effort during that period to engage Jewish organizations in Washington to help lobby on their behalf in Congress (Dahl and Slutzky, 2006). See also İlker Aytürk, "The Coming of an Ice Age? Turkish–Israeli Relations Since 2002," *Turkish Studies*, Vol. 12, No. 4, 2011, pp. 676, 683.

[19] Aytürk, 2011, p. 676.

operation not only ended the Israeli-Syrian peace process but also transformed Israeli-Turkish relations. Not informed of Israel's plans, and having a strong emotional tie with Gaza and its leadership,[20] Erdoğan saw this as both a personal insult and, more generally, a blow to Israeli-Turkish bilateral ties.[21] Shortly afterward, then–Israeli President Shimon Peres and Erdoğan clashed publicly on stage at the World Economic Forum in Davos, Switzerland.[22] The heated rhetoric influenced leaders on both sides. The Israeli deputy foreign minister threatened to recognize Turkey's actions against Armenians during and after World War I as genocide if Turkey continued to refer to Israel's actions in Gaza as genocide.[23]

In October 2009, after a few months of attempts on both sides to soothe the groundbreaking animosity, including a meeting of the foreign ministers,[24] Erdoğan blocked Israel from participating in the Anatolian Eagle military exercises. The United States and Italy pulled out of the exercises in protest, which led to their cancelation,[25] but Erdoğan did not budge, choosing to exacerbate bilateral tensions and domestic outrage with anti-Israel actions, including harsh rhetoric.[26] Israel did not settle for traditional diplomatic protest. Then–Deputy Foreign Minister Danny Ayalon publicly humiliated the Turkish ambassador Oğuz Çelikkol, whom he summoned to protest anti-Israeli television programs in Turkey.[27] Despite a formal apology, the incident led to further deterioration of relations.[28]

---

[20] Liel, 2017.

[21] Selin Nasi, *Turkey-Israel Deal: A Key to Long-Term Reconciliation?* Ramat Gan, Israel: Global Political Trends Center, Mitvim Institute, and Friedrich-Ebert-Stiftung, January 2017. Erdoğan stated that he lost confidence in Olmert, declared that he no longer considered Olmert a "partner for peace," and condemned Israel and the international community for accepting Israel's behavior (Aytürk, 2011, p. 677).

[22] Erdoğan told Peres, "When it comes to killing, you know well how to kill," and left the stage angrily (Katrin Bennhold, "Leaders of Turkey and Israel Clash at Davos Panel," *New York Times*, January 29, 2009).

[23] Harut Sassounian, "Israel May Retaliate Against Turkey by Recognizing the Armenian Genocide," *Huffington Post*, May 25, 2011.

[24] Barak Ravid, "Livni, Turkish FM Hold Reconciliation Talks in Brussels," *Haaretz*, March 6, 2009.

[25] Julian Borger, "Turkey Confirms It Barred Israel from Military Exercise Because of Gaza War," *The Guardian*, October 12, 2009.

[26] This sentiment trickled down to public opinion, and two television series, one on the Turkish public network and another on a private network, portrayed Israel and the Jewish religion extremely negatively. In the series on Turkish public television, IDF soldiers were portrayed as monstrous murderers of Palestinians in the West Bank and Gaza (Michael Weiss, "Turkish TV Depicts IDF as Bloodthirsty," *Tablet*, October 15, 2009). The show on a private channel was described as anti-Semitic (Kevin Flower and Shira Medding, "Israel-Turkey Tensions High over TV Series," CNN, January 12, 2010).

[27] Alon had Çelikkol sit on a lower stool in a meeting that was open to the media and said, "The main thing is that you see that he is seated low and that we are high . . . that there is one flag on the table (the Israeli flag) and that we are not smiling" (Flower and Medding, 2010).

[28] Barak Ravid, "Peres: Humiliation of Turkey Envoy Does Not Reflect Israel's Diplomacy," *Haaretz*, January 13, 2010. When then–Defense Minister Ehud Barak went to Ankara to mend ties, neither then-President Gül

The *Mavi Marmara* incident in May 2010, the first violent conflict in the 60-year history of bilateral relations, weakened the already frayed ties. Purchased by the Humanitarian Relief Foundation (İnsani Yardım Vakfım [İHH]), a Turkish Islamic nongovernmental organization, the *Mavi Marmara* was the largest ship taking part in the Gaza Freedom Flotilla seeking to break Israel's naval blockade on Gaza. After the ship did not heed Israeli navy warnings, IDF commandos raided the ship, leading to the death of ten Turkish activists (one of whom was a dual U.S.-Turkish citizen), as well as injuries of other activists and IDF soldiers. The incident is still controversial.[29] Following several months of attempted reconciliation efforts, pushed vigorously by the U.S. government,[30] Turkey again downgraded its ties with Israel to the second secretary level—30 years after the last downgrading following Israel's annexation of East Jerusalem. Israel withdrew its ambassador to Turkey, and the two countries entered a turbulent six-year period of estrangement.

Normalization Achieved After a Six-Year Process

The *Mavi Marmara* incident exacerbated an ongoing crisis in Israeli-Turkish relations that has resulted in enduring damage to all levels of ties and influenced public opinion in both countries. Since the 2010 crisis, the United States attempted to broker a reconciliation of these two U.S. allies, but neither side was in a rush to make the first step. Ankara demanded three conditions for reconciliation—an Israeli apology, compensation for the *Mavi Marmara* victims, and the lifting of the blockade on Gaza. Of the three conditions, the apology did not come easy for Israel, despite sustained U.S. pressure.[31]

---

nor Erdoğan was willing to see him, and he met only with then–Foreign Minister Davutoğlu (Sami Moubayed, "Israel and Turkey Are Drifting Apart," *Gulf News*, January 19, 2010).

[29] Israeli sources argue that the Islamic nongovernmental organization that owned the ship on board, İHH, supports Hamas and has helped provide weapons and funds for "Islamic terrorist elements in the Middle East" ("Profile: Free Gaza Movement," BBC News, June 1, 2010). Flotilla activists accused Israeli commandos of immediately shooting, but, according to Israeli officials, the soldiers opened fire only after being attacked with clubs, knives, and a gun ("Mavi Marmara: Why Did Israel Stop the Gaza Flotilla?" BBC News, June 27, 2016). A United Nations inquiry found the Israeli naval blockade of Gaza to be legal and acknowledged that there were "serious questions about the conduct, true nature and objectives of the flotilla organizers, particularly İHH." See R. Buchan, "II. The Palmer Report and the Legality of Israel's Naval Blockade of Gaza," *International and Comparative Law Quarterly*, Vol. 61, No. 1, January 2012; and Geoffrey Palmer, Alvaro Uribe, Joseph Ciechanover Itzhar, and Süleyman Özdem Sanberk, *Report of the Secretary-General's Panel of Inquiry on the 31 May 2010 Flotilla Incident*, New York: United Nations, September 2011.

[30] Dan Arbell, *The U.S.-Turkey-Israel Triangle*, Washington, D.C.: Brookings Institution, Analysis Paper No. 34, October 2014. An official with Israel's National Security Council explained, "The Obama Administration strongly pressured us to apologize, and, for three years, Israel did not know what to say in response, but we didn't want to apologize. I don't think it is smart to apologize to someone like Erdoğan" (Israeli National Security Council official, discussion with the author, Jerusalem, January 24, 2017).

[31] Israeli National Security Council official, discussion with the author, Jerusalem, January 24, 2017.

Although Israel did not officially apologize, it embarked on several confidence-building measures in 2012–2013 that helped pave the way for later reconciliation.[32] In March 2013, U.S. President Barack Obama visited Israel, where he facilitated and eventually joined a phone conversation between Netanyahu and Erdoğan in which, according to an official statement, Netanyahu apologized and "agreed to complete the agreement for compensation." Turkey, for its part, agreed to cancel all the legal proceedings against IDF officers and soldiers that were opened in the wake of the *Mavi Marmara* flotilla incident. Furthermore, the two leaders agreed to normalize relations and return their respective ambassadors.[33] Despite this breakthrough, the diplomatic promises to restore relations did not materialize, partly because of Erdoğan's inflammatory rhetoric regarding Israel.[34] Negotiations continued, and even though the two sides could narrow their differences, the reconciliation process stagnated.[35] Turkey insisted that Israel lift the blockade on Gaza, and Israel demanded that Ankara shut down Hamas's offices in Turkey.[36]

Several major shifts in the region since 2015 have helped facilitate rapprochement between Israel and Turkey. The first shift came via the countries' shared interests in stabilizing Syria, including mitigating adverse spillover effects and outcomes of the civil war. At the outset of the Syrian uprising, both governments advocated regime change but tempered this goal as it became clear that Assad was winning the civil war in Syria and that a complete collapse of the regime could wreak wider instability.[37] The two governments now have distinct objectives in Syria. Turkey's highest priority, as elaborated in Chapter Two, is to prevent the emergence of a Kurdish autonomous region in Syria that would provide safe haven for terrorist operations in Turkey and a building block for an independent Kurdish state. Israel wants to ensure that Iran and Hezbollah do not emerge with a stronghold along its northern border to sustain the "rejectionist front" against Israel.[38]

---

[32] One such step was the sale of Israeli technology for upgrading the Turkish Air Force's early-warning systems, a deal reportedly pushed by U.S. officials seeking to support reconciliation between the two countries (Anshel Pfeffer, "Israel Supplies Turkey with Military Equipment for First Time Since Gaza Flotilla," *Haaretz*, February 18, 2013).

[33] Herb Keinon, "Netanyahu Apologizes to Turkey over Gaza Flotilla," *Jerusalem Post*, March 22, 2013.

[34] As one Israeli said, Erdoğan's rhetoric "sounded as if it came directly from Tehran" (former Israeli diplomat who served in Turkey, discussion with the author, Jerusalem, January 24, 2017).

[35] Selin, 2017.

[36] Additional events prolonged the process. Protests in Turkey drew Erdoğan's attention to domestic affairs, and Israel was also worried about instability in Turkey. Furthermore, Operation Protective Edge in Gaza in July 2014 caused the two sides to drift apart again over Israel's policies in the Gaza Strip, as Turkish public opinion turned against Israel (Selin, 2017).

[37] Israeli diplomat with Turkey expertise, telephone discussion with the author, March 1, 2017.

[38] Israeli think tank analyst with Turkey expertise, telephone discussion with the author, January 25, 2017.

Second, Turkey and Israel were brought back together by a shared anxiety over Iran. Both countries have long been worried about Iran, and several interlocutors indicated that this feeling reached a new high in 2015 as it became clear that Tehran could fulfill its regional aspirations in both Syria and Iraq. The nuclear agreement with Iran and what has been perceived as a U.S. retreat from the region have further exacerbated Israeli and Turkish concerns.[39]

Finally, developments related to natural gas interest in each country were the ultimate game changers leading to Israeli-Turkish reconciliation. The event that spurred Turkey to renew ties with Israel was the aftermath of Turkey's downing of the Russian bomber that violated its airspace in November 2015. Turkey imports approximately 60 percent of its gas from Russia. The subsequent crisis, discussed in Chapter Six, reminded Ankara of the need to diversify its energy sources away from Russia and to seek other allies in the region. This opened the door again to Israel, which, as elaborated later, is poised to become an exporter of natural gas. Some Israeli officials agree that, although the shared interests with Turkey over Syria and Iran were indeed important, the natural gas interest was the main catalyst for reconciliation.[40] On the Israeli side, the main advocate for renewal of ties was Energy Minister Yuval Steinitz. Steinitz's rationale developed as follows. After an international arbitration court ordered Egypt in December 2015 to pay a fine of almost $1.73 billion to Israel over gas that was supplied to Egypt through a Sinai pipeline, the Egyptian government ordered its oil and gas companies to freeze all business related to Israeli gas.[41] Worried about the loss of the Egyptian market for its newly discovered gas fields, Israel felt the need to turn to the other potential large market in the region—Turkey. Fewer than ten days after the Egyptian announcement, Turkish and Israeli delegates signed a preliminary normalization deal, which included an agreement over a compensation fund of $20 million for the *Mavi Marmara* victims and Turkey's extradition of a senior Hamas leader based there.[42]

In late June 2016, the reconciliation agreement was signed. It stipulated that, in addition to the compensation, Israel would enable Turkey to set up infrastructure projects in Gaza (e.g., a hospital, a power station, and a desalination facility).[43] Israel's

---

[39] The Joint Comprehensive Plan of Action set restrictions on Iran's nuclear program. It was signed in Vienna on July 14, 2015, between Iran, the five permanent members of the United Nations Security Council (China, France, Russia, the United Kingdom, and the United States), Germany, and the EU.

[40] Israeli Ministry of Foreign Affairs official, discussion with the author, March 1, 2017.

[41] For more details, see Tamim Elyan and Abdel Latif Wahba, "Egypt to Freeze Israeli Gas Import Talks After Court Ruling," *Bloomberg*, December 6, 2015.

[42] Selin, 2017.

[43] Israel journalist and Turkey scholar, email correspondence with the author, March 1, 2017. All the materials for these projects would be transported via Israel's Port of Ashdod. According to an Israeli journalist and Turkey scholar, Turkey presented this as an achievement; however, Turkey could always have helped Gaza as long as it shipped goods through the Port of Ashdod and met Israel's security requirements.

gain from the agreement, in addition to rapprochement with its long-time ally, was that Ankara committed to passing a law that would bar and prevent claims against IDF personnel. Also, Ankara vowed that Hamas would not carry out any terrorist or military activity against Israel from Turkish territory and promised to seek the return of two Israeli citizens and the remains of two soldiers held in the Gaza Strip.

Turkey later waived its demand that Israel remove the blockade on the Gaza Strip, and Israel came to terms with continued Hamas presence in Turkey. Pragmatism and shared interests made both parties set aside their key demands—the same demands that allegedly forestalled the reconciliation for six years.[44]

Post-Reconciliation Status of Israeli-Turkish Relations

The normalization of ties between Israel and Turkey in late 2016 represented an important milestone. Whether the two countries can sustain and deepen the rapprochement in the long run is unclear. In the months after the rapprochement, both governments sought to gain from the renewed ties on multiple levels—the economy, energy, security cooperation, and even diplomacy vis-à-vis post-war Syria. Since then, some of the key incentives, including economic incentives, that brought Ankara and Jerusalem together have dissipated. The relationship still faces multiple obstacles, particularly the mistrust between political leaders and the public in both countries and substantial differences on the Palestinian question. A deepening divide over Kurdish independence and Israel's growing strategic and energy cooperation with Cyprus and Greece designed to counterbalance Turkey could further limit the scope of ties. This section explores the main areas in which bilateral developments are most meaningful both in the present day and in the short term.

Expected Economic Gains in Tourism and Trade

Israel and Turkey have, for the most part, been able to separate economic from strategic-security relations. Despite their diplomatic freeze between 2010 and 2016, bilateral trade during those years increased.[45] However, there was a decrease in the number of Israeli companies operating in Turkey during those years, and 33 percent of the Israeli companies that operated in Turkey before the flotilla incident have stopped work-

---

[44] "All You Need to Know About the Israel-Turkey Reconciliation," *Haaretz*, June 27, 2016.

[45] "Turkish-Israeli Economic, Trade Ties Expected to Soar After Deal," *Hürriyet Daily News*, June 27, 2016. This trend might be misleading. It includes flows from a growing number of multinational companies that have set up factories and plants in Turkey, where they produce goods and from where they distribute to countries in the region (Israeli expert on Turkey, discussion with the author, Tel Aviv, January 25, 2017).

ing there.[46] Because of fears of instability and the anti-Israel climate, Israeli investors viewed Turkey as risky.[47]

Following the normalization of ties, bilateral trade has been on the rise. In 2017, total trade volume grew by 10 percent, and Israel was one of the top ten export markets for Turkey.[48] Ankara is interested in continued expansion of trade to support the AKP's economic growth goals, and the advancement of Turkish business interests is a high priority for Erdoğan. Thus, the Israeli market matters.[49] Turkey is Israel's fifth-largest trading partner after the United States, the United Kingdom, China, and the Netherlands.[50] With 75 million consumers in Turkey, Israeli economists estimate the potential bilateral trade at $8 billion per year, approximately twice the 2016 amount.[51]

Another Israeli economic interest is reaching an agreement that would reopen the Turkish aviation market to Israeli airlines. An initial agreement, which was drafted in 2009, was tabled after the *Mavi Marmara* crisis and then revisited. However, Israeli carriers remain locked out of the Turkish market, mostly because of differences over security procedures. Despite various hurdles, resuming flights by Israeli carriers to Turkey would provide substantial economic benefits for Israel.[52] Turkey also has an interest in establishing Qualifying Industrial Zones with Israel, like those that exist in Egypt and Jordan.[53] Israeli officials are disinclined to offer this benefit unless there is progress with Turkey on the aviation agreement or restraint in Turkey's Palestinian engagement, and the Turkish government has not pursued the issue since 2016.

One area of possible improvement in Israeli-Turkish relations is tourism. Israelis did not stop visiting Turkey entirely during the crisis years, but the number of visi-

---

[46] See Yuval Azulay, "Machon Ha'Yetzu: Ha'Piyus Im Turkkya Yiten 'Boost' Nosaf Le'Kishrey Ha'Sachar," *Globes*, June 27, 2016.

[47] Turkish businesspeople have told Israeli counterparts that, during the crisis years, they were waiting for a green light from the government to do business in Israel. As one official noted, "While it was not formally forbidden, Turks did not feel comfortable working with Israelis when their leader said that Israelis are murderers and child killers" (Israeli Ministry of Foreign Affairs official, telephone discussion with the author, March 1, 2017).

[48] "Turkish Businesspeople Seek Trade Boost with Israel," *Hürriyet Daily News*, November 27, 2017; and Daniel Heinrich, "Turkey and Israel: Animosity Ends When It Comes to Money," *Deutsche Welle*, December 12, 2017.

[49] Sharon Udasin, "Turkish Industrial Leaders Call for Trade Increase with Israel," *Jerusalem Post*, May 16, 2017.

[50] Ramzi Gabai, "Lenatzel et Hamomentum Hachiyuvi," *Marker Magazine*, trans. by Shira Efron, March 1, 2017.

[51] Israeli Ministry of Foreign Affairs official, telephone discussion with the author, March 1, 2017.

[52] Istanbul is an important global aviation hub. Turkish Airlines operates the second-most flights (after Israeli airline El Al) at Israel's national Ben Gurion Airport. There are about ten flights per day from Tel Aviv to Turkey, none of which is operated by an Israeli airline. A key hurdle is that Turkey does not want Israeli security personnel carrying weapons in its airports. See Raphael Ahren, "In Battle for the Skies, Turkey Beats Israel 112:0," *Times of Israel*, October 31, 2013; and Israeli Ministry of Foreign Affairs official, telephone discussion with the author, March 1, 2017.

[53] Qualifying Industrial Zones are industrial parks that house manufacturing operations and were established to take advantage of the free-trade agreements between the United States and Israel (Israeli Ministry of Foreign Affairs official, telephone discussion with the author, March 1, 2017).

tors did plunge to about 80,000 annually in the worst times (after the *Mavi Marmara* incident); by 2013, the number had increased to 164,917. In 2016, prior to the reconciliation, 200,000 Israelis visited Turkey, and the number jumped to close to 300,000 by the end of the year.[54] Although the number of Israelis visiting Turkey is currently relatively small—in better times, 560,000 Israelis visited annually, compared with millions of visitors from Germany and Russia—such tourism is important for certain Turkish cities, such as Antalya, that have traditionally drawn most Israeli visitors.[55] Concerns about terrorist attacks in Turkey have also slowed the revitalization of tourists from Israel. Turkey, for its part, wants Israel to make it easier for Turkish citizens to travel to Israel. However, Israel is unlikely to do so, because security risk assessments concerning Turkish citizens visiting Israel have not changed dramatically since the normalization agreement.[56] Turks do not visit Israel in large numbers, but because of the civil war in Syria, Israel's Haifa Port turned into a key transit point for Turkish exports to Jordan, which could no longer be shipped by truck through Syria. In 2018, some 30–40 trucks arrived in freighters to the port every week and, from there, traveled through Israel to Jordan.[57]

Israel and Turkey have generally been able to separate their economic interests from diplomatic tensions; however, in May 2018, following the dispute over Gaza and the U.S. embassy in Jerusalem, commentators in Israel warned that this separation could be at risk.[58]

Waning Bilateral Interest in Energy Trade

Whether energy trade will be a key factor in sustaining limited Israeli-Turkish reconciliation over the coming decade will turn on complex political, economic, and technical

---

[54] Daniel K. Eisenbud, "Turkey Remains Popular Tourist Destination for Israeli Arabs," *Jerusalem Post*, January 1, 2017; and "Israeli Tourists Flock to Turkey as Relations Normalize, Number of Tourists Rise 80 Percent," *Daily Sabah*, February 5, 2017.

[55] In May 2017, almost a year after reconciliation, an official delegation headed by Antalya's governor visited Israel with the aim of reviving Israeli tourism to Antalya, a city that was Israel's most preferred vacation destination in the previous decade. While 170,000 Israelis visited Antalya in 2016, that is still half of the 330,000 who visited in 2008 (Amir Alon, "Turkish Ambassador to Israel Trying to Coax Israelis Back to Antalya," *Ynet News*, May 25, 2017).

[56] Israeli analyst with Turkey expertise, telephone discussion with the author, January 25, 2017. From the Israeli perspective, there is a concrete concern that some Turks would cause provocations on the Temple Mount. Israel is worried about Turkish religious activism in Jerusalem and has even barred Turkish worshippers wearing shirts with the Turkish flags from entering the Temple Mount (Nadav Shargai, "Ha'Pe Shel Erdoğan, Ha'Milim Shel Hamas," *Israel Hayom*, December 28, 2017).

[57] Sami Peretz, "An Angry Erdogan Stands to Harm Israel-Turkey Economic Ties," *Haaretz*, May 17, 2018.

[58] Peretz, 2018.

factors involving several other governments with stakes in the development of natural gas in the Eastern Mediterranean.[59]

The 2010 discovery of the Leviathan gas field off Israel's coast, which is estimated to hold between 470 billion and 620 billion cubic meters of natural gas, has the potential of transforming Israel into an energy-exporting country.[60] Realizing the potential of Leviathan, which lies within Israel's maritime exclusive economic zone, depends on developing the field, which could cost some $4 billion.[61] This large investment hinges, in turn, on identifying a substantial export market in the region—a prospect constrained by Israel's geopolitical situation.[62] Israeli proponents assess that the Turkish market is technically viable and would be lucrative financially. Despite its improved relations with Russia and Iran, Turkey has an enduring, albeit diminished, interest in diversifying its gas supply. Skeptics question whether gas from Leviathan would be competitive with Russian and other gas in the Turkish market, and they cite the estimated $2 billion–$4 billion cost of constructing the undersea pipeline to Turkey, challenges of securing the pipeline, and potential for political clashes with Turkey to disrupt energy flows. In early 2017, with diplomatic support from the Obama administration, the companies developing Leviathan approved a $3.75 billion investment and declared that a new, 300-mile pipeline could be conveying Israeli gas to southern Turkey by the end of 2020.[63]

Another major factor in the construction of an Israeli-Turkish pipeline is Cyprus. Cypriot officials have made clear that they would not allow this pipeline to pass through their exclusive economic zone unless the conflict with Turkey is resolved and Israel supports the Cypriot position.[64] With the collapse of the Turkish-Cypriot peace talks in July 2017, discussed in Chapter Eight, the political impediments to the Israeli-Turkish pipeline have hardened. Russia has substantial influence in Cyprus and might

---

[59] For a comprehensive analysis of Eastern Mediterranean gas developments, see Tareq Baconi, *A Flammable Peace: Why Gas Deals Won't End Conflict in the Middle East*, London: European Council on Foreign Relations, policy brief, December 2017.

[60] Shaul Chorev, Mary Landrieu, Ami Ayalon, Seth Cropsey, Charles D. Davidson, Douglas J. Feith, Arthur Herman, Ron Prosor, Gary Roughead, and Eytan Sheshinski, *Report of the Commission on the Eastern Mediterranean*, Washington, D.C.: University of Haifa and the Hudson Institute, September 2016. Prior to the 2009 discovery of the Tamar gas field in its coastal waters, Israel was dependent on imported energy supplies. Tamar, estimated to be half the size of Leviathan, is in operation and supplies more than half of Israel Electric Corporation's needs, providing power to Israel and the Palestinian Authority.

[61] Israeli energy expert, discussion with the author, Herzliya, Israel, January 22, 2017.

[62] Gabriel Mitchell, *The Risks and Rewards of Israeli-Turkish Energy Cooperation*, Ramat Gan, Israel: Global Political Trends Center, Mitvim Institute, and Friedrich-Ebert-Stiftung, January 2017.

[63] Tova Cohen and Ari Rabinovitch, "Leviathan Gas Field Developers Approve $3.75 Billion Investment," Reuters, February 23, 2017; and "Israel-Turkey Gas Pipeline Could Be Ready in Four Years—Company," Reuters, March 2, 2017.

[64] Michele Kambas, "Cyprus Blocks Israel-Turkey Gas Pipeline Until Ankara Mends Ties," *Haaretz*, July 6, 2016.

also press the Cypriot government to slow the approval process to protect Moscow's market interests, particularly its gas exports to Turkey.[65]

Israel is actively pursuing alternatives for Leviathan development that would not involve Turkey.[66] Israel's relations with Cyprus and Greece have been deepening since Israeli-Turkish ties soured following the *Mavi Marmara* incident.[67] Jerusalem signed an agreement in December 2017 with Cyprus, Greece, and Italy, with financial support from the EU, to explore construction of the 1,200-mile EastMed Pipeline Project. While politically less risky than the Turkish deal, this pipeline is of questionable feasibility because of its estimated $6 billion cost, and Turkey could create obstacles through its control of Northern Cyprus.[68] Israel has also been exploring arrangements with Jordan and, in light of improved bilateral relations, Egypt to develop Leviathan, but these also face financial and political challenges. Turkey and Israel had explored development of a gas pipeline, but as of mid-2019, chances of a deal were remote. These other options, coupled with strains in bilateral relations, make near-term progress highly unlikely.[69]

Once the Bedrock of Bilateral Ties, Security Cooperation Unlikely to Grow Soon

Although security and defense ties were historically the bedrock of Israeli-Turkish relations, cooperation on those issues is now limited because of the two countries' divergent policies and interests concerning Palestinian issues, Syria, Iran, and the Eastern Mediterranean. Under former Israeli Defense Minister Avigdor Lieberman, all defense deals with Turkey were blocked. The only exception has been intelligence-sharing pertaining to terrorism, which continued even during the six-year crisis between the two countries.[70] Israelis, for the most part, do not see Turkey as a security threat but consider Erdoğan an unreliable partner and expect that his Islamist agenda will become stronger.[71]

Furthermore, Israel is deeply concerned about Ankara's ties with Hamas. Unless Turkey terminates those ties, a robust security relationship—including combined exer-

---

[65] Sara Stefanini, "Cyprus Fears Russia Could Wreck Reunification," *Politico*, January 12, 2017.

[66] For a discussion on Israel's other gas resources and market options, see Shira Efron, *The Future of Israeli-Turkish Relations*, Santa Monica, Calif.: RAND Corporation, RR-2445-RC, 2018, pp. 13–14.

[67] Israeli National Security Council official, discussion with the author, Jerusalem, January 24, 2017.

[68] Simone Tagliapietra, "Is the EastMed Gas Pipeline Just Another EU Pipe Dream?" *Bruegel*, May 10, 2017.

[69] Israeli Ministry of Foreign Affairs officials, discussion with the author, Jerusalem, December 13, 2017. See also Yaacov Benmeleh and David Wainer, "Fraying Israel-Turkey Ties Threaten Planned Natural Gas Venture," *Bloomberg*, February 5, 2018.

[70] Former Israeli ambassador to Turkey, discussion with the author, Jerusalem, January 24, 2017.

[71] Israeli National Security Council official, discussion with the author, Jerusalem, January 24, 2017; and former Ministry of Foreign Affairs official who served in Turkey, discussion with the author, Jerusalem, January 24, 2017.

cises, weapon trading, and knowledge exchanges—with Israel is out of the question.[72] For Erdoğan, the Palestinian cause and the relationship with Hamas are important emotional issues that represent an area where ideology competes with his pragmatism.[73]

In the past, Israeli-Turkish security cooperation aimed at rolling back Iranian influence and achieving mutual regional objectives. But because of Turkey's engagement with Iran (and Russia) on Syria, such cooperation is not viable in the near term. Ankara's engagement with Tehran has exacerbated Israeli suspicions that the Turks have passed Iran information detrimental to Israeli intelligence services.[74] The Turkish military may value Israel's ability to disrupt Iranian military activities in Syria and to keep pressure on Assad, and those benefits could give Turkey a reason to restore some defense cooperation. However, such a move would not advance Erdoğan's domestic political agenda and therefore seems unlikely.

Some Israelis still contend that the two countries' shared interests and Turkey's actions—including sending an airplane to help Israel extinguish an outbreak of wildfires in November 2016[75]—prove Ankara's pragmatism.[76] Some experts believe that, despite Israel's current veto on advancing defense ties with Turkey, security cooperation between the two countries could resume if conditions change. These experts project that counterterrorism cooperation could grow and that Israel and Turkey will elaborate their strategic dialogue on regional issues, where their interests regarding Syria and Iran are somewhat aligned.[77]

Although official Israeli policy blocks weapon sales to Turkey, the defense industries in both countries are eager to collaborate again, and the strong defense lobby in Israel is likely to pressure the Ministry of Defense to be more lenient in its Turkey policy if relations improve.[78] In terms of weapon sales and training, the TSK would be interested in purchasing Israeli reconnaissance and surveillance systems, including sensor suites, to modernize their F-4 fighter aircraft and additional Heron unmanned aerial vehicles.[79] The Turks are also interested in acquiring Israeli cyber technologies and the Iron Dome missile defense system. In the past, Israel has provided Turkey with

---

[72] Israeli National Security Council official, discussion with the author, Jerusalem, January 24, 2017. A Turkish journalist and scholar agreed with this assessment (Turkish journalist and scholar, roundtable at RAND Corporation, Arlington, Virginia, April 19, 2017).

[73] Turkish journalist and scholar, roundtable at RAND Corporation, Arlington, Virginia, April 19, 2017.

[74] Cengiz Çandar, "Turkey: The Self-Fulfilling Prophecy of the Hakan Fidan Story," *Al-Monitor*, October 21, 2013.

[75] "PM Netanyahu Thanks Turkey for Plane to Fight Israel's Wildfires," *Daily Sabah*, November 24, 2016.

[76] Former Israeli ambassador to Turkey, discussion with the author, Jerusalem, January 24, 2017.

[77] Israeli expert on Turkey, discussion with the author, Tel Aviv, January 25, 2017.

[78] Israeli expert on Turkey, discussion with the author, Tel Aviv, January 25, 2017; and Israeli diplomat, telephone discussion with the author, March 1, 2017.

[79] Ari Yashar, "Turkey Wants Normalization to Buy Israeli Weapons," *Arutz Sheva*, December 24, 2015.

technologies that the United States was not ready to sell, and Ankara may again seek to purchase such technologies from Israel.[80] The Turkish military is also interested in learning from the Israeli experience in urban warfare and apply these lessons to Turkey's fight against Kurdish insurgents.[81]

Given the tense state of relations, bilateral military exercises between Israel and Turkey are unlikely to resume anytime soon. This is not a major loss for Israel because the IDF have been conducting a growing number of combined air, ground, and naval exercises with both Cyprus and Greece, and these exercises provide the freedom to maneuver and varied terrain that cooperation with Turkey previously afforded.[82] This cooperation is becoming multidimensional. The heads of the Israeli, Cypriot, and Greek governments have met several times to discuss energy, defense, and other elements of cooperation, which might reflect an effort to establish a new geopolitical bloc in the Eastern Mediterranean, partly as a counterweight to Turkey. Israeli officials give high importance to maintaining close ties with Cyprus and Greece because both countries help Israel in managing tensions with the EU.[83] In 2015, Cyprus ordered a coastal patrol vessel from Israel Shipyards, with an option to buy three more, to protect the country's exclusive economic zone and Aphrodite gas field in the Eastern Mediterranean.[84] Turkish officials have expressed concerns about the implications of this new trilateral security cooperation, and Ankara has undertaken military exercises in the Eastern Mediterranean to demonstrate resolve and challenge Cypriot energy claims.[85] Cyprus was concerned about Israel's rapprochement with Turkey and has been wary of past Israeli weapon sales to the Turks. Israeli restraint on military sales to Turkey is one way of keeping Cyprus as a reliable partner.[86]

Israeli officials have varying views on how the United States should handle its Turkey policy, and the officials try to find a balance between Turkey's geostrategic

---

[80] Israeli expert on Turkey, discussion with the author, Tel Aviv, January 25, 2017.

[81] Israeli think tank analyst with Turkey expertise, telephone discussion with the author, January 25, 2017.

[82] For example, the Israeli Air Force has conducted a series of exercises with the Hellenic Air Force. The exercises enable Israeli pilots to train for long-range missions and to operate against Russian S-300 anti-aircraft systems, which the Greek—and Syrian and Iranian—armies possess. Furthermore, special commando units of the IDF have conducted exercises in areas of Cyprus that have a topography similar to northern Lebanon. See Gabi Siboni and Gal Perl Finkel, "The IDF Exercises in Cyprus and Crete," Tel Aviv: Institute for National Security Studies, Insight No. 945, June 28, 2017.

[83] Israeli diplomat, telephone discussion with the author, March 1, 2017.

[84] The first vessel was delivered in December 2017 (Igor Bozinovski, "Cyprus Boosts Maritime Capabilities with First Offshore Patrol Vessel," Jane's Navy International, January 16, 2018; and George Tsiboukis, "Cyprus Buys 1+3 Offshore Patrol Vessels," Dartmouth Center for Seapower and Strategy News, Plymouth University, United Kingdom, November 4, 2015).

[85] Gili Cohen, "Turkey Holds Naval Drill Off Cyprus in Heated Response to Israeli Commando Exercise on Its Doorstep," *Haaretz*, June 15, 2017.

[86] Israeli diplomat, telephone discussion with the author, March 1, 2017.

importance and what they see as Erdoğan's ideology and unreliability. On one hand, Israelis advise Washington to be very cautious and even to restrict certain aspects of defense cooperation with Turkey.[87] Other Israeli officials believe that the United States should work to strengthen its alliance with Turkey and keep Ankara as a balancing Sunni counterweight in the conflict between Shi'a and Sunni extremists.[88] These officials argue that Turkey's size and location make it too important to lose, and they fear that a change in policy toward Ankara may push it into Russia's arms. As long as NATO exists, they contend, Turkey should remain a member. Some Israeli officials assess that Turkey's membership in NATO, particularly the nuclear deterrent mission and the Nuclear Planning Group, serve to prevent Turkey from seeking to acquire its own nuclear weapons.[89]

Limited Israeli-Turkish defense cooperation could emerge in the context of NATO. Drawing closer to NATO has been a high Israeli priority for many years. Turkey enabled its formal ties with the Alliance to advance in 2016 when it removed its veto over the establishment of an Israeli mission at NATO headquarters in Brussels.[90] An important milestone was a meeting between Turkey's then–Chief of the General Staff Hulusi Akar and IDF Deputy Chief of Staff Yair Golan on the margins of a meeting of NATO military leaders in January 2017, a first such meeting since before the *Mavi Marmara* incident. Although the meeting was reportedly symbolic, its mere existence was interpreted as a sign of warming security relations.[91]

Washington has traditionally relied on these two longtime allies to work together to foster regional stability, but significant Israeli-Turkish defense cooperation is likely to remain on hold in the near term.

Precarious Political Ties Stemming from Disagreement on the Palestinian Issue

Turkish-Palestinian relations are long-standing and complex, partly because the Ottoman Empire ruled Palestine for 400 years before the British Mandate that followed World War I. Although Turkey remained a champion of the Palestinian cause over the years, it balanced its positions carefully to maintain close ties with Israel. The ups and downs in relations between Turkey and Israel have always been linked to developments on the Israeli-Palestinian front. This was true before the AKP came to power, but tensions have escalated more quickly and intensely under AKP rule. Intra-Palestinian factional rivalry between Fatah and Hamas has further complicated Turkish-Palestinian relations and added another layer of complexity to the Turkish-Israeli-Palestinian tri-

---

[87] Israeli National Security Council official, discussion with the author, Jerusalem, January 24, 2017.

[88] Former Israeli ambassador to Turkey, discussion with the author, Jerusalem, January 24, 2017.

[89] Israeli think tank analyst with Turkey expertise, telephone discussion with the author, January 25, 2017.

[90] Barak Ravid, "NATO Okays Israel Office in Its Brussels Headquarters After Turkey Lifts Veto," *Haaretz*, May 4, 2016.

[91] Herb Keinon, "Israeli, Turkish Generals Meet for First Time in Years," *Jerusalem Post*, January 19, 2017.

angle. Turkish-Israeli disagreements concerning the Palestinians concentrate in two main arenas—Gaza and East Jerusalem. The IDF killing dozens of Palestinians in violent protests in Gaza—which occurred at the same time as the opening of the U.S. embassy in Jerusalem in May 2018—hit those two exposed nerves.

One of Turkey's demands during its rift with Israel was to lift the blockade on Gaza. Israel demanded that Turkey stop sheltering leaders of Hamas's military wing in its territory. Even though Turkey expelled some Hamas military leaders, Israel is worried that this demand has not entirely been fulfilled. The AKP's ties with Hamas and the affiliated Muslim Brotherhood are strong, long-standing, and multifaceted. These ties are worrisome to Israel and other countries in the region, especially Egypt and Jordan, because they are not necessarily based on interests but rather a reflection of shared ideology and desire to assert a Turkish dominance in the region.[92] In addition, some Israeli officials believe that members of Hamas's military wing continue to operate in Turkey and that Hamas receives financial support from organizations affiliated with the AKP.[93] Turkey has, at times, separated its ideological ties with Hamas from dealings with Israel, but it has linked the two relationships in other times.[94]

Israel and Turkey share some objectives related to Gaza. Both countries want to prevent a humanitarian disaster there, and Israel welcomes Turkey's reconstruction efforts.[95] Turkey's current assistance to Gaza is less ambitious than it was before the reconciliation, presumably because it is stretched thin on the Syrian front, but that assistance is still significant.[96] While Israel seeks to prevent further deterioration of living conditions in Gaza and welcomes Turkey's assistance, it is worried that too much support would strengthen Hamas's position in the Palestinian arena and undermine the Palestinian Authority, which is Israel's negotiation partner. As noted in Chapter Four, Egypt, which pressured Israel not to reconcile with Turkey, has its own redlines on Turkish involvement in Gaza. The diplomatic retaliation and vitriolic

---

[92] Mohammad Abdel Kader, "Turkey's Relationship with the Muslim Brotherhood," Al Arabiya Institute for Studies, October 14, 2013.

[93] Shargai, 2017.

[94] Gallia Lindenstrauss and Süfyan Kadir Kıvam, "Turkish-Hamas Relations: Between Strategic Calculations and Ideological Affinity," *Strategic Assessment*, Vol. 17, No. 2, July 2014.

[95] Turkey's support includes building a new hospital, cleaning water wells, constructing housing units, and shipping humanitarian aid (including fuel through Israel's Port of Ashdod). A religious Turkish network renovates mosques in Gaza, and Turkey has collaborated with Germany in building a power plant in the Strip (Avi Issacharoff, "Hamas Says Turkey to Send Fuel to End Gaza Electricity Crisis," *Times of Israel*, January 14, 2017a; and Israeli think tank analyst with Turkey expertise, telephone discussion with the author, January 25, 2017).

[96] As one interlocutor said, "It is true though that, under the new framework, Turkey can do much more for the Gazans in terms of infrastructure, water and humanitarian supply than it did until now. Since the agreement, however, it seems that Ankara has lost its appetite to help" (Israeli journalist and Turkey scholar, email correspondence with the author, March 1, 2017).

exchanges between Erdoğan and Netanyahu following the May 2018 clashes in Gaza, for example, suggest that this issue could lead to another serious crisis in relations.[97]

Although Gaza was Ankara's main reason for not reconciling with Israel earlier, Turkey's focus in the Palestinian arena is now East Jerusalem. The Turkish media constantly discusses Jerusalem, and the popular narrative is that Israel seeks to change the status quo in Jerusalem and around the Temple Mount. Turkey is also politically active in supporting Islamic groups in East Jerusalem, again upsetting not only Israel but also Jordan.[98] Erdoğan has increased Turkey's involvement in East Jerusalem and the Muslim holy sites and strengthened ties with Palestinian citizens and residents of Israel—including with the northern branch of the Islamic Movement, an affiliate of the Muslim Brotherhood that is outlawed in Israel. In May 2017, Erdoğan lashed out at Israel in response to the Israeli Parliament's passing of a law restricting early-morning Muslim calls to prayer.[99] A terrorist attack on the Temple Mount on July 14, 2017, and Israel's response led to escalation in Israeli-Turkish tensions over Jerusalem.[100] Perhaps more than any other Muslim leader, Erdoğan was the most vocal in his opposition to the U.S. recognition in December 2017 of Jerusalem as Israel's capital. Erdoğan rebuked both Israel and the United States and recognized East Jerusalem as the capital of an independent Palestine. In turn, Prime Minister Netanyahu denounced Erdoğan and Turkey's policies toward the Kurds, internal dissent, and terrorism. After the May 2018 opening of the U.S. embassy in Jerusalem and the deadly May 2018 protests in Gaza, Turkey recalled its ambassadors to the United States and Israel. Unlike in the past when Israel often restrained its response, Israel's post-rapprochement strategy has been to pungently attack Erdoğan personally. Turkey's behavior on such a sensitive issue may have pushed Netanyahu to be the first world leader to announce support for the Kurdish independence referendum.[101]

---

[97] Noa Landau and Jonathan Lis, "Turkey and Israel Expel Envoys Over Gaza Deaths," *Haaretz*, May 16, 2018.

[98] Israeli think tank analyst with Turkey expertise, telephone discussion with the author, January 25, 2017.

[99] Eyal Lehman and Roi Kais, "Erdoğan Rebukes Israel over Muezzin Bill and Calls on Muslims to Go en Masse to Al-Aqsa," *Ynet News*, May 8, 2017.

[100] On Israel's response, see Isabel Kershner, "Israel Agrees to Remove Metal Detectors at Entrances to Aqsa Mosque Compound," *New York Times*, July 24, 2017. Of the Temple Mount incident, Erdoğan said, "When Israeli soldiers carelessly pollute the grounds of Al-Aqsa with their combat boots by using simple issues as a pretext and then easily spill blood there, the reason is we [Muslims] have not done enough to stake our claim over Jerusalem" (Barak Ravid, "Israel Responds to Erdogan: Temple Mount Statements 'Unfounded and Distorted,'" *Haaretz*, July 25, 2017). Israeli Foreign Ministry Spokesman Emmanuel Nahshon responded,

> Turkish President Erdoğan['s] statements to his party's activists are wacky, unfounded and distorted. It would be better for him to deal with the problems and difficulties of his country. The days of the Ottoman Empire are long gone. The capital of the Jewish people had been, is and will be Jerusalem. Unlike in past years, it is a city whose government is committed to security, liberty, religious freedom and respect for the rights of all minorities. He who lives in a glass house shouldn't throw stones. (Ravid, 2017)

[101] Jeffrey Heller, "Israel Endorses Independent Kurdish State," Reuters, September 13, 2017.

Ankara's ability to mediate between Fatah and Hamas is hampered by its tense relations with regional players; in addition, the Palestinian Authority does not see Turkey as a fair broker because of Erdoğan's ideological alignment with Hamas.[102] Nevertheless, ties between Turkey and the Palestinian Authority have been solid. Ankara was very active in helping the group push for recognition at the United Nations, and there are current and planned Turkish projects in the West Bank, including industrial zones. When United Nations Secretary-General António Guterres visited the Palestinian territories in August 2017, Palestinian President Mahmoud Abbas canceled his meeting with Guterres and instead went to Turkey to meet with Erdoğan. It is not clear whether the visit to Ankara indicates closer ties with Turkey or expression of dissatisfaction with both the United Nations and Egypt.[103] Nevertheless, improvement of ties between Ramallah and Ankara seems more plausible after Erdoğan became the key champion against the recognition of Jerusalem as Israel's capital; the Palestinian Authority's main allies (Saudi Arabia, Jordan, Egypt, and the UAE) were seen as only paying lip service by objecting to the announcement.

Some in Israel's diplomatic corps do see a role for Ankara as a mediator between Israel and Hamas, but that is not something Israeli officials discuss publicly.[104] Reports about an attempt at such mediation surfaced in March 2017 when Turkish Foreign Minister Mevlüt Çavuşoğlu announced during a meeting in Washington that his country had "pressured Hamas to shift away from armed resistance" and negotiate with Israel; he also stated that Hamas showed willingness to recognize Israel. Hamas's negative response followed quickly with both an official statement dismissing the report and an anonymous Hamas source on an Iranian website denying caving into Turkish pressure on Israel.[105] The Iranian link is important because it might indicate that Turkey's ability to bring Hamas closer to Israel's position is diminished. Indeed, Turkey still shelters elements of Hamas's military wing, but its support for Hamas is more on the political front, which is becoming less influential relative to its military wing. The key backer of the military wing is Iran, and as the military wing becomes stronger, so does Iran's ability to influence the movement at the expense of Turkey.

---

[102] Former Palestinian official, telephone discussion with the author, April 28, 2017. Even though the Palestinian Authority and Hamas signed a reconciliation agreement in October 2017, implementation is expected to be challenging, and their rivalry is likely to continue because their fundamental differences remain. Israel is refusing to deal with Hamas until it renounces violence and abides by other conditions.

[103] Pinhas Inbari, "Why Did the PA's Mahmoud Abbas Avoid the UN Secretary-General When He Toured the Region?" Jerusalem Center for Public Affairs, September 4, 2017.

[104] Israeli diplomat, telephone discussion with the author, March 1, 2017.

[105] Adnan Abu Amer, "Is Turkey Trying to Bypass Abbas in Gaza?" *Al-Monitor*, March 30, 2017.

Israeli-Turkish Ties Face Formidable Challenges

Israeli-Turkish relations since the June 2016 rapprochement have been fitful. The first 11 months after the agreement were characterized almost solely by positive trends, mainly in improving economic connections but also in restoring and maintaining diplomatic ties; there were also signs of initial military discussions, primarily about NATO. Since then, however, diplomatic tensions have arisen reflecting that fundamental differences remain between these two former partners. In multiple recorded incidents, Erdoğan lashed out at Israel after the latter instituted controversial policies related to the Palestinians. Israel responded harshly, attacking Erdoğan's autocratic rule and treatment of the Kurds—two sensitive issues in Turkey.

Israel's policy on the Kurdish issue remains a wild card in the relationship. Israel has maintained discreet military, intelligence, and business ties with the Kurds since the 1960s, partially to create a buffer against common Arab adversaries (primarily Saddam Hussein's Iraq) and Iran. In June 2014, Netanyahu was the first world leader to express support for the establishment of an independent Kurdish state in northern Iraq. Although earlier support for Iraqi Kurds was not overly troubling to Ankara, that changed when Netanyahu strongly endorsed the KRG's independence referendum just two weeks before the September 25, 2017, vote. When Netanyahu realized that Washington opposed the referendum, he toned down the rhetoric, but this gambit stimulated further recriminations from Erdoğan, and Turkish media reported that Kurdish groups signed a secret agreement with Israel to gain their independence by resettling Jews in the region.[106]

The personal nature of Israeli responses to Erdoğan is not coincidental. In Israeli eyes, the once multifaceted Turkey is now ruled completely by its unreliable, autocratic, and possibly anti-Semitic president. The outcome of Turkey's April 16, 2017, constitutional referendum granting sweeping powers to Erdoğan (discussed in Chapter Two) only reaffirmed Israel's suspicions. The Israeli Ministry of Foreign Affairs was relieved that, unlike in previous cases when Turkish campaigns invoked issues with Israel to rally support, Israel was not even mentioned in the referendum campaign.[107] For Israel, decisions by the ever-more-empowered Erdoğan, combined with the countries' several domestic and foreign challenges, will have implications for Israeli-Turkish ties in all areas—the economy, energy, security cooperation, and diplomacy. In the short run, economic ties could grow and the two countries could still pursue some energy trade, but cooperation on these and more-sensitive issues (specifically, security and diplomacy) are not forecasted to improve meaningfully anytime soon.

---

[106] Tom O'Connor, "Turkey Tries to Scare Voters with Warning About Jews Ahead of Kurdish Referendum," *Newsweek*, September 15, 2017.

[107] Israeli diplomat in Turkey, email correspondence with the author, April 21, 2017.

Over the next decade, notwithstanding multiple shared interests in again deepening diplomatic, economic, and security cooperation, several questions remain about how Israel and Turkey handle their rapprochement. These questions concern broad regional dynamics, including Turkey's ties with Jordan, Egypt, and Saudi Arabia; the aftermath of the war in Syria; the Israeli-Palestinian conflict; and domestic politics in both Israel and Turkey. Thus, although the issues at hand in both countries are broader than the bilateral relations and both have an interest in working toward some shared goals, their bilateral ties could be affected by other developments. Table 5.1 provides a summary assessment of where Turkish and Israeli interests are convergent, divergent, or in conflict.

Moreover, whereas Israel previously had almost no alternative to Turkey as an economic, diplomatic, or security partner in the region, the situation is different now. Greece, Cyprus, and other countries have replaced Turkey in joint and combined military exercises after Turkish airspace was closed to IDF flights. Furthermore, although Turkey was an important export market for the Israeli defense industries during the 1990s and most of the early 2000s, other, larger markets are now available and offer lucrative opportunities.[108] In addition, Turkey was historically Israel's only Muslim-majority ally, but Israel now enjoys back-channel relations with Saudi Arabia and the UAE.[109] Ties with Egypt and Jordan, with which Israel has peace agreements, have been steadily improving.[110] Turkey's relations with these countries have been declining.

Table 5.1
Alignment of Turkish Interests with Israeli Interests

Neighbor or Partner	Converging Interests	Diverging Interests	Conflicting Interests
Israel	• Trade • Possible development of the Leviathan natural gas field as a driver of reconciliation • Humanitarian relief in the Gaza Strip • Limited Iranian influence	• Political, economic, and security relations with countries in the wider Middle East • Israeli facilitation of U.S. regional presence and involvement	• Palestine: statehood, East Jerusalem, Gaza closure, and Hamas • Israel's support for Kurdish autonomy • Israeli cooperation with Egypt's Abdel Fattah al-Sisi government • Growing Israeli partnership with Cyprus and Greece

---

[108] Amos Harel, "Israel's India Missile Deal Will Be Partially Implemented After Netanyahu's Attempts at Persuasion," *Haaretz*, January 21, 2018.

[109] Clive Jones and Yoel Guzansky, "Israel's Relations with the Gulf States: Toward the Emergence of a Tacit Security Regime?" *Contemporary Security Policy*, Vol. 38, No. 3, 2017.

[110] See, for example, Zena Tahhan, "Egypt-Israel Relations 'at Highest Level' in History," *Al Jazeera*, September 20, 2017.

Greece and Cyprus have substituted for Turkey as nearby affordable tourism destinations for large parts of the Jewish population, and, while Israel and Turkey were initially interested in a gas deal, Israel is examining other alternatives, such as the EastMed pipeline being negotiated with Cyprus, Greece, and Italy. Jerusalem and Ankara have been historically effective at separating economics from politics, but the "poisonous" political atmosphere between the two countries adds political risks that investors and businesspeople may wish to avoid, possibly hampering progress on the economic front.[111]

All of these factors do not mean that Israel and Turkey no longer share some common interests. But if the seven-decade-old record of bilateral ties teaches one lesson, it is that Israeli-Turkish relations in the short to medium term will be linked primarily to developments on the Israeli-Palestinian front. Presumably, if present trends continue, ties will remain the same: Political and security relations will stay cold, while business sectors work to expand relations. Periodic outbursts related to the Palestinian issue are expected. Under this scenario, the relationship may not break down completely, although threats to cut ties and mutual expulsion of each other's envoys are certainly unhelpful.[112]

Israel and Turkey will continue to share common objectives and should find ways to agree on an approach to rehabilitate Gaza. Both countries are interested in preventing a humanitarian disaster in Gaza, and Israel continues to welcome Turkey's reconstruction efforts.[113] One of the challenges for Israel is that Turkey's aid to Gaza is channeled through several governmental and nongovernmental organizations, including the İHH, which has been linked to support for Hamas.[114] Israel and Turkey have previously found ways to handle such disagreements delicately when working toward a shared objective.[115]

The June 2017 crisis over the Temple Mount was also an example of possible mitigation approaches that Turkey and Israel may adopt. Following their mutual

---

[111] Israeli think tank expert on Turkey, email correspondence with the author, January 19, 2018.

[112] "Turkish FM: No Danger to Israel-Turkey Relations," *Arutz Sheva*, January 7, 2018.

[113] Issacharoff, 2017a.

[114] Yonah Jeremy Bob, "Israel Arrests Head of Turkish Humanitarian Group in Gaza for Financing Hamas," *Jerusalem Post*, March 21, 2017.

[115] In March 2017, Israel arrested the manager of the Gaza branch of the Turkish Cooperation and Coordination Agency (Türk İşbirliği ve Koordinasyon İdaresi Başkanlığı [TİKA]) on suspicion that he funneled aid money to Hamas's military wing activities. This operative was also linked to İHH. The Turkish Foreign Ministry expressed solidarity with the TİKA worker arrested, risking possible escalation between Ankara and Jerusalem. Nevertheless, despite warnings that this incident demonstrates the strong Turkey-Hamas military ties to Israel's detriment, the Israeli government asserted that Ankara was not aware of this mishandling and that Hamas took advantage of Turkey's generosity. See "Turkish Foreign Ministry Voices Solidarity with TIKA Worker Arrested by Israel," *Hürriyet Daily News*, March 22, 2017; and Avi Issacharoff, "Arrest of Gaza Manager Exposes Hamas's Turkish Connection," *Times of Israel*, March 21, 2017b.

slander over the holy site, Erdoğan requested to speak with Israeli President Reuven Rivlin instead of his counterpart head of government Netanyahu. Rivlin took the call despite objections from the Israeli Ministry of Foreign Affairs,[116] as well as political rhetoric suggesting that Israel should retaliate with a review of relations with Turkey, recognition of an independent Kurdistan, and acknowledgement of the Armenian genocide.[117] This phone conversation illustrated that Israel and Turkey can maintain diplomatic ties even during the height of a crisis, helping eventually to lower the flames—until the next time.

A substantial change, for good or bad, in the Israeli-Palestinian arena could shift Israeli-Turkish relations in one of two directions. Another war in Gaza between Israel and Hamas is only a matter of time.[118] From Israel's perspective, bilateral relations could endure as long as Ankara separates its strong ideological and practical ties with Hamas and support for the Palestinians from its pragmatic bilateral ties with Israel. This may not be that simple. Israelis in the defense realm have feared that, in the next round of fighting, Turkey would withdraw its ambassador and ties would freeze again. This prediction materialized in May 2018. At the time of writing this report, it is unclear whether this estrangement is permanent; however, it is evident that negative developments on the Palestinian front will continue to pose formidable obstacles to Israeli-Turkish ties, especially if it comes down to a more extreme scenario of a third intifada or Israeli annexation of parts of the West Bank, as proposed by some members of government.[119] The already fragile trust that exists between Jerusalem and Ankara will shatter, affecting public opinion.

Alternatively, it is safe to assume that a meaningful breakthrough in the Israeli-Palestinian peace process would lead to changes in Turkey's approach toward Israel and help bring the two countries closer together. As with the Madrid peace conference in 1991, the Oslo Accords, and Israel's disengagement from Gaza, Ankara is likely to respond positively to progress on the Palestinian front and strengthen its ties with Israel. Furthermore, having sought a mediator role in the past, Ankara is still interested in mediating talks between Israelis and Palestinians and helping advance a two-state solution to the conflict.[120]

Absent a meaningful development on the Israeli-Palestinian front or substantial political changes in Israel, Turkey, or the region—none of which seems likely in the near future—Jerusalem and Ankara need to be more motivated to sustain and improve

---

[116] Ravid, 2017.

[117] Raphael Ahren, "Lapid Calls for More Aggressive Stance on Turkey," *Times of Israel*, July 27, 2017.

[118] Amos Harel, "Gaza Power Crisis Explained: Why Israel and Hamas Are Heading for a Face-Off Neither Side Wants," *Haaretz*, June 12, 2017.

[119] Peter Beaumont, "Far-Right Israeli Minister Plans Bill to Annex One of Biggest Settlements," *The Guardian*, January 3, 2017.

[120] "Turkish FM: No Danger to Israel-Turkey Relations," 2018.

relations. Although the anti-Israeli rhetoric has become a standard operating procedure on Erdoğan's part, this is not something Jerusalem is willing to get used to. Its rebukes of Erdoğan, however, may not be the most effective way of stopping the slander. Despite lower incentives for cooperation, seven decades of bilateral relations have shown that, when Israel and Turkey want to collaborate, they find ways to do so, despite divisions.

Conclusion and Implications for the United States

The United States was pivotal in achieving Israeli-Turkish reconciliation after the six-year rift. After the Obama administration attempted, unsuccessfully, to prevent the downgrading of diplomatic ties,[121] it facilitated confidence-building measures during the crisis years.[122] In 2013, it worked diligently with both sides to arrange an apology by Netanyahu to Erdoğan.[123] What could explain U.S. efforts to mediate between Jerusalem and Ankara? Clearly, the nature of Israeli-Turkish relations has several implications for the United States. First, good Israeli-Turkish relations could enable a trilateral strategic U.S.-Israeli-Turkish dialogue to enhance regional stability (or, at the very least, not add an additional strenuous component to a complicated region) and promote shared economic interests. The three countries have traditionally had mutual interests regarding Iran, Syria, and counterterrorism. Israel's new association with NATO is another avenue for trilateral cooperation, which serves U.S. interests and hinges on continued Turkish consent. The first U.S. permanent military base in Israel, an air defense facility established in September 2017 under U.S. European Command, is another indication of the importance the United States attributes to security ties with Israel in the context of the Middle East, Europe, and (by extension) NATO.[124]

The United States also has geostrategic and economic interests in the emerging Israeli-Cypriot-Greek gas deal. From a U.S. perspective, a NATO member (Greece), an EU partner (Cyprus), and an important ally (Israel) could be the beneficiaries of Mediterranean gas discoveries at the expense of Russia and Iran. Economically, the Texas-based Noble Energy, Inc. is the second-largest partner in the Leviathan gas field, with holdings of 39.7 percent.[125] Moreover, despite notable challenges, Turkey's ideological and pragmatic ties with Hamas could be helpful as the United States and its other allies in the region seek to promote an Israeli-Palestinian peace process.

---

[121] Arbell, 2014.

[122] Pfeffer, 2013.

[123] Arbell, 2014.

[124] Judah Ari Gross, "In First, U.S. Establishes Permanent Military Base in Israel," *Times of Israel*, September 18, 2017.

[125] Yaacov Benmeleh and David Wainer, "Israel and Turkey Seek to Shield Natural Gas Ties From Politics," *Bloomberg*, December 12, 2016.

Ankara has traditionally played a balancing game, maintaining close ties with the United States and other NATO allies and cooperating, to varying degrees, with Iran, Syria, and Russia. However, recent developments suggest that the balancing act has become less delicate. The strident Turkish response to the U.S. recognition of Jerusalem as Israel's capital and the withdrawal of Turkey's ambassador to the United States after the opening of the new embassy in Jerusalem suggest possible further deterioration of U.S.-Turkish ties.

In the long run, however, the United States also sees Turkey as an important regional player—large, populous, technologically advanced, and militarily capable—that can contribute to the Sunni balance of Iran. Better Israeli-Turkish ties in this context would be important for advancing regional stability and rallying a regional coalition that includes both countries to roll back Iranian influence. Although Ankara's ties with both Washington and Jerusalem are at a low point, the United States still has leverage over Israel and Turkey and can use it to continue facilitating positive interactions between the two sides on multiple levels. If it chooses to do so, the U.S. government can push the two sides to separate their ideological differences from their pragmatic ties and to avoid escalatory rhetoric on sensitive issues—be it the Temple Mount or Kurdish independence. In addition, the United States can help shape Israeli-Turkish relations in the long term by pursuing a serious Israeli-Palestinian peace process. If history is any indication, improvement in Israeli-Palestinian relations will be followed by improvement in Israeli-Turkish relations.

CHAPTER SIX

The Russian-Turkish Bilateral Relationship: Managing Differences in an Uneasy Partnership

Anika Binnendijk

The relationship between Turkey and Russia has historically been turbulent, defined by competition for influence and power across the Black Sea region. A circumspect warming in relations that began in the waning days of the Cold War—driven, in part, by common interests in trade and energy—has periodically left observers speculating about prospects for a deep and durable partnership. Today, the states remain pulled between interests that induce cooperation and those that induce potential conflict.

To Russia, Turkey represents a geopolitically important neighbor and major energy market, and it presents opportunities to expand gas routes to Europe, constrain the influence of NATO and the EU, bolster another increasingly autocratic government, and strengthen Russia's position in the Middle East. Recent bilateral military and diplomatic coordination in Syria, joint exercises in the Black Sea, a planned gas pipeline through Turkey to Europe, and a Turkish purchase of Russian air and missile defense systems represent tangible manifestations of improved relations. However, persistent areas of friction continue to threaten the scope and longevity of the Russian-Turkish relationship.[1] The Turkish government's relationship with Russia proceeds from a recognition that Russia is the more powerful partner intent on using all its instruments of national power to dominate the Black Sea region. To Turkey, Russia is a leading trade partner, energy supplier, business customer, and source of tourist revenue. Potential flashpoints could emerge from divergent interests and several contentious areas of interaction, such as the recent surge in Russian ambitions and relative military power in the Black Sea region, enduring differences over each country's approach to the Middle East (especially Syria), competition for energy transit routes from Central Asia and the Caspian Basin, and a tension between Turkey's NATO identity and Russia's desire to undermine the Alliance. This chapter examines areas of cooperation and conflict through the lens of several key interests in the bilateral relationship between Russia and Turkey.

---

[1] For additional reading on Russian-Turkish rivalries, see Dimitar Bechev, *Rival Power: Russia in Southeast Europe*, New Haven, Conn.: Yale University Press, 2017, Chapter 5 ("The Russian-Turkish Marriage of Convenience"); and Jeffrey Mankoff, "Why Russia and Turkey Fight: A History of Antagonism," *Foreign Affairs*, February 24, 2016a.

Historical Context

Turkey and Russia engaged in intense regional rivalries over much of their modern history. Competition during the Ottoman and Russian empires over control of territories across the Black Sea, Caspian, and Balkan regions led to more than a dozen wars between the two powers between the 16th and 20th centuries. In the 1768 Russo-Turkish war for control of the Black Sea, the Russian empire under Catherine the Great annexed Crimea, bringing the peninsula—and its Turkic population—under Russian rule until the breakup of the Soviet Union. During the 19th century, Russian influence over Slavic populations in southeastern Europe and Russian-Ottoman competition in the Balkans roiled the relationship even as the Ottoman Empire grappled with its own gradual decline. Bilateral competition within the Black Sea had not abated by the eve of World War I: Russia's ambition to control the strategically located city of Constantinople (now Istanbul) was a driving force behind its entry into the war, and—perhaps unsurprisingly—the Ottoman Empire's first move during World War I was an October 1914 naval assault on Russian positions in Odessa and Sevastopol.[2]

Post-imperial internal dynamics in both countries—as well as shared suspicions about the Western powers—led to a March 1921 friendship treaty between Turkey and the Union of Soviet Socialist Republics (USSR). In the wake of Russia's 1917 revolution, a new Bolshevik government had supported Mustafa Kemal Atatürk during and after the Turkish war for independence. Despite this fresh start, conflicts over regional ambitions ultimately prevailed. Beginning in the mid-1930s, Soviet claims on Kars and Ardahan provinces in northeastern Turkey and assertive policies in the Bosporus eventually led to the Turkish Straits crisis in 1946, prompting a Turkish backlash against the Soviet Union and a turn to the United States for assistance. Then–U.S. President Harry Truman concluded that the United States could not let the straits come under Soviet control because it would give the USSR a major strategic gateway between the Black Sea and the Mediterranean and possibly lead to a Communist takeover of Turkey. The resulting U.S. military support to Turkey and strengthened security ties under the Truman Doctrine, culminating with the entry of Turkey and Greece into NATO in 1952, led the Soviet Union to view Turkey largely as a client of the United States throughout the Cold War.[3] For its part, the United States considered Turkey to be a critical bulwark against Soviet expansionism and penetration of the eastern Mediterranean and the Middle East.

---

[2] Dmitri Trenin, "Russia in the Middle East: Moscow's Objectives, Priorities, and Policy Drivers," Carnegie Endowment for International Peace and Chicago Council on Global Affairs, 2016; and Vefa Kurban, *Russian-Turkish Relations from the First World War to the Present*, Newcastle, United Kingdom: Cambridge Scholars Publishing, 2017, p. 5.

[3] For additional details, see F. Stephen Larrabee, *Turkey as a U.S. Security Partner,* Santa Monica, Calif.: RAND Corporation, MG-694-AF, 2008.

The waning of the Cold War presented new opportunities for improved bilateral relations, as the countries' economic interests increasingly converged. Complementary energy interests paved the way: Turkey needed a reliable source of energy, and the USSR was seeking additional export markets for its natural gas resources. The first deliveries of natural gas to Turkey began flowing in June 1987 through the Trans-Balkan pipeline, under a contract that called for export of up to 6 billion cubic meters of gas annually through 2011.[4] A 1988 bilateral gas swap deal that permitted Turkey to pay for 70 percent of its gas imports with goods and services helped to double bilateral trade into the early 1990s.[5] Tourism also took off, as Soviet vacationers began to flock to affordable Turkish beaches and resorts. For both countries, a need to prioritize domestic challenges constrained any broader regional ambitions. Moscow grappled with Russian economic and political weakness after the breakup of the USSR, and Ankara had to deal with a volatile economy, a deepening counterinsurgency against Kurdish separatists, the growth of political Islam, and periodic backlashes from the Turkish military during what became known as the "lost decade" of the 1990s.

While economic relations remained strong, Turkey's support for Islamist groups in the Caucasus fueled continued distrust by a Russian government battling an Islamist insurgency in Chechnya. The Russian government accused Ankara of supporting Chechen separatists in 1996 during the First Chechen War, and a classified Russian Special Services White Book that year reportedly described Turkey as an aspiring regional power with "pan-Turkic ideas" that maintained support for "Muslim movements."[6]

Trends in the relationship since Turkey's 2002 election of the AKP to office have generally been positive, especially in light of Prime Minister and then President Tayyip Recep Erdoğan's prioritization of trade, investment, and limited security cooperation with Russia.[7] By 2008, Russia had become Turkey's leading national trade partner (after the EU), and a 2010 visa-free travel agreement further bolstered tourism ties. Warm personal relations between Erdoğan and Russian leader Vladimir Putin appeared to seal the strengthening ties, which were codified with great fanfare in a

[4]   Gazprom Export, "Foreign Partners: Turkey," webpage, undated-b.

[5]   Andrew C. Kuchins and Alexandros Petersen, "Turkey, Russia, the Black Sea, the Caucasus, and Central Asia," in Stephen J. Flanagan, Samuel J. Brannen, Bulent Aliriza, Edward C. Chow, Andrew C. Kuchins, Haim Malka, Julianne Smith, Ian Lesser, Eric Palomaa, and Alexandros Petersen, *Turkey's Evolving Dynamics: Strategic Choices for U.S.-Turkey Relations*, Washington, D.C.: Center for Strategic and International Studies, March 2009.

[6]   Igor Torbakov, "Turkey-Russia: Competition and Cooperation," *Eurasianet*, December 27, 2002.

[7]   Torbakov, 2002. Erdoğan worked to expand trade and investment and develop limited security cooperation. The 2002 AKP platform stated that the "relations established with the Russian Federation, Central Asia and the Caucasus will be based not on competition but friendly cooperation" and that Ankara's relations with Moscow exhibit marked "dualism" (Fatih Özbay, "The Relations Between Turkey and Russia in the 2000s," *Perceptions*, Vol. 16, No. 3, Autumn 2011, p. 71; and Igor Torbakov, "The Turkish Factor in the Geopolitics of the Post-Soviet Space," Foreign Policy Research Institute, E-Notes, January 1, 2003).

2010 strategic partnership agreement that called for annual summits and established a High-Level Cooperation Council and multiple subordinate bodies to advance a wide range of bilateral cooperation.[8]

However, the relationship remained more transactional than strategic, and conflicting regional priorities—this time to the south—once again roiled relations, as festering differences over the war in Syria came to a head after Turkish air forces shot down a Russian Su-24 fighter-bomber in November 2015. Amid inflammatory diplomatic rhetoric and media coverage on both sides, Russia responded with damaging sanctions on Turkey and threats to annul the 1921 friendship treaty. In June 2016, after seven months of economic sanctions and political isolation, Erdoğan was forced to apologize to Russia in return for rapid restoration of diplomatic and trade relations.[9] Although the Turkish and Russian governments currently enjoy a positive relationship—and are pursuing diplomatic and military cooperation in Syria—their mutual history and persistent points of friction suggest that the exiting state of harmony cannot be taken for granted.

A Lasting Partnership?

The extent to which the current rapprochement will endure over the longer term is likely to hinge on the convergence or divergence of several critical Turkish and Russian interests and the prioritization that each government gives to disparate interests.

This chapter considers the prospects for a lasting partnership through the lens of five key interests in bilateral relations and those interests' role as drivers of future relations. The first is Russia's interest in expanding bilateral trade and energy ties, including access to Turkey as an additional transit country for sending energy sources from Russia to Europe. The second Russian interest, articulated in the rhetoric and actions of Putin over the past decade, is in presenting an alternative to traditional Western institutions, such as NATO and the EU. A third factor that could influence Russia's future relations with Turkey is the autocratic character of the current Russian government, as well as Putin's interest in consolidating domestic rule. Russia's enduring interest in preserving regional autonomy in the Black Sea region constitutes a fourth factor—one that has historically proven a source of conflict but has more often led to cooperative ventures. Finally, a recent surge in Russia's interest in expanding its influence in the Middle East has highlighted some fundamental differences in Russian and Turkish policy objectives but has also yielded opportunities for diplomatic and operational collaboration.

---

[8] Stephen Flanagan, "The Turkey-Russia-Iran Nexus: Eurasian Power Dynamics," *Washington Quarterly*, Vol. 36, No. 1, 2013.

[9] Jim Zanotti and Clayton Thomas, *Turkey: Background and U.S. Relations*, Washington, D.C.: Congressional Research Service, R41368, August 26, 2016; and "Russia, Turkey Sign Gas Pipeline Deal," Radio Free Europe/Radio Liberty, October 10, 2016.

Each of these interests has some conjunction with key Turkish interests and has the potential to drive Turkey and Russia closer together. However, each could also yield friction points for the partnership. Turkey is committed to deepening economic and energy ties with Russia, but it also wants to diversify its energy sources and serve as a regional hub for energy from sources in the Caspian Basin and Eastern Mediterranean, which compete with Russia for market share. Ankara remains wary of growing Russian assertiveness and growing military power in the Black Sea and sees the collective defense commitments of Turkey's NATO allies as an essential check on potential Russian aggression. The following sections consider both sides of the ledger, as well as potential future flashpoints for the relationship.

Economic Ties

In recent decades, Turkish analysis has frequently cited the strengthening economic relationship between Russia and Turkey as the major reason why a return to a contentious regional rivalry is unlikely to occur.[10] Both countries maintain economic interests in a positive energy relationship. However, energy has also served as a source of competition at times, as Russia has sought to expand its energy monopoly in southern Europe and Turkey has sought to leverage its geographic position to become a critical energy transit hub, particularly for natural gas from the Caspian Basin and Central Asia. Although the broader trade and tourism relationships between the two countries are strong—and have continued to grow substantially over the past 30 years—Russia has demonstrated a willingness to jeopardize these ties to advance its political or military objectives, as evidenced by its efforts to restrict trade with Turkey during the 2008 Georgia War and its imposition of broad sanctions against Turkey in 2015 following Turkey's downing of a Russian bomber aircraft.[11]

For Turkey, Russia represents a critical source of natural gas, providing about one-third of Turkey's overall consumed energy.[12] In 1998, Turkey's state-owned energy company BOTAŞ signed a long-term contract to increase gas imports from Russia by an additional 8 billion cubic meters per year via the Trans-Balkan pipeline through 2022. And in 2003, gas started flowing directly between Russia and Turkey through the Blue Stream pipeline under the Black Sea, with a maximum annual capacity 16 billion cubic meters. With around 55 percent of Turkey's gas imported from Russia today, the Turkish government has periodically sought to diversify gas imports in order to

---

[10] Suat Kiniklioglu, *The Anatomy of Turkish-Russian Relations*, Washington, D.C.: Brookings Institution and Sabanci University, 2006.

[11] Igor Torbakov, *The Georgia Crisis and Russia-Turkey Relations,* Washington, D.C.: Jamestown Foundation, 2008, pp. 14–16.

[12] Alan Makovsky, "Turkey's Growing Energy Ties with Moscow," Center for American Progress, May 6, 2015.

reduce its dependence.[13] However, analysts have noted that the TurkStream project—a second pipeline being constructed under the Black Sea with landfall on Turkey's European coast north of Istanbul, which will help reduce gas prices for Turkish consumers—reflects a growing comfort within the Turkish government with Russia's role as its primary gas supplier.[14] Russian gas exports to Turkey reached a nine-year high in 2016–2017.[15] Russia was once the largest single-country source of Turkey's crude oil imports, but this percentage has been declining and stood at 11 percent in 2015 as a result of Turkish diversification efforts and Russia's focus on Asian export markets.[16]

Turkey offers Russia its second-largest individual gas export market (24 percent share in 2016) after Germany.[17] Perhaps more important is Turkey's potential role as a transit country from Russia to western and southern Europe—particularly after the failure of the Gazprom-funded South Stream project for a pipeline under the Black Sea to Bulgaria.[18] The South Stream project had unraveled following the Ukraine crisis, and President Putin attributed its breakdown to European opposition.[19] During a state visit to Turkey in December 2014, Putin announced Russia's intent to build a gas pipeline to Turkey after the cancellation of South Stream.[20] Formal negotiations began shortly after Turkey and Russia signed a memorandum during that 2014 visit.[21]

Following Turkey's November 24, 2015, downing of a Russian bomber aircraft, progress on TurkStream talks temporarily halted. Both Turkey and Russia claimed to be the side that had put the project on hold.[22] The Russian government attributed the

---

[13] U.S. Energy Information Administration, *Country Analysis Brief: Turkey*, Washington, D.C., February 2, 2017; and Asli Aydıntaşbaş, *With Friends Like These: Turkey, Russia, and the End of an Unlikely Alliance*, London: European Council on Foreign Relations, policy brief, June 2016.

[14] Makovsky, 2015.

[15] "Russian Gas Flows to Europe, Turkey Break New Records in 2017: Gazprom," *S&P Global Platts*, January 9, 2017. Gazprom reported that Turkey was the destination of 24 percent of its gas exports (Gazprom Export, "Delivery Statistics," webpage, undated-a).

[16] U.S. Energy Information Administration, 2017.

[17] Aydıntaşbaş, 2016.

[18] "Russia Drops South Stream Gas Pipeline Plan," BBC News, December 1, 2014; and "Russia's Gazprom Starts Building TurkStream Gas Pipeline Under Black Sea," *Deutsche Welle*, May 7, 2017.

[19] "Russia Drops South Stream Gas Pipeline Plan," 2014; "Russia's Gazprom Starts Building TurkStream Gas Pipeline Under Black Sea," 2017.

[20] "Russia Drops South Stream Gas Pipeline Plan," 2014.

[21] Emre Peker, "Russia, Turkey Complete Initial Turk Stream Gas Pipeline Talks," *Wall Street Journal*, December 11, 2014.

[22] Russian energy minister Aleksandr Novak stated, and Russian media reported, that Russia had suspended TurkStream as a result of the plane incident. Erdoğan dismissed this account as untrue and instead claimed that Turkey had stopped the project even before the aircraft downing because Russia had not met Turkish demands ("Russia Halts Turkish Stream Project over Downed Jet," *RT*, December 3, 2015; and "Turkey Has Shelved Turkish Stream Gas Pipeline Project, Says President Erdoğan," *Hürriyet Daily News*, December 5, 2015).

halt to the downed jet, and Erdoğan claimed that the project had run aground prior to the incident and emphasized that Turkey could find alternative suppliers for its oil and gas, a point punctuated by senior Turkish leaders visiting Qatar and Azerbaijan.[23]

After Erdoğan's June 2016 letter of apology and the restoration of mutual economic relations, the TurkStream project was resumed, and the project reportedly was a topic of discussion during the August 2016 meeting between the Putin and Erdoğan in St. Petersburg.[24] Construction on the pipeline began in May 2017, as did Russian discussions with Bulgaria and Greece regarding a potential entry point to Europe for TurkStream, which is expected to come on line in late 2019.[25]

In addition to gas and oil, Russia has become the Turkish government's exclusive partner in its plans to have three nuclear power plants operating by 2023, the centennial of the Turkish Republic.[26] In 2013, Turkey commissioned Russia's state-owned company Rosatom to build four 1,200-megawatt nuclear reactors in a $20 billion project.[27] Turkish energy officials expressed some uncertainty about the project's future immediately after the 2015 downed plane incident, but during a February 2017 visit to the Akkuyu plant's construction site, then–Energy and Natural Resources Minister Berat Albayrak announced plans to have the plant in service in 2023.[28]

Despite the countries' significant mutual interests in the realm of energy, Russia's desire to dominate regional energy transit has caused some frictions with Turkey. Even as Turkey has sought to establish itself as a critical route for gas flows from the Caspian Basin and Central Asia to points west and south, Moscow has warned that projects such as the Trans-Caspian pipeline—which Turkey has strongly supported but which circumvents Russia—run counter to its interests.[29] To curb the diversification of energy routes, Russia has offered commercial incentives to enhance bilateral energy cooperation with Azerbaijan, Kazakhstan, Turkmenistan, and Uzbekistan and

---

[23] "Turkey Has Shelved Turkish Stream Gas Pipeline Project, Says President Erdoğan," 2015.

[24] Nick Tattersall and Alexander Winning, "As Turkey's Coup Strains Ties with West, Detente with Russia Gathers Pace," Reuters, August 6, 2016; and Kalyeena Makortoff, "Major Russian Pipeline Faces Revival After Rapprochement with Turkey," CNBC, August 11, 2016.

[25] "Russia's Gazprom Starts Building TurkStream Gas Pipeline Under Black Sea," 2017; "Russia Discussing Turkish Stream Entry Point with European Countries, Russian PM Says," Daily Sabah, May 22, 2017.

[26] Ziya Onis and Şuhnaz Yılmaz, "Turkey and Russia in a Shifting Global Order: Cooperation, Conflict, and Asymmetric Interdependence in a Turbulent Region," Third World Quarterly, Vol. 37, No. 1, 2015, pp. 86–87.

[27] Polina Devitt, Dmitry Solovyov, and Jack Stubbs, "Factbox: Impact of Russian Sanctions on Trade Ties with Turkey," Reuters, June 27, 2016.

[28] Orhan Coskun, "Update 1—Russia Halts Turkey Nuclear Work, Ankara Looks Elsewhere," Reuters, December 9, 2015; and "Turkey's First Nuclear Power Plant Akkuyu to Be Operational by 2023," Daily Sabah, February 3, 2017.

[29] "Russia Keeps a Wary Eye on the Trans-Caspian Pipeline," Stratfor, November 19, 2014. In August 2019, Russian Energy Minister Alexander Novak announced that the second leg of the TurkStream pipeline will go through Bulgaria, Serbia, and Hungary, not Greece ("A Change of Route for TurkStream Second Leg," Oil & Gas Observer, August 2, 2019).

demonstrated to Kazakhstan and Turkmenistan its readiness to leverage control over major export routes in order to ensure energy dominance and force price concessions.[30]

More broadly, economic ties between Turkey and Russia have been steadily expanding since the end of the Cold War. By 2015, Russia had become Turkey's third-largest trading partner, and Russian direct investment—including by Gazprom, Lukoil, and Sberbank—had established Russia's presence in Turkish markets.[31] Although Turkish companies have sold as much as $6 billion of food, chemicals, textiles, and other goods in Russian markets, a perennial trade imbalance—Turkey registered a trade deficit close to $7 billion with Russia in 2005—has reportedly been a persistent area of concern among Turkish economic officials.[32]

Moscow and Ankara have used the bilateral High-Level Cooperation Council noted earlier as a vehicle to deepen economic, political, and cultural cooperation.[33] Presidents Putin and Erdoğan co-chaired the sixth such council at the Kremlin in March 2017. The meeting focused on advancing trade and economic ties, and the leaders endorsed a 2017–2020 program of cooperation, along with an agreement to establish a Russian-Turkish sovereign investment fund. The governments also signed MOUs on training of diplomatic personnel and intellectual property and agreed to cooperation in the small and medium-sized business sector and between their official news agencies, TASS and Anadolu. Erdoğan said the session, his fourth meeting with Putin in a year, "finalized normalization of bilateral relations," and he urged that remaining economic restrictions be removed so that the two countries could realize their goal of raising total annual trade volume to $100 billion.[34] Trade volume has yet to top $38 billion in any year and fell to $17 billion in 2016.

Beyond trade, construction has long represented a major area of economic cooperation between Turkey and Russia, with Turkish contractors reaching approximately $65 billion business volume in 2015, nearly 20 percent of Turkey's $350 billion abroad.[35]

---

[30] Andrew S. Weiss, F. Stephen Larrabee, James T. Bartis, and Camille A. Sawak, *Promoting International Energy Security*, Vol. 2: *Turkey and the Caspian*, Santa Monica, Calif.: RAND Corporation, TR-1144/2-AF, 2012; Bruce Pannier, "Russia Flexes Muscles in Turkmenistan," Radio Free Europe/Radio Liberty, June 13, 2016; and Bruce Pannier, "The End of the (Gas Pipe-) Line for Turkmenistan," Radio Free Europe/Radio Liberty, March 6, 2017.

[31] Jeffrey Mankoff, "Russia and Turkey's Rapprochement: Don't Expect an Equal Partnership," *Foreign Affairs*, July 20, 2016b; and Aydıntaşbaş, 2016.

[32] Aydıntaşbaş, 2016; Kiniklioglu, 2006.

[33] Ayla Gürel and Harry Tzimitras, "Beyond Energy: Remarks About the Direction of Turkish-Russian Relations and Their Implications for the Cyprus Problem," *Euxeinos: Governance and Culture in the Black Sea Region*, Vol. 18, 2015.

[34] President of Russia, "High-Level Russian-Turkish Cooperation Council," press release, March 10, 2017a; and President of Russia, "Joint News Conference with President of Turkey Recep Tayyip Erdoğan," transcript, March 10, 2017b.

[35] The number of projects totaled 1,930 ("Turkish Contractors Hopeful as Russia Relaxes Sanctions," *Hürriyet Daily News*, June 2, 2017).

Tourism—an industry that accounts for more than 10 percent of Turkey's gross domestic product—has also been a major pillar of bilateral economic relations. According to one Turkish news source, about 3.65 million Russians visited Turkey in 2015 and 4.5 million visited in 2014; during Russia's ban on travel to Turkey (following the downed plane incident), this number dropped dramatically to 866,256 overall, but it rebounded in 2017.[36]

These economic ties have fostered some political cooperation. In 1992, Russia and Turkey established the Organization of the Black Sea Economic Cooperation (BSEC) and later collaborated to limit U.S. participation.[37] Although the forum has not been particularly dynamic—and initially was stymied by a Russian reluctance to participate—foreign ministers have recently met more regularly, as was the case at the July 2016 BSEC meeting in Sochi.[38]

The imbalance in the economic relationship and Turkey's relative energy dependence on Russia have translated into Russian leverage in the political and diplomatic arena. Turkey's refusal to join the U.S. and EU sanctions against Russia in response to Russian military aggression in Ukraine after Russia's 2014 invasion—and Turkey's muted response to the suppression of the rights of the sizable population of pro-Turkish Tatars in Crimea—can be seen as a willingness to prioritize economic interests over other regional considerations. However, the Turkish government's decision to shoot down the Russian Su-24 bomber in November 2015 indicated a willingness to put those ties at risk. Similarly, Russia has demonstrated that it is willing to sever such ties in order to coerce Turkey to comply with its political and diplomatic prerogatives. In response to the 2015 downed bomber incident, Russia put an embargo on many Turkish agricultural imports, restricted Russian tourism to Turkey, ended visa-free travel for Turkish citizens, and ceased construction of the TurkStream gas pipeline.[39] The impact of the Russian sanctions against Turkey was significant: Turkish news reports cited loss of tourism revenues ranging from $5 billion to $10 billion, and the European Bank for Reconstruction and Development estimated that, had the sanctions stayed in place for a year, it would have reduced Turkey's gross domestic product by 0.7 percent in 2016.[40] Erdoğan's letter of apology, though a bitter pill to swallow, flowed partly from domestic pressures to protect Turkish interests in the areas of tourism, trade, and energy.

---

[36] "Russian Tourist Numbers to Turkey Skyrocket in January but Foreign Arrivals Keep Declining," *Hürriyet Daily News*, February 28, 2017; and "Update 1—Turkey's 2017 Tourism Revenues Jump as Russians Return," Reuters, January 31, 2018.

[37] Kuchins and Petersen, 2009, p. 67.

[38] Organization of the Black Sea Economic Cooperation Permanent International Secretariat, "Press Release on the 34th meeting of the BSEC Council of Ministers of Foreign Affairs," Sochi, July 1, 2016.

[39] Idil Bilgic-Alpaslan, Bojan Markovic, Peter Tabak, and Emir Zildzovic, "Economic Implications of Russia's Sanctions Against Turkey," European Bank for Reconstruction and Development, December 7, 2015.

[40] Aydıntaşbaş, 2016; Mankoff, 2016b.

Although economic ties with Russia appear to have influenced some Turkish foreign policy positions, this approach could potentially backfire in the future. Efforts by Moscow to use gas prices or trade to manipulate Ankara could provoke Turkish backlash and lead to Turkey's renewed efforts to diversify its markets and energy sources to reduce its dependence on Russia.

Russian Efforts to Undermine Western Institutions

Russia's efforts to undermine NATO and the EU and establish alternatives to Western institutions—particularly those dominated by the United States—represents a second major Russian interest that is a source of tension in the relationship, given Turkey's interest in NATO security guarantees and integration into Europe. In recent years, Russia has increasingly played to Turkey's troubles with Western partners—as well as its enduring Eurasian ambitions—to seek to drive a wedge between Turkey and its NATO allies in what one team of analysts dubbed the "axis of the excluded."[41] Although shared frustrations with Western institutions and governments appear to have contributed to certain aspects of political and security cooperation between Turkey and Russia, frictions have endured and could intensify if Turkey aligns closely with NATO allies (as happened during 2015–2016 crisis) or becomes an obstacle to Russia's efforts to assert regional hegemony. Putin has also publicly warned about the potential difficulties that could arise if Turkey joins the EU.[42]

Turkey has sometimes taken positions in opposition to U.S. and Western policies, which Russia has welcomed or shared. Turkey's traditionally strong relations with the United States were undermined by overwhelming public opposition to the 2003 U.S. invasion of Iraq. Turks feared that the war would be devastating to their economy and lead to an independent Kurdish state, which resulted in the Turkish Parliament's refusal in March 2003 to allow U.S. troops to launch military operations into northern Iraq from Turkish territory.[43] Frustration with failure to gain significant traction on its EU accession process has contributed to increased ambivalence within Turkey about the EU as an institution. Turkish leaders, like their Russian counterparts, have bridled at criticism by Western allies of the authoritarian drift of internal political developments, which has led to strains in cooperation with Germany and other NATO countries, as outlined in Chapter Eight.[44]

---

[41] Fiona Hill and Ömer Taşpınar, "Turkey and Russia: Axis of the Excluded?" *Survival*, Vol. 48, No. 1, Spring 2006b.

[42] Kiniklioglu, 2006.

[43] Hill and Taşpınar, 2006b.

[44] Leonid Bershidsky, "Turkey's Troubled NATO Status," *Bloomberg*, March 14, 2017.

The trend has been reinforced by an unfulfilled desire within Turkey and Russia for recognition as European great powers—likely a remnant of both states' former imperial status. The Russian government regularly cites its desire to preserve an active role in global affairs, and Turkey has emphasized its unique position as a crossroads between Europe and the Middle East.[45] A common observation by Turkish officials that Russians "treat us with respect" underscores the significance of status from the Turkish perspective.[46] Within Turkey, this perspective is perhaps most explicitly articulated in the pro-Russian Eurasianism espoused by the small but vocal Turkish Homeland Party, which advocates an alliance with Russia akin to Atatürk's early anti-imperialist collaboration with the Soviet Union.[47]

The partnership also offers practical benefits to the two countries in the absence of EU membership. For Turkey, strong economic ties with Russia present an important alternative to European markets, particularly for Turkey's agricultural products and construction services. Although the EU maintains a customs union with Turkey, that union covers only industrial goods and stipulates requirements for Turkish trade policy reform.[48] For Russia, collaboration with Turkey on the TurkStream gas pipeline allows it to circumvent EU regulatory hurdles that had banned a Gazprom monopoly on the abandoned South Stream project and, ultimately, to undermine EU energy independence goals.

Russia has also sought to court Turkey through enhanced defense cooperation and arms sales. Growing security cooperation between Turkey and Russia has elicited concerns within NATO—an upshot almost certainly not lost on Moscow. Joint Russian-Turkish Black Sea exercises in April 2017 offered Moscow the opportunity to demonstrate that a NATO ally was willing to work individually with it on regional security cooperation, despite isolation after annexing Crimea.[49] In July 2019, Turkey acquired Russian S-400 air defense systems—a move that has raised deep concerns in the United States and NATO because the S-400 is unable to integrate with NATO common air defense systems and poses intelligence risks to advanced NATO aircraft.[50] In a development that would herald new levels of cooperation between Russia and a

---

[45] Foreign Minister Sergey Lavrov's 2007 quote presents one example: "Russia is now in a favorable international position. But such a position is never guaranteed in an evolving international environment. We can preserve, as well as increase, our achievements only through our active involvement in international affairs" (Sergey Lavrov, "The Present and the Future of Global Politics," *Russia in Global Affairs*, May 13, 2007).

[46] Hill and Taşpınar, 2006b.

[47] Metin Gurcan, "The Rise of the Eurasianist Vision in Turkey," *Al-Monitor*, May 17, 2017c.

[48] Nihat Zeybekci, "Turkey Deserves a Better EU Trade Deal," *Bloomberg*, April 12, 2017.

[49] Dave Majumdar, "Why Are Russia and Turkey Holding Joint Naval Exercises in the Black Sea?" *National Interest*, April 5, 2017.

[50] In response to NATO concerns, the Turkish Ministry of Defense has criticized Western technology transfer policies and pricing ("Turkey Seeks Advanced S-400 Anti-Air Missiles from Russia," Military.com, May 22, 2017).

NATO ally, Rosoboroneksport (the Russian company responsible for defense-related imports and exports) announced in May 2017 that it was discussing joint arms development and production with Turkey's Ministry of Defense.[51]

While common skepticism of Western-led institutions and policy disputes with the United States and Europe may currently serve as a source of cohesion between Russia and Turkey, the two governments are far from forming an unbreakable bond. Ankara continues to manage important policy differences with Moscow and remains wary of the Kremlin's long-term intentions. Turkish leaders have demonstrated that they still see the United States and NATO as their most reliable security partners. During Turkey's 2015 diplomatic crisis with Russia, for example, Erdoğan urged a stronger NATO commitment to maintaining security in the Black Sea region. Erdoğan is also one of the few NATO leaders to invoke the North Atlantic Treaty's Article 4 within the Alliance,[52] and Turkey's defense establishment remains heavily dependent on NATO equipment and is likely to remain closely tied to the U.S. and NATO defense industry for at least a decade to come.[53] A Turkish decision to join NATO allies in taking actions against significant Russian interests, such as restricting transit of the Black Sea fleet through the Turkish Straits in the context of a future contingency in Syria or the Eastern Mediterranean, could fundamentally rupture the bilateral relationship with Moscow. Conversely, a Turkish decision to support the Russian action in such a crisis could cause significant strains in relations with NATO allies.

Consolidation of Domestic Power and Mutual Support for Authoritarianism

Putin's concerns about potential threats to his domestic power have been well examined by Western analysts.[54] In Turkey, Erdoğan's gradual consolidation of power and crackdown on Turkish media and opposition forces has brought him closer to autocracy. In both states, highly centralized governmental decisionmaking with consistent state leadership make the personal relationships between Putin and Erdoğan all the more significant. Both leaders view political opponents and popular protests through an authoritarian lens, and the two have provided one another with mutual support against Western pressure for democratic reform. However, domestic political agendas in both states could also prove a source of friction.

---

[51] "Turkey Discusses Joint Weapons Development with Russia," *Middle East Monitor*, May 3, 2017.

[52] NATO, North Atlantic Treaty, Washington, D.C., April 4, 1949.

[53] Eric Edelman and Merve Tahiroglu, "It's Time for NATO to Call Turkey's Bluff," *Weekly Standard*, May 25, 2017.

[54] See, for example, Stephen Crowley, "Why Protests Keep Putin Up at Night," *Foreign Affairs*, April 19, 2017.

A friendly personal relationship between Putin and Erdoğan has, at times, been celebrated as an assurance of a robust bilateral bond. During the year following Putin's December 2004 visit to Turkey—the first by a Russian head of state in 32 years—the two leaders met no fewer than four times, including a seven-hour private meeting in Sochi.[55] In the 13 months following Erdoğan's June 2016 apology for downing the aircraft, the two leaders met five times, including at the much-touted March 2017 meeting of the High-Level Cooperation Council. In both Russia and Turkey, traditions of strong central governments and highly personalized leadership styles make the individual ties between Putin and Erdoğan all the more significant.[56] Consistent efforts by both leaders to cripple domestic civil society organizations that could serve as a check to executive leadership further accentuate this factor.

Each leader has sought to strengthen his control over domestic governance amid Western criticism for undemocratic practices and human rights abuses. Both are concerned about the potential for popular revolt. In Russia, Putin has made his antipathy toward "color revolutions" a guiding principle of his domestic and foreign policy, and Erdoğan's reactions to the Gezi Park protests demonstrate his own concerns about the potential for sudden regime change.[57] Notably, Erdoğan followed the Russian public line during Ukraine's Maidan protests in late 2013 and early 2014.

Ultimately, mutual support for authoritarianism helped repair the bilateral rift during the last diplomatic crisis. Following the July 15, 2016, coup attempt in Turkey, Putin and Russia nearly immediately expressed solidarity with the Turkish government, while Turkey's western allies were slower and more qualified in their responses. Unconfirmed reports circulated in Russian media that Russia had even warned Turkey of the coup prior to its unfolding (see Box 6.1).[58]

However, domestic considerations within both states could also contribute to tensions in the relationship. Diplomatic fallout from the shootdown crisis of 2015 demonstrated the potential downside of centralized leaderships that take populist positions with few institutional constraints on power. Following critical rhetoric from Putin in which he characterized the event as an "enemy act" and a "stab in the back," the Russian press and public became highly critical of Turkey and Erdoğan personally, with one Levada Center poll showing Turkey among the top three enemies of Russia, along

---

[55] Kiniklioglu, 2006.

[56] Dimitar Bechev, "Erdoğan and Putin: Unalike Likeness," *Open Democracy*, November 28, 2015.

[57] As a 2017 RAND report explains, "Since the end of the Cold War, a series of pro-democracy and pro-Western protests have led to changes in government in the post-Soviet space; these have been referred to as *color revolutions* because participants often used flowers or colors as symbols" (Andrew Radin and Clint Reach, *Russian Views of the International Order*, Santa Monica, Calif.: RAND Corporation, RR-1826-OSD, 2017).

[58] See, for example, "Russia Warned Turkey of Imminent Army Coup, Says Iran's FNA," TASS, July 21, 2016.

Box 6.1
Russia's Use of the Media and Information Operations to Support Its Foreign Policy Goals in Turkey

Katherine Costello

Russian media have sought to undermine Turkey's political and security cooperation with the United States and Europe by exacerbating mutual skepticism and highlighting policy differences.[a] In Turkey, Russian media efforts have contributed to anti-American discourse and have reinforced and informed the Turkish government's own propaganda pursuits. This section describes how, following three key events in Turkey, Russian media responses employed the propaganda strategies of amplifying existing uncertainty, creating opportunistic fabrications, and using multiple contradictory narratives.[b] These strategies supported Russian foreign policy objectives, including sowing discord within NATO, disrupting Turkey's relationship with its Western allies, and making Turkey a more compliant partner for Russia.[c]

Amplification of Existing Uncertainty: Allegations of Turkish Sponsorship of ISIS After the Downing of a Russian Plane

After Turkey shot down a Russian bomber on November 24, 2015, Russian media began aggressively portraying Turkey as a supporter of terrorism that funded ISIS through illegal oil purchases.[d] With these allegations, Russian media amplified a genuine, preexisting uncertainty: Credible Western and Turkish domestic media sources had already questioned Turkey's commitment to combating ISIS.[e] Russian reports after the plane incident then added new allegations to this reporting trend by claiming that Erdoğan and his family had links to ISIS oil smuggling.[f] In doing so, Russian media may have sought to generate curiosity and fuel further discussion beyond just Russian outlets. Indeed, U.S., European, and Turkish outlets then amplified Russia's desired message by reporting about the new Russian accusations.[g] These legitimate reports, even when they acknowledged that Russian claims were false, still gave the claims further publicity. Thus, they added to the existing international and domestic discourse that cast doubt on the Turkish government's dedication to counterterrorism and to security—and that, by extension, questioned its commitment to its allies and to its public.

Opportunistic Fabrications: Anti-U.S. Disinformation Following Turkey's Coup Attempt

After the July 15, 2016, coup attempt in Turkey, Russian media crafted conspiracy theories alleging U.S. and Western involvement in the failed coup. These opportunistic fabrications included, for example, a false report by a Moscow-based website alleging that the late former U.S. National Security Adviser Zbigniew Brzezinski had acknowledged U.S. backing of the Turkish coup attempt.[h] The piece widely circulated on Turkish social media.[i] This and other Russian conspiracy theories alleging U.S. involvement in the coup target Turkish public opinion. They attempt to direct negative attention toward the United States and away from Russia in order to enable the Turkish-Russian cooperation that followed the countries' reconciliation.[j] Yet, although the ability of Russian disinformation to infiltrate Turkish news reports and social media feeds is cause for concern, Turkish-origin conspiracy theories alleging U.S. plots have been mainstream in Turkey for decades. Thus, negative and false Russian and Turkish media narratives about U.S. policy reinforce one another.

Multiple Contradictory Narratives: Various Insinuations of Blame After the Assassination of the Russian Ambassador

Following the assassination of the Russian ambassador in Turkey on December 19, 2016, an op-ed published in *RT* titled "Who Profits from Turkey's 'Sarajevo Moment'?" offered a representative example of the primary—and contradictory—interpretations of the event promoted by Russian media.[k] It pointed out that three groups—the Gülen network, Islamic terrorists, and Western powers—all had something to gain from the event (thus insinuating that any one of those groups could be responsible for the act), while Turkey did not. These points focused potential blame away from failures of the Turkish police and security services and offered more-sinister, alternative explanations based on the three insinuations offered, each of which held appeal for a different audience. The *RT* narrative provided a context that supported the Russian government's decision to continue its rapprochement with Turkey, despite this damaging incident, which it portrayed as caused by forces that want to disrupt the relationship.

Implications

Russian media and information operations seek to sow discord in NATO and to manipulate discussion in Turkey, the United States, and Europe. The media activities associated with the three events described in this box are part of what is an ongoing, wide-reaching, and opportunistic propaganda effort. Russian media take action whenever a Turkey-related subject can be shaped or an event exploited to Russia's advantage.

In Turkey, Russian media efforts have contributed to anti-American discourse, which some Turkish politicians employ for their own purposes and popularity.[l] Turkish leaders can also use this discourse to justify foreign policy decisions that disrupt U.S.-Turkish security cooperation. Such a situation occurred when Turkish politicians cited strong public opposition as a key reason behind the 2003 Turkish parliamentary decision that failed to allow U.S. troops access to Iraq through Turkey.[m] Similar dynamics could influence future Turkish decisions relating to NATO and İncirlik Air Base. Former Turkish military adviser and *Al-Monitor* columnist Metin Gurcan wrote that he has "frequently been hearing in Ankara an increasing dose of 'Isn't it time for Turkey to withdraw from the military wing of NATO?'"[n] Russian media are hard at work to inspire and reinforce such trends and to promote the idea that Turkey's most valuable ally is actually Russia.[o]

Finally, Turkish government efforts to create propaganda may emulate well-honed Russian practices. In the aftermath of government shutdowns of opposition media and continuing intimidation, surviving Turkish news outlets offer increasingly one-sided and sometimes blatantly false reports favorable to the government. The Turkish government has also developed its own propaganda arm, *TRT World*, a television channel of the Turkish state broadcasting corporation that resembles *RT* in many respects.[p] In March 2017, Putin and Erdoğan endorsed an agreement between their two countries' official news agencies, TASS and Anadolu, to exchange information and photos, with the prospect for expanded cooperation.[q] Although it is too soon to tell exactly where these initiatives will lead, enhanced understanding of state-supported Russian and Turkish media efforts could help safeguard Turkey's ties to NATO and impede the efforts of those who would like to disrupt the long-standing U.S.-Turkish alliance in favor of stronger Turkish-Russian ties.

---

[a] This analysis of Russian media examines Turkey-related internet material produced by the Russian state-supported media outlets *RT* (formerly *Russia Today*) and *Sputnik* (which has a Turkish-language edition),

articles from other Russian broadcasts, and Russia-based websites. For a fuller discussion of the issues in this box, see Katherine Costello, *Russia's Use of Media and Information Operations in Turkey: Implications for the United States*, Santa Monica, Calif.: RAND Corporation, PE-278-A, 2018.

[b] For an analysis of overall characteristics of Russian propaganda, the effects this propaganda might have, why it is concerning, and potential options to counter it, see Christopher Paul and Miriam Matthews, *The Russian "Firehose of Falsehood" Propaganda Model: Why It Might Work and Options to Counter It*, Santa Monica, Calif.: RAND Corporation, PE-198-OSD, 2016.

[c] For more on the dynamics of the Turkish-Russian relationship, see Pavel K. Baev and Kemal Kirişci, *An Ambiguous Partnership: The Serpentine Trajectory of Turkish-Russian Relations in the Era of Erdoğan and Putin*, Washington, D.C.: Brookings Institution, Turkey Project Policy Paper No. 13, September 2017. For further information on recent developments in Turkish-Russian interactions, see Jeffrey Mankoff, "A Friend in Need? Russia and Turkey After the Coup," Center for Strategic and International Studies, July 29, 2016c. For more on Eurasian power dynamics involving Turkey and Russia and their historical roots, see Flanagan, 2013.

[d] Paul Sonne, "Russian Media Takes Aim at Turkey," *Wall Street Journal*, November 30, 2015.

[e] For a list of prominent Western and Turkish media reports alleging Turkey-ISIS oil trade in 2014, see David L. Phillips, "Research Paper: ISIS-Turkey Links," *Huffington Post*, November 9, 2014. For such reports in 2015, see David L. Phillips, "Research Paper: Turkey-ISIS Oil Trade," *Huffington Post*, December 14, 2016.

[f] "Ankara's Oil Business with ISIS," *RT*, November 25, 2016; and "Rusya: Erdoğan ve Ailesi, IŞİD'in Suriye'deki Yasadışı Petrol Sevkıyatıyla Doğrudan İlişki" ["Russia: Erdoğan and His Family Directly Involved in ISIS's Illegal Oil Shipment in Syria"], *Sputnik*, December 2, 2015.

[g] For example, a *Time* article that ultimately discounted Russian claims nevertheless used the clickbait title, "Is Turkey Really Benefiting from Oil Trade with ISIS?" (Tara John, "Is Turkey Really Benefiting from Oil Trade with ISIS?" *Time*, December 2, 2015).

[h] F. William Engdahl, "Top USA National Security Officials Admit Turkey Coup," *New Eastern Outlook*, August 31, 2016.

[i] Mustafa Akyol, "Did Zbigniew Brzezinski Blame CIA for Turkey's Coup?" *Hürriyet Daily News*, September 7, 2016.

[j] Jack Stubbs and Dmitry Solovyov, "Kremlin Says Turkey Apologized for Shooting Down Russian Jet," Reuters, June 27, 2016.

[k] Pepe Escobar, "Who Profits from Turkey's 'Sarajevo Moment'?" *RT*, December 20, 2016.

[l] For more on the history and political use of anti-Americanism in Turkey, see Burak Kadercan, "Turkey's Anti-Americanism Isn't New," *National Interest*, August 23, 2016.

[m] Karen Kaya, "The Turkish-American Crisis: An Analysis of 1 March 2003," *Military Review*, July–August 2011, p. 74.

[n] Metin Gurcan, "Russia's Winning the War for Turkish Public's Trust," *Al-Monitor*, November 20, 2017e.

[o] Gurcan, 2017e.

[p] Ali Ünal, "TRT World Ceo Ibrahim Eren: We Will Tell the Truth, Even If It Is Inconvenient or Disturbing," *Daily Sabah*, November 20, 2016; and Mehul Srivastava and Henry Mance, "Turkish TV Station Aims to Switch Western Views," *Financial Times*, March 11, 2016.

[q] "Russia's TASS Signs Cooperation Deal with Turkey's Anadolu News Agency," Radio Free Europe/Radio Liberty, March 11, 2017.

with the United States and Ukraine.[59] Erdoğan's initial refusal to apologize for the incident may also have reflected his need to continue to project strength to domestic audi-
ences. The incident highlighted how the domestic political dynamics of authoritarian
or semi-authoritarian governments can risk creating a spiral effect during moments of
diplomatic downturn, as well as the danger of inadvertent conflict given both governments' use of state propaganda to demonize adversaries.

Erdoğan's political power base in moderate political Islam presents another potentially complicating domestic factor. Erdoğan's public image as an authentic conservative
could also push him to take steps that would be of concern to Putin, who has long been
concerned about an Islamist separatist movement in the Caucasus.[60] The Russian and
Turkish governments made a breakthrough in the early 2000s when Turkey agreed to
cease permitting Chechen and other separatists to operate from Turkey and Russia shut
down PKK offices within its borders.[61] Putin's tough actions against radical Islamist
groups in the Russian Federation have sometimes proven embarrassing to Erdoğan in
relations with his base. Turkish support for Islamic groups in Syria have also led to tensions with Russia; after the 2015 aircraft downing, some Russian news sources even
suggested that Erdoğan's government had provided covert assistance to ISIS.

Finally, Russia's willingness to meddle in Turkish domestic affairs could provoke
a backlash from Erdoğan, particularly if such meddling threatened Erdoğan's domestic priorities. For example, Russia permitted the Syrian Kurdish PYD, which the AKP
views as a terrorist group, to open an office in Moscow with great fanfare during the
nadir of the relationship in 2016—a move that, as analysts noted, demonstrated that
the Russian government was willing and able to exacerbate Turkish internal problems
if it so desired.[62] Should Russia seek to interfere domestically to destabilize Turkey
during a future diplomatic crisis, it could create a rift that would be difficult to repair.

Uneasy Partnership in the Black Sea

Russia and Turkey have significant and somewhat convergent security interests in the
Black Sea, a commonality that has been, at times, a source of cooperation but more frequently an arena of competition. Russia is interested in working with Turkey—albeit
as a junior partner—to limit other NATO forces in the Black Sea, and Russia currently seeks to ensure eased transit for its Black Sea fleet to support Russian operations
in the Eastern Mediterranean and the Middle East. Concurrently, Russian rhetorical

[59] Victor Vladimirov and Taras Burnos, "Poll: Russians See US, Ukraine, Turkey as Top 3 Enemies," Voice of
America, June 3, 2016.

[60] Bechev, 2015.

[61] Kuchins and Petersen, 2009.

[62] Michael A. Reynolds, "Vladimir Putin, Godfather of Kurdistan?" *National Interest*, March 1, 2016.

bluster and military buildup in the Black Sea appear to demonstrate Russian desire to assert dominance across the Black Sea region and beyond. Unsurprisingly, this stance has regularly created frictions with Turkey and could well lead Turkey to increasingly return to NATO for regional security needs.

Both Russia and Turkey have long resisted attempts by outside powers to penetrate the region.[63] A revealing illustration of this mutual interest was the creation of the Black Sea Economic Council and Turkey's decision not to support U.S. candidacy, which ultimately had to be championed by other Black Sea littoral states.[64] Militarily, the multinational force of the Black Sea Naval Cooperation Task Group has periodically been cited by Moscow and Ankara as evidence that a NATO presence is not necessary in the Black Sea.[65] Within NATO, Turkey has generally advocated a minimalist presence in the Black Sea, in an effort to avoid provoking Russia. Turkish policymakers have sought to ensure Russian cooperation in the region because of a conviction that "without Russia we cannot fulfill our objectives. Russia needs to be on board."[66] Turkish leaders appreciate that Moscow's military might and substantial political and economic influence in the region can thwart Turkish ambitions.

From Russia's perspective, Turkey's legal rights, under the 1936 Montreux Convention Regarding the Regime of the Straits, to limit the passage of civilian and military ships through the Dardanelles and Bosporus straits provides a relatively compelling rationale for cooperation.[67] According to the convention, Ankara has the right to stop ships it suspects of carrying supplies to its enemies—a provision that could include, for example, Russian logistics ships providing assistance to the Syrian government.[68] Turkey can also deny the United States and other NATO allies access to Black Sea coasts through strict application of the Montreux provisions when Turkey feels threatened by the potential for war. Turkey employed this power following the 2008 Russian invasion of Georgia by refusing the passage of two U.S. Navy hospital ships that were seeking to provide humanitarian relief but that exceeded the Montreux Convention's tonnage limitations.[69]

---

[63] Hill and Taşpınar, 2006b.

[64] Hill and Taşpınar, 2006b.

[65] Kiniklioglu, 2006.

[66] Kiniklioglu, 2006, p. 10; the quotation comes from a presentation by Turkish Ministry of Foreign Affairs official Osman Yavuzalp.

[67] Under the Montreux Convention, while merchant vessels enjoy freedom of passage through the Turkish Straits, military vessels are subject to restrictions on tonnage, type of vessel, duration of stay in the Black Sea, and notification procedures.

[68] Turkiye'nin Nabsi, "Is Turkey Turning Its Stern on the West in the Black Sea?" *Al-Monitor*, December 2016.

[69] Turkey subsequently allowed three smaller U.S. vessels (one a Coast Guard cutter) passage to the Black Sea (Nabsi, 2016). See also Bulent Aliriza, "Turkey and the Crisis on the Caucasus," Center for Strategic and International Studies, September 9, 2008.

In recent decades, some of Turkey's emphasis on Black Sea cooperation has rested on an assumption of relative Turkish strength. Since the 1991 collapse of the Soviet Union and division and decline of the Russian Black Sea Fleet, no other littoral navy has been able to maintain a robust and modern naval presence in the Black Sea.[70] In this vacuum, Turkey has sought to rely on its own naval superiority to initiate and retain control over regional naval security cooperation frameworks.[71]

Recent Russian assertiveness and efforts to strengthen Russia's relative position in the Black Sea and ability to project maritime power could derail this cooperative approach. In September 2016, Russian General Valeriy Gerasimov boasted, just before a visit to Turkey, that the military balance in the Black Sea had already shifted toward Russia "with the deployment of reconnaissance assets, submarines with Kalibr [cruise missiles], new aircraft, and the Bastion coastal defense missiles with 350 km range in Crimea."[72] In 2016, Russia announced that it intended to spend a further $2.4 billion over the next four years to strengthen and modernize its Black Sea Fleet, including the procurement of more-modern surface ships and submarines outfitted with advanced cruise missiles, as well as integrated air defense and amphibious-landing capacities.[73] There is debate among experts about whether Moscow can realize this naval modernization program on the timeline envisioned. In July 2017, President Putin approved a new Russian naval doctrine, which declares that it is designed to counter the ambitions of the "United States and its allies to dominate the high seas, and to press for overwhelming superiority of their naval forces." The document identified strengthening the Black Sea Fleet and Russian forces in Crimea, as well as maintaining a constant naval presence in the Mediterranean, as the most critical geographic priorities for future development of the Russian Navy.[74] The enhancements to the Black Sea Fleet that have already been achieved have strengthened Moscow's ability to project power in that region and expand its influence in the Eastern Mediterranean, the Balkans, and the Middle East.

Russia's annexation of Crimea, improvements in the size and readiness of ground forces in the Southern Military district, continuing patronage of breakaway Georgian province Abkhazia, and enhancements of Russian military presence in Armenia have

---

[70] Oktay F. Tanrısever, *Turkey and Russia in the Black Sea Region: Dynamics of Cooperation and Conflict*, Washington, D.C.: German Marshall Fund of the United States, Edam Black Sea Discussion Paper Series 2012/1, 2012, p. 13.

[71] Tanrısever, 2012.

[72] Joshua Kucera, "Russia Claims 'Mastery' over Turkey in Black Sea," *Eurasianet*, September 25, 2016b. General Valeriy Gerasimov, chief of general staff of the Russian armed forces, said, "Several years ago the capability of the fleet was sharply contrasted, in particular, with the Turkish navy, when it was said that Turkey is virtually the master of the Black Sea. Now everything is different."

[73] F. Stephen Larrabee and Stephen J. Flanagan, "Making Waves on the Black Sea," *U.S. News and World Report*, July 7, 2016.

[74] Dimitry Gorenburg, "Russia's New and Unrealistic Naval Doctrine," *War on the Rocks*, July 26, 2017.

strengthened Russian military posture and power projection capabilities in the Black Sea littoral region. Russia's 2014 intervention in Crimea provided it with full control of Sevastopol, as well as three other former Ukrainian naval bases.[75] In July 2016, Russia unveiled plans for a new $1.4 billion Black Sea Fleet base near Crimea by 2020 that will serve as Black Sea Fleet headquarters, with ships continuing to dock in Crimea.[76] Some Turkish analysts have concluded that, "with the annexation of Crimea, Russia became the greatest immediate military threat to Turkey once again, as it was during the Cold War and in the previous two centuries."[77]

Although Black Sea security considerations have not yielded frictions between Turkey and Russia in recent years, growing Russian ambition and relative power in the region, paired with Turkey's tendency to turn to NATO during times of threat, could well present a roadblock to deep and enduring bilateral security relations between the two nations. Official Turkish statements during and after the 2015–2016 crisis in relations with Russia reflect a wariness about Russia's military capabilities and intentions that appears to persist.[78] During the crisis, Erdoğan reversed his traditional reluctance about a NATO presence in the Black Sea, lamenting that NATO is "absent from the Black Sea. The Black Sea has almost become a Russian lake. If we don't act now, history will not forgive us."[79] When NATO allies agreed at the July 2016 Warsaw Summit to initiate a tailored forward presence for the Black Sea region, the Turkish Ministry of Defense announced that it would contribute to the initiative—despite vocal Russian opposition.[80] A future contingency in which Russia uses its military might to intimidate Turkey or undermine its security interests in the Black Sea or Middle East will likely be the true test of how this shifting regional military balance will affect the future course of Turkey's relations with its NATO allies and with Russia.

Middle East Ambitions

For Russia, a cooperative relationship with Turkey could serve as an important cornerstone as it seeks to expand influence in the Middle East. Divergent approaches by each government to regional politics, however, seem likely to limit the scope of this

---

[75] Larrabee and Flanagan, 2016; and Adam Ereli, "Putin's Newest Satellite State," *Forbes*, February 24, 2016.

[76] Kucera, 2016b.

[77] Şener Aktürk "The Crisis in Russian-Turkish Relations, 2008–2015," *Russian Analytical Digest*, No. 179, Center for Security Studies, February 12, 2016; p. 4.

[78] Senior Turkish and U.S. officials, discussion with the authors, Ankara, June 2017.

[79] Sam Jones and Kathrin Hille, "Russia's Military Ambitions Make Waves in the Black Sea," *Financial Times*, May 13, 2016.

[80] NATO, "Press Conference by NATO Secretary General Jens Stoltenberg Following the Meeting of the North Atlantic Council at the Level of NATO Defence Ministers," Brussels, transcript, October 27, 2016b.

partnership. Deep Russian concern about Islamist instability in the Caucasus and the flow of fighters from that region to and from conflicts in the Middle East, as well as the Kremlin's penchant for autocratic partners, has underpinned Russian support for status quo forces across the region, including support for Assad in Syria and for military rule in Egypt and Libya. Turkey, on the other hand, has sided primarily with forces for change and is far more comfortable with the forces of political Islam. Additionally, the relationship could suffer if Turkey's enduring concerns about the potential for an independent Kurdish statelet are ignored by a utilitarian Russian approach to the Syria conflict.

Because of a convergence in regional perspectives and policies, prospects for cooperation looked favorable during the first decade of the 21st century. Both Turkey and Russia adamantly opposed the U.S. invasion of Iraq, an event that would dramatically shape the dynamics of the region.[81] During Ahmet Davutoglu's early tenure as Turkey's foreign minister, his "zero problems with neighbors" and "normalization with the neighborhood" policies were consistent with the Russian emphasis on Middle Eastern stability.[82] However, as Turkey took on a more assertive role in supporting forces of political Islam during and after the 2011 Arab Awakening, Ankara's regional agenda increasingly came in conflict with Moscow's priorities.[83] This tension could be seen, for example, in the two capitals' support for opposing sides in the struggles between the Muslim Brotherhood and military establishments in Egypt and Libya.

Syria has been the major source of bilateral friction since 2011, with Russian support for Assad initially conflicting with Turkey's policy favoring regime change in Syria. For Moscow, the emphasis on maintaining the Assad regime stemmed from a desire to maintain a close ally in the Middle East region—and specifically a Russian naval base in Tartus, Syria—as well as a preference for autocratic continuity over regime change and genuine security concerns about the growth of radical Islamist forces. In 2014, notably, ISIS identified the Caucasus region as a priority sphere of interest.[84] For Turkey, its initial impulse to convince the Assad regime to reform—an impulse borne from two decades of engagement with Damascus that had led to normalization of relations—evolved into firm calls for regime change, direct support for the Syrian opposition, and a willingness to permit fighters and weapon shipments to pass through Turkish territory, which raised concerns both for Russia and for Turkey's Western allies. Turkey has also been critical of Russian military and political support for Syrian Kurdish groups—including the PYD and its militias, which Ankara views as closely linked to the insurgent PKK in Turkey. The November 2015 airplane inci-

---

[81] Kiniklioglu, 2006.

[82] Kiniklioglu, 2006.

[83] Flanagan, 2013.

[84] Sergey Markedonov and Natalya Ulchenko, "Turkey and Russia: An Evolving Relationship," Carnegie Endowment for International Peace, August 19, 2011.

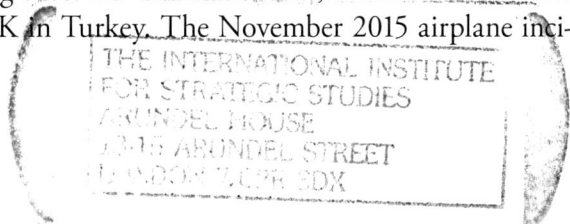

dent thus can best be understood as a manifestation of deep underlying differences around the countries' respective Syria policies.

Russian and Turkish coordination on Syria has been a major element of the recent rapprochement between the two governments since the latter half of 2016. Following the reconciliation, Turkey backed away from its position on the necessity of removing Assad from power and has collaborated with Russia on military and diplomatic initiatives in Syria. Direct consultations on Syria—and bilateral coordination of military operations—have yielded some concrete initiatives, including a May 2017 agreement among Russia, Turkey, and Iran to establish four "de-escalation zones" in predominantly opposition-held parts of Syria. Coming out of the discussions, Erdoğan announced that Russia and Turkey "have very serious work on our shoulders and a very big responsibility. And I am sure that the steps we take together will change the destiny of the whole region."[85] Russia remains the dominant power in Syria, and Ankara, which previously had a relatively free hand, is forced to coordinate its Syria policies with Moscow.

Despite Erdoğan's optimism, Turkish-Russian cooperation on the Middle East may be tenuous. The accidental February 2017 killing of Turkish soldiers by Russian air strikes in northern Syria demonstrated that incidents can take place when two countries are backing opposing sides in conflict—even if they actively seek to deconflict and even collaborate. The future of regional collaboration could be threatened by conflict end states that do not take into account Turkish interests, including potential territorial empowerment of the PYD Kurds. Beyond Syria, Moscow has lately been seeking to cast itself as a responsible actor in the region to maintain good relations with all the current governments in the Middle East, including Israel—which have welcomed Russian engagement.[86] This contrasts sharply with Turkey's recent support for the Muslim Brotherhood in Egypt and elsewhere, tense relations with Israel, and efforts to back Qatar in its conflict with the other Arab Gulf states. Additionally, if Russia were to find hard evidence of Turkish support for radical Islamist groups—particularly if these groups were connected to insurgent groups in Russia's North Caucasus region—it would represent a major flashpoint for the relationship.

Table 6.1 provides a summary assessment of where Turkish and Russian interests are convergent, divergent, or in conflict. Trade and energy have recently been a core area of cooperation—and the anticipated TurkStream project is likely to further that trend. Given Russia's desire to expand its control over European energy markets, Turkey may need to manage its own ambitions for profit as an energy transit hub. Internally, Turkey will also need to become more comfortable with its own energy dependence on Russia, because the deal's lower gas prices reduce market incentive to diversify energy sources.

---

[85] "Turkey, Russia Steps 'May Influence Middle East,'" *Hürriyet Daily News*, May 3, 2017.

[86] Mark N. Katz, "Russia's Middle East Policy and the Trump Administration," Arab Gulf States Institute in Washington, January 13, 2017; and James Sladden, Becca Wasser, Ben Connable, and Sarah Grand-Clement, *Russian Strategy in the Middle East*, Santa Monica, Calif.: RAND Corporation, PE-236-RC, 2017.

Table 6.1
Alignment of Turkish Interests with Russian Interests

Neighbor or Partner	Converging Interests	Diverging Interests	Conflicting Interests
Russia	• Trade expansion • Energy cooperation (Russian gas supplies; nuclear plant) • Tensions with the EU and West • Arms trade • Illiberalism and authoritarian governance	• Energy transit corridors • Counterterrorism issues • Russian role in the Middle East, the Caucasus, and Central Asia • Relations with the United States	• Endgame and Russian presence in Syria • Russian engagement with the PYD and the YPG • Russian military buildup in the Black Sea • Turkey's NATO membership, especially its missile defense site and other deployments

Conclusion and Implications for the United States

Examination of five key elements of the Russian-Turkish relationship (expanding bilateral trade and energy ties, undermining Western institutions, supporting authoritarianism, preserving regional autonomy in the Black Sea region, and expanding influence in the Middle East) indicates that, although some forces may continue to draw the two countries together in the coming years, there are also significant points of friction and divergent interests. Whether Russia and Turkey are able to reach a new modus vivendi or will continue to muddle through in a mix of cooperation and conflict while managing important differences will likely depend, in large part, on Turkish willingness to acquiesce to expanding Russian ambition in each of the five elements. Even if Turkey is willing to accommodate Russia on many issues, unintended conflict in any one of the five could well derail a long-term rapprochement. Nevertheless, U.S. policymakers should expect Turkey to remain an unpredictable ally that is more willing to work with Russia at cross purposes on certain issues when its shifting national interests dictate.

The developments in the energy relationship between Russia and Turkey run contrary to U.S. interests that Turkey and other European countries reduce their dependence on Russian energy, and they could limit the U.S. goal of developing multiple pipeline routes for transmission of Caspian and Central Asian energy. Although the Russian-Turkish trade relationship has benefited both parties—particularly Turkey—Russia's willingness to use trade sanctions as a punitive tool could lead Turkish exporters to look elsewhere for markets. These concerns and likely economic slowdowns in both countries seem likely to keep total trade volume well below the $100 billion goal.

Russia's desire to contest and undermine Western institutions presents another set of opportunities and potential challenges for the relationship. While frustration with a failed EU membership process and Eurasianist strains within Turkey may fuel near-term cohesion with Russia, long-term strategic alignment would require that Turkey take a permanent turn away from its NATO allies—or at least ensure that it did not side with Western institutions against Russia. This would be a risky course at a time when Russia is increasingly challenging European security norms and flexing its military prowess. Turkish leaders remain wary of Russian intentions and military capabilities and have repeatedly shown an inclination to turn to the United States and NATO when times get rough—even though the response has sometimes been disappointing to Ankara. If Turkey remains closely aligned with NATO policies, military plans, and operations—particularly on Russia's periphery—Russia will remain wary of Turkey as a long-term partner.

A clear trend toward authoritarian rule in both countries has led to mutual support in the face of Western criticism and underscored the role of individual leaders in determining the course of the bilateral relationship. To ensure that this factor continues to contribute positively to the relationship, Erdoğan—assuming he remains in power—would need to continue to personally prioritize his relationship with Putin and avoid the temptation to lash out rhetorically if and when diplomatic crises arise. He might also need to pursue policies that are sensitive to Russian concerns about radicalism in the South Caucasus and independence movements in the North Caucasus. However, as was seen during the shootdown crisis, both leaders' propensity for nationalist rhetoric and an absence of checks on their judgment mean that any bilateral crisis could quickly spiral should either leader believe that a confrontational stance would strengthen his domestic position. In general, this development is damaging to U.S. interests in strengthening democratic institutions in Turkey and combating Russian efforts to undermine democratic institutions in Europe and the United States, and it could reemerge as a future source of friction between the United States and Turkey.

Recent Russian investments in its Black Sea Fleet and territorial gains in the littoral region have tipped the Black Sea balance of power in Russia's favor. Because of its vulnerability to Russian military and economic pressure, Turkey has pursued a balancing strategy between NATO and Russia. This has led to continued bilateral exercises with the Russian Navy in the Black Sea, as well as regular TGS and service staff talks. In light of Russia's desire to assert Black Sea regional hegemony, Turkey would need to accept expanding Russian posture and continue to pursue a cooperative approach to keep the U.S. and NATO presence limited. Such an approach could have tangible implications for U.S. maritime access during a crisis, as was the case following Russia's 2008 invasion of Georgia. Alternatively, Russian expansion of maritime military power in the region could reignite a more zero-sum approach, prompting additional requests from Ankara for NATO attention to the Black Sea.

Russia's efforts to expand its influence in the Middle East have featured increasingly assertive policies in Syria while seeking to maintain good relations with governments across the region. To avoid allowing this to become an area of competition, Turkey would need to accept that Russia's fundamentally different priorities could sometimes lead to policy outcomes that diverge from Turkey's own regional priorities—and ensure that such differences are managed constructively. Such an approach could be challenging, given the history of AKP support to political Islam across the region and deep Turkish concerns about potential Kurdish autonomy. Specifically, Turkey would need to accept Russian support for status quo military leaderships in Egypt and Libya and tread carefully with Islamist groups that Russia deems a security threat. Turkish connection to violent Islamist activity in the Caucasus could prove a deal-breaker for the Russians. Russian support for a Kurdish state on Turkey's borders could send shockwaves through the relationship, although tacit Russian support for the Turkish assault on Afrin, Syria, may indicate that, on this matter, Moscow prioritizes its relationship with Ankara. The overall relationship with Ankara is an important element of Moscow's larger strategy of expanding its influence in the Middle East and challenging the U.S. predominance in the region.

Of the five elements of the relationship, potential competition in the Black Sea and conflicting interests in the Middle East appear most likely to present roadblocks to a deep and enduring partnership between Turkey and Russia. The shootdown crisis of 2015 demonstrated that economic ties, while currently strong, initially did little to constrain diplomatically escalatory steps by increasingly autocratic leaders unencumbered by domestic checks and balances. President Erdoğan's public solicitation of Western support in the Black Sea following the crisis provided evidence of Turkish insecurity with Moscow's naval buildup and instinctive turn toward NATO to counter a perceived threat.

For the United States, warm, though turbulent, ties between Ankara and Moscow have exacerbated fractures in a historically close alliance and raised questions about the future of relations with an ally willing to conduct joint maritime exercises, coordinate military operations in Syria, and purchase air defense systems from a potential NATO adversary. But competing interests and potential flashpoints in Turkey's relations with Russia make it too early to consider this a new paradigm. As one of the few allies to have invoked NATO's collective security commitments in times of duress, Turkey could well solicit Alliance support during a future crisis with Russia, leaving Washington with a set of policy challenges wholly different from those of today.

CHAPTER SEVEN

Turkey's Relations with the Caucasus and Central Asia: Unrealized Ambitions

James Hoobler

The Caucasus has often been an arena for imperial competition among regional powers. The Ottoman, Russian, and Persian empires have been dominant at different points in history, and today their successor states continue to compete for geopolitical influence and economic access. Throughout the Cold War, the Caucasus and Central Asia remained largely closed off to Turkey, as Moscow worked aggressively to undermine pan-Turkic sentiment and links, especially in such countries as Azerbaijan.[1] The independence of former Soviet republics presented new opportunities for Turkish engagement in the region and fed anticipation that Turkey would move to fill some of the vacuum left after the collapse of the USSR. These expectations were unmet, however, and Turkey's engagement in the 1990s and early 2000s remained surprisingly limited.[2] Since then, historical legacies, resource constraints, and contemporary politics have combined and continue to present significant obstacles to Turkish strategy in its eastern neighborhood (see Figure 7.1).[3]

Despite the governing AKP's ambitious aspirations to become a major regional and global power, broader Turkish foreign policy has experienced a series of profound setbacks in recent years. Contentious relations with the EU and stalemated accession talks, disagreements within NATO, squabbles with the United States, and backsliding from democratic norms have all severely strained relations with the West. Turkey's regional policy after the Arab Spring and amid the Syrian civil war has been similarly frustrated. There is some evidence in this context that the Caucasus might present Ankara with an attractive neighborhood for redirected strategic attention, as it appeared to do in the years following the collapse of the Soviet Union.[4] Although the

---

[1] Svetlana Savranskaya and Vladislav Zubok, "Cold War in the Caucasus: Notes and Documents from a Conference," *Cold War International History Project Bulletin*, No. 14/15, Winter 2013–Spring 2014.

[2] Fiona Hill and Ömer Taşpınar, *Russia and Turkey in the Caucasus: Moving Together to Preserve the Status Quo?* Paris: Institut Français des Relations Internationales, Russie.Nei.Visions No. 8, 2006a.

[3] For a fuller discussion of other factors complicating Turkey's post-USSR engagement with Central Asia and the Caucasus, see Larrabee and Lesser, 2003, p. 99.

[4] For a broader discussion of rising schools of international security strategy in Turkey, see Gurcan, 2017c.

Figure 7.1
Map of Turkey, the Caucasus, and Central Asia

region might present a more benign environment for Ankara's engagement than the Middle East does, Turkey's domestic turmoil and ongoing purges of the state bureaucracy will undermine capacity for sustained and coherent leadership, and Turkey's economic slowdown and the deterioration of the rule of law may dampen appetites for investment and eventually trade volume. Additionally, much of Ankara's appeal to Tbilisi and, to a lesser extent, Baku was as a bridge to Euro-Atlantic political and security frameworks. The more decisively Turkey turns its back on these ties, the less useful it is to those in regional governments seeking closer relations with the West. The same is true if Turkey continues to turn to Russia as a security partner.

At the end of the Cold War, then–Turkish President Turgut Özal envisioned rekindling historic economic and cultural ties with the five newly independent Turkic states in Central Asia and the Caucasus (Azerbaijan, Kazakhstan, Kyrgyzstan, Turkmenistan, and Uzbekistan) and opening new trade and energy transit routes, with Turkey potentially serving as a hub of a new Eurasian community. However, during the 1990s and early 2000s, Turkey lacked the resources to advance these goals. The economic, political, and infrastructural ties developed during the Soviet era gave Russia a favored position in Central Asia at that time, and Russia sought to limit Turkish inroads. Moreover, most Central Asian governments were focused on consolidating their sovereignty and national identities and were not eager to trade a Soviet Big Brother for a Turkish one. Over the past decade, China has emerged as the most dynamic trade and investment partner for Central Asian countries, with the capacity to realize its vision of One Belt and One Road as a modern version of the Silk

Road.[5] Indeed, the land component of this vision, the Silk Road Economic Belt concept encompasses billions of dollars of investments in connectivity and infrastructure projects to facilitate China's expansion into new markets and build relationships with states across the region.[6] Although Chinese projects are also viewed with suspicion by many Central Asians, Turkey has neither the strategic vision nor the financial heft to compete with Chinese engagement in the region.

Furthermore, despite the hostility of official rhetoric and frequent provocations, Turkey's relations with Europe, Russia, the Middle East, and the United States will remain higher priorities. Thus, even with any attempts at strategic realignment, the Caucasus and Central Asia will continue to be second- and third-tier theaters for Turkey, respectively.

Domestic Forces Driving Regional Policy

As discussed in Chapter Two, President Erdoğan has sought to co-opt nationalist votes to shore up his majority in Parliament. Courting the MHP has been limited,[7] however, even as Erdoğan has adapted his rhetoric and narrative to more readily incorporate conventional nationalist symbolism.[8] To the extent that the AKP continues to rely more heavily on MHP constituencies for a governing coalition, it is likely that these ethno-nationalist strains of historical ideology will play a more prominent role in narratives of Turkish history and identity—narratives that lend themselves well to expressions of affinity with and overtures to the Caucasus and Central Asia. Indeed, the MHP's manifesto has emphasized the history, culture, and values that Turkey shares with the Caucasus and Central Asia; Turkey's role as a bridge to and leader in these regions; and the commonality of interest and need for increased political and economic cooperation with these neighboring nations.[9] While this historical kinship and Eurasian vision is thus likely to be cited with growing frequency and fervor in the short to medium term, practical shortcomings and the reality of Turkey's geopolitical situation mean that such solidarity is likely to remain as much rhetorical as it is concrete.

---

[5] Victoria Kelly-Clarke, "Why Is Central Asia Dumping Russia for China?" *Global Risks Insights*, May 23, 2016. For the Chinese official exposition of the concept, see China Internet Information Center, "The Silk Road Economic Belt," webpage, undated.

[6] International Crisis Group, *Central Asia's Silk Road Rivalries*, Brussels, Report No. 245, July 2017b. For an assessment of the security implications, see Richard Ghiasy and Jiayi Zhou, *The Silk Road Economic Belt: Considering Security Implications and EU–China Cooperation Prospects*, Stockholm: Stockholm Peace Research Institute, 2017, pp. 19–43.

[7] Blaise Misztal, Nicholas Danforth, and Jessica Michek, *What's Next for Turkey: Authoritarian Stability or Chaos?* Washington D.C.: Bipartisan Policy Center, May 2017.

[8] Nicholas Danforth, "The New Turkey: One Nation, Indivisible, Under God," *War on the Rocks*, June 24, 2017.

[9] Nationalist Movement Party, *Ülkenin Geleceği* [*Future of the Country*], Ankara, November 2015.

Similarly, although Tbilisi and Baku look to Ankara as a partial counterbalance to Moscow's power in the region, Turkey will continue to approach regional security with some circumspection, aware that it cannot afford to be too confrontational with Russia. This was painfully clear to Tbilisi in 2008, when Ankara expressed tepid rhetorical support for Georgia following the Russian invasion of South Ossetia but also sought to balance relations with Russia by advancing a vague regional stability dialogue and accommodating Russian security concerns in the Black Sea by limiting U.S. access and even hosting a Russian commander aboard a Turkish Navy frigate.[10] More-recent developments, detailed in Chapter Six, have likely led Georgian officials to conclude that Turkey has neither the ability nor the intention to forcefully oppose Russian preponderance in the region. Wariness over Moscow's role is not misplaced: Crimea and South Ossetia loom large in recent memory, and Russia continues to assertively exercise hard and soft power in the region, arming both Armenia and Azerbaijan, enhancing and possibly expanding its military presence in Armenia, and occasionally stoking frozen conflicts to ensure that they remain unresolved.[11]

Nevertheless, Turkey remains committed to soft integration in the region and development of an east-west economic and security axis. Georgia and Azerbaijan have cooperated since the 1990s to maintain a corridor to Turkey that has facilitated the development of (1) a range of energy and other infrastructure projects and (2) bilateral and trilateral security cooperation, described later in this chapter.[12] Turkey's trade with Azerbaijan and Georgia has increased substantially over the past two decades. In 1995, Turkey's total annual trade volume was $183.1 million with Azerbaijan and $118.3 million with Georgia. By 2014, this trade had increased to $3.2 billion and almost $1.7 billion, respectively, making Turkey Azerbaijan's fourth-largest and Georgia's second-largest trading partner after the EU as a whole. Baku and Tbilisi do not rank among Turkey's top ten import or export markets, however, which underscores the asymmetry of the countries' economic relations.[13] Turkish companies have also

---

[10] See Aliriza, 2008. Erdoğan advanced a Caucasus Cooperation and Stability Pact, which included the two combatants plus Armenia and Azerbaijan, as the main element of Turkish policy. The idea, consistent with Turkey's "zero problems" strategy at that time, gained no support from either Moscow or the Caucasus governments. As noted in Chapter Six, following the 2008 Russian invasion of South Ossetia, Turkish authorities denied a U.S. request to transit two hospital ships, which exceeded Montreux Convention weight limits, through the Turkish Straits, but the authorities did approve the passage of three smaller U.S. military vessels to provide humanitarian relief to Georgia.

[11] Ereli, 2016.

[12] See Andrew C. Kuchins, Jeffrey Mankoff, and Oliver Backes, *Azerbaijan in a Reconnecting Eurasia: Foreign Economic and Security Interests*, Washington, D.C.: Center for Strategic and International Studies, June 2016, pp. 9–10.

[13] European Commission, Directorate-General for Trade, "European Union, Trade in Goods with Turkey," June 11, 2018.

undertaken major construction projects in Azerbaijan and been significant investors in the tourism and manufacturing sectors.[14]

Several semi-overlapping, high-level dialogue platforms, trade initiatives, and regional cooperation mechanisms have emerged in the Black Sea and Caucasus region since the end of the Cold War, some of which have been heavier on process than substance.[15] Most prominent among them is BSEC, a Turkish government initiative launched in 1992 with the goal of fostering a new era of economic cooperation, regional integration, and stability. The member countries, including several energy suppliers and transit countries, had realized significant growth between 2000 and the 2008 global financial crisis, driven largely by expanding trade with EU countries.[16] Although BSEC and affiliated bodies have contributed to the expansion of intraregional commerce, divergent political and economic interests of member states have limited integration, and the institution played no role in either the Georgia or the Ukraine conflicts. Ahead of Turkey's hosting of the 25th BSEC summit in Istanbul in 2017, government media highlighted the organization's potential for Turkey in light of the "all-time low" in relations with the EU and Turkey's "search for alternatives to the EU."[17] However, the heterogeneity of regional economies, unresolved conflicts, and competing Russian economic integration efforts seem likely to thwart those aspirations.

Russia has sought to use the Commonwealth of Independent States and the Eurasian Economic Union to promote regional economic integration with post-Soviet states and to reestablish a dominant sphere of influence in the region. The Collective Security Treaty Organization (CSTO), a military alliance of six post-Soviet states (including Armenia, Belarus, Kazakhstan, Kyrgyzstan, Russia, and Tajikistan), has also been used by Moscow as a mechanism for advancing this agenda in the security domain, including for regional peacekeeping missions.[18]

Russia has also used frozen conflicts in the region to reinforce these divisions, particularly the conflict between Armenia and Azerbaijan in Nagorno-Karabakh. The Organization for Security and Co-operation in Europe's Minsk Process, launched in 1994 and chaired by Russia, France, and the United States, has failed to resolve the

---

[14] Kemal Kirişci and Andrew Moffatt, "Turkey and the South Caucasus: An Opportunity for Soft Regionalism?" *Regional Security Issues: 2015*, April 25, 2016, pp. 74–75. All trade figures in this paragraph are in current dollars.

[15] For a list of the various forums, see Commission on the Black Sea, *A 2020 Vision for the Black Sea Region*, Gütersloh, Germany: Bertelsmann Stiftung, May 2010, pp. 45–48.

[16] Ludwig Schulz and Colin Dürkop, "The Organization of the Black Sea Economic Cooperation (BSEC)—A Mechanism for Integration in a Geopolitically Sensitive Area," Konrad-Adenauer-Stiftung, Country Report, November 10, 2014, pp. 3–4, 8.

[17] "Black Sea Economic Cooperation Organization: Turkey's Third Option," *Daily Sabah*, December 15, 2016.

[18] There was speculation in 2017 that CSTO exercises in Russia, Armenia, and Kazhakstan were preparing forces for a peacekeeping mission in Syria (Joshua Kucera, "As Russian Military Exercises in Armenia, Is Syria on Its Mind?" *Eurasianet*, October 10, 2017).

conflict between Armenia and Azerbaijan. There is little prospect of a peaceful settlement any time soon, and there have been recent flare-ups in violence along the lines of contact. Although Turkey is a member of the Minsk Group, it has criticized the platform for being too slow in helping Azerbaijan recover its lost territory, and Ankara has played a secondary role in the negotiations.[19] Over the past five years, Turkey has increased military and defense industrial cooperation with Azerbaijan, discussed further later in this chapter.[20]

Turkey has also hoped to facilitate the transfer of Turkmen and Central Asian gas to Europe across the Caspian and through Azerbaijan, lessening European reliance on Russian gas and undermining Russian energy leverage. Thus far, however, these hopes have been unmet: The only pipelines out of Turkmenistan are heading east to China, and plans for the Trans-Caspian Gas Pipeline have stalled due to costs, declining relevance and European demand, concerns about Turkmen reserves, and legal disputes over the status of the Caspian arising from Russian and Iranian obstruction.[21] Russia has also pressured Turkmenistan by backing out of contracts and offering more-favorable terms to its neighbors, and Ashgabat's situation is worsened by its debt to China, the probable loss of Iran as a gas customer, and the likely insurmountable hurdles facing a proposed Turkmenistan-Afghanistan-Pakistan-India pipeline.[22] The obstacles facing the Trans-Caspian pipeline are thus profound, undermining Turkish efforts to connect Caspian and Central Asian gas to European markets.

As discussed in Chapter Six, Moscow has thwarted development of the Trans-Caspian pipeline; offered commercial incentives to enhance bilateral energy cooperation with Azerbaijan, Kazakhstan, Turkmenistan, and Uzbekistan; and used its control over major export routes to ensure energy dominance and force price concessions.[23]

Turkey and the Caucasus

Azerbaijan and Turkey: One Nation, Two States

Strong cultural, linguistic, and historical ties have contributed to the close political and security alliance between Ankara and Baku. Turkey views Azerbaijan as a trade and energy partner and link to the resource-rich Caspian and Turkic Central Asia, while Azerbaijan looks to Turkey as a patron, major ally, and link to the Euro-Atlantic world.

---

[19] Kuchins, Mankoff, and Backes, 2016, p. 34.

[20] Joshua Kucera, "Azerbaijan Has Advantage over Armenia in U.S. Military Aid," *Eurasianet*, May 17, 2016a.

[21] Elena Kosolapova, "Some in Europe Still Interested in Trans-Caspian Gas Pipeline—Expert," *Trend News Agency*, May 19, 2017.

[22] Pannier, 2017; and Paul Stronski, "Turkmenistan at Twenty-Five: The High Price of Authoritarianism," Carnegie Endowment for International Peace, January 30, 2017.

[23] Weiss et al., 2012; Pannier, 2016; Pannier, 2017.

These ties are as strong on the popular level as they are politically, and polls show that more than 70 percent of Turks view Azerbaijan as their nation's best friend.[24]

While eschewing substantive liberal reforms, Baku has sought closer ties with the West to balance Russian support for Armenia and regional hegemony. In this respect, Turkey's illiberal backsliding may lead it to sense more affinity with Azerbaijan, because both countries seek to reap selective benefits of political and economic alignment with the West while opting out of the democratic norms associated with full integration. This like-mindedness, however, is somewhat qualified by the AKP's growing religiosity and social conservatism—inclinations that Azerbaijan's secular government does not share.

Ankara's relations with Moscow have been tested in recent years. Although the initial crises following the downing of the Russian jet in late 2015 and assassination of the Russian ambassador to Turkey in late 2016 were subsequently addressed, they did highlight to Ankara the importance of diversified energy sources, adding urgency to the acceleration of domestic capacity and partnerships with Azerbaijan, such as the Trans-Anatolian Natural Gas Pipeline.[25]

More generally, such energy and connectivity projects continue to form the broader bedrock of bilateral ties between Baku and Ankara, because the projects tend to align with the countries' geostrategic aspirations and economic incentives. Public and private Azerbaijani firms also continue to invest extensively in strategic sectors of the Turkish economy, further solidifying ties and influence.[26]

Though initially caught somewhat off guard by the progress of the Zurich Protocols in 2009, Baku moved quickly to ensure that Ankara did not normalize relations with Yerevan in the absence of a satisfactory resolution to the Nagorno-Karabakh dispute. The restoration of the lost provinces of Nagorno-Karabakh remains the lodestar of Azerbaijan's foreign policy, and the issue remains the biggest stumbling block to regional development and long-term stability. Despite whatever peacemaking ambitions Turkey might once have had,[27] its ability to serve as a mediator is obviously complicated by its own fraught history with Armenia.[28]

Because of Moscow's influential role with respect to the Nagorno-Karabakh issue and in an effort to play a regional peacemaker, Azerbaijan has sought to balance relations with NATO members and Russia. The Azeris joined NATO's Partnership for

[24] "Fight Against Terror Number One Foreign Policy Issue in Turkey, Says Poll," *Hürriyet Daily News*, July 21, 2017.

[25] Mehmet Cetingulec, "Can Turkey Break Its Russian Gas Habit?" *Al-Monitor*, April 7, 2016.

[26] Nuran Erkul, "SOCAR's Investments in Turkey to Exceed $18 Billion," Anadolu Agency, December 2016.

[27] Ahmet Davutoğlu, "Turkey's Mediation: Critical Reflections from the Field," *Middle East Policy*, Vol. 20, No. 1, Spring 2013.

[28] "Turkey's Mediation in Nagorno-Karabakh Peace Process Ruled Out—Armenian MP," *Tert*, November 8, 2016.

Peace in 1994 and have pursued limited military training and technology coopera-tion with Turkey since then. Baku also signed the Collective Security Treaty with nine other post-Soviet states but did not agree to its extension in 1999. Dissatisfac-tion with the Minsk Process and deepening security cooperation between Russia and Armenia—including a 2010 agreement that extends Moscow's lease on its military base in Gyumri, Armenia, to 2044—moved the Azeris to deepen cooperation with Turkey. In response to a bilateral defense agreement signed between Moscow and Yere-van a couple of months before that 2010 agreement, Baku and Ankara signed a sym-bolic but somewhat vague Agreement on Strategic Partnership and Mutual Support in late 2010, in which they pledged to deploy "all possible means" to assist one another in the case of armed aggression and pursue more combined exercises and expanded arma-ments cooperation.[29] This did not, however, lead to deployments of Turkish troops on Azerbaijani soil, reflecting both countries' desire to not provoke Baku's neighbors excessively. Georgia also participates in some aspects of this cooperation, including tri-lateral security consultations and initiatives to protect critical infrastructure.[30]

Armenia

Armenia's bilateral relationship with Turkey is dominated not just by the 1992–1994 war over Nagorno-Karabakh but also by the legacies of 1915. At the end of World War I, the Turkish government massacred or forcibly expelled most of the Armenians living in the Ottoman Empire, and Armenia, other governments, and most historians consider these events to have amounted to a genocide.[31] Historical memory in both countries has since remained highly sensitive and politicized, and nationalist politics have continued to complicate hopes for resolution and closure around the incidents.[32]

Following a limited opening in 2008, the two governments negotiated bilateral protocols in Zurich in October 2009. These Zurich Protocols set out a pathway for reestablishing formal diplomatic relations, opening the neighbors' shared border, and creating a joint history commission to address the issue of the Armenian genocide,

---

[29] Shahin Abbasov, "Azerbaijan-Turkey Military Pact Signals Impatience with Minsk Talks—Analysts," *Eurasianet*, January 2011.

[30] Tamaz Papuashvili, "The Future of Azerbaijani-Turkish Military Cooperation," Meydan TV, May 22, 2017; Kuchins, Mankoff, and Backes, 2016, pp. 14–15; and Samuel Ramani, "Why the Russia-Azerbaijan Alliance Is Weaker Than It Looks," *Huffington Post*, August 23, 2017.

[31] Fiona Hill, Kemal Kirişci, and Andrew Moffatt, "Armenia and Turkey: From Normalization to Reconcilia-tion," *Turkish Policy Quarterly*, Vol. 13, No. 4, Winter 2015.

[32] Some contemporaneous analysis suggested that Moscow cultivated Armenian agitation against Turkey in the final years of the USSR, ensuring that the issue remained central to troubled relations between the two countries. See, for example, Paul B. Henze, *Georgia and Armenia: Troubled Independence*, Santa Monica, Calif.: RAND Corporation, P-7924, 1995.

but they were never ratified.[33] The 2015 centennial highlighted the ongoing relevance of this dispute: On the same day as Yerevan's formal anniversary observance, Ankara held commemorations of the Ottoman Empire's success in the Gallipoli Campaign during World War I, leading to dueling remembrances and the speculation by some that Turkey was seeking to distract from the Armenian ceremony. This suspicion was expressed candidly in Yerevan and was at least partly responsible for then–Armenian President Serzh Sargsyan's decision to withdraw the 2009 Zurich Protocols from parliamentary consideration.[34] Though already then stalled, the talks had been part of an initially promising effort at Turkish-Armenian diplomatic normalization that had run aground largely over Azerbaijan's protestations that the protocols did not precondition the restoration of diplomatic ties on the resolution of the Nagorno-Karabakh conflict and on Armenian demands regarding the designation of the events of 1915. Although the Turkish government has made some conciliatory statements around the 100th anniversary of 1915 and formally expresses its willingness to solve the ongoing border closure and blockade dating to the Nagorno-Karabakh war,[35] neither dispute appears near solution, and bilateral ties remain suspended. The role of the Armenian diaspora and nationalist politics in these issues has hardened Yerevan's position and made pragmatic diplomacy difficult, which complicates Armenia's efforts to alleviate its economic and strategic isolation.[36]

For its part, Ankara continues to link the restoration of diplomatic ties with Yerevan to "improvement" in Armenian-Azerbaijani relations,[37] and the resumption of sporadic violence in April 2016 and January 2017 along the line of contact in the disputed region suggests that such progress is unlikely in the near future. Indeed, the security situation has declined markedly since 2016, and observers warn that the likelihood of escalation has increased significantly.[38] Turkey remains closely aligned with

---

[33] Republic of Turkey and Republic of Armenia, "Protocol on Development of Relations Between the Republic of Armenia and the Republic of Turkey," October 10, 2009a; and Republic of Turkey and Republic of Armenia, "Protocol on the Establishment of Diplomatic Relations Between the Republic of Turkey and the Republic of Armenia," October 10, 2009b.

[34] Erik Davtyan, "Armenia Recalls the Zurich Protocols," *Eurasia Daily Monitor*, Vol. 12, No. 40, March 4, 2015.

[35] "Erdoğan Marks Armenian Dead from 1915 Events in Message," *Daily Sabah*, April 25, 2017; and Republic of Turkey Ministry of Foreign Affairs, "Turkey's Relations with Southern Caucasus Countries," webpage, undated-e.

[36] Emil Sanamyan, "The Armenian Diaspora and Armenia: A New Relationship?" *Eurasianet*, November 14, 2016c.

[37] Republic of Turkey Ministry of Foreign Affairs, "Relations Between Turkey and Armenia," webpage, undated-c.

[38] International Crisis Group, *Nagorno-Karabakh's Gathering War Clouds*, Brussels, Report No. 244, June 1, 2017a.

Azerbaijan,[39] and growing trilateral defense cooperation among Ankara, Baku, and Tbilisi has led to increasing concern in Yerevan.[40] Armenia also watches economic slumps and political turmoil in Turkey and Azerbaijan with unease, fearing that instability in its unfriendly neighbors could increase chances of conflict arising from resurgent nationalism.[41]

Armenia's economic and political isolation in the region following the Nagorno-Karabakh conflict has left it heavily dependent on Russia for trade, energy, and security. This reliance is both evidenced and compounded by Armenian participation in the Eurasian Economic Union and CSTO,[42] despite attempts to balance engagement with the West and hedge against full dependence on Russia. As elsewhere in the neighborhood of the Commonwealth of Independent States, Moscow's policy toward Yerevan involves a heavy mix of inducement and coercion and the maintenance of political, economic, and security leverage over its former satellites. Turkey's attempt at normalization with Armenia in 2009 miscalculated the salience of several factors in the regional balance, including Russia's determination that Armenia's strategic vulnerability remain acute.

This exposure is increased not just because Eurasian Economic Union and CSTO membership are designed to be exclusive of broader Western integration but also because Armenia has remained under a partial economic blockade since the end of its war with Azerbaijan in 1994, with both the Turkish and Azerbaijani borders closed. Armenia's only open borders are with Iran to the south and Georgia to the north. Although Armenia's bilateral trade with both countries has grown in recent years, it remains limited. Yerevan is seeking to serve as a broker for Iranian transit trade with the Eurasian Economic Union; however, it faces competition from Baku, and Tbilisi wants concessions from Russia on the breakaway issues before helping Armenia develop this corridor.[43] Armenia's economic isolation is thus compounded by Iran's economic constraints and the volatility of Georgia's relations with Russia.

Armenia's defense ties with Russia also have continued to deepen in recent years, including the sale of a joint air defense system and Iskander short-range ballistic missiles, as well as the establishment of joint ground forces in late 2016.[44] Although the

---

[39] Ercan Gurses, "Turkey Stands by Azerbaijan in Nagorno-Karabakh Conflict: Davutoglu," Reuters, April 5, 2016.

[40] Fuad Shahbazov, "Azerbaijan-Turkey-Georgia: A Geopolitical Axis or an Accidental Alliance?" *Eurasia Daily Monitor*, Vol. 14, No. 75, June 7, 2017.

[41] Paul Stronski, "Armenia at Twenty-Five: A Rough Ride," Carnegie Endowment for International Peace, December 7, 2016.

[42] "Armenia and Russia: Stuck with Each Other," *The Economist*, March 20, 2015.

[43] Bradley Jardine, "Armenia and Azerbaijan Compete to Attract Iranian Cargo," *Eurasianet*, April 9, 2018.

[44] Hasmik Mkrtchyan and Margarita Antidze, "Armenia Ratifies Agreement on Joint Air-Defense System with Russia," Reuters, June 30, 2016; Emil Sanamyan, "Armenian Parade Reveals Iskander Ballistic Missiles," *Jane's*

air defense system apparently does not cover Nagorno-Karabakh and the joint ground forces remain operationally untested, these efforts clearly represent an attempt to build on the arms sales and troop presence that have been the foundation of Russia's security relationship with Armenia since independence. Indeed, a weapon sale amounting to $200 million was announced in early 2016, which included rocket launchers, anti-tank guided missiles, anti-tank rockets, man-portable air defense systems, and electronic warfare systems, as well as upgrades to various vehicles and tanks.[45] Furthermore, some 5,000 Russian troops are posted at the Russian 102nd military base at Gyumri, a short distance from the Turkish border and the city of Kars in Turkey's northeast.[46]

Yerevan's isolation is worsened by major infrastructure and connectivity projects bypassing Armenia, including the Baku-Tbilisi-Ceyhan pipeline,[47] the Baku-Tbilisi-Kars railway,[48] and the International North-South Transport Corridor.[49] Rival north-south infrastructure projects, such as the proposed gas pipeline linking Georgia and Iran through Armenia, have sputtered,[50] failing to relieve the country's economic seclusion.

Georgia

Turkey values Georgia as a trade and energy partner and a crucial link to Azerbaijan, through which it reaches the Caspian, Central Asia, and China. Georgia's primary geostrategic goal for some time has been NATO and EU accession and proactive alignment with broader Euro-Atlantic institutions. Georgia traditionally saw Turkey as a link to this order and a bridge to Europe and the West. This has also been confluent with Georgia's energy and trade strategy, in which Georgia has sought to maximize its role as an east-west transit corridor in such initiatives as the Interstate Oil and Gas Transportation to Europe program, the Central Asian Regional Economic Cooperation program, the Trans-Anatolian Natural Gas Pipeline, the Transport Corridor

---

Defence Weekly, September 23, 2016b; and Eduard Abrahamyan, "Russia and Armenia Establish Joint Ground Forces," *Central Asia Caucasus Analyst*, December 2016.

[45] Emil Sanamyan, "Russia Details USD200 Million Arms Sale to Armenia," *Jane's Defence Weekly*, February 19, 2016a.

[46] Nikolai Litovkin, "Russia and Armenia to Create Joint Defense Force in Caucasus," *UPI*, November 16, 2016.

[47] Svante E. Cornell and Fariz Ismailzade, "The Baku-Tbilisi-Ceyhan Pipeline: Implications for Azerbaijan," in S. Frederick Starr and Svante E. Cornell, eds., *The Baku-Tbilisi-Ceyhan Pipeline: Oil Window to the West*, Washington, D.C.: Central Asia-Caucasus Institute and Silk Road Studies Program, 2005.

[48] Vasili Rukhadze, "Completion of Baku–Tbilisi–Kars Railway Project Postponed Again," *Eurasia Daily Monitor*, Vol. 13, No. 42, March 2, 2016.

[49] Zaur Shiriyev, "Will the North–South Transport Corridor Overshadow the Baku–Tbilisi–Kars Railway?" *Eurasia Daily Monitor*, Vol. 14, No. 53, April 24, 2017.

[50] Ilgar Gurbanov, "Armenia Seeks to Boost Its Role in the Iran-Georgia Gas Talks," *Central Asia-Caucasus Analyst*, October 17, 2016.

Europe Caucasus Asia program, the Baku-Tbilisi-Ceyhan pipeline, and the Baku-Tbilisi-Kars railway.[51]

Ministers from both countries also work together closely in such forums as the High Level Strategic Cooperation Council (a bilateral forum) and trilateral meeting mechanisms with Azerbaijan. These relations add high-level impetus to working-level diplomatic and defense coordination, strong trade and investment links, and regular business interaction. The three governments initiated trilateral meetings of defense ministers in 2012 and have held regular talks among their chiefs of defense staff and several field training exercises. At high-level meetings in Georgia in May and October 2017, the three agreed to expand defense ties, including additional combined exercises and cooperation in defense industry, counterterrorism, military education, and military medicine.[52] In June 2017, special forces from the three countries conducted a field training exercise in Georgia called Caucasian Eagle, which focused on protecting regional energy pipelines and rail lines.[53] Unlike the frequently negative coverage of Ankara's Western allies, the coverage from government-controlled media in Turkey is often very positive about cooperation with Georgia, emphasizing the commonality of interest and partnership between the countries.[54]

Although these extensive and diverse ties have helped Turkish-Georgian relations remain strong on multiple levels, Georgia has also been disappointed to realize that

---

[51] Specifically,

- The Interstate Oil and Gas Transportation to Europe program was a technical assistance initiative between 1996 and 2016 aimed at enhancing energy cooperation, security, and market harmonization between the EU and the regional states of the Caspian and Black seas.
- The Central Asian Regional Economic Cooperation program is a regional forum created to promote the economic integration of Central Asian states.
- The Trans-Anatolian Natural Gas Pipeline brings natural gas from the Shah Deniz 2 field and elsewhere in Azerbaijan to Turkey and Europe as part of the Southern Gas Corridor.
- The Transport Corridor Europe Caucasus Asia initiative is a regional effort intended to promote economic dialogue around trade and transportation in the Black Sea, the South Caucasus, and Central Asia.
- The Baku-Tbilisi-Ceyhan pipeline carries oil from the Azeri-Chirag-Deepwater Gunashli field and condensate from Shah Deniz along nearly 1,800 km to Ceyhan on Turkey's Mediterranean coast. There is also a South Caucasus gas pipeline—also known as the Baku-Tbilisi-Erzurum pipeline—that follows the same land corridor.
- The Baku-Tbilisi-Kars railway, which became operational in October 2017, connects the Caspian port of Baku to Turkey's east and beyond to Europe. It will have an initial capacity to transport 1 million passengers and 5 million tons of freight a year ("Baku-Tbilisi-Kars Railway Line Officially Launched," Radio Free Europe/Radio Liberty, October 30, 2017).

[52] Michael Hikari Cecire, "Georgia-Turkey-Azerbaijan Cooperation: Pragmatism Proves Durable Formula," *Eurasianet*, June 1, 2017; and "Georgia, Azerbaijan and Turkey Signed an Agreement on Military Cooperation," *Front News International*, October 18, 2017.

[53] Shahbazov, 2017; and Bakhtiyar Hasanov, "Caucasus Eagle 2017 Military Drills Underway," CBC News Azerbaijan, June 10, 2017.

[54] "Turkey, Azerbaijan, Georgia Unity Help Regional Stability: Experts," *Daily Sabah*, June 6, 2017.

Turkey, while always an indispensable neighbor, will not be a reliable security partner against Russia and will likely be progressively less helpful as a link to the West.

In addition, bilateral ties are somewhat strained by lower-level concerns. For example, some Georgians resent perceived Turkish economic dominance, and the presence of the others' minority populations and cultural and religious heritage sites in each country leads to occasional tension. Turkey's continued contact with the de facto government of separatist Abkhazia remains a sore point in Georgia, as well.[55]

Turkey and Central Asia

Turkish policy toward Central Asia has gone through several relatively distinct periods. After maintaining a largely deferential posture toward Moscow during the Cold War, Ankara saw opportunities for expansion into the region after the fall of the Soviet Union, partly enabled by ethno-linguistic ties and a sense of historical connection. When the Central Asian countries gained independence after 1991, Turkish leaders envisioned reviving cultural and economic links among Turkic peoples and forming a Turkic Union that would enhance the sovereignty and development of their new partners and expand Turkey's influence. President Özal convened a summit of the presidents of the five Turkic-speaking states in 1992 to initiate this cooperation. There were nine more gatherings that issued declarations of goodwill and openness to cooperation, but they produced few concrete results.

By the time of the AKP's rise to power in the early 2000s, Turkey's ambitions in Central Asia moderated in the face of a reassertive Russia, and Ankara increasingly prioritized the more proximate Caucasus and Caspian littoral states.[56] Turkey's diminished attentions in the 2000s may also have been due, in part, to the AKP's prioritization of religious over ethnic affinity, leading to greater focus on the Middle East, where Islam found greater political and social salience.[57] The coolness of Turkey's relations with the region may also have resulted from the reluctance of the Turkic Central Asian states to exchange Soviet tutelage for that of a Turkish "elder brother."[58]

At the 2009 summit of the presidents of the Turkic-speaking states, the presidents of Azerbaijan, Kazakhstan, Kyrgyzstan, and Turkey signed the Nakhchivan Agreement, which established the Cooperation Council of Turkic Speaking States to

---

[55] Vasili Rukhadze, "Defying Georgia, Turkey Gradually Cultivates Its Influence in Separatist Abkhazia," *Eurasia Daily Monitor*, Vol. 12, No. 177, October 1, 2015.

[56] Unal Cevikoz, *Turkey in a Reconnecting Eurasia: Foreign Economic and Security Interests*, Washington, D.C.: Center for Strategic and International Studies, April 2016.

[57] M. K. Kaya, "The 'Eastern Dimension' in Turkish Foreign Policy Grows," *Turkey Analyst*, Vol. 2, No. 18, October 2009.

[58] Kaya, 2009.

promote trade and investment among member states (Turkmenistan and Uzbekistan chose not to join). While Özal's vision has not been realized and these summits have not undertaken grand initiatives, the Central Asian governments do appear to value them as another forum where they have equal standing with a leading developed country in the context of deepening geopolitical competition in the region between Russia and China.[59]

The Turkish government has provided considerable development assistance to Central Asian countries, and several nongovernmental organizations, including the Gülen movement, have been active in promoting education and civil society. Since 1992, the Turkish government has provided the Central Asian states with billions of dollars of credit and financing support through TİKA, which was founded with the express purpose of supporting development in these "ancestral lands." TİKA's assistance supported economic, social, and cultural programs in its early years and, since 1995, has concentrated on education and culture.[60] Overall, Turkish official development assistance has grown substantially between 2002 and 2015, and total grants to the five Central Asian states totaled $265 million in 2015.[61] Turkey is not the only economic player in the region, however, and Turkish engagement is heavily outweighed by Chinese investment. Beijing's trade with Uzbekistan was worth $3 billion in 2015, and its investment in Kazakhstan reached nearly $24 million in the same year. China's military aid and energy investment in Turkmenistan has also been profound, and energy ties in other Central Asian countries have grown similarly.[62]

Turkey's relations with the Central Asian states have also ebbed and flowed in response to Ankara's relations with Moscow. The Central Asian states continue to pursue a delicate balancing act in their own relations with Moscow. During the 2015–2016 crisis in Turkish-Russian relations following the Turkish downing of a Russian jet, Central Asian governments appeared concerned that they too could be subject to sanctions. To Ankara's dismay, at a December 2015 summit of the Commonwealth of Independent States in Moscow, the Central Asian governments joined other members in calling on Turkey to apologize to Russia for the incident. Moscow took other actions to undermine Turkey's relations with Central Asian countries, including suspending negotiations with Ankara on establishing a free-trade zone with the Eurasian Economic Union and freezing transit permits to Turkish truckers, which disrupted Turkish exports to Central Asia.[63]

---

[59] Alim Bayaliyev, "The Turkic Council: Will the Turks Finally Unite?" *Central Asia-Caucasus Analyst*, February 19, 2014.

[60] TİKA, "About Us," webpage, undated.

[61] TİKA, *Turkish Development Assistance Report 2015*, Ankara, 2015.

[62] Kelly-Clarke, 2016.

[63] Zülfikar Doğan, "First the Middle East, Now Central Asia Slipping Away from Turkey," *Al-Monitor*, January 6, 2016a.

Turkey has also pursued modest bilateral security and defense cooperation with several Central Asian governments, particularly Kazakhstan and Kyrgyzstan. Hundreds of military personnel from have been trained in Turkey, and Ankara has supported various law enforcement training efforts.[64] Turkish military sales to Central Asia are relatively modest, however, and Russia and Israel are much bigger suppliers. With equal funding from their two governments, the Turkish defense company Aselsan concluded a $44 million agreement in 2013 with Kazakhstan Engineering to co-produce military equipment, including thermal imaging and night vision devices for export, and the companies have been seeking contracts in helicopter maintenance.[65] Turkey has also provided $13 million in military aid to Kyrgyzstan.

Turkish cooperation with Central Asian militaries is also pursued in multilateral settings. Turkey hosts one of the six NATO Partnership for Peace training centers, where Central Asian forces have engaged in exercises. Turkey also contributes in the NATO-led exercise Steppe Eagle, which involves NATO and Central Asian partner militaries and takes place in Kazakhstan, despite its membership in the CSTO.[66] Although these areas of cooperation and exchange contribute to some linkages, they are heavily outweighed by Russian preponderance in the region's security architecture.

Table 7.1 provides a summary assessment of where Turkish interests are convergent, divergent, or in conflict with those of states in the Caucasus and Central Asia.

Table 7.1
Alignment of Turkish Interests with Caucasian and Central Asian Interests

Neighbor or Partner	Converging Interests	Diverging Interests	Conflicting Interests
Caucasus	• Development of connectivity and infrastructure for trade and energy • Facilitation of wider economic links with Europe • Turkey's alignment with Azerbaijan on the Nagorno-Karabakh conflict	• Baku's and Tbilisi's efforts for closer political and security ties with Europe • Georgia's desire for stronger support against Russia • Turkish deference to Russia in the Black Sea region	• Differences between Turkey and Armenia on the Nagorno-Karabakh conflict and whether to refer to Turkey's actions in 1915 as genocide • Armenian provision of military basing to Russia
Central Asia	• Some trade and development ties • Minor security cooperation	• Alignment with Russia • Turkic integration limited by Central Asian nations' quest to deepen national identity	• Official secularism versus Islamism

---

[64] Ryskeldi Satke, Casey Michel, and Sertaç Korkmaz, "Turkey in Central Asia: Turkic Togetherness?" *The Diplomat*, November 28, 2014.

[65] Bilal Khan, "Kazakhstan Aselsan Engineering Begins Posting Exports," *Quwa Defence News and Analysis Group*, February 1, 2017.

[66] Özge Nur Öğütcü, "The Current State of Relations Between Kazakhstan-Turkey," Avrasya İncelemeleri Merkezi, Analysis No. 2017/29, September 13, 2017.

Conclusion and Implications for the United States

Potential trajectories of Turkish involvement in the Caucasus and Central Asia can be grouped into three broad scenarios.

First, continued erosion of ties with the West and a frustrated policy toward the Middle East and North Africa could lead Turkey to turn eastward, reprioritizing its neighborhood and investing in leadership with the states of the Caucasus and Turkic Central Asia. This scenario might see ambitious Turkish courtship of economic partnerships and a reemphasis of pan-Turkic culture that would appeal to resurgent nationalisms and shared history while playing to Turkey's regional strengths and strategic geography to effectively exploit opportunities in trade and energy development.

A second scenario could see a moderately increased level of Turkish outreach, characterized by constrained and limited commitment and uneven appetite for new engagement. This reorientation would see mixed success, with its efficacy undermined by structural factors, inconsistent execution, persistently low oil prices, and a somewhat impaired capacity for strategic planning.

A third scenario could see a Caucasus and Central Asia policy of deep neglect and inertia, in which Turkey is consumed by domestic instability and successive crises and loses interest and capacity to achieve this strategic vision in its diplomacy. Hamstrung by political infighting and micromanagement, a purged and sidelined foreign policy apparatus would be incapable of sustaining a coherent policy or effective engagement.

There is little historical or present evidence to suggest the likelihood of the first scenario. Turkey's ambitions in these regions were disappointed even during the relatively permissive and opportune 1990s, and there is little reason to expect more success as Turkey's geostrategic position and relevant relationships have become only more complex in the decades since.

Under current circumstances, the second scenario is most probable in light of Turkey's current trajectory, in which repeated setbacks and miscalculations have undermined Ankara's regional strategy and tempered its aspirations. Increasing descent into the third scenario also remains a significant possibility if Turkey's domestic climate continues to deteriorate and the national security establishment continues to suffer from politicization and the sustained loss of human capital.

As is evident in Table 7.1, Turkey's relations with the Caucasus and Central Asia will likely remain secondary to its ties with Russia and the West. Given the extent to which Ankara's political and economic links with its eastern neighbors have been built around connectivity to Europe, their relevance will likely decline further if Turkey's ability to bridge East and West continues to diminish.

Nevertheless, Turkey's ongoing commitment to advancing integration among the South Caucasus states through measured security cooperation with Georgia and Azerbaijan is confluent with U.S. and European interests in the region because it helps bolster the sovereignty and independence of these states. U.S. and Turkish interests also remain aligned insofar as both still wish to see Turkey become an increasingly important and strategic partner for European energy needs and grow in its role as an east-west economic corridor.

Turkey's continued, though limited, engagement in Central Asia broadly supports U.S. strategic interests, as articulated in the 2017 U.S. National Security Strategy, of helping states in the region strengthen their integration into the global economy, resist domination by Russia and China, and support global counterterrorism efforts.[67] The development assistance provided by the Turkish government and various non-governmental organizations, along with growing commercial trade, investment, and construction projects, can help diversify and broaden Central Asian economies and their foreign policy orientations. Such broadening can then contribute to political stability and a gradual lessening of the nations' diplomatic reliance on Russia and China.

Turkey also engages with its Central Asian partners in modest bilateral security and defense cooperation efforts, supports NATO Partnership for Peace exercises, and assists in the training of Central Asian military and police forces. To the extent that these contribute to the professionalization of these forces and their competence as responsible security actors, these efforts will also be positive and constructive. Turkey will not be an effective partner in encouraging democratic reforms in the Caucasus and Central Asia, however, and Ankara's approach to its southern border during much of the Syrian civil war suggests that partnering in counterterror efforts may not be a high priority in its engagement with Central Asian states.

Finally, Ankara's long-standing political and cultural ties to Afghanistan are likely to ensure its continued involvement in the NATO Resolute Support mission in Afghanistan, as discussed in Chapter Eight.

Ultimately, although Turkish engagement in the Caucasus and Central Asia faces profound obstacles, these are regions where most U.S. and Turkish interests are broadly aligned, and the United States will seek to encourage Turkish success and the positive trends noted in this chapter. However, Ankara will continue to be considerate of the fact that the regions are more central to the security calculations of Moscow than those of Washington and that Russia remains more willing and able to bring to bear sustained pressure on its neighboring regions.

---

[67] White House, *National Security Strategy of the United States of America*, Washington, D.C., December 2017.

CHAPTER EIGHT

Turkey's Relations with Europe, the European Union, and NATO: Reaching an Inflection Point

Magdalena Kirchner and Stephen J. Flanagan

EU governments have long viewed Turkey not only as one of the Union's most important neighbors and trading partners but also as a membership candidate whose strategic relevance had been reconfirmed in recent years by the dramatically increased challenges of migration and foreign terrorist transit. The question of whether Turkey is a part, partner, or neighbor of Europe has been highly contested on both sides. Hopes that EU membership would resolve this issue were frustrated by an accession process that has stalled since 2005. Given developments over the past few years, many experts now see this delay as Turkish EU membership's deathbed (meaning formal suspension). How successful Turkey and the EU manage differences on migration, travel, counterterrorism efforts, NATO and EU cooperation, and Cyprus will determine the longevity of the accession process and the development of alternative futures for the relationship.

Turkey's security relationship with NATO allies has had its ups and downs over the past six decades. Throughout the Cold War, Turkey's European and North American allies saw it as a reliable and capable, albeit sometimes difficult, ally in a dangerous part of the world and as the cornerstone of the southern flank against Soviet expansion and the spread of the Iranian revolution after 1979. This view has generally prevailed since 1989, as Turkey has made valuable contributions to NATO efforts to deal with evolving Euro-Atlantic and global security challenges. However, shifting Turkish interests and pursuit of policies that are sometimes at odds with the NATO consensus, as well as the Alliance's hesitancy about assisting Turkey in countering threats from its southern neighbors, have triggered intermittent strains in Alliance relations. Some circles in Turkey have also begun to question whether NATO is relevant in addressing the country's most pressing security concerns—countering terrorism and separatism—and argue that Turkey engagement in Eurasian political and security arrangements would better serve Turkish interests.

Turkey's relationships with both the EU and NATO may be reaching critical inflection points with important implications for U.S. interests and transatlantic security.

Relations with the European Union

Turkey's Bid for Membership

Turkey's relationship with an integrating Europe has followed a long and torturous course over the past six decades. Turkey applied for associate membership in the European Economic Community in 1959. The two parties signed an association agreement in 1963, and that cooperation framework led to the establishment of a limited customs union in 1995. The European Parliament conditioned ratification of the customs union on Turkey's pursuit of certain political reforms, which Ankara undertook. The introduction of conditionality at the outset of the relationship helped set Turkey on a reform course and ultimately paved the way for it to become an EU candidate country.[1]

The customs union covers all industrial goods but does not address agriculture (except processed agricultural products), services, or public procurement. Certain bilateral trade concessions apply to agricultural, coal, and steel products. The EU countries have been Turkey's leading trading and investment partner, by far, over the past 30 years. Of Turkey's global trade, 41 percent is with the EU. Turkey's exports to EU countries have grown enormously, from 35 percent of volume in 1950 to more than 55 percent by the mid-1990s. As of 2019, 44 percent of Turkey's exports are bound for EU countries, making it the Union's fifth-largest source of imports. About 38 percent of Turkey's imports today come from Europe, making it the EU's fourth-largest export market.[2] More than 70 percent of foreign direct investment in Turkey has come from EU member states in recent years.[3]

Although then–Turkish Prime Minister Turgut Özal applied for full membership in 1987 and Turkey was declared eligible to join in 1999, it was not until 2004 that EU leaders agreed to start accession negotiations on October 3, 2005. The negotiations were to happen after Ankara completed additional reforms and extended its association agreement and customs union with the European Economic Community to the EU's ten new member states, including the Republic of Cyprus—a decision that was, however, never ratified by the Turkish Parliament. In contrast to other enlargement projects, the Turkish negotiations took a negative turn almost immediately after their initiation.[4] In October 2006, the EU's enlargement commissioner Olli Rehn warned that differences over Cyprus, Turkey's record on human rights and media freedom, and other issues could lead to a "train crash."[5] Two months later, the European Coun-

---

[1]   Kemal Kirişci and Onur Bülbül, "The EU and Turkey Need Each Other. Could Upgrading the Customs Union Be the Key?" Washington, D.C.: Brookings Institution, August 29, 2017.

[2]   European Commission, "Turkey," webpage, February 15, 2019a.

[3]   "FDI into Turkey Upward Despite Political Rift with EU," *Daily Sabah*, August 7, 2017.

[4]   Hanna-Lisa Hauge, Atila Eralp, Wolfgang Wessels, and Nurdan Selay Bedir, "Mapping Milestones and Periods of Past EU-Turkey Relations," Future of EU-Turkey Relations Working Paper, September 2016.

[5]   "EU Warns Turkey to Step Up Reforms to Avoid 'Train Crash,'" *Deutsche Welle*, March 10, 2006.

cil decided to suspend negotiations on eight of 35 chapters because of Turkey's refusal to open its ports and airports to Greek Cypriot ships and aircraft in accordance with a 1970 protocol to the association agreement with the European Economic Community.[6] Ankara had linked these actions to further steps by the EU and Greek Cypriots to end the economic isolation of the Turkish Republic of Northern Cyprus.[7]

European leaders, including then–French President Nicolas Sarkozy and German Chancellor Angela Merkel, became more explicit in articulating their opposition to Turkey's membership in the EU and suggested a "privileged partnership" as an alternative. Mounting doubts in Turkey about Europe's willingness to ultimately offer membership led to a diminished commitment by officials and the public to pursue the requisite reforms. In addition, the EU's expectation that it would take Turkey a decade or more to implement those reforms was at odds with Turkey's expectations that it should be granted membership quickly. Ankara's frustration led to a series of rhetorical excesses and brinkmanship.[8] In the context of contentious debates in member countries on enlargement following the 2008 European debt crisis and official statements from Ankara that Turkey would be "proudly and pretentiously becoming a self-declared regional power with no need of EU norms,"[9] the European Commission launched a so-called Positive Agenda to overcome stagnation in fields of mutual interests.[10]

Turkey made fitful progress on some of the *acquis communautaire*, with the Commission agreeing to open negotiations on one or two new chapters each year until 2013.[11] Progress stalled, however, because of the ongoing Cyprus conflict and the German and Dutch veto to the opening of Chapter 22 (regional policy and coordination of structural instruments) in June 2013 in response to Ankara's violent repres-

---

[6] Belgium, Germany, France, Italy, Luxembourg, the Netherlands, the Council of the European Communities, and Turkey, "Additional Protocol and Financial Protocol Signed on 23 November 1970, Annexed to the Agreement Establishing the Association Between the European Economic Community and Turkey and on Measures to Be Taken for Their Entry into Force—Final Act—Declarations," Brussels, November 23, 1970.

[7] Hauge et al., 2016.

[8] See Julianne Smith, "Turkey and Europe: A Widening Gap," in Stephen J. Flanagan, Samuel J. Brannen, Bulent Aliriza, Edward C. Chow, Andrew C. Kuchins, Haim Malka, Julianne Smith, Ian Lesser, Eric Palomaa, and Alexandros Petersen, *Turkey's Evolving Dynamics: Strategic Choices for U.S.-Turkey Relations*, Washington, D.C.: Center for Strategic and International Studies, March 2009, pp. 19–20.

[9] Cengiz Aktar, "The Positive Agenda and Beyond: A New Beginning for the EU-Turkey Relations?" *Insight Turkey*, Vol. 14, No. 3, 2012.

[10] The Commission set up the following eight working groups: Judiciary and Fundamental Rights; Justice, Freedom, and Security; Right of Establishment and Freedom to Provide Services; Information Society and Media; Consumer and Health Protection; Financial Control; Company Law; and Statistics.

[11] The *acquis communautaire* is the accumulated body of EU laws and obligations from 1958 to the present day. It comprises all the EU's treaties and laws (e.g., directives, regulations, decisions), declarations and resolutions, international agreements, and the judgments of the Court of Justice.

sion of domestic protests.[12] As discussed in Chapter Two of this report, the authorities' brutal eviction of participants in a sit-in protesting the development of Taksim Gezi Park in central Istanbul triggered anti-government demonstrations by more than 3 million people across Turkey, and the demonstrations were forcefully repressed by police. Ankara's actions sparked harsh criticism in European capitals and from the European Parliament.[13]

Both Turkish and European commitment for Turkey's accession diminished during this period, and the question of whether either side will walk away from the negotiation table resurfaces frequently.[14] In Turkey, those who perceive the accession talks as an "annoying reminder of the country's deficits as a liberal democracy" would be eager to follow Erdoğan in his repeated call to "cut our own umbilical cord" if the EU will not finally "make up its mind" on Turkey's membership.[15] Still, leaving the EU track would have an impact on trade and investment policy and would be accompanied by economic costs that are not yet foreseeable. Experts assume that, if nego-

---

[12] Ebru Turhan, "Europe's Crises, Germany's Leadership and Turkey's EU Accession Process," *Focus*, Vol. 17, No. 2, Summer 2016a.

[13] The European Parliament officially decried "the disproportionate and excessive use of force by the Turkish police in its response to the peaceful and legitimate protests" (Michael Curtis, "The European Union vs. Turkey," *American Thinker*, June 24, 2013).

[14] Annual surveys conducted by the German Marshall Fund between 2003 and 2013 reflected an enduring ambivalence in EU member states and Turkey with respect to Turkish membership in the EU. By 2008, while 60 percent of Europeans polled expected that Turkey would join the EU, only 26 percent of Turkish participants thought that goal would be attained. In 2013, while a majority of Turkish respondents still favored joining the EU, their commitment declined dramatically. Forty-four percent of Turks surveyed said that EU membership would be a good thing, down from 73 percent in 2004. Thirty-four percent said that it would be a bad thing, as opposed to 9 percent in 2004. In the 2013 survey, only 20 percent of European respondents said that Turkey's accession would be good, while 33 percent said that it would be bad and 37 percent said that it would be neither good nor bad. See Constanze Stelzenmueller and Joshua Raisher, *Transatlantic Trends 2013: Key Findings*, Washington, D.C.: German Marshall Fund of the United States, September 18, 2013, pp. 46–47.

A 2017 survey conducted in nine EU countries for the center-right European People's Party found that 77 percent of respondents did not want Turkey to join the EU, with the strongest opposition in Germany (86 percent), followed by the Netherlands (84 percent). The lowest resistance was recorded in Spain, where 60 percent of respondents said that they would not support a Turkish EU bid. See Cynthia Kroet, "Resistance Against Turkish EU Membership Highest in Germany: Poll," *Politico*, May 19, 2017.

A 2017 nationwide poll conducted by Kadir Has University found that 51.6 percent of Turks surveyed did not want Turkey to become a member of the EU and 48.4 percent did—which reflect the highest and lowest results, respectively, in annual surveys conducted since 2013. Of those surveyed, 81.3 percent believed that membership in the EU will never occur; however, more than 70 percent believed that neither the EU nor Turkey would suspend accession talks soon. See Kadir Has University, Center for Turkish Studies, "Public Perceptions on Turkish Foreign Policy," Istanbul, July 20, 2017.

[15] Nathalie Tocci, "Turkey and the European Union: Scenarios for 2023," Future of EU-Turkey Relations Background Paper, September 2016, p. 7; Mehul Srivastava, "Erdogan Moves in on Executive Presidency After Crackdown on Kurds," *Financial Times*, November 7, 2016; and Ece Toksabay, Tuvan Gumrukcu, and Nick Tattersall, "Turkey Could Put EU Talks to a Referendum Next Year: Erdogan," Reuters, November 14, 2016. In November 2016, Erdoğan publicly suggested taking the question of continuing the negotiations to a popular vote in 2017.

tiations were suspended, at least some of the enormous European investments would be redirected. In addition, the contractual basis for EU-Turkish economic relations would be "scaled down from a customs union to a free trade agreement."[16] Being in a customs union without the membership perspective would be highly disadvantageous for Turkey because Turkey would then be obliged to implement more than 50 free trade agreements that the EU has with other states, and regional organizations without these entities would, in turn, be obliged to open their markets to Turkish exports.[17] Giving up on the customs union would untie Turkey's hands in trade issues, but economic experts are concerned that this would result in political interference in the markets and incomplete structural reforms.[18] It would be difficult for Turkey to raise its standards of production, and its economy would face severe difficulties to overcome the so-called middle-income trap.[19] Given its lack of hydrocarbon resources, Turkey would still have to seek ways to stay integrated in the global economy, and the EU would likely continue to be the first economic partner of Turkey in an even more asymmetric relationship.[20]

On the European side, experts agree that it is "hard to tell whether there is still a Member State which genuinely supports Turkey's membership today."[21] Although the EU's southern states, (Portugal, Italy, and Spain) fear that further enlargement could drain some of the resources they need for economic recovery after the 2008 financial crisis, the scenario of mass immigration of Turkish labor to the United Kingdom became a factor in the 2016 Brexit vote. Scandinavian members, especially Finland and Sweden, dropped their earlier support for Turkish membership tacitly against the background of Turkey's creeping authoritarianism, and most eastern member states are highly wary of Ankara's collaboration with Russia.[22]

Amid the background of Turkey's dramatic domestic developments (see Chapter Two), the European Parliament has turned especially critical of continuing the accession process and called for a temporary freeze on November 24, 2016. In its resolution, the Parliament invoked Paragraph 5 of the 2005 Negotiation Framework, which stipulates that the European Commission could suspend negotiations if Turkey should seriously and persistently breach the "principles of liberty, democracy, respect

---

[16] Nathalie Tocci, *Turkey and the European Union: A Journey in the Unknown*, Washington, D.C.: Brookings Institution, Turkey Project Policy Paper No. 5, November 2014, p. 6.

[17] Turkey must automatically comply with the terms of free trade agreements that the EU signs with third-party countries without the latter having an obligation to conclude free trade agreements with Turkey.

[18] Tocci, 2016, p. 8.

[19] Tocci, 2016, p. 8.

[20] Kemal Kirişci, "The Transformation of Turkish Foreign Policy: The Rise of the Trading State," *New Perspectives on Turkey*, No. 40, 2009.

[21] Tocci, 2016, p. 6.

[22] Tocci, 2016, p. 6.

for human rights and fundamental freedoms and the rule of law."[23] The next day, European Commission President Jean-Claude Juncker, reflecting the position of such key member states as Germany, warned "Europe to refrain from giving lessons to Turkey."[24] Austria's then–Foreign Minister Sebastian Kurz also faced criticism from both Berlin and Brussels for his failed push to freeze negotiations during an EU foreign minister meeting in mid-December 2016, but his efforts did secure a public statement that the EU is not considering opening new chapters any time soon.[25] In response to an unprecedented German-Turkish bilateral crisis, including the detention of at least 12 German citizens in Turkey after July 2016, Berlin has been blocking the modernization of the customs union with Turkey since August 2017.[26] Germany also urged other members in October 2017 to reduce the €4.5 billion pre-accession funds that the EU had allocated to Turkey to support rule of law, civil society, fundamental rights, democracy, and governance for 2014 through 2020.[27] On March 26, 2018, after talks with Erdoğan, President of the European Council Donald Tusk, and Bulgarian Prime Minister Boyko Borissov, Juncker pledged to personally guarantee the survival of the accession process.[28] However, on September 30, 2019, the European Parliament approved a nonbinding resolution calling on the European Commission and member states to officially suspend negotiations on Turkey's EU accession, citing Turkey's lack of respect for justice and fundamental rights, including freedom of expression and the media.[29]

Despite mutual disillusionment, neither party has moved to suspend the accession talks or seems likely to do so in the near term. Other issues have dominated the

---

[23] European Parliament, "European Parliament Resolution on the 2004 Regular Report and the Recommendation of the European Commission on Turkey's Progress Towards Accession," September 15, 2005. On March 13, 2019, the Parliament passed a nonbinding resolution calling on the European Commission and member states to formally suspend accession talks with Turkey in accordance with the 2005 Negotiation Framework. The resolution cited continuing concerns about excessive presidential power and continuing limits on freedom, human rights, the media, and civil society in Turkey. The vote was 370 in favor and 109 against, with 143 abstentions. See European Parliament, "Parliament Wants to Suspend EU Accession Negotiations with Turkey," press release, March 13, 2019.

[24] "EU Commission President Warns Europe Not to Lecture Turkey over Migration," *Euronews*, November 25, 2016.

[25] Florian Eder, "Austria to the EU: We Need to Talk About Turkey," *Politico*, December 12, 2016; and Jacopo Barigazzi, "EU Ministers Reject Austria's Call to Freeze Turkey Membership Talks," *Politico*, December 13, 2016.

[26] Patrick Kingsley and Alissa J. Rubin, "Turkey's Relations with Europe Sink amid Quarrel with Netherlands," *New York Times*, March 12, 2017; and Magdalena Kirchner, "Will the German Election Outcome Change Berlin's Turkey Policy?" German Marshall Fund of the United States, September 26, 2017b, p. 2.

[27] Andrew Rettman and Eric Maurice, "Merkel: EU to Cut Turkey Pre-Accession Funds," *EUobserver*, October 20, 2017.

[28] Simon Osborne, "EU Torn in Two over Turkey—Austria Calls for End to Talks as Juncker Seeks Accession," *Sunday Express*, April 3, 2018.

[29] The vote was 370 members in favor, 109 against, and 143 abstentions. See Philip Pangalos, "European Parliament Calls for Suspension of Turkey EU Accession Talks," *Euronews*, September 30, 2019.

bilateral agenda over the past few years, and discussions of a "new model" for the relationship have gained traction. After the September 2013 German elections, Chapter 22 was opened in November, and a dialogue on readmission and visa liberalization initiated.[30] Although the agreement in late 2013 already pointed to a more transactional direction, this trend was reinforced in 2015 amid the flow of hundreds of thousands of asylum seekers to Europe via Turkey.

Migration

Migration from Turkey to the EU has been a key issue in bilateral relations for decades. Beginning in 2002, the EU attempted to negotiate a readmission agreement with Turkey that would commit it to take back third-country nationals who had entered the EU illegally after transiting through Turkey. For several reasons, this agreement was not realized until late 2013. Besides Ankara's general mistrust of the European Neighborhood Policy as a potential placebo for full membership, fears that a readmission agreement would turn Turkey into a buffer zone for unwanted migration, little progress regarding visa liberalization, and concerns over Turkey's border management capacity slowed down negotiations.[31]

Joint Action Plan

In 2015, the Eastern Mediterranean route via Turkey and Greece became the center of gravity for human smuggling and trafficking routes into the Schengen Area.[32] Facing the enormous pressure of the refugee crisis, EU members pushed for speeding up negotiations and offered Turkey major financial assistance if the 2013 readmission agreement would be implemented swiftly. In addition, both sides agreed to open new chapters in the accession negotiations and to increase resettlement numbers of Syrian refugees in Turkey to Europe.[33] Under the EU-Turkey Joint Action Plan, which was agreed *ad referendum* in October 2015 and formalized in March 2016, the two parties pledged to address the root causes of the massive influx of Syrians, support Syrians under temporary protection in Turkey and their host communities, and strengthen bilateral cooperation to prevent irregular migration flows to the EU.[34]

---

[30] Ebru Turhan, "The Struggle for the German-Turkish Partnership: Preventing the 'Train Crash,'" E-International Relations, December 4, 2016b.

[31] Kemal Kirişci, "Will the Readmission Agreement Bring the EU and Turkey Together or Pull Them Apart?" Centre for European Policy Studies, February 4, 2014.

[32] European Border and Coast Guard Agency, "Migratory Map," webpage, November 6, 2018. The Schengen Area comprises 26 European countries that abolished their internal borders to allow the unrestricted movement of people.

[33] European Council, "EU-Turkey Statement," press release, March 18, 2016.

[34] In addition, the plan aims at being consistent with the 2013 Visa Liberalization Dialogue (see European Commission, "EU-Turkey Joint Action Plan," fact sheet, October 15, 2015a).

On March 18, 2016, following intensive diplomatic efforts over the previous six months, the EU and Turkey reconfirmed their commitment to the Joint Action Plan. This plan requested Ankara to open domestic labor markets to Syrians under temporary protection, to introduce visa requirements for Syrians and other nationalities entering Turkey from third countries, and to step up both border control efforts and information-sharing. The EU committed to disburse €3 billion to projects under the umbrella of the newly established Facility for Refugees in Turkey; move forward with visa liberalization; and open new chapters of the accession process, such as Chapter 17 (Economic and Monetary Policy), which was opened on December 14, 2015.[35] Ankara had earlier agreed to readmit rejected asylum seekers who had entered Greece from Turkey, as well as "all irregular migrants intercepted in Turkish waters."[36] Both sides also pledged to further step up measures against trafficking, among other things, in the framework of stronger EU-NATO cooperation.[37]

In light of this deal, both parties reconfirmed their commitment at that time to reenergize the EU accession process. Their decision to open Chapter 33 (Financial and Budgetary Provisions) was implemented in late June 2016.[38] In addition to the €3 billion allocated to the Facility for Refugees in Turkey in November 2015, the EU announced its intent to mobilize an additional €3 billion to the facility up to late 2018, once the resources initially provided were "about to be used to the full, and provided the [other stated] commitments are met."[39] Despite little enthusiasm for this procedure by Turkish authorities, the EU largely refused direct budget support, and the projects funded by the Facility for Refugees were jointly identified—most of them in the areas of health, education, infrastructure, food, and other living costs.[40]

---

[35] European Council, 2016.

[36] European Council, 2016.

[37] The March 18 deal also added further specifications to the Joint Action Plan. First, all future irregular migrants crossing from Turkey into Greek islands should be returned to Turkey. Ankara also pledged to readmit all migrants who did not apply for or were not granted asylum in Greece. The EU agreed to cover the costs of these returns. Second, for every Syrian returned, another should be resettled to an EU member state (the "1:1 initiative"), up to 72,000 people. In exchange for Turkey's enhanced border controls, the EU offered to establish a scheme that would replace the 1:1 initiative but would not entail a fixed quota for member states. The deal also foresaw upgrading of the customs union through an extension to services, public procurement, and agriculture, as well as the fulfillment of the 2013 visa liberalization roadmap by the end of June 2016. See European Commission, *Fourth Report on the Progress Made in the Implementation of the EU-Turkey Statement*, Brussels, December 8, 2016b.

[38] As of November 2017, 16 of the 35 chapters of the acquis had been opened to negotiations with Turkey and one of them (Chapter 25: Science and Research) had been provisionally closed.

[39] European Council, 2016.

[40] European Council, 2016. In July 2016, however, the EU signed two major direct grants to the Ministry of National Education and the Ministry of Health, including €600 million for access to formal education and primary health care services for Syrian refugees in Turkey (see European Commission, 2016b, p. 12).

Turkish critics of the EU-Turkey deal condemned it as an unethical "bargaining over an international humanitarian issue,"[41] asserting that the benefits for Turkey were both natural rights of EU candidates and part of Europe's humanitarian obligations. Human rights organizations have fiercely objected the EU's disregard for the fact that Turkey—just as Lebanon, Jordan, and Egypt, which have become secondary gate-keepers when Ankara imposed visa restrictions for Syrians traveling by air or sea in January 2016—cannot provide all necessary support to refugees within its borders.[42] This concerns not only access to education, health care, and lawful employment in order to maintain livelihood but also timely registration and protection against exploitation or even refoulement.[43]

Has the Joint Action Plan Been a Success?

Despite the July 2016 military coup attempt, the massive crackdown by the Turkish government on perceived coup plotters and alleged terrorism supporters (including parliamentarians, academics, and journalists), and daily recriminations from both sides, the refugee deal has not collapsed because it serves the interests of the parties. When arguing that the agreement has been successful, EU leaders frequently point to the substantial drop of monthly sea arrivals to Greece from more than 67,000 in February 2016 to about 1,700 in May the same year.[44] Daily arrivals had gone down to fewer than 200 people by November 2017.[45] By the end of December 2017, the full envelope of €3 billion had been contracted, and €1.95 million had been disbursed to more than 72 projects.[46] Despite Turkish complaints about the slow pace of the disbursement, EU officials described this as fast and extensive compared with similar EU projects.[47]

On the other side, the European Commission evaluated the pace of returns to Turkey as too slow, adding further pressure on crowded reception centers on the Greek islands and, at times, triggering violent incidents.[48] Cooperation was further slowed by the attempted military coup in July 2016, which led Turkey to recall its liaison offi-

---

[41] Seçil Paçacı Elitok, *A Step Backward for Turkey? The Readmission Agreement and the Hope of Visa-Free Europe*, Istanbul: Istanbul Policy Center, Sabanci University, December 2015, p. 4.

[42] "Turkey Does a U-Turn, Imposes Entry Visas on Syrians," *New Arab*, December 29, 2015.

[43] "EU: Don't Send Syrians Back to Turkey," Human Rights Watch, June 20, 2016.

[44] United Nations High Commissioner for Refugees, "Refugees & Migrants Sea Arrivals in Europe," monthly data update, Regional Bureau Europe, August 2016.

[45] United Nations High Commissioner for Refugees, "Operational Portal, Refugee Situations: Mediterranean Situation," web tool, October 29, 2017b.

[46] European Commission, "The EU Facility for Refugees in Turkey," fact sheet, December 2018b.

[47] European Commission, 2018a, p. 3; EU officials, discussion with the authors, Ankara, November 2016; and European Commission, 2016b, p. 2.

[48] European Commission, 2016b, p. 5.

cers on the Greek islands, and these officers were not redeployed until October 25.[49] Among 1,484 migrants who were returned from Greece to Turkey between April 2016 and the end of 2017, only 236 were Syrian nationals.[50] These numbers show that the Syrian civil war is not the only root cause of displacement that needs to be addressed by both partners. In December 2016, an EU report ascribed the overall slow pace of returns to the frequent delay or even absence of a response by Turkish authorities to Greek requests for return operations.[51] Until December 31, 2017, 11,711 Syrian refugees were resettled under the deal to at least 15 EU member states.[52]

With regard to visa liberalization as a condition for the survival of the deal, Turkey, as of mid-2019, had yet to meet all of the benchmarks required to achieve a positive decision by both the European Council and the European Parliament.[53] Most observers see little room for progress on this front, especially with regard to the revision of Turkey's terrorism legislation.[54] Ankara's attempts to engage in a public bargain over a quick implementation and threats to back out of the deal have also failed so far and were met by demands from then–Austrian Foreign Minister Kurz (now prime minister) that the EU should invest more in unilaterally protecting its external borders instead of giving in to "blackmailing" by Turkey.[55] Others, like Germany's then–Finance Minister Wolfgang Schäuble (now president of the Bundestag), called for continued cooperation and emphasized Europe's dependence on Turkey.[56]

---

[49] European Commission, 2016b, p. 4

[50] European Commission, 2018a, p. 46; and United Nations High Commissioner for Refugees, "Returns from Greece to Turkey," Greece, October 6, 2017a.

[51] European Commission, 2016b, p. 5.

[52] European Commission, 2018a, p. 46.

[53] The seven benchmarks remaining to be met were

- issuing *biometric travel documents* fully compatible with EU standards
- adopting the measure to prevent *corruption* foreseen by the [visa liberalization] Roadmap
- concluding an *operational cooperation agreement with Europol*
- revising legislation and practices on *terrorism* in line with European standards
- aligning legislation on personal *data protection* with EU standards
- offering effective *judicial cooperation in criminal matters* to all EU Member States
- implementing the *EU-Turkey Readmission Agreement* in all its provisions. (European Commission, *Seventh Report on the Progress Made in the Implementation of the EU-Turkey Statement*, Brussels, September 6, 2017, p. 10; see also European Commission, "Key Findings of the 2019 Report on Turkey," press release, Brussels, May 29, 2019b)

[54] EU officials, discussion with the authors, Ankara, November 2016.

[55] Cynthia Kroet, "Austrian Minister: EU Doesn't Need Turkey," *Politico*, August 16, 2016a; Matthew Holehouse, "Turkey to Get Visa-Free Travel Despite Failing to Meet EU Targets," *The Telegraph*, May 4, 2016; "Turkey out of Migrant Deal If EU Fails on Visa-Free Travel: Cavusoglu," *Deutsche Welle*, July 31, 2016; and "EP's President Schulz Opposes Liberalisation of Visa Regime with Turkey," *News for Turkey*, December 28, 2016.

[56] Cynthia Kroet, "Wolfgang Schäuble: EU Needs Turkey for Migration Crisis," *Politico*, August 17, 2016b.

On the Turkish side, President Erdoğan and other leading AKP politicians issued several ultimatums throughout 2016 to walk away from the agreement and to "open the gates" if the EU would not implement the visa liberalization.[57] Many observers question both Erdoğan's political will to end the refugee deal and his leverage. First, because the Turkish government had been presented with clear benchmarks, the call for ultimatums could backfire because it primarily pressures Ankara to meet them.[58] Second, a 2017 survey underlined that the vast majority of more than 3.2 million Syrians prefer to stay in Turkey if returning to their home country would not be possible.[59] Many have successfully integrated in the labor market there, and those who aimed for Western Europe had mostly left Turkey in the past few years. In addition, the idea of a life in Europe has been tarnished by reports of the hardships of reception and integration, while new Turkish visa restrictions make it difficult for Syrians to return once they have received European papers.[60] When comparing the situation in Turkey with the economic and legal conditions in Lebanon and Jordan, many Syrians see Turkey as their best option.[61] Further incentives for refugees to stay in Turkey were created by the Turkish government itself, which announced plans to grant citizenship to some 50,000 Syrians, and more than 36,000 had been naturalized in 2017.[62]

Counterterrorism

Discussions on terrorism and how to counter it encompass three sets of threats:

- radical jihadist groups, such as ISIS or al Qaida, with a special focus on the challenge of foreign terrorist fighters of European origin transiting to and from Syria and Iraq through Turkey
- violent Kurdish nationalism, as represented by the PKK and the Kurdistan Freedom Falcons[63]
- the Gülen movement (often referred to as the *Hizmet* movement by its followers), which has been designated a terrorist organization by Turkish authorities but,

---

[57] Şafak Timur and Rod Nordland, "Erdogan Threatens to Let Migrant Flood into Europe Resume," *New York Times*, November 25, 2016.

[58] Bernd Riegert, "Opinion: An Absurd Threat from Ankara," *Deutsche Welle*, August 1, 2016.

[59] Kristin Fabbe, Chad Hazlett, Tolga Sinmazdemir, "What Do Syrians Want Their Future to Be?" *Foreign Affairs*, May 1, 2017.

[60] Syrian civil society activist, discussion with the authors, Istanbul, November 2016.

[61] Fabbe, Hazlett, and Sinmazdemir, 2017.

[62] European Commission, 2018a, p. 47; "Erdogan Offers Citizenship to Syrian and Iraqi Refugees," *Al Jazeera*, January 7, 2017; and "Turkey Processing Citizenship for 50,000 Syrians." *Daily Sabah*, September 23, 2017.

[63] The Kurdistan Freedom Falcons have been designated a terrorist organization by the United States and by the EU at least since 2006 (Council of the European Union, "Council Common Position 2006/1011/CFSP of December 21, 2006," *Official Journal of the European Union*, L 379/129, December 28, 2006).

despite pressure from Ankara, has not been outlawed by any EU member state so far (see Chapter Two).

The number of Europeans traveling to Syria to join jihadist militias and terrorist organizations has increased dramatically, from up to 600 in mid-2013 to nearly 4,000 in early 2015, and has confronted the EU with the risk that internationally connected, well-trained, and radicalized returnees would conduct attacks on European soil.[64] In 2016, Europol reported that Turkey had been these recruits' main transit country, partly because EU citizens do not require visas to enter the country; in addition, there were frequent reports and complaints, by U.S. President Obama and others, that Turkish authorities would turn a blind eye to the flow of thousands of fighters into Syria and back.[65] Ankara initially rejected these allegations and called on the EU to prevent the fighters' departure in the first place; in May 2014, Turkey announced that 1,100 ISIS recruits had been deported to their home countries—a number that rose to some 5,000 people by August 2017.[66]

Following the terrorist attacks in Paris on November 13, 2015, and in Brussels on March 22, 2016, it was confirmed that a lack of information-sharing between EU and Turkish authorities was key to the failure to arrest suspects in time. In both cases, Ankara had warned French, Belgian, and Dutch services of several of the perpetrators, among them European jihadists that had been detained in Turkey or even deported but freed upon arrival in Europe.[67] According to Turkish officials, EU intelligence services had declined the officials' demands in late 2012 to provide a "pooled list" of potential radicals that could be banned from entering Turkey.[68] In response to the foreign terrorist fighter challenge, Germany, for instance, established a bilateral task force with

---

[64] International Centre for the Study of Radicalisation, "Up to 11,000 Foreign Fighters in Syria; Steep Rise Among Western Europeans," London, December 12, 2013; and Peter R. Neumann, "Foreign Fighter Total in Syria/Iraq Now Exceeds 20,000; Surpasses Afghanistan Conflict in the 1980s," London: International Centre for the Study of Radicalisation, January 25, 2015.

[65] Europol, *European Union Terrorism Situation and Trend Report 2016*, The Hague, Netherlands: European Police Office, 2016a, p. 28; Daniel Byman and Jeremy Shapiro, "Be Afraid. Be A Little Afraid: The Threat of Terrorism from Western Foreign Fighters in Syria and Iraq," Washington, D.C.: Brookings Institution, November 2014; Senada Sokollu, "European Jihadists Use Turkey as Transit Country," *Deutsche Welle*, May 14, 2014; Adam Entous and Joe Parkinson, "Turkey's Spymaster Plots Own Course on Syria," *Wall Street Journal*, October 10, 2013; and Jonathan Schanzer, "An Unhelpful Ally: ISIS and Other Violent Factions Have Benefited from Turkey's Loose Border Policies," *Wall Street Journal*, June 25, 2015.

[66] Sokollu, 2014; Kareem Shaheen "Turkish Officials: Europe Wanted to Export Extremists to Syria," *The Guardian,* March 25, 2016; and "Turkey, France Work Closely in Deporting Foreign Fighters," *Daily Sabah*, August 23, 2017.

[67] Shaheen, 2016.

[68] Shaheen, 2016. On July 6, 2017, Erdoğan said that Turkish authorities had barred the entry of more than 53,000 terrorist suspects ("Turkey Banned 53,000 Foreign Fighters So Far: Erdoğan," *Hürriyet Daily News,* July 6, 2017).

Turkey.[69] In March 2016, Turkey and Europol signed a bilateral Liaison Agreement, offering enhanced cooperation that would also provide Ankara with regular access to Europol expertise and a wide network of more than 40 other liaison countries; Turkey and the EU held a Counter-Terrorism Dialogue later that year.[70] According to high-ranking EU officials, however, Turkey's current data protection laws, preference for bilateral arrangements with individual EU member states, and other frictions continue to impede full implementation of the agreement.[71]

Another focus of cooperation and contention between Ankara and its European partners had been the operations of the PKK, which has been designated a terrorist organization by the EU since 2002. Given Turkey's refusal to assist the PKK's Syrian affiliate the YPG in defending against ISIS's attack on the mostly Kurdish populated border town of Kobanî in September 2014 (as examined in Chapter Two) and the escalation of violence between the PKK and the TSK, consensus on cooperation eroded rapidly since mid-2015. On the one hand, Ankara's policy of military escalation in the southeast in the face of increasing PKK attacks and an increasingly positive assessment of the YPG in the campaign against ISIS led to a growing sentiment, especially among European leftists, that the ban on the PKK should be lifted.[72] On the other hand, Turkish authorities have increasingly criticized the lack of cooperation on the part of their European counterparts with regard to both the failure to rein in PKK activity in their countries and the slow and limited responses to extradition requests by Turkey. Germany—which had outlawed the PKK in 1994 and where, according to its own domestic intelligence service, 14,000 active PKK members live—has become the focal point of this criticism.[73] German officials point to their commitment to joint prosecu-

---

[69] Emine Kart, "Ankara, Berlin in Joint Anti-Terror Mechanism," *Hürriyet Daily News*, January 27, 2016.

[70] Europol, "Turkey and Europol Sign Liaison Agreement," press release, March 21, 2016b. In addition to discussing ways to improve law enforcement and judicial cooperation, the two parties also pledged to do more to address the root causes of radicalization and recruitment (European Union External Action, "Turkey-EU Counter Terrorism Dialogue," press release, June 8, 2016).

[71] EU officials, discussion with the authors, Ankara, November 2016. For example, in response to Ankara's decision to issue Interpol "red notice" arrest warrants against German citizens since late August 2017, Berlin condemned what it deemed a misuse of international organizations to repress nonviolent dissidents outside the country (Thomas Escritt and Daren Butler, "Merkel Attacks Turkey's 'Misuse' of Interpol Warrants," Reuters, August 20, 2017; Kirchner, 2017b).

[72] Sertan Sanderson, "European PKK Ban Could Undermine Turkish Democracy," *Deutsche Welle*, November 25, 2016; and "Turkish Min. Criticizes EU 'Double Standards' on PKK," *World Bulletin*, November 7, 2016.

[73] Sanderson, 2016. In early November 2016, Erdoğan publicly called Germany "an important harbor for terrorists" and claimed that Berlin not only turned a blind eye to the PKK's activity but also had followed up on only six of the 4,500 PKK files Ankara had sent to German authorities ("Deutschland ist ein wichtiger Hafen für Terroristen," *Zeit Online*, November 3, 2016).

tion of the group and opening of more than 4,000 legal proceedings against alleged PKK affiliates, as well as other steps.[74]

Ankara's conflict with the Gülen movement and the failed coup attempt in July 2016 added another controversial issue to EU-Turkish counterterrorism efforts. Turkish requests for the extradition of potential coup plotters were met with little success. Turkish media reported that, after the failed coup attempt, some 4,000 members of the Gülen group had fled to Germany, which is home to at least 70,000 followers of Gülen.[75] Between July 2016 and October 2017, Ankara formally requested the extradition of 81 Turkish citizens, although it is unclear from public sources how many of them were charged as members of the Gülen movement.[76] Berlin granted asylum to 196 Turkish citizens, among them a significant portion of the 615 diplomatic and service passport holders and their families (including some previously stationed at NATO bases in Germany) who had applied between July 2016 and August 2017.[77] The rapid increase of asylum applications was accompanied by a rising number of complaints by Gülenist schools and cultural centers in several European countries that they face intimidation, death threats, and physical attacks on their property.[78] By May 2017, Greek courts had rejected the asylum applications of seven of the eight soldiers, including two majors, who had fled Turkey after the coup attempt, yet the courts also subsequently blocked Turkish extradition requests.[79] Turkish media and even Foreign Minister Mevlüt Çavuşoğlu stated concerns that, based on the ongoing activities of the movement in Albania, Bosnia, Macedonia, and Kosovo, those countries would

---

[74] Sanderson, 2016; Hannes Heine, "De Maiziere will mit der Türkei kooperieren," *Der Tagesspiegel*, November 16, 2016; and Yunus Paksoy, "Germany Insists It Does Not Support PKK Despite Own Intelligence Reports," *Daily Sabah*, November 17, 2016. However, in discussions with us, German diplomatic sources reported that the accusations have negatively affected bilateral counterterrorism cooperation in a broader sense and led to, among other things, the cancellation of high-ranking German visits to Ankara (German diplomats, discussion with the authors, Ankara, November 2016). Since March 2017, German authorities banned symbols associated with the PKK and the YPG, as well as the PKK's jailed leader Abdullah Öcalan, and rejected at least one request for asylum by a former YPG fighter (Kirchner, 2017b).

[75] "Germany Sees No FETÖ Presence Despite Hundreds of Schools and Fugitives," *Daily Sabah*, November 2, 2016. According to the Turkish News Agency, 22 of the 37 alleged Gülenists in Europe that Ankara had formally requested to be extradited were living in Germany ("Germany Becomes Magnet for FETO Suspects," Anadolu Agency, September 11, 2017).

[76] "Türkei verlangte seit Putschversuch 81 Auslieferungen" ["Turkey Has Demanded 81 Extraditions Since Coup Attempt"], *Welt*, October 23, 2017.

[77] "Germany Becomes Magnet for FETO Suspects," 2017; and Sertan Sanderson, "Germany Grants Asylum to Turkish Military Personnel," *Deutsche Welle*, May 8, 2017.

[78] Maïa De La Baume and Guilia Paravicini, "'Sleepless Nights' for Gülen's Supports in Europe," *Politico*, August 24, 2016.

[79] "Greek Court Overturns Extradition Decision Against Two More Turkish Coup-Plotting Soldiers," *Hürriyet Daily News*, December 8, 2016; and "Greece Says Court Decision Not to Extradite Turkish Soldiers Must Be Respected," *VOA News*, June 19, 2017.

have been "seized by Gülenists."[80] Although no EU member state, as of October 2017, had responded to extradition requests or complied with Turkish demands to launch an inquiry about the group, official statements about the MİT's abduction of some 80 suspected Gülenists in 18 countries, including six men from Kosovo in March 2018, likely increased tensions.[81]

Turkey's Security Cooperation with the European Union and NATO

From Ankara's perspective, multilateral crisis management operations had been traditionally understood as useful to underline Turkey's Western and European identity. Even before Turkey and the EU formally agreed in June 2006 on a framework for Turkey's participation in EU crisis management operations, Turkey joined the EU's first military operation in Macedonia in 2003.[82] Based on that framework, Ankara deployed military and police forces to EU missions in the Western Balkans and the Democratic Republic of Congo.[83] By March 2017, Turkey had participated in at least eight operations and been a major contributor to the European Union Force's Operation Althea in Bosnia-Herzegovina, where Turkey's 250 deployed ranked second in number of troops.[84]

From the EU's perspective, integrating Turkey into the EU's Common Security and Defense Policy (CSDP) security architecture comes with three important assets. First, as the debate over İncirlik Air Base has demonstrated, Turkey's geographic location is of high strategic importance, especially with regard to current and future theaters of EU stabilization missions, and Turkey's political influence in these regions can also contribute to conflict management and the success of reconstruction efforts. Second, Turkey's NATO membership and veto rights in the North Atlantic Council make it an indispensable player for any form of EU-NATO cooperation. Third, despite the purges and subsequent decline in certain military capabilities, particularly

---

[80] Fatjona Mejdini, "Albania Weighs Turkey's Claim to Be Gulenist Hub," *Balkan Insight*, November 3, 2016; and Barçın Yinanç, "Turkey's New Foreign Policy Item: FETÖ Diaspora," *Hürriyet Daily News*, August 11, 2016.

[81] "Germany Sees No FETÖ Presence Despite Hundreds of Schools and Fugitives," 2016; "EU Loses Ankara's Trust," *AzerNews*, October 16, 2017; and "Turkey's Spy Agency Has Captured 80 FETÖ-Linked Suspects from 18 Countries: Bozdağ," *Hürriyet Daily News*, April 5, 2018.

[82] European Union and Republic of Turkey, "Agreement Between the European Union and the Republic of Turkey Establishing a Framework for the Participation of the Republic of Turkey in the European Union Crisis Management Operations, of December 21, 2006," *Official Journal of the EU*, Brussels, L 189/17, June 29, 2006; and Steven Blockmans, "Participation of Turkey in the EU's Common Security and Defence Policy: Kingmaker or Trojan Horse?" Leuven Centre for Global Governance Studies, Working Paper No. 41, March 2010, p. 16.

[83] "Turkey Takes Pragmatic Approach to International Peacekeeping," *World Politics Review*, January 20, 2015; and Blockmans, 2010, p. 16.

[84] Thierry Tardy, "CSDP: Getting Third States on Board," Paris: European Union Institute for Security Studies, issue brief, March 2014, p. 1.

air power, Turkey has one of the largest armies in Europe and a growing defense industry supporting its military operations.[85]

Turkey's participation as a third party in CSDP missions is based not only on hopes that this could speed up the accession process but also on Ankara's own security interests in stabilizing both its neighborhood and areas to which it has developed strong ties—such as Africa, where, in May 2019, the EU was involved in eight missions and operations.[86] Hence, even if the accession process were suspended, Turkey would continue to have a genuine interest in security cooperation with the EU. Turkey has, however, been highly skeptical about, and sometimes openly hostile toward, more-institutionalized EU-NATO cooperation in general terms and in the concrete case of NATO's support for the EU's border agency Frontex in the Aegean Sea since February 2016.[87] Turkey's previous privileges in the Western European Union were not equally transferred into the CSDP, where Turkey has not become a part of decisionmaking and operation or mission structures and has been excluded from the European Defence Agency.[88] This, in addition to the unresolved crisis between Turkey and Cyprus, led to a feeling in Ankara of exclusion and lack of trust, which was reflected in Turkey's vetoes of EU-NATO intelligence-sharing and of Cypriot participation in CSDP missions that would involve NATO intelligence and resources.[89] In 2007, Ankara blocked approval of new activation orders for NATO's missions in Kosovo because it involved support to an EU mission, and Ankara took a similar stance against NATO-EU cooperation in Afghanistan.[90]

Turkey's current alienation from the EU and the uncertainty around its accession prospects make it unlikely that Ankara would support significant steps to allow the further institutionalization of EU-NATO cooperation, especially if the Cyprus conflict remains unresolved.[91] Turkey did reluctantly agree in February 2016 to endorse a German initiative to authorize the Standing NATO Maritime Group 2 to provide

---

[85] Blockmans, 2010, p. 19; and "Turkey's Defence Sector to Boost Exports as It Transitions from Arms Procurement to Manufacture and Sale," in Oxford Business Group, *The Report: Turkey 2015*, London, 2016.

[86] Antonio Cascais, "Turkey Seeks Greater Role in Africa," *Deutsche Welle*, June 2, 2016; and European Union External Action, "Military and Civilian Missions and Operations," webpage, May 3, 2019.

[87] NATO, "NATO-EU Relations," Brussels, fact sheet, July 2016a; and Sertif Demir, "Turkey's Contribution to the European Common Security and Defense Policy," *Turkish Public Administration Annual*, Vol. 38, 2012, pp. 5–6.

[88] Oya Dursun-Özkanca, "Turkish Soft Balancing Against the EU? An Analysis of the Prospects for Improved Transatlantic Security Relations," *Foreign Policy Analysis*, Vol. 13, No. 4, October 1, 2017.

[89] Demir, 2012, pp. 4–5, 19–20; Esra Çayhan, "Towards a European Security and Defense Policy: With or Without Turkey?" in Ali Çarkoglu and Barry Rubin, eds., *Turkey and the European Union: Domestic Politics, Economic Integration and International Dynamics*, London: Frank Cass, 2003, p. 46; and İhsan Kızıltan, "Improving the NATO-EU Partnership: A Turkish Perspective," *Turkish Policy Quarterly*, Vol. 7, No. 3, Summer 2008.

[90] See Kızıltan, 2008.

[91] Dursun-Özkanca, 2017, p. 910.

information to the EU's Frontex, as well as to Greece and Turkish coast guards and other authorities, in their efforts to staunch human trafficking and illegal migration in the Aegean Sea.[92] However, Turkey reportedly obstructed implementation of the EU-NATO joint declaration at NATO's Warsaw Summit in July 2016.[93] Ankara's willingness to grind NATO operations to a halt on this matter of principle has angered other allies and could be damaging to Turkey's long-term standing in the Alliance. This is another reason for the United States and the EU to work urgently with Turkey and other relevant parties to resolve the Cyprus issue (see Box 8.1).

NATO-Turkey Relations

Shifting Security Priorities and Hard Realities

There are many elements of continuity in Turkey's relations with NATO. The Turkish government remains committed to NATO, which plays a central role in Turkey's national security strategy and defense plans. Turkey actively engages in Alliance political institutions, which provide it a unique forum to influence Euro-Atlantic security policy deliberations.[94] The TSK participate in NATO's integrated military structure and exercise program and continue to make substantial contributions to current operations, standing forces, and the NATO Response Force.[95] Turkey hosts NATO forces at its İncirlik and Konya air bases, the NATO Land Forces Command in Izmir, and a U.S. early-warning radar system in Kürecik that is part of the European Phased Adaptive Approach to missile defense. The TGS created a Partnership for Peace Training Center in 1998, which provides training to military and civilian personnel to enhance interoperability of NATO's partner nations, and inaugurated the NATO Centre of

---

[92] According to European diplomats we spoke with, the operation had been opposed by the Turkish Ministry of Defense from the start, partly because of fear that it might give Greece some advantage in unresolved disputes over certain islets, whereas the Foreign Ministry argued in favor of the cooperation to bolster relations with Germany (European diplomats, discussion with the authors, Ankara, November 2016). In October 2016, the Turks informed NATO that the Standing NATO Maritime Group along the Turkish coast was no longer needed, given the sharp drop in sea arrivals, and should not be extended beyond December 2016. EU and other NATO members disagreed, and Germany offered to retain responsibility for the Aegean component of Standing NATO Maritime Group 2 for the first half of 2017 before handing over command to the United Kingdom on June 30, 2017. NATO's defense ministers decided in February 2017 to continue the mission "as long as there are prospective illegal migrants or refugees on the other side of the Aegean" (Andrea Shalal, "NATO Nearing Solution to Continue Aegean Migrant Mission: UK General," Reuters, November 30, 2016; and "NATO's Aegean Patrols to Continue," *Ekathimerini*, February 16, 2017).

[93] Donald Tusk, Jean-Claude Juncker, and Jens Stoltenberg, "Joint Declaration by the President of the European Council, the President of the European Commission, and the Secretary General of the North Atlantic Treaty Organization," press release, North Atlantic Treaty Organization, July 8, 2016.

[94] Republic of Turkey Ministry of Foreign Affairs, "Turkey's Relations with NATO," webpage, undated-d.

[95] Republic of Turkey Ministry of Foreign Affairs, "IV. Turkey's International Security Initiatives and Contributions to NATO and EU Operations," webpage, undated-a.

Box 8.1
Cyprus

Magdalena Kirchner

The decades-long division of the island of Cyprus between Greeks in the south (Republic of Cyprus) and Turks in the north (Turkish Republic of Northern Cyprus) has been a central impediment to Turkey's EU membership and integration into EU security structures, as well as aspects of EU-NATO cooperation, especially since the Republic of Cyprus became a member of the EU in 2004.[a] The AKP's initially "proactive policy" toward a solution of the crisis slowed down substantially when Greek Cypriots rejected the Annan Plan for reunification in a 2004 referendum and were welcomed into the EU nonetheless.[b] This decision by the EU granted the Republic of Cyprus a veto over all aspects of Turkey's relations with the EU, eroded Turkish trust in the accession process, and reinforced economic and political disparities between the two Cypriot communities.

Turkey continued to play a pivotal and active role as one of the three security guarantors of Cyprus (along with Greece and the United Kingdom), including when United Nations–sponsored talks resumed in late 2008 and again in 2015. The talks in 2015 opened with great promise because the moderate leaders of two communities were committed to reunification. However, differences over property issues and security arrangements on the island again proved intractable, and talks collapsed on July 7, 2017.[c] A major sticking point was Turkey's refusal to disband the Cyprus Turkish Peace Force Command and withdraw some 40,000 soldiers from the island, deployed there since 1974.[d] From its outset, the latest round of negotiations was undermined by growing nationalist sentiment in Turkey and by the AKP's assessment that Turkey had little to gain from the negotiations' success, especially with its own EU membership aspirations stalled.[e] Success of the talks would have enhanced Ankara's reputation and prestige as a capable conflict manager in its neighborhood and would have benefited Turkey economically.[f] In October 2017, new tensions erupted with the European Commission over statements from Northern Cyprus and Ankara hinting at the establishment of an "autonomous republic" quasi-annexed by Turkey.[g]

Given the enduring stalemate between the two communities on the island and Ankara's hard line on security, it appears that resolution will remain elusive for the foreseeable future and that the Cyprus factor will continue to constrain effective Turkish-EU and NATO-EU security cooperation.

---

[a] Dursun-Özkanca, 2017, p. 904.

[b] The Annan Plan, named for United Nations Secretary General Kofi Annan, would have formed a federation of two constituent states joined together by a federal government apparatus. It would have allowed both Greece and Turkey to maintain permanent military presence on the island, following phased force reductions (Dursun-Özkanca, 2017, p. 904).

[c] Sara Stefanini, "Cyprus Reunification Talks Break Down in Switzerland," *Politico*, November 22, 2016b.

[d] Troop withdrawal remains highly unpopular among Turkey's nationalist circles and could be interpreted as surrender or sellout (Sara Stefanini, "Erdoğan Shadow over Cyprus Peace Bid," *Politico*, February 2, 2016a; Eric Maurice, "Turkey Holds Key at Last-Ditch Cyprus Talks," *EUobserver*, January 9, 2017; Tocci, 2016, p. 6; and former Turkish diplomat, discussion with the authors, Istanbul, November 2016).

[e] Maurice, 2017.

[f] Helena Smith, "Cyprus Reunification Talks Collapse amid Angry Scenes," *The Guardian*, July 7, 2017.

[g] Sarantis Michalopoulos, "EU Tells Ankara to Stay Calm, Respect UN Framework for Cyprus," *EURACTIV*, October 17, 2017.

Excellence for the Defence Against Terrorism in Ankara in 2005. When regional tensions have risen in recent years, Turkey has turned to the United States and its other NATO allies for military support.

However, doubts among the Turkish public and political elite about the reliability of NATO's collective defense commitment and relevance in addressing the country's most-immediate security threats have been growing in recent years, and particularly in nationalist circles. Turkey's rapprochement with Moscow, military cooperation in the Black Sea and Syria, and acquisition of the Russian S-400 missile defense system have led to concerns in other NATO capitals that Turkey is seeking to balance ties to the United States and Europe with new links to Russia. There is also some evidence that advocates of a more fundamental foreign policy reorientation (the Eurasian power option; see Chapter Two) have gained leadership positions in the Foreign Ministry and armed forces as a result of the purges that followed the June 2016 attempted military coup.[96]

Turks who doubt the solidity of NATO's commitment cite several lessons over the past three decades. First, on the eve of the Gulf War in 1991, several NATO allies initially resisted but ultimately approved the deployment of NATO air and air defense capabilities to deter Iraqi attacks against Turkey. In 2003, several allies refused a U.S. request to undertake contingency planning to deter or defend against a possible Iraqi threat to Turkey.[97] And the lack of a coherent NATO response to the Georgia crisis in August 2008 was also troubling to many Turks who wondered how the Alliance might respond in the face of similar aggression against a member state. The episode was seen as a partial justification for Ankara's cautious response and limited consultation with NATO allies in pursuing Turkey's separate diplomatic engagement with Russia and its Caucasus neighbors in the wake of the crisis.

Polling conducted by the German Marshall Fund from 2004 to 2014 found that support for NATO in Turkey was among the lowest of any Alliance country surveyed. The number of Turks who felt "that NATO is still essential for their country's security" dropped steadily, from 53 percent in 2004 to 34 percent in 2007, rising only slightly to 37 percent in 2008 after the Russian attacks on Georgia. Some of this drop can be accounted for by the wave of anti-American sentiment in Turkey in the aftermath of the Iraq War. Support for NATO then rose to 49 percent in 2014 following Russia's illegal annexation of Crimea and intervention in Eastern Ukraine. When asked in 2014 what NATO should be doing, Turks were divided and somewhat conflicted. Fifty-

---

[96] Turkish and European officials and experts, discussion with the authors, Ankara, November 2016 and June 2017; and Turkish and European officials and experts, discussion with the authors during a RAND Corporation workshop on Turkey's foreign policy, Arlington, Va., July 21, 2017.

[97] See Stephen J. Flanagan and Samuel J. Brannen, "Implications for U.S.-Turkey Relations," in Stephen J. Flanagan, Samuel J. Brannen, Bulent Aliriza, Edward C. Chow, Andrew C. Kuchins, Haim Malka, Julianne Smith, Ian Lesser, Eric Palomaa, and Alexandros Petersen, *Turkey's Evolving Dynamics: Strategic Choices for U.S.-Turkey Relations*, Washington, D.C.: Center for Strategic and International Studies, March 2009, pp. 86–87.

seven percent supported NATO's collective defense mission, and a 43 percent plurality supported NATO's work attempting to establish stability in such places as Afghanistan; however, a 42 percent plurality opposed its operating outside the North Atlantic area, and a 47 percent plurality opposed its providing arms and training to other countries (41 percent if Ukraine was mentioned specifically).[98] And in more recent years, public support for NATO appears to have increased further. Annual national polling conducted by Kadir Has University revealed that an average of 67 percent of Turks surveyed between 2015 and 2017 thought that Turkey's membership in NATO should be continued, with a spike of 73 percent in 2016 during the crisis with Russia.[99]

Earlier research found that some in the Turkish national security policy community believe that NATO has been diluted by its expansion in the 1990s and that its members' military capabilities and willingness to meet commitments are not as serious as they used to be. Officials reported that invoking NATO obligations or commitments no longer carried the same weight they once did in Turkish policy deliberations.[100] There is also a sense of ambivalence about NATO among some segments of the Turkish military, particularly in the junior officer corps. Officers who have served in NATO missions and command assignments are reportedly more likely to see NATO's enduring value. However, many of those whose service has focused on Turkey's counterterrorism operations in the southeast see NATO as placing increasingly costly demands for expeditionary operations on the TSK but providing few benefits to Turkish security in return.[101] Responding to concerns expressed by General Petr Pavel, the chairman of NATO's Military Committee, about Turkey's plans to purchase the Russian S-400 missile defense system, MHP leader Devlet Bahçeli responded, "We can buy weapons from whoever we want, and we never have to justify this to NATO. . . . We're not looking at NATO but Qandil," referring to the PKK's safe haven in northern Iraq. "We're engaged in a life and death struggle with murderers. What measures did NATO take against [the Fethullah Terrorist Organization's] July 15 coup attempt, what preventive measures has NATO put into effect?"[102]

A political firestorm erupted in Turkey on November 17, 2017, when a Norwegian civil contractor used a picture of Turkey's founding father Mustafa Kemal Atatürk among "hostile leaders' biographies" in a war game during NATO's 2017 Trident Javelin exercise at its Joint Warfare Centre in Norway. The staffer also set up a dummy chat account called "Erdoğan" for a collaborator with a "leader of an enemy state,"

---

[98] German Marshall Fund of the United States, *Transatlantic Trends 2008*, Washington, D.C., September 20, 2008; and Constanze Stelzenmueller and Joshua Raisher, *Transatlantic Trends 2014*, Washington, D.C.: German Marshall Fund of the United States, September 10, 2014, p. 29.

[99] Kadir Has University, Center for Turkish Studies, 2017.

[100] Flanagan and Brannen, 2009, pp. 86–87.

[101] Turkish and U.S. officials and experts, discussion with the authors, Ankara, June 2017.

[102] "Update—Turkey: Opposition Leader Slams NATO Dig at Defense Buy," *Haberler*, October 31, 2017.

distributing anti-NATO messages. NATO Secretary General Stoltenberg, Norwegian Defense Minister Bakke-Jensen, and the Joint Warfare Centre commander quickly made formal apologies and announced disciplinary action against the staffer, whose actions did not reflect the views of NATO.[103] However, Turkish politicians across party lines asserted that the episode belied a fundamental mistrust of Turkey within some quarters of the Alliance or maybe even Gülenist subterfuge, and the demand "Let's leave NATO" (#*NATO'dan cikalim*) was trending on Turkish social media for at least a day. Erdoğan's spokesman stated, "The case should not be covered up and NATO should not allow anti-Turkey circles to affect the alliance."[104] These incidents have left lingering doubts in Turkey about allies' intentions and the depth of their commitments.

Recent NATO Operations

Turkey has participated in all NATO-led operations in the Balkans since 1995 and continues to provide forces to NATO's Kosovo Force mission and the EU's Operation Althea in Bosnia-Herzegovina—under the mechanisms of NATO support to EU operations.[105] Turkey has also been a major contributor to NATO missions in Afghanistan since 2003. It led International Security Assistance Force VII in 2005 and has had responsibility for the management of Kabul's Hamid Karzai International Airport and the command of the city's Regional Command Capital for an extended period. Turkey has also made major contributions to training the Afghan National Police. High-level Turkish officials have twice served as NATO's senior civilian representative in Afghanistan, and Turkey established two provincial reconstruction teams. Turkey is the only NATO member state that did not reduce the number of troops in Afghanistan after NATO's combat mission ended in 2014. Rather, it expanded its military presence and assumed a larger role in NATO's ongoing Resolute Support mission to provide training, advice, and assistance to the Afghan security forces.[106]

On the other side, NATO allies have undertaken recent operations to defend Turkey. After a Turkish F-4 reconnaissance jet was shot down by Syrian air defenses on June 22, 2012, Ankara invoked Article 4 of the Washington Treaty, which allows a NATO member to ask for consultations with other allies when its territorial integrity, political independence, or security is threatened.[107] NATO allies, as had been expected, publicly condemned the attack as unacceptable, and Ankara refrained from invoking the collective defense provisions in Article 5. Still, Ankara succeeded in putting the

---

[103] "NATO Apologises to Turkey for War Games Blunders," *Al Jazeera*, November 17, 2017.

[104] "Turkey Calls on NATO to 'Not Cover Up' Scandal," *Hürriyet Daily News*, November 20, 2017.

[105] NATO, "Kosovo Force (KFOR): Key Facts and Figures," Brussels, November 19, 2017d; and Republic of Turkey Ministry of Foreign Affairs, undated-a.

[106] Republic of Turkey Ministry of Foreign Affairs, undated-a; and NATO, "Resolute Support Mission (RSM): Key Facts and Figures," Brussels, November 19, 2017e.

[107] NATO, 1949.

Syrian civil war on NATO's agenda.[108] When Syria's shelling of the Turkish border city of Akçakale killed five civilians on October 3, 2012, Ankara again invoked Article 4, and NATO demanded the "immediate cessation of aggressive acts against an ally."[109] Despite fears, especially among European politicians, that NATO could be dragged into the conflict or into the enforcement of a no-fly zone in northern Syria, which Turkey had been advocating, allies responded positively to Turkey's official request on November 21, 2012, to augment its air defense capabilities.[110] Beginning in February 2013, Germany, the Netherlands, and the United States deployed two Phased Array Tracking Radar to Intercept of Target (PATRIOT) batteries each to one of three sites in southern Turkey under NATO operational command and control.[111] The Dutch withdrew their batteries in January 2015 because of resource constraints, and those two were replaced by a single Spanish battery. Because the U.S. PATRIOT batteries are in high demand in other theaters and because U.S. officials assessed that the threat to Turkey could be handled by other capabilities, including NATO aircraft based there, the United States withdrew its batteries in October 2015, despite an appeal by Ankara. Germany followed suit in January 2016. To reassure Ankara, NATO issued statements that allies were prepared to send ground forces to defend Turkey. As of January 2017, and after the withdrawal of the initial six deployed batteries, Italy and Spain were continuing to contribute one PATRIOT missile battery and one Aster Sol-Air Moyenne Portee Terrestre (SAMP/T) battery each.[112]

Despite Turkey's rapprochement with Russia since President Erdoğan apologized in early 2016 for the downing of a Russian bomber in 2015, Erdoğan remains deeply concerned about Russian military activities in the Black Sea region. On the eve of the 2016 Warsaw Summit, he lamented NATO's lack of a visible military presence in the region and called on allies to take steps to prevent the Black Sea from becoming "a Russian lake."[113] In addition, Russia's military buildup in Crimea since 2014, plans for expanding its Black Sea Fleet, and military operations in Syria and the Eastern Mediterranean, discussed in Chapter Six, have been a reminder to Turks of the value of NATO's collective defense commitment.

---

[108] Sami Kohen, "NATO Stands Behind Turkey, Condemns Syria for Downing Jet," *Al-Monitor*, June 26, 2012; and Tülin Daloğlu, "Syrian Downing of Turkish Plane Adds to Strain on Both Regimes," *Al-Monitor*, June 25, 2012.

[109] NATO, "NATO Support to Turkey: Background and Timeline," Brussels, February 19, 2013.

[110] NATO, 2013; and Ayhan Simsek, "Confusion over Turkey's Request for Patriots," *Deutsche Welle*, November 23, 2012.

[111] NATO, 2013.

[112] Eric Schmitt, "After Delicate Negotiations, U.S. Says It Will Pull Patriot Missiles from Turkey," *New York Times*, August 16, 2015; NATO, "Augmentation of Turkey's Air Defence," Brussels, fact sheet, January 2017a; and Burak Bekdil, "Germany Pulls Patriot Systems from Turkey," *Defense News*, December 23, 2015b.

[113] Jones and Hille, 2016.

Impact of Bilateral Political Tensions

Turkey's strained bilateral relations with several NATO member states have also been a difficult balancing act for the Alliance and have sometimes complicated operations and cooperation with the EU.

At NATO's 2016 Warsaw Summit, just days prior to the July 15, 2016, military coup attempt in Turkey, members tentatively agreed to Erdoğan's offer to hold the next summit in 2018 in Istanbul.[114] By late May 2017, however, German media reported that at least 18 member states, among them Germany and Canada, opposed the summit being held in Turkey based on bilateral tensions and to "avoid the impression that NATO supports the Turkish government's internal policy."[115] Although Ankara called these claims unfounded, Secretary General Stoltenberg announced at the defense ministers meeting in June 2017 that the next summit would be held in Brussels.[116]

When Austria, a NATO partner country that has contributed more than 400 soldiers to the Kosovo Force since 1999, began calling for ending Turkey's EU membership talks, Ankara started to veto NATO cooperation with Vienna in November 2016, therefore effectively blocking all cooperation programs, including education, training, and military exercises, with nonmember states.[117] NATO members managed in May 2017 to lift the overall blockade on partnership through a technical amendment. Austria, however, continued to be excluded from partnership programs, which could cause problems (e.g., for preparing missions in Kosovo).[118]

The German-Turkish bilateral crisis, simmering since the 2013 Gezi Park protests, negatively affected security cooperation prior to the coup attempt and escalated further in 2017, putting NATO deployments in Turkey at risk. On June 2, 2016, the Bundestag declared that the mass killings of Armenians by Ottoman Turks in 1915 amounted to a genocide. Three weeks later, Ankara denied German parliamentarians access to visit the 260 German soldiers supporting Tornado surveillance jets and tanker aircraft at İncirlik Air Base; Berlin had deployed these troops in December 2015 under a bilateral agreement as a national contribution to the Global Coalition to Defeat ISIS. Furthermore, Ankara stalled German plans to expand future deploy-

---

[114] Saim Saeed, "EU Countries Move to Block Turkey from Hosting NATO Summit: Report," *Politico*, May 31, 2017; and Tom Körkemeier and Shadia Nasralla, "Turkey Blocks Some Cooperation with NATO Partners as EU Row Escalates," Reuters, March 15, 2017.

[115] Saeed, 2017.

[116] Uğur Çil, "Turkey Slams German Daily over NATO Summit Accusations," Anadolu Agency, May 2, 2017; and David M. Herszenhorn and Jacopo Barigazzi, "Snubbing Turkish Offer, NATO Plans Next Summit in Brussels," *Politico*, June 29, 2017.

[117] Peter Baugh, "Turkey Vetoes NATO-Austria Partnership," *Politico*, May 23, 2017.

[118] "NATO Ends Partnership Deadlock over Turkey-Austria Dispute," *New Arab*, May 24, 2017; and Körkemeier and Nasralla, 2017.

ments at the İncirlik base.[119] On-site visits to military missions are an important part of the Bundestag's constitutional function to monitor the government's foreign and security policy. Lawmakers were allowed to visit the base only in October 2016, after the German government had publicly declared the Bundestag vote as nonbinding.[120] Tensions over the air base flared up again in May 2017, when Ankara barred German lawmakers again from visiting İncirlik, and on June 7, 2017, Berlin decided to redeploy soldiers and aircraft to the Muwaffaq Salti Air Base in Jordan.[121]

Although Stoltenberg deemed formal NATO mediation unnecessary in the İncirlik case, he cautioned against linking that case to NATO's deployment of the Airborne Warning and Control System in Konya, where Germany provides 30 percent of all personnel.[122] When Berlin rejected Turkish efforts to remove individual lawmakers from a delegation list to Konya in July 2017 and protested in Brussels under pressure from parliamentarians who were calling for unilaterally withdrawing troops from the mission, NATO took a formal mediation role and facilitated the visit of seven German parliamentarians as part of a NATO delegation led by Deputy Secretary General Rose Gottemoeller in September 2017.[123]

Policy differences between Turkey and the United States, particularly with respect to the decision to train and equip the Kurdish YPG militias in the campaign against ISIS in Syria and the U.S. refusal to extradite Fethullah Gülen, have led to concerns that Turkey might evict U.S. forces and aircraft from İncirlik, thereby disrupting coalition air operations against ISIS. While there was a brief disruption of coalition air operations following the June 2016 coup attempt, this fear has not been realized. Nevertheless, as Murat Yetkin, editor of *Hürriyet Daily News*, noted, the United States is "the locomotive force of NATO," and these disputes are "prompting both Americans and Turks to question the long-running alliance between their countries."[124]

---

[119] Matthias Gebauer, "Türkei untersagt Besuch von deutschem Staatssekretaer," *Spiegel Online*, June 6, 2016; and "Germany to Invest €58 Million in Turkish Airbase: Report," *The Local*, September 6, 2016.

[120] "Turkey Grants Germany Access to İncirlik After Meeting 'Expectations,'" *Rudaw*, September 8, 2016.

[121] Magdalena Kirchner, "'Out-Cirlik': After Months of Tensions, Domestic Pressure Drives German Cabinet to Vacate Turkey's Incirlik Airbase Diminishing Support for the Assault on Raqqa," American Institute for Contemporary German Studies, June 14, 2017a.

[122] NATO, "Joint Press Statements by NATO Secretary General Jens Stoltenberg and the President of Montenegro, Filip Vujanović—Secretary General's Remarks," Brussels, press statement, June 7, 2017b; and Julian E. Barnes and Emre Peker, "Disputes Between Germany and Turkey Threaten to Affect NATO Mission," *Wall Street Journal*, July 24, 2017.

[123] Matthias Gebauer, "Türkei blockiert Abgeordneten-Besuch auf Nato-Basis," *Spiegel Online*, July 14, 2017; "Turkey Confirms German MPs Will Visit Troops in Konya Under NATO Flag," *Hürriyet Daily News*, August 10, 2017; and NATO, "NATO Deputy Secretary General Leads Parliamentary Delegation to Konya," Brussels, September 8, 2017c.

[124] Dorian Jones, "Turkey Hosts Iranian, Russian FMs as Ankara-NATO Dispute Festers," Voice of America, November 19, 2017.

Table 8.1 provides a summary assessment of where Turkish interests are convergent, divergent, or in conflict with those of members of the EU and most other NATO allies.

Conclusion and Implications for U.S. and Allied Interests

The unprecedented crisis between Turkey and the EU, including disputes with individual EU members, has major implications for Turkey's membership aspirations, bilateral and multilateral cooperation in several fields, and the domestic stability of a long-standing U.S. strategic ally in Europe. The crisis in Turkey's relations with Europe, combined with Ankara's deepening policy differences with the United States and Canada, are also undermining the cohesion of NATO and effective defense and security cooperation with Turkey during a volatile period in the Middle East and Eurasia.

Although there is no formal agreement among EU members to formally suspend Turkey's membership bid, negotiations have been de facto frozen since Turkey's 2017 constitutional referendum, and no EU member is expected to take the initiative to convince its peers to give Turkey, under the current conditions, another try. In contrast,

Table 8.1
Alignment of Turkish Interests with European Union and NATO Interests

Neighbor or Partner	Converging Interests	Diverging Interests	Conflicting Interests
EU	• Trade and energy • Economic ties	• Migration crisis • Counterterrorism and the flow of foreign fighters • EU visa liberalization	• Democratic backsliding in Turkey • Turkish diasporas in Europe • Syria policy • European asylum to Gülenists and coup suspects • Irregular detention of EU citizens in Turkey • Turkey's competing maritime claims with Greece and Cyprus in the Eastern Mediterranean and the Aegean
NATO	• Solidarity against threats to Turkish territorial integrity • Turkish role in Afghanistan • Denial of Russian dominance in and power projection from the Black Sea	• Democratic backsliding in Turkey • Approach to Russia • Restrictions on Incirlik Air Base, which affect U.S. and German operations	• Acquisition of non-NATO defense systems • Aggressive Turkish challenges to Greek and Cypriot maritime claims, which risk conflict

resumed debates in Turkey about reintroducing capital punishment could further isolate the country, because the necessary denouncement of the European Convention on Human Rights would cost Ankara its seat in the Council of Europe. Hence, even an alternative transactional model of EU-Turkish relations limiting cooperation to free trade, immigration, and counterterrorism would be hard to establish in the near future. This is particularly true since the EU in June 2018 conditioned initiation of a new round of trade talks with Ankara on democratic reforms and the full restoration of the rule of law in Turkey. In addition, Ankara is likely to continue to resist EU pressure to make changes in its terrorism laws in order to gain visa liberalization for Turkish citizens traveling to EU countries.

From a U.S. perspective, a full collapse of Turkey's EU membership would demonstrate, on the one hand, the limitations of the EU's efforts to anchor policy reforms in third countries as a means of projecting stability. On the other hand, the collapse would make it necessary, albeit more difficult, to engage Turkey directly on sensitive issues in an extremely polarized environment.

Against this backdrop, foreign investors and credit rating agencies express grave concerns about the effect of political developments in Turkey and the lack of economic and legal reforms. In the months after the military coup attempt, S&P Global Ratings, Moody's, and Fitch have downgraded Turkey to noninvestment grades, citing a difficult investment climate, worries about the rule of law, risks from external financing, and slow growth. Inflation reached a nine-year high of 11.9 percent in October 2017, with the U.S. dollar hitting an all-time high against the Turkish lira at 3.9780 in late November.[125] An economic situation that volatile could easily spill over into politics, especially as political leaders accuse the mentioned rating agencies of being part of an external conspiracy against Turkey.

In terms of security cooperation, the bilateral crisis with the EU and the significantly lowered enthusiasm of Turkish decisionmakers to join Western missions as a way of anchoring itself in the West could reduce Ankara's readiness to deploy troops to CSDP missions. Multiple incidents have also demonstrated both Ankara's and EU members' willingness to drag bilateral conflicts into NATO, which publicly undermines Alliance cohesion. This spillover has led to instances in which Ankara has blocked consensus on important policy documents and on activation orders for NATO missions in Kosovo and Afghanistan involving support to the EU.

While the Turkish government officially professes its continuing commitment to the Alliance's core missions and remains a significant contributor to operations and the command structure, there is growing disillusionment with NATO in Turkey. Nevertheless, Turkish leaders still look to the collective defense commitments Alliance membership affords whenever they face a serious military threat and recognize that there is

---

[125] Selcan Hacaoglu and Onur Ant, "Turkey Core Inflation Hits Its Highest Level in 13 Years," *Bloomberg*, November 3, 2017.

no viable alternative. At the same time, NATO member governments are increasingly fatigued by the transactional nature of the relationship in that it regularly takes high-level political intervention and bargaining to gain Ankara's assent to important operational and policy decisions. This suggests continuing frictions with Turkey in Alliance management but no rupture in relations.

Voices in the Turkish political establishment and military leadership are openly questioning how relevant NATO is to Turkey's most-pressing security concern—countering terrorism at home and in its immediate neighborhood; in addition, these voices are concerned that, in the case of Syria, the United States and other allies are pursuing strategies that are inimical to Turkish security. There is a small but vocal number of Turkish political figures openly calling for Turkey to reassess its relationship with NATO and advocating deeper cooperation with Russia and Iran to deal with regional security challenges. As discussed in Chapter Six, Moscow has been adept in exploiting and amplifying these fissures and casting itself as Turkey's more reliable economic and security partner. Lingering unease in Ankara about Moscow's recent actions, long-term intentions, and growing military capabilities have limited the effectiveness of this appeal and left Turkey trying to straddle the fence between its longtime allies and newfound partner. The outrage in Turkey over the Trident Javelin exercise in Norway illustrates, however, how volatile the political situation has become in Turkey and how quickly Russia can exploit these missteps to try to cause a crisis. There is little doubt that Moscow is engaged in an intensive campaign to win the hearts and minds of the Turkish political establishment and public and is steadily gaining ground.

The United States and Europe are not without significant leverage over Ankara and should not be reluctant to use it in seeking to manage policy differences. At the same time, better coordination is needed to prevent Ankara from playing its Western partners against each other, especially with regard to bilateral security cooperation or their citizens in Turkish detention. Despite differences over strategy, the United States and Europe still share many common interests with Turkey in combating terrorism, limiting Iranian influence, maintaining stability in the Middle East, and even deterring further Russian aggression. U.S. and allied leaders will need strategic patience and steady engagement to manage those differences as Turkey sorts out its internal political turmoil, copes with a deteriorating regional security situation, and charts a more effective foreign and security policy.

CHAPTER NINE

Implications for the U.S.-Turkish Partnership and the U.S. Army

Stephen J. Flanagan and Peter A. Wilson

In this chapter, we consider the implications of the trends in Turkey's internal affairs and foreign and security policies (documented in Chapters Two through Eight) for relations with the United States, particularly U.S. defense plans, military posture, and the U.S. Army over the coming decade. We begin with a summary assessment of the political and social forces that are likely to sustain Turkey's internal turmoil. We then outline how the likely developments in Turkey's relations with its neighbors and other key countries, based on earlier analysis of where national interests are convergent, divergent, or in conflict, will affect U.S. strategic interests, particularly preventing the development of a regional hegemon. We also summarize how U.S. and Turkish interests align or diverge and the likely points of friction and suggest ways to manage them and sustain critical elements of bilateral and multilateral political, defense, and military cooperation. We close the chapter by postulating four plausible future geostrategic orientations for Turkey.

Turkey's Uncertain Trajectory

Domestic Polarization

As explored in Chapter Two, Turkey remains highly polarized on political, religious, and ethnic lines as President Recep Tayyip Erdoğan and the AKP move to implement fundamental changes in governance and society that, if fully realized, will result in the establishment of an authoritarian state with political power centralized in the president and the dominant party. Erdoğan is more openly embracing ethnic Turkish nationalism as his guiding ideology while taking steps to enlarge the role of religion in public life and to marginalize his opponents and a large segment of the population that still supports the parliamentarian political system and secular order.

Erdoğan and the AKP retain an upper hand in political life, and the main opposition parties—the CHP and the HDP—have been marginalized by the government's domination of the media and legal challenges; furthermore, parliamentary oversight is limited. CHP leadership demonstrated that it can still mobilize protests, and the party's dynamic presidential candidate in the June 2018 presidential elections energized the CHP base and forged an inclusive alliance with four opposition parties. On the political right, polls showed greater support for Meral Akşener and the İP, in opposition to AKP rule, than for the AKP's electoral ally, the MHP. Despite vigorous campaigns by opposition parties, Erdoğan and the AKP proved unstoppable, given their domination of the media and a distorted electoral process under a state of emergency that offered them every advantage. Erdoğan won a decisive first-round victory with 52.6 percent of the vote, and the MHP earned a critical 11 percent of seats in Parliament, allowing it to play an influential role in future government policy initiatives. Nevertheless, these results, as well as the 2019 election of CHP candidates to be mayors in six of Turkey's ten largest cities—particularly the decisive victory of Ekrem İmamoğlu in Istanbul—illustrate that Erdoğan and the AKP are not invincible.

Turkey's internal security situation will remain fraught (1) in the absence of a sustained effort to address the concerns of the Kurds and other national minorities and (2) with the continuation of harsh measures to combat the continuing transnational insurgency being waged by the PKK and other violent Kurdish groups. There is little prospect of the AKP reviving the peace talks with the PKK, which continued on and off since 2008 and collapsed in 2015, in the near future, especially as Ankara remains focused on defeating the Kurdish YPG militias in Syria, to the dismay of many Turkish Kurds. In the first four weeks of Operation Olive Branch in early 2018, Turkish authorities arrested 845 people on "terrorism propaganda" charges for participating in protests against the operation or criticizing it in social media outlets.[1] The threat of mass casualty attacks in Turkey remains a major domestic concern in light of past attacks and the substantial presence of ISIS affiliates and other terrorist groups. These threats have placed increased demands on security and police forces, whose ranks have been diminished by purges of alleged Gülenists and targeted attacks. Since the Gezi Park protests of 2013, the police have been militarized and granted extensive authorities to suppress domestic dissent. To fill some gaps in police capabilities, local governments have increasingly turned to hiring heavily armed neighborhood guards and private security officers, who have limited training and whose firms have varying agendas.

Foreign and Defense Policy: From "Zero Problems" to "Precious Loneliness"
The AKP has moved away from the strategy of its first years in power, which gave priority to European integration, good relations with the United States, and the leveraging of Turkey's economic strength and Ottoman heritage to build good relations with all its neighbors—a policy that was dubbed "zero problems." Erdoğan is now pursuing a realist balancing strategy in foreign affairs, seeking to leave open options that will best advance his consolidation of power and Turkish national interests. Erdoğan's

---

[1]   Media and Law Studies Association, "845 People in Turkey Detained for Criticizing Military Campaign in Syria," February 27, 2018.

often provocative actions and rhetoric that express his disappointment with Europe, the United States, and Israel have further strained relations with these longtime allies. Erdoğan is more focused on building the country's stature in the Islamic world and forging new ties with Russia and China. He has not given up on the West but appears to hope that he can elicit favorable policy changes from allies and partners by demonstrating that he has options. Up until U.S. President Donald Trump announced his decision to move the U.S. embassy in Israel to Jerusalem in December 2017, Turkish officials expressed hopes that Trump would bring a fresh start in relations with Washington, and Erdoğan has been using his budding relationship with French President Emmanuel Macron to bring a reset in relations with the EU.

Turkish leaders have tried to forge wary partnerships with historic rivals Russia and Iran, particularly as these two gained control over the end game in the Syrian civil war since 2015. Differences with Iraq, many Gulf states, and Egypt over the AKP's ties to the Muslim Brotherhood, policies in the wake of the Arab Spring, and stance on Qatar have seemed to diminish the stature in the Arab world that Turkey had around 2010. As policy differences with nearly all its neighbors and allies have mounted, leaders of the AKP and the MHP have argued that Turkey must be more self-reliant in protecting its interests and accept a "precious loneliness" in taking principled stands to defend its values and national interests. The AKP's foreign policy continues to reflect an anticolonial nationalism borne of this period and a suspicion of globalization and foreign influence widespread in all segments of Turkish society. Polls conducted in November 2017 indicated that more than 84 percent of Turks overall agree at least somewhat that global economic and political elites have too much power over Turkey and should be resisted, and 83 percent of respondents stated that they hold unfavorable views of the Unites States.[2] If a viable opposition leader or coalition were to emerge in Turkey and dislodge Erdoğan and the AKP from power after 2023, one could expect a more conciliatory approach from Turkey, because the three leading opposition parties in the 2018 elections ran on platforms calling for revitalizing relations with NATO allies and the EU. Nevertheless, deep public suspicion of the United States and Europe would constrain the pace and scope of a future rapprochement.

Continuation of current trends over the next five to ten years likely will lead to Turkish foreign and defense policies that are contrary, in varying degrees, to the interests of the United States and other NATO allies and that undermine long-standing aspects of defense and security cooperation. This situation warrants a fundamental reassessment of U.S. and European strategy toward Turkey, preparations for disruptive developments in all aspects of relations, and initiatives that could maintain cooperation on abiding mutual interests over the next decade and help restore long-standing ties if these trends are reversed.

---

[2] See Halpin et al., 2018, p. 22.

Impact on the Turkish Armed Forces

Erdoğan and the AKP have systematically strengthened civilian authority over the military since 2010 by gaining a decisive hand in the promotion and selection process, overseeing purges of military personnel, and increasing legal authorities for command and control. The AKP seized on the 2011 resignations of the chief of the TGS and service commanders, who were protesting show trials against their fellow officers, to appoint more-compliant and loyal military leaders. The AKP has deepened political influence over annual promotion decisions in the YAŞ and through the purge of almost half of the general and flag officers since the failed July 2016 military coup. Under post-coup reforms, the chief of the TGS now reports to the president, and service commanders come under the immediate control of the civilian minister of defense. Under the approved constitutional changes, the president is able to issue orders directly to those commanders, diminishing the authority of the TGS chief to more of a coordinator. These organizational reforms have muddied the chain of command, increased interservice rivalry, and led to a politicization of the officer corps. Parliamentary oversight of the TSK budget and posture is likely to diminish further under the constitutional changes.

As noted in Chapter Two, TGS Chief Hulusi Akar's retention of his position in the August 2017 YAŞ meeting and subsequent appointment as Minister of Defense in July 2018 in the first presidential decree under the new executive presidential system suggest that he will remain the leading figure in Turkish military affairs. Akar has been a key interlocutor for U.S. and other foreign counterparts. At that same 2017 YAŞ meeting, Erdoğan approved new commanders for the Turkish Land Forces and Air Force, as well as a major shakeup in the leadership of the Navy, which left the service with a commander who has the lowest seniority among his fellow chiefs. The 2017 YAŞ meeting also extended the terms of an unusual number of senior officers who qualified for retirement, and others were promoted to one-star rank. These actions may be designed to help deal with the effects of post-coup purges, which created a significant gap between the number of four-star and one-star general and flag officers. The leadership changes make clear that Erdoğan wants the armed forces to focus on succeeding at operations in Syria, combating terrorism, and rooting out Gülenists, with priority being given to the Turkish Land Forces and the Gendarmerie.

The TSK ranks have been severely reduced by post-coup purges. Of 325 general and flag officers in the Army, Navy, and Air Force, 150 (46 percent) have either been cashiered or involuntarily retired. By December 2018, 15,154 members of the TSK, including 7,595 officers (about 23 percent of early 2016 totals), had been dismissed.[3] The National Defense University, established after the 2016 coup attempt, is supervising all levels of professional military education and appears to have a mandate to break down the TSK's insular culture as guardians of secularism and ensure that more-diverse recruits are being enlisted from civilian universities. However, as of early 2018,

---

[3] "Turkey Remands in Custody 118 Soldiers over Suspected FETÖ Links," 2018.

the number of cadets who had graduated from the university was insufficient to restore the TSK's pre-coup force levels.[4] In January 2018, the TSK announced plans to recruit 42,938 new personnel to fill its depleted ranks, but we do not yet know the outcome of this effort.[5]

The purges and military reforms have adversely affected the TSK's strategic and tactical capacity, readiness, and morale. The purges have been most damaging to the Turkish Air Force and have created a substantial shortage of experienced combat pilots. Before the failed coup, the Air Force had nearly two pilots for each of its 333 combat-capable aircraft. The dismissal of 280 pilots reduced that ratio to less than one pilot per aircraft as of September 2017. By mid-2018, the Air Force reportedly had 400 combat-ready pilots (a 1.2 pilot-to-aircraft ratio), but knowledgeable officials and experts expect that it will take at least three to five years to restore the Air Force's combat readiness. There also appear to be lingering shortages of Army helicopter pilots after the dismissal of 40 personnel. These shortfalls create stresses on forces that are engaged in strikes on the PKK, patrolling Turkish airspace, and supporting TSK ground operations in Syria.[6] There are also reports that many helicopter pilots and other commissioned and noncommissioned officers in the Air Force's elite Combat Search and Rescue unit, as well commanders of the Navy's Underwater Assault Unit, were dismissed on charges of supporting the coup.[7]

As for the other services, one of the keenest Turkish observers of the TSK, Metin Gurcan, has advanced the following assessment of the purges among the Turkish Land Forces:

> In the army, most of the purges are from the general staff and service command headquarters in Ankara, and from corps and brigades in Istanbul and Ankara, as those were the ones that overwhelmingly participated in the July 15 uprising. The Second Army Command in Malatya, which is responsible for combating terrorism in the southeast, and soldiers who served in Turkish operations in Syria have been the least affected so far, with a high probability of being purged later. This speaks to the government's pragmatic approach to de-Gulenification of the military. Today, about 20 brigades of the Second Army Command are operationally active with new commanders.[8]

The Navy has been the service least affected by the purges; most of its dismissals were in the command offices in Ankara or of personnel serving in rear headquarters.

---

[4] Gurcan, 2018.

[5] "Turkish General Staff to Recruit over 40,000 Personnel as Compensation for Post-Coup Attempt Dismissals," 2018.

[6] Gurcan, 2018; and Turkish experts, discussion with the authors, Ankara, June 2017.

[7] Gurcan, 2018.

[8] Gurcan, 2018; and Turkish experts, discussion with the authors, Ankara, June 2017.

The purges of hundreds of mid-level officers who received advanced training in the United States and were involved in transformation projects could slow modernization efforts. The full transfer of the Gendarmerie to the Ministry of Interior could result in a force that is loyal to the AKP and could reduce the joint capabilities for the Army and the Gendarmerie to conduct counterterrorism and wartime territorial defense missions. Unusual political activity by the military leadership and a general decline in professionalism has alienated lower ranks of the TSK. Mid-level officers are reported to be extremely frustrated with the military leadership and concerned about being removed in the continuing post-coup purges. This discontent could even lead to another coup attempt at some point, and Erdoğan appears to take the threat seriously. Public trust in the military, previously seen as the guardian of order and the secular state, has eroded, and many Turks feel that there is no institution left that can reliably assure their security.

Relations with Neighbors: Implications for U.S. Interests

The Levant and the Wider Middle East: Problems in All Directions

As Turkish leaders survey the country's regional environment, wherever they look, they are faced with upheaval and changes that complicate their strategic choices. The challenges in dealing with Turkey's neighbors to the south are particularly vexing.

Despite lingering mutual suspicions and deep religious and political differences, Turkey and Iran have pursued pragmatic relations over the past 20 years when certain interests have converged. The Syrian civil war and growing Iranian influence in Syria and Iraq have strained relations between Tehran and Ankara. Ankara has had trepidation about the major role Iranian and Iranian-backed forces have played in operations to defeat ISIS, fearing that these forces' enduring presence in Iraq and Syria would expand Tehran's regional influence. During the height of the civil war, Tehran denounced Turkey's support to the Syrian opposition as abetting terrorists, and Iranian leaders remain suspicious of Ankara's dealings with both rebels and jihadi groups in Syria. Shared concerns about the possible emergence of an independent Kurdish state in Iraq led to parallel political efforts and military threats to prevent this development in 2017.

Although leaders of the two governments agreed in 2017 to intelligence-sharing and coordinated exercises and tactical operations to enhance border security, including to restrict smuggling that has benefited the separatist PKK and PJAK, Tehran is unlikely to support combined operations with Turkey against PKK strongholds in Iraq.[9] Tehran has played a double game in dealings with various Kurdish groups. With

---

[9] Metin Gurcan, "Turkey, Iran Could Unite to Overcome Their Kurdish Worries, *Al-Monitor*, October 10, 2017d. Turkey and Iran have shared tactical intelligence and coordinated air strikes in 2008–2009 to cut PKK and PJAK transit routes in the Qandil Mountains along their borders with northern Iraq (Malka, 2009, p. 46).

ISIS defeated, the basis for Turkish-Iranian cooperation is Syria has narrowed. Given Tehran's continuing support for the Assad regime, it decried Ankara's Operation Olive Branch to cut off the YPG militias in northwestern Syria from their brethren east of the Euphrates. Mutual interests in expanding limited trade, particularly in energy, and cooperation on securing borders, reducing transnational crime, and limiting the influence of extraregional powers in their neighborhood constitute a base for future cooperation. This was also underlined by the lack of criticism from Ankara of the crackdown on protests in several Iranian cities in early 2018. Nevertheless, Turkish-Iranian relations are likely to remain circumspect, given the overall divergence of their regional and security interests, Ankara's concerns about Tehran's nuclear weapon program, and abiding distrust and sectarian sentiments.

Given mutual mistrust between Turkey and the Iraqi central government, relations are likely to remain uneven. Ankara has concerns about Iranian influence over Baghdad and retains a strong interest in protecting the Turkmen population in northern Iraq. Despite periods of tension, economic interests have helped stabilize bilateral relations, and the two governments came together in 2017 to thwart the independence referendum by the KRG. Nevertheless, Turkey continues to value an autonomous KRG as an important trading partner and a balance against Iranian influence over Baghdad. Both Ankara and Baghdad have increased leverage over the KRG since the fall of Kirkuk, but it remains to be seen whether this will bolster cooperation among all three parties in countering the PKK in the post–Masoud Barzani era. There are several flashpoints that could lead to conflicts in northern Iraq: the enduring presence of about 2,000 Turkish troops in Bashiqa near Mosul, the role of the Shi'a Popular Mobilization Units, and the PKK presence in Sinjar in northwestern Iraq.

Turkey will continue to welcome U.S. efforts to counter Iran's drive for regional hegemony, but specific Turkish policies toward Iran, Iraq, and Syria will often be at odds with U.S. approaches. Ankara supports the unity of Iraq but has lingering impulses to intervene in Iraqi politics and harbors latent territorial claims. Ankara also shares U.S. support for maintaining the territorial integrity of Syria, but its priority there is to prevent the emergence of a Kurdish mini-state along Turkey's southern border, which it sees as being fostered by U.S. support for the YPG. Ankara also shares U.S. and European concerns that Iran plans to develop a military supply and oil pipeline corridor through parts of Iraq and Syria to the Mediterranean that would run along that same border. In addition, Turkey shares the U.S. and European interest of limiting Russian influence in Syria and the Eastern Mediterranean, even as Ankara has been forced to deal with both Moscow and Tehran in trying to end the conflict.

The Arab states to Turkey's south have long looked to Ankara as a highly capable Sunni partner in blunting the Iranian challenge to the regional order—a need that has become more acute with the growth in Iranian influence in Iraq and Syria. Ankara's more-pragmatic policies toward Iran and Syria have disappointed the Arab world, but maintaining Turkey as key partner remains a priority for those states. The AKP's embrace of the forces of change, particularly support for the Muslim Brotherhood, disrupted Turkey's relationships with the UAE and Egypt. In contrast, Qatar and Turkey are building a genuine strategic partnership based on deepening economic and military cooperation and a shared vision that political Islam plays a crucial role in the region's development. The complex relationships between Turkey and the Arab states could improve or deteriorate in response to diminished salience of recent political turmoil or a shift in national priorities (described in Chapter Four) but will likely constrain advancement of U.S. foreign policy and security interests. The overarching challenge is that the differing priorities of Ankara and Arab capitals are likely to continue to create obstacles for the United States gaining partner support for regional initiatives, as happened in the efforts to assemble the counter-ISIS coalition. The second major challenge for the United States stemming from intraregional competition is the impact of Turkish involvement in the intra-GCC rift. On the one hand, the rift is beneficial insofar as it may deter the Saudi-led bloc from military action against its neighbor, but on the other hand, the rift will almost certainly prolong the dispute, which Washington wants to resolve quickly because Turkey's support for Doha puts Qatar on closer parity with its GCC challengers. One benefit of these intraregional fissures is that they limit the risk that a Sunni coalition would feel it had the strength to mount an offensive against Iran, which could fuel an inadvertent regional war that the United States would feel compelled to enter.

Meanwhile, Turkish-Israeli relations will continue to be closely linked to developments on the Arab-Israeli and Israeli-Palestinian fronts. After a long period of close economic, diplomatic, and military ties, bilateral relations between Turkey and Israel soured during the 2000s. The second Palestinian uprising, the AKP's more confrontational stance toward Israel, the Second Lebanon War, and clashes over Israel's Gaza policies exacerbated tensions, culminating in a six-year rift between the countries from 2011 to 2016. Their partial reconciliation in mid-2016 encouraged stakeholders in each country who were eager to resume aspects of collaboration, but little progress has been made. Improved Israeli-Turkish relations face formidable obstacles, primarily deep mistrust between the current political leaderships in both countries and divergences on the Palestinian issue. Washington could use its leverage to encourage both governments to avoid escalatory rhetoric on sensitive issues and dampen ideological differences. Doing so might allow pragmatic cooperation or parallel efforts that would advance mutual interests in developing energy sources and infrastructure, countering Iran's regional aspirations, and combating terrorism. Israel's new association with NATO is another avenue for U.S.-Turkish-Israeli cooperation that aligns with U.S. interest and hinges on continued Turkish consent. Furthermore, the United States has geostrategic and economic interests in the emerging Israeli-Turkish-Cypriot gas deal. Turkey's ties with Hamas could, in a changed political context, also be helpful to the United States and its other allies in the region in advancing an Israeli-Palestinian peace process.

Russia, the Caucasus, and Central Asia

Turkish-Russian relations historically have been adversarial, defined by competition for influence and power across the Black Sea region. A circumspect warming in relations since the end of the Cold War has been driven, in large measure, by mutual interests in expanded economic and energy ties. Today, the two governments claim to be pursuing a strategic partnership but are pulled between elements of cooperation and potential for conflict. Examination of five key elements of the Russian-Turkish relationship—economic and energy ties, Western institutions, authoritarian domestic politics, Black Sea issues, and Middle East ambitions—indicates that, although some convergent interests may continue to draw the two countries together in the coming years, there are also significant points of friction and divergent interests. Deepening energy and economic ties, including a new TurkStream gas pipeline under the Black Sea; close personal ties between Presidents Erdoğan and Putin; recent bilateral diplomatic and military coordination in Syria; and Turkey's purchase of Russian S-400 air and missile defense systems represent tangible manifestations of improved relations. The surge in Russian ambitions and relative military power in the Black Sea region, enduring differences between each country's policies and goals in the Middle East (especially Syria), and the tension between Turkey's interest in retaining a NATO security guarantee and Russia's efforts to lure Ankara away from the Alliance and diminish its unity present sizable roadblocks to a deep bilateral partnership.

The crisis of 2015–2016, following Ankara's downing of a Russian bomber that violated Turkish airspace, demonstrated that economic and leadership ties, while currently strong, have failed to prevent volatile shifts in bilateral relations. Whether Russia and Turkey are able to reach a new modus vivendi or will continue to muddle through in a mix of cooperation and conflict by managing important differences will likely depend, in large measure, on Turkish willingness to acquiesce to expanding Russian ambitions and accept growing energy dependence. Even if Turkey is willing to accommodate Russia on many issues, unintended conflict in any one of the five areas noted in this report could well derail a long-term rapprochement. Nevertheless, U.S. policymakers should expect Turkey to remain an unpredictable ally that is more willing to work with Russia at cross purposes to NATO when its shifting national interests dictate.

Turkey's aspirations to become a more influential force in the Caucasus and Central Asia and a hub for regional energy and trade routes are likely to continue to be constrained by resource limitations, domestic turmoil, and other priorities. Turkey remains committed to advancing integration in the South Caucasus through its cooperation with Georgia and Azerbaijan to strengthen and protect the east-west economic and energy transit corridor and limited bilateral and trilateral security cooperation. Turkey's efforts help bolster the sovereignty and independence of these states, thereby supporting U.S. and European interests in the region. However, Ankara's appeal to Georgia and Azerbaijan as a bridge to Euro-Atlantic political and security frameworks has been diminished by Turkey's strained ties with the EU and its NATO allies, as well as its cooperation with Russia. Tbilisi and Baku still look to Ankara as a partial counterbalance to Moscow's power in the region, but Ankara will continue to approach regional security with some circumspection, aware that it cannot afford to be too confrontational with its powerful neighbor.

Ankara's early 1990s vision of reviving cultural and economic links among Turkic peoples in Central Asia and the Caspian to form a Turkic Union that would enhance regional development and expand Turkey's influence has not been realized. Nevertheless, the Turkish government and various nongovernmental organizations have provided considerable development and educational assistance to Central Asian countries, and commercial trade, investment, and construction projects have grown considerably over the past decade. Turkey has also pursued modest bilateral security and defense cooperation with several Central Asian governments; such steps include some arms sales and training for military and law enforcement personnel. Turkey also supports NATO Partnership for Peace exercises in Central Asia and has trained Central Asian militaries at its Partnership for Peace Training Center. In addition, Turkey contributes in the NATO-led exercise Steppe Eagle, which involves NATO and Central Asian partner militaries and takes place in Kazakhstan, despite its membership in the CSTO. Governments in the region value Turkey's engagement with them but also have to balance relations with Moscow, which retains and has not hesitated to exercise significant leverage over those governments and their relations with Turkey. Furthermore, over the past decade, China has emerged as the most dynamic trade and investment partner for Central Asian countries, with the capacity to realize its vision of One Belt and One Road as a modern version of the Silk Road. Ultimately, a moderately increased level of Turkish outreach to Central Asia and the Caucasus is likely in the coming years, characterized by constrained resources, limited commitment, and uneven appetite for new engagement.

EU-Turkish Relations

Turkey's relations with the EU have reached an acrimonious, 30-year low point that threatens the collapse of membership accession talks, stalled since 2005 and effectively frozen since Turkey's April 2017 constitutional referendum. How successful Turkey and the EU are at managing differences on migration, travel, counterterrorism policies, NATO-EU cooperation, and Cyprus will determine the longevity of the accession process and the development of alternative futures for the relationship. The two sides have sparred over implementation of a 2013 readmission deal, in which Turkey agreed to provide temporary relief to refugees from Syria in return for EU humanitarian assistance. Turkey has taken a strident stance, even prior to the July 2016 coup attempt, as Europe's concerns about Erdoğan's authoritarian rule, restrictions on civil and political rights, and various foreign policy moves have deepened. Although Ankara made gestures in early 2018 that suggest it may be seeking a reset of relations in the midst of Turkey's growing isolation, a broad reconciliation is improbable. EU-Turkish relations are likely to become even more transactional and focused narrowly on free trade, immigration, and counterterrorism, but, given lingering differences on these issues and conditions for resolving them, even this model for the relationship will be hard to establish in the near future.

So far, the EU has not started to implement visa liberalization for Turkish citizens because Turkey continues to fail to meet EU benchmarks on domestic reforms, yet it is unlikely that Erdoğan will put earlier threats to break off accession talks into action. At the same time, authoritarian developments in Turkey increase the risk that EU member governments suspend the talks, although the members remain divided on the issue. A full collapse of Turkey's EU membership would have profound economic and political costs to both sides and would be detrimental to U.S. interests. It would mark a significant failure of the EU's ability to bolster policy reforms in third countries (i.e., non-EU countries) as a means of projecting stability and would make it both more urgent and more difficult for Washington to engage Turkey directly on several sensitive issues.

Given this context, Ankara is unlikely to support further institutionalization of EU-NATO cooperation, especially if the Cyprus conflict remains unresolved. The enduring stalemate between the two communities on the island and Ankara's hard line on security issues makes resolution of the Cyprus dispute elusive for the foreseeable future. Turkish leaders are also less inclined to join EU missions as a way of anchoring their country to the West, which will not only reduce Ankara's engagement in CSDP missions but also continue to drag bilateral conflicts into NATO, thus undermining Alliance cohesion.

Turkey and NATO

There are many elements of continuity in Turkey's engagement in NATO. The Alliance still plays a central role in Turkey's national security strategy and its plans for defense against high-intensity threats. NATO membership provides Turkey a seat at the North Atlantic Council, where key policy decisions on Euro-Atlantic security are developed. Turkey remains engaged in other Alliance political institutions, the integrated military structure, and the exercise program and continues to make substantial contributions to current operations, standing forces, and the NATO Response Force. In addition, Turkey hosts forces from other NATO countries at its İncirlik and Konya air bases, the NATO Land Forces Command in Izmir, and the U.S. early-warning radar system in Kürecik that is part of the European Phased Adaptive Approach to missile defense. When regional tensions have risen in recent years, Turkey has promptly turned to the United States and other NATO allies for military support, twice calling for consultations under Article 4 of the North Atlantic Treaty.[10]

---

[10] Article 4 allows a NATO member to ask for consultations with other allies when its territorial integrity, political independence or security is threatened. It has been viewed as a step toward invoking the collective defense provisions in Article 5 of the Treaty (NATO, 1949).

However, doubts among the Turkish public and political elite about the reliability of NATO's collective defense commitment and the Alliance's relevance in addressing the country's most-immediate security threats—countering terrorism and separatism at home and in Turkey's neighborhood—have grown in recent years. Most Turks also see the policies that the United States and other allies have been pursuing in Syria as inimical to Turkey's security. In the wake of the July 2016 coup attempt, serious political figures contended that NATO had "supported every military coup in Turkey" and has regularly undermined Turkish interests.[11] Others aptly observe that, even if this claim were true, being a NATO member puts Turkey in a better position to prevent moves against it than not being a NATO member does.[12] Discussion of the *Eurasian vision*—that is, disengaging from NATO and pursuing deeper cooperation with Russia, Iran, and other major powers to address Turkey's security challenges more effectively—has gained resonance in political and academic circles, particularly following the U.S. decision in May 2017 to provide heavy weapons to the YPG. Advocates of this reorientation have reportedly gained bureaucratic influence now that they have assumed some positions in the Foreign Ministry and armed forces that were vacated by Atlanticists purged in the wake of the coup.

Moscow has been adept at exploiting and amplifying these fissures within Turkey and among allies, thus casting itself as a more reliable political and security partner. At the same time, Moscow has made clear to Ankara that Russia's military buildup in the Black Sea region and upper hand in the Syrian conflict give it considerable leverage. Lingering unease in Ankara about Moscow's long-term intentions and growing military capabilities have limited the effectiveness of this appeal. Turkey has reacted to geopolitical realities and the duality of Russian strategy by trying to balance relations with its longtime allies and newfound partner. Turkey's rapprochement with Moscow, military cooperation in the Black Sea and Syria, and acquisition of the Russian S-400 missile defense system are one side of this balancing effort. Turkish leaders remain deeply concerned, however, about Russia's military buildup in Crimea since 2014, plans for expanding its Black Sea Fleet, and military operations in Syria and the Eastern Mediterranean.

On the on the eve of NATO's 2016 Warsaw Summit, Erdoğan lamented NATO's lack of a visible military presence in the Black Sea and called on allies to take steps to prevent it from becoming "a Russian lake."[13] Although Turkey subsequently muted its rhetoric, it also pledged to contribute to NATO' s tailored forward presence for the Black Sea region, announced at the Warsaw Summit, despite vocal Russian opposition. On missile defense, Ankara is pursuing cooperation with the Franco-Italian Eurosam consortium to jointly develop and produce a long-range air and missile defense system

---

[11] Semih Idiz, "NATO Blunder Ignites Turkish Calls to Leave Alliance," *Al-Monitor*, November 21, 2017.

[12] Idiz, 2017.

[13] Jones and Hille, 2016.

with Turkish defense industry partners. The depth of current cooperation with Russia is uncertain, and interoperability concerns, as well as lingering suspicions, would likely limit the scope of future arms deals. Turkey's defense establishment remains heavily dependent on NATO equipment and is likely to remain reliant on the U.S. and NATO defense industry over the next decade.

Allied governments have also been increasingly dismayed by some of Ankara's confrontational rhetoric and periodic brinkmanship and by the fact that gaining Ankara's assent to important NATO operational and policy decisions regularly requires top-level political intervention with President Erdoğan. It required concerted U.S. diplomatic efforts to convince the Turkish government to endorse the development of NATO's missile defenses at the 2010 Lisbon Summit and, a year later, the deployment of U.S. missile defense radars on Turkish territory; Ankara was concerned that the action would damage its relations with Iran. It took similar engagement with Ankara to convince Turkish authorities to close Turkey's borders to foreign fighters heading to Syria and to finally participate in strike missions as a member of the counter-ISIS coalition in 2015. The acrimony between Berlin and Ankara discussed in Chapter Eight led Germany to redeploy its military personnel and aircraft supporting the counter-ISIS coalition from İncirlik to Jordan in 2017, when, for the second time, the Turks barred German lawmakers from visiting German forces.

Despite policy differences, allies still share many common interests with Turkey in combating terrorism, deterring further Russian aggression in southeastern Europe and the Eastern Mediterranean, limiting Iranian influence, and promoting stability in the Middle East. The United States and other allies are not without significant leverage over Ankara and should not be reluctant to use that leverage in seeking to manage policy differences. Turkish leaders know that NATO remains the only viable framework for maintaining their nation's security. U.S. and allied leaders will need strategic patience and steady engagement to manage those differences as Turks sort out their internal political differences and cope with their deteriorating security situation. This engagement could, over time, lead future Turkish governments to pursue foreign and security policies that are more-convergent with U.S. policies. Given Turkey's geostrategic position and regional influence, it is far better to have it cooperating in various ways from inside NATO than seeking to thwart the Alliance's efforts from the outside.

Thorny Bilateral Issues Add to Strains with the United States

In addition to policy differences concerning Syria, the Kurds, Iran, Russia, and Israeli-Palestinian issues, there are several bilateral problems that have strained the strategic partnership between the United States and Turkey. The Obama administration came to office in 2009 determined to deepen regional and global cooperation with Turkey, calling for the development of a "model partnership" to advance mutual interests in a changing Middle East and more widely.[14] However, disagreements over Libya, the Iranian nuclear issue, the Muslim Brotherhood, and the early phases of the Syrian civil war limited the realization of that vision. Erdoğan's periodic brinkmanship and tight control over policy decisions, which regularly required top-level political interventions to gain Ankara's support for key foreign policy initiatives, led to disappointment in Washington. Erdoğan, in turn, felt rebuffed when Washington refused to pursue his initiatives to solve the Iranian nuclear issue in 2011, take military action to oust the Assad regime in Syria, and establish safe zones to protect Syrian civilians from regime brutality. Erdoğan bristled as Washington expressed its concerns about the authoritarian drift in Turkish politics and what he saw as a hesitant denunciation of the July 2016 attempted military coup and affirmation of support for the Turkish government.

Erdoğan expressed hopes that President Donald Trump would bring a fresh start to the relationship and that he could persuade Trump to stop supporting the Syrian YPG. These hopes faded when Trump announced that he would provide the YPG with heavy weapons and were dealt a severe blow when Trump announced his decision to move the U.S. embassy in Israel from Tel Aviv to Jerusalem. Erdoğan and other Turkish leaders have decried the fact that the United States not only has failed to act on their 2016 request to extradite Fethullah Gülen—who they contend masterminded the July 2016 coup and is the head of what Turkey brands a terrorist organization—but also has allowed Gülen to live in great comfort and without interference. These tensions have led to vitriolic statements by Turkish leaders that the United States can no longer be considered an ally because it is providing a safe haven to one of the country's leading enemies and arming another that is waging a separatist insurgency. Anti-American sentiment has deepened in Turkey, as have doubts about the reliability of the U.S. commitment to Turkey's stability and security.

Bilateral relations have been further complicated by Turkey's arrests of American and European nationals and two Turkish employees of U.S. consulates on questionable terrorism charges, as well as by Turkish security personnel's assaults on protesters in Washington during Erdoğan's May 2017 visit there.[15] A case that gained considerable attention involved an American pastor, Andrew Brunson, who was charged in Turkey in 2016 as a supporter of the Gülen movement. Tensions were strained further with the sensational trial in the United States of gold trader Reza Zarrab, who was accused of orchestrating a large money-laundering scheme designed to circumvent sanctions against Iran in coordination with senior officials in the Turkish government. The case received high-profile press coverage, and Erdoğan himself reportedly raised the issue

---

[14] Bulent Aliriza, "President Obama's Trip to Turkey: Building a 'Model Partnership,'" Center for Strategic and International Studies, April 8, 2009b.

[15] See Eric Edelman and Aykan Erdemir, "Turkey's President Is Holding Americans Hostage. Why Aren't We Doing Anything About It?" *Washington Post*, April 15, 2018; and Richard Gonzales, "Feds Drop Prosecution of 7 Turkish Bodyguards Involved in Assault of Protesters," National Public Radio, March 22, 2018.

with senior U.S. figures on at least two occasions. Zarrab also retained the services of former New York Mayor Rudolph Giuliani, who attempted to negotiate a "state-to-state" settlement for the case outside of court.[16] Zarrab ultimately pleaded guilty to fraud, testified against a senior executive in a state-owned Turkish bank, and claimed that President Erdoğan had personally approved of his operations. Turkish officials were quick to dismiss the case as politically motivated "theater" and the result of a Gülenist plot against Turkey.[17] Though soon overtaken by a series of other bilateral disputes, the case remains a major point of tension between Washington and Ankara and retains the potential to place considerable strain on the already volatile relationship.

Overall Assessments

Table 9.1 provides a summary assessment of where Turkish interests are convergent, divergent, or in conflict with those of key neighbors and other allies; the table is a compilation of our analysis in Chapters Two through Eight.

As exhibited in Table 9.1, Turkey, the United States, and other NATO allies still have many convergent strategic interests, including countering terrorism, promoting peace in the Middle East, constraining the growth of Russian and Iranian power, and expanding energy transit corridors. However, differences over the policies to best advance these interests have become more pronounced and exacerbated by deepening mutual suspicions. The foregoing analysis suggests four potential Turkish futures, as outlined in Chapter Two and further described here:

1. *Difficult ally*: Turkey continues to be a difficult and sometimes wavering ally but remains committed to NATO operations and policies and reliant on the Alliance's collective security guarantee. Relations with Europe and the United States remain transactional, but differences are managed without too much strain or disruption.
2. *Resurgent democracy*: An opposition political leader or coalition is able to defeat Erdoğan after 2023, walk back the constitutional changes approved in the 2017 referendum, and resume a more Western-oriented foreign and security policy. This could lead to enhanced U.S. and European policy and defense cooperation with Turkey, improved Turkish relations with Israel and the Arab states, and progress on the Kurdish and Cyprus issues.
3. *Strategic balancer*: Turkey moves to more openly balance its ties with its NATO allies and emerging partners in Eurasia (particularly Russia, Iran, and China),

---

[16] "Trump Adviser Seeks Political Deal to Settle Iran Sanctions Case," Radio Free Europe/Radio Liberty, April 21, 2017.

[17] "Reza Zarrab Case: Gold Trader Implicates Turkish President Erdogan," BBC News, December 1, 2017.

Table 9.1
Alignment of Turkish Interests with Neighbor and Partner Interests

Neighbor or Partner	Converging Interests	Diverging Interests	Conflicting Interests
Iran	• Expanded trade in goods and energy; economic cooperation • Opposition to the development of Kurdish mini-states in Iraq and Syria • Limited influence of outside actors • Border security • Caution toward Russia • Turkish facilitation of Iranian sanctions avoidance • Turkish support for Qatar in disputes with GCC and other Arab states	• Iran's political and military ties to Baghdad • Approach to Kurdish separatism • Settlement in Syria (Turkey wants to limit Iranian influence) • Relations with the United States and Europe • Counterterrorism • Iranian regional activities and influence	• In Syria: Iranian cooperation with the PKK to achieve an energy transit corridor • Religious differences between the Sunni and Shi'a denominations • Turkey's NATO membership • Iran's nuclear program • Resettlement of depopulated areas in Syria and Iraq • Turkish support to Sunni Islamist and jihadist groups
Iraq	• Opposition to the development of Kurdish mini-states in Iraq and Syria • Trade and energy transit	• Influence of Iran and Shi'a militias in Iraq • Relations with the KRG, particularly on energy flows	• Turkish military presence in northern Iraq • Turkish ties to Sunni separatist Turkmen in Iraq
Arab Middle East	• Opposition to Iranian regional influence, although the Arab Gulf states question Turkey's commitment • Opposition to Syria's Bashar al-Assad regime, although the Arab states were concerned that Turkey has been more focused on countering the YPG than aiding the Sunni-Arab opposition; the states were also concerned with Turkey's support to jihadis and the Free Syrian Army	• The endgame and settlement terms in Syria, which are affected by Turkey's dealings with Iran and jihadi groups • Palestine: Turkey has ties to Hamas and the Muslim Brotherhood; others have ties to the Palestinian Authority • Turkey's cross-border operations against the PKK and the YPG, which raise sovereignty concerns	• Muslim Brotherhood: Turkey and Qatar support the group; others oppose • Turkish support of other Islamist groups in Syria and Libya, as well as its enabling of some jihadist groups • Turkey's deepening ties to Qatar • Rift with Egypt over Muslim Brotherhood and Palestinian issues • Management of shared water resources
Israel	• Trade • Possible development of the Leviathan natural gas field as a driver of reconciliation • Humanitarian relief in the Gaza Strip • Limited Iranian influence	• Political, economic, and security relations with countries in the wider Middle East • Israeli facilitation of U.S. regional presence and involvement	• Palestine: statehood, East Jerusalem, Gaza closure, and Hamas • Israel's support for Kurdish autonomy • Israeli cooperation with Egypt's Abdel Fattah al-Sisi government • Growing Israeli partnership with Cyprus and Greece

Table 9.1—Continued

Neighbor or Partner	Converging Interests	Diverging Interests	Conflicting Interests
Russia	• Trade expansion • Energy cooperation (Russian gas supplies; nuclear plant) • Tensions with the EU and West • Arms trade • Illiberalism and authoritarian governance	• Energy transit corridors • Counterterrorism issues • Russian role in the Middle East, the Caucasus, and Central Asia • Relations with the United States	• Endgame and Russian presence in Syria • Russian engagement with Syria's PYD and the YPG • Russian military buildup in the Black Sea • Turkey's NATO membership, especially its missile defense site and other deployments
Caucasus	• Development of connectivity and infrastructure for trade and energy • Facilitation of wider economic links with Europe • Turkey's alignment with Azerbaijan on the Nagorno-Karabakh conflict	• Baku's and Tbilisi's efforts for closer political and security ties with Europe • Georgia's desire for stronger support against Russia • Turkish deference to Russia in the Black Sea region	• Differences between Turkey and Armenia on the Nagorno-Karabakh conflict and whether to refer to Turkey's actions in 1915 as genocide • Armenian provision of military basing to Russia
Central Asia	• Some trade and development ties • Minor security cooperation	• Alignment with Russia • Turkic integration limited by Central Asian nations' quest to deepen national identity	• Official secularism versus Islamism
EU	• Trade and energy • Economic ties	• Migration crisis • Counterterrorism and the flow of foreign fighters • EU visa liberalization	• Democratic backsliding in Turkey • Turkish diasporas in Europe • Syria policy • European asylum to Gülenists and coup suspects • Irregular detention of EU citizens in Turkey • Turkey's competing maritime claims with Greece and Cyprus in the Mediterranean and Aegean Seas
NATO	• Solidarity against threats to Turkish territorial integrity • Turkish role in Afghanistan • Denial of Russian dominance in and power projection from the Black Sea	• Democratic backsliding in Turkey • Approach to Russia • Restrictions on Incirlik Air Base, which affect U.S. and German operations	• Acquisition of non-NATO defense systems • Aggressive Turkish challenges to Greek and Cypriot maritime claims, which risk conflict

Table 9.1—Continued

Neighbor or Partner	Converging Interests	Diverging Interests	Conflicting Interests
United States	• Solidarity against threats to Turkish territorial integrity • Turkish role as energy supplier to Europe • Turkish role in Afghanistan • Concerns about Russian efforts to dominate and project power from the Black Sea	• Democratic backsliding • Approach to Russia • Iran sanctions • Approach to foreign fighters and Islamist groups in Syria • Restrictions on Incirlik, which affect U.S. operations • Wider Turkish role in the region and Muslim world • Turkish desire for increased defense industrial self-sufficiency	• Syria policy • U.S. tactical engagement with the YPG, the PYD, and Syrian Democratic Forces • Extradition of Gülen • U.S. court case against gold trader Reza Zarrab, who implicated Erdogan in criminal activity • Anti-U.S. propaganda in Turkish government rhetoric and in official and semi-official press • Turkey's acquisition of non-NATO defense systems, particularly Russia's S-400 system • Turkey's detention of U.S. citizens

sometimes supporting Western positions but often forming shifting coalitions. This is a strategy outlined in Erdoğan's 2018 election manifesto, and it reflects the worldview of many AKP and MHP politicians. It has attendant risks for Turkey and would complicate U.S. deterrence and defense efforts against Russia, Iran, and China. This future is more likely to be pursued if contentious issues with the United States and European governments remain unresolved.

4. *Eurasian power*: As mutual suspicions and policy differences with Europe and the United States reach a breaking point, Turkey moves to formally leave NATO and pursue closer cooperation and various alignments with partners in Eurasia and the Middle East. This results in distant, more-adversarial relations and the risk of military incidents.

To arrive at these four plausible, future geostrategic orientations for Turkey, we employed a simplified scenario-axes approach whereby we identified the most-significant driving forces in Turkish domestic and external affairs. We then outlined the types of policies that Turkey would likely pursue if these forces prevailed, as well as the implications for the United States and other allies under each future orientation (see Table 9.2). We did not seek to assess the probability of each alternative unfolding or advance the futures in an effort to predict Turkey's course in global affairs. Rather, these four futures are alternatives that may unfold as a consequence of certain internal and external developments. We offer these as a heuristic device to provide U.S. decisionmakers with a set of indicators of evolving alternative futures against which various policy courses of action might be assessed to shape outcomes in directions more favorable to U.S. interests.[18]

Implications for U.S. Defense Planning and the U.S. Army

The developments in Turkey's domestic politics, foreign and defense policies, and military posture, along with the strains in bilateral relations with Washington, have significant implications for U.S. defense planning and the U.S. Army. In this section, we examine the state of military-to-military relations and how U.S. and Turkish defense policies and force postures align or diverge in three of the most-pressing regional security challenges: stabilizing post-ISIS Syria and the evolving counterterrorism struggle in the Middle East, containing Iranian influence in the Middle East and the Persian Gulf, and containing Russian influence and military activities in the Black Sea region and beyond.

---

[18] For a discussion of this method and its limitations, see David G. Groves and Robert J. Lempert, "A New Analytic Method for Finding Policy-Relevant Scenarios," *Global Environmental Change*, Vol. 17, No. 1, 2007.

Table 9.2
Pathways, Policies, and Implications of the Four Potential Turkish Futures over the Next Decade

Alternative	Pathways	Policies	Implications
Difficult ally	• Domestic political polarization persists; Erdogan dominant; opposition divided • Authoritarian rule under new constitution • Kurdish insurgency and terrorist threat remains high • Economy stable • Differences with NATO on Russia and the Black Sea • Differences with United States on Iran and Israel policies	• Acrimonious dealings with Europe; accession talks continue fitfully • Reluctant to support NATO presence in Southeast Europe and the Black Sea • Differences with the United States and the coalition on Syria and the Kurds • Growing cooperation with Russia and Iran • Persisting tensions with Israel and Cyprus	• Relations with U.S. and Europe remain transactional; differences managed • Periodic crises require high-level engagement to avoid fissures; growing frustrations • Defense and military cooperation with the United States and NATO weakens
Resurgent democracy	• Growing discontent with Erdogan and AKP rule • Economic downturn; foreign direct investment falters; capital flight • Opposition parties unite • Possible PKK ceasefire • AKP ousted in elections • Presidential powers tempered	• Efforts to improve ties with the United States, Europe, and Israel • Economic and energy ties with Russia and Iran • Differences on Syria and the Kurds persist but are managed better • Restart of peace process with the Kurds	• Defense and military cooperation with the United States and NATO improves • Progress with the EU on customs union and visa liberalization • More pragmatic Middle East role • Managed tensions with Greece and Cyprus
Strategic balancer	• More nationalist drift under the AKP or if the MHP or a new right-wing party displaces the AKP • Accession talks with the EU collapse; talks on customs union enhancements and visa liberalization stall • Economic and security cooperation with Russia deepens; modus vivendi in the Black Sea region and the Caucasus • Deeper economic and security cooperation with Iran and China	• Authoritarian rule consolidated • Limit NATO presence in Southeast Europe and passage through Turkish Straits • Opt out of NATO missions in Afghanistan and the Balkans • Periodic alignment with Russia, Iran, and China to limit or offset U.S. influence in the Middle East, North Africa, and Eurasia	• Regular crises require high-level engagement to avoid confrontations • Waning commitment to NATO policies and missions • Defense and military cooperation with the United States and NATO wanes significantly; access to Turkish bases is sometimes restricted or denied

Table 9.2—Continued

Alternative	Pathways	Policies	Implications
Eurasian power	• More nationalist drift under the AKP or if the MHP or a new right-wing party displaces the AKP • EU membership process collapses; trade with and travel to Europe drop sharply • Economic and security cooperation with Russia deepens; new modus vivendi in the Black Sea region and the Caucasus • Deeper cooperation with Iran, China, and Muslim-majority countries	• Block allied policies and missions or withdraw from NATO • Block tailored forward presence in Southeast Europe, as well as U.S. and NATO passage through the Turkish Straits • Withdraw from missions in Afghanistan and Syria • New ties with the Eurasian Economic Union and the Shanghai Cooperation Organisation • Deeper involvement in the Organisation of Islamic Cooperation	• Relations with the United States and Europe become distant, sometimes adversarial • Routine alignment with Russia, Iran, and China to limit or offset U.S. influence • Defense and military cooperation with the United States and NATO curtailed; access to bases denied • Possible military incidents

State of Bilateral Military-to Military and Defense Industrial Relations

The U.S. and Turkish militaries have a long history of close cooperation, which has evolved in light of shifting priorities. The U.S. military presence in Turkey was close to 15,000 personnel in the late 1980s, reflecting Cold War priorities on NATO's southern flank. In contrast, there are about 2,200 U.S. military personnel stationed in Turkey today, about 1,500 of whom are at İncirlik Air Base. Relations suffered a major setback after 2003, when the Turkish Parliament did not support the U.S. request for the 4th Infantry Division to use Turkish territory to launch operations into Iraq, and the U.S. subsequently declined the Turkish government's offer to send 10,000 troops to Iraq as members of the coalition. U.S. efforts to curtail Turkish military operations in Iraqi Kurdistan against the PKK and a high-profile incident between the U.S. and Turkish forces there led to further strains and limited senior contacts.[19] The United States took steps to enhance intelligence-sharing on the PKK with the TSK in 2007, which helped pave the way for improved military-to-military relations and a restoration of high-level contacts. But restrictions and bureaucratic red tape that Turkey has placed on U.S. use of İncirlik Air Base have sometimes been an irritant.

---

[19] On July 4, 2003, U.S. forces raided a Turkish special forces safe house in Suleymaniyah, Iraq. The U.S. team cuffed the 11 Turkish officers and enlisted personnel using zip ties and placed black hoods over their heads as they were taken into custody—an image that would later be compared countless times to the treatment of prisoners in U.S. custody at Abu Ghraib prison. After two days in U.S. custody in Baghdad, the Turkish soldiers were released unharmed, but the political damage was enormous. The incident generated front-page headlines of outrage for weeks in the Turkish media, which portrayed it as a loss of face and an American betrayal. It was also the inspiration for what would be the country's highest-grossing film ever, *Valley of the Wolves: Iraq* (*Kurtlar Vadısı: Irak*), and a best-selling book, *Metal Storm* (*Metal Fırtına*).

The depth of U.S. military-to-military interactions with the TSK has varied by service. Cooperation with the Turkish Air Force has generally been consistently strong over the years, including continuing operations at İncirlik and the regular Anatolian Eagle exercises, which involve other NATO and partner countries. Considerable interaction between the U.S. and Turkish navies takes place in NATO operations and exercises, as well as regular staff talks. For many years, there were limited formal dialogues between the U.S. Army and the Turkish Land Forces, even though the Land Forces are the biggest component of the TSK. The first ever talks between the U.S. Army Staff and the TGS took place in January 2009, leading to a plan of future command post exercises and unit-level exchanges.[20] Cooperation among special operations forces also saw marked improvement after 2008 and continued for operations in Afghanistan and Syria.

Despite political differences with the Turkish government and turmoil within the TSK, bilateral defense and military-to-military cooperation with the United States has continued to function fairly well over the past few years, with some bumps in the road. The TSK has demonstrated that it wants to work effectively with U.S. forces, but the relationship has retained a transactional character.[21] Turkey's ministers of defense and chief of the TGS have met regularly with their U.S. counterparts in recent years, and Chairman of the Joint Chiefs of Staff Gen. Joseph Dunford, Jr., was the first senior U.S. official to visit Turkey two weeks after the July 2016 attempted coup.[22] The pace and nature of the TSK's engagement with U.S. counterparts had been improving before the coup, and although such engagement slowed somewhat in the immediate months after the coup, almost 95 percent of planed operations and activities with United States Army Europe forces resumed the following year. In fact, the TSK participated in ten United States Army Europe exercises during 2016, which was a significant increase over previous years. Since the coup attempt, TSK officers have been more circumspect in engagements with U.S. counterparts, hew closely to approved talkers, and are less flexible in decisions. They are sometimes accompanied by officials from the Ministry of Foreign Affairs or the MİT. No doubt, lingering concerns about arrest remain. The TSK recalled officers attending U.S. professional military education institutions in July 2016 and has not been making full use of its sizable allocation for international military education and training.[23]

---

[20] Flanagan and Brannen, 2009, p. 86.

[21] U.S. officials and military officers, discussion with the authors, Headquarters, United States Army Europe, Wiesbaden, Germany, February 2017; U.S. officials and military officers, discussion with the authors, United States European Command, Stuttgart, Germany, February 2017; and U.S. officials and military officers, discussion with the authors, Ankara, June 2017.

[22] Jim Garamone, "Dunford Visit to Turkey Is First by Senior U.S. Official Since Coup Attempt," DoD News, August 1, 2016.

[23] U.S. officials and military officers, discussion with the authors, Headquarters, United States Army Europe, Wiesbaden, Germany, February 2017; U.S. officials and military officers, discussion with the authors, United

In addition, the United States and Turkey maintain a long-standing defense trade relationship. This has included a consortium between U.S. and Turkish aerospace firms to coproduce most of Turkey's 240 F-16s in Turkey during the 1980s and 1990s and a similar $3.5 billion deal finalized in 2014 to produce 109 Turkish-version Black Hawk helicopters in Turkey. Turkey was a level 3 partner in the Joint Strike Fighter program, committed to purchasing 116 F-35A Lightning aircraft, before its suspension from the program in July 2019. Turkey's defense industry has made significant strides over the past decade, and the government has been pursuing coproduction and codevelopment projects with many countries, with the goal of being self-sufficient by 2023, the centennial of the Turkish Republic. In this context, and in the face of the growing missile threat in the region, Turkey entered into negotiations with the United States to purchase and coproduce the PATRIOT Advanced Capability (PAC)-3 air and missile defense system, but the talks collapsed because of costs and disagreements over technology transfers. This was an important factor in Turkey's decision to seek alternatives, including a Chinese system and then the Russian S-400, as well as the Franco-Italian option. Despite these efforts to achieve self-reliance and diversification of supply, the TSK will remain heavily dependent on U.S.-origin military equipment for at least the next decade, which is another positive factor in sustaining the military-to-military relationship between the United States and Turkey.

Stabilization of Syria and Future Counterterrorism Efforts

Differences between the United States and Turkey over goals, strategy, and tactics for ending the Syrian civil war have grown more pronounced. Having become reconciled to the fact that its previous objective of removing Bashar al-Assad from power is beyond reach following the 2015 Russian intervention, Ankara's top priority has been to prevent the Syrian PYD and its YPG militias, which it views as integral elements of the outlawed PKK, from gaining control of the entire length of Turkey's 500 mile-long southern border with Syria.[24] The Turks fear that such a development would lead to consolidation of PYD control over an autonomous region in Syria, which the Kurds call Rojava. The Turks launched Operation Euphrates Shield in September 2016 to prevent the YPG from moving units west of the Euphrates River, thereby closing one gap in the border not under YPG control.[25] The Turks have viewed the 2015 U.S. decision to train and equip the Syrian Democratic Forces (SDF), which include many YPG fighters, and then to supply them with heavy weapons and equipment two years

---

States European Command, Stuttgart, Germany, February 2017; and U.S. officials and military officers, discussion with the authors, Ankara, June 2017.

[24] For background on the relationship between the PYD and the PKK, see Andrew Tabler, Soner Cagaptay, David Pollock, and James F. Jeffrey, "The Syrian Kurds: Whose Ally?" remarks to a policy forum at the Washington Institute for Near East Policy, PolicyWatch 2597, March 29, 2016.

[25] Rex W. Tillerson, "Remarks on the Way Forward for the United States Regarding Syria," Hoover Institute at Stanford University, January 17, 2018.

later in advance of the assault on ISIS in Raqqa as the equivalent of an ally arming an enemy. Erdoğan was incensed that assurances from U.S. officials that the SDF would not be left in control of the Syrian towns of Manbij and Jarbulus after ISIS was evicted and that the United States would stop providing the SDF with ammunition and support after the fall of Raqqa have not been honored. Indeed, Erdoğan noted that the January 2018 announcement that the United States was planning to start training members of the SDF into a new Syrian Border Security Force with up to 30,000 members was tantamount to creating a "terrorist army" on Turkey's borders (see discussion of this border force later in this section).[26] From Ankara's perspective, the announcement underlined U.S. resolve to extend cooperation with the SDF beyond the immediate battle against ISIS and develop the relationship from a tactical alignment, as it had been repeatedly portrayed by U.S. officials, to a strategic political alliance in northeastern Syria. Although then–U.S. Secretary of State Rex Tillerson denied such plans shortly after, the TSK launched Operation Olive Branch against YPG forces in Afrin on January 20, 2018, after days of fierce anti-American rhetoric, and the operation was portrayed in Turkish media as an anti-imperialistic act of defiance. Erdoğan declared that Turkish and allied Free Syrian Army forces will establish a 30-km-deep buffer zone in Afrin, and he and TGS Chief Akar threatened to clear the YPG out of Manbij and possibly the entire border region. The Turkish move into Afrin brought into stark relief the contradictions and limitations of U.S. policy in Syria. U.S. forces advising and assisting SDF forces near Manbij and other places east of the Euphrates were at risk of being attacked by their Turkish treaty allies.

Defusing confrontations over Syria will require agile U.S. diplomatic engagement with Turkey and Kurdish partners, as well as some policy adjustments. Despite the harsh rhetoric emanating from Ankara and the hard line taken by the PYD and the YPG, there are some convergent interests. For example, Turkey and the United States support resolution of the conflict between the Syrian people and the Assad regime through the United Nations–led political process that would result in a unitary Syrian state with Assad's transition from power. Ankara, Washington, and the PYD (despite some cooperation with Tehran) want to limit Iranian influence in Syria. U.S. officials have some leverage to convince the PYD to take concrete steps to distance itself from the PKK, although this would be hard to achieve in the short to middle term, given a shared ideology and the long-standing ties between both organizations. Turkey and the PYD did cooperate as late as 2015 on efforts to defend Kobanî in Syria. In addition, Washington could help broker a dialogue among Turkey, the PYD, and moderate Syrian opposition to avoid conflict with each other and to work together against Assad and his Iranian backers. Finally, Washington should take steps to prevent YPG weapons and assistance

---

[26] Patrick Wintour, "Erdogan Says US Is Creating 'Terrorist Army' in Syria," *Irish Times*, January 15, 2018; and Joanne Stocker, "Coalition Retraining 15,000 Veteran SDF Fighters to Serve as Syrian Border Force," *Defense Post*, January 13, 2018.

from flowing to the PKK, guarantee Ankara that the United States will vigorously oppose Kurdish secession in Syria, and work to dissuade Turkey from launching further attacks on enclaves under PYD control. This strategy faces many hurdles, but the Turkish reconciliation and partnership with the Iraqi Kurds over the past decade, despite their previous conflicts, suggests that it is in the realm of possibility.[27]

In the conduct of operations to support U.S. and Global Coalition efforts to prevent the reemergence of ISIS and stabilize Syria and Iraq, the U.S. Army will need to be mindful of tensions with Ankara concerning the Kurds and other elements of U.S. policy.[28] In one development that has especially strained the relationship, leaders of the Combined Joint Task Force – Operation Inherent Resolve announced plans in January 2018 to maintain a small (reportedly 1,500 personnel) U.S. ground force to train and assist in the development of a 30,000-strong Syrian Border Security Force composed of veteran fighters under the leadership of the SDF. The core of the force was expected to be formed of 15,000 members of the SDF as operations against ISIS were completed. The force would reportedly be stationed along the Iraqi and Turkish borders and the Euphrates River Valley, the western edge of the territory in Syria being controlled by the SDF. Because the Syrian Border Security Force units would have been drawn from the areas that they would protect, Turkish authorities feared that the YPG would become predominant in northeastern Syria, where the Kurds are a majority of the population; more Arabs live along the Euphrates River Valley and the border with Iraq.[29] In early 2019, the United States and Turkey were negotiating joint U.S and Turkish patrols of a 20-mile safe zone along the border.[30]

As diplomatic and civilian stabilization initiatives in Syria and Iraq unfold, Army training efforts could support a sustainable end state by

- ensuring that training programs for SDF forces are as inclusive as possible so that areas with mixed Kurdish, Arab, and Turkmen residents develop a more diverse force
- working with the TSK to mitigate tensions along east-west lines of control in northern Syria between those dominated by the YPG and those under control of the Turkish-backed Free Syrian Army

---

[27] For more on this approach see James F. Jeffrey and David Pollack, "How to Stop the War Between Turkey and the Syrian Kurds," *Foreign Policy*, January 25, 2018.

[28] Center for Army Lessons Learned, *Strategic Landpower in Europe: Special Study*, Washington, D.C.: U.S. Army, No. 18-05, December 2017, p. 80.

[29] Stocker, 2018.

[30] Karen DeYoung, "U.S. and Turkey Negotiate Plan for Their Troops to Jointly Patrol Safe Zone in Syria," *Washington Post*, April 25, 2019. These negotiations ended in October 2019, when President Trump announced the withdrawal of U.S. forces from northwestern Syria, and Turkey launched an operation to take control of the border region in Syria.

- providing security and support to U.S. State Department and Agency for International Development personnel working in northern Syria with the United Nations, partners in the Global Coalition to Defeat ISIS, and various nongovernmental organizations to help local and regional authorities restore essential services in liberated areas and establish an environment conducive to resettlement of refugees
- taking steps to enhance U.S. Army cooperation with the Turkish Land Forces and special operations forces, which are likely also operating in Syria to protect safe zones and monitor border areas; doing so could enhance the stabilization mission in Syria and future regional counterterrorism efforts
- initiating a focused dialogue with TSK counterparts—in addition to whatever efforts are taken to sustain the Global Coalition—on how regional efforts to combat terrorism should unfold following the complete defeat of ISIS.

The Black Sea and the Eastern Mediterranean

Both Russia and Turkey have long sought to limit maritime operations by nonlittoral powers in the Black Sea. In 2001, Turkey led efforts with Bulgaria, Romania, Ukraine, Russia, and Georgia to create the Black Sea Naval Cooperation Task Group to undertake combined maritime operations against terrorism, organized crime, and trafficking. Turkey worked with some littoral states to establish Operation Black Sea Harmony in 2004, which sought to disrupt terrorist activities by tracking and boarding suspicious ships and was intended as a counterpart to NATO's Operation Active Endeavor in the Mediterranean. To avoid provoking Moscow or triggering dangerous incidents, Turkey had advocated a limited NATO maritime presence in the Black Sea, operating from an assessment that Turkey's then-superior naval forces could manage relations with the Russians in a cooperative maritime framework. Turkey's legal rights, under the terms of the 1936 Montreux Convention, to limit the passage of civilian and military ships through the Dardanelles and Bosporus straits have given Moscow a compelling rationale for cooperation.

Russian aggression against Georgia and Ukraine, as well as efforts to strengthen its position in the Black Sea and its ability to project maritime power, have strained the cooperative approach between Russia and Turkey. Russia suspended participation in the Black Sea Naval Cooperation Task Group in 2015, and in September 2016, Russian General Valeriy Gerasimov boasted that the military balance in the Black Sea had already shifted toward Russia. The deployment of new reconnaissance assets, submarines with Kalibr cruise missiles, new aircraft, and the Bastion coastal defense missile system have given Russia an even more robust anti-access/area denial capability against NATO navies and air forces and have strengthened Russia's ability to project power into the Eastern Mediterranean and Middle East. Russia intends to spend an additional $2.4 billion by 2022 to strengthen and modernize its Black Sea Fleet, including the procurement of more surface ships and amphibious-landing capacities. There is debate among experts about whether Moscow can realize this naval modernization program in the timeline envisioned, but many analysts agree that the balance has shifted in Moscow's direction.[31] The 2017 Russian naval doctrine identified strengthening the Black Sea Fleet and Russian forces in Crimea and maintaining a constant naval presence in the Mediterranean as the most critical geographic priorities for future development of the Russian Navy.[32] Moscow's improvements in the size and readiness of ground forces in the Southern Military district, continuing patronage of the breakaway Georgian province of Abkhazia, and enhancements of its military presence in Armenia have strengthened Russian ground and air power in the Black Sea region.

Turkish perceptions have shifted with the recognition that Russia has again become Turkey's most formidable military threat. Official Turkish statements during and after the 2015–2016 crisis in relations with Moscow reflect a deep wariness about Russia's military capabilities and intentions. On the eve of NATO's 2016 Warsaw Summit, Erdoğan lamented NATO's absence from the Black Sea and noted that it is in danger of becoming "a Russian lake." When NATO allies agreed at the summit to establish a tailored forward presence in southeastern Europe, the Turkish Ministry of Defense announced that it would contribute to the initiative—despite vocal Russian opposition. Moreover, despite Russian and Iranian objections, Ankara has continued to support NATO's European Phased Adaptive Approach missile defense operations in Turkey.

Nevertheless, because of its vulnerability to Russian military and economic pressure, Turkey's balancing strategy between NATO and Russia has led to continued bilateral exercises with the Russian Navy in the Black Sea, as well as regular TGS and service staff talks with Russian counterparts. Moscow has highlighted this cooperation to demonstrate that a NATO ally is willing to work individually with it on regional security cooperation. A Turkish decision to join NATO allies in taking actions against significant Russian interests, such as restricting transit of the Black Sea Fleet through the Turkish Straits in the context of a future contingency in Syria or the Eastern Mediterranean, could rupture Ankara's bilateral relationship with Moscow. Conversely, a Turkish decision to support Russian actions in such a crisis could cause a crisis in NATO. A future contingency in which Russia uses its military might to intimidate Turkey or undermine its security interests in the Black Sea or the Middle East will likely be the true test of how this shifting regional military balance will affect the future course of Turkey's relations with its NATO allies and Russia. This has the following implications for U.S. defense and security cooperation plans:

- The U.S. Army and other services should continue to deepen their engagement with Turkish counterparts in the development of NATO's tailored forward pres-

---

[31] Paul Schwartz, "Amphibious Plans and Posture in Support of NATO," presentation at a RAND Corporation workshop related to the Amphibious Leaders Expeditionary Symposium, Arlington, Va., January 19, 2018.

[32] Gorenburg, 2017.

ence in Southeastern Europe and in U.S. European Command's Black Sea exercise program, particularly the Saber Guardian and Sea Breeze series. Such engagement in U.S. and NATO planning and exercises could help build consensus with the Turkish government on assessments of the Russian threat and how best to counter it. It would also assure the Turks that their security concerns are being factored into U.S., combined, and NATO contingency planning for the region.

- Given uncertainty about how the TSK might respond in a period of heightened tensions with Russia, the U.S. Army should design and deploy flexible logistic options to support any NATO peacetime deterrent or crisis flexible deterrent options for Bulgaria and Romania.
- Now that Turkey is proceeding with the deployment of Russian S-400s, the U.S. Army, as the owner and operator of the PATRIOT and Terminal High Altitude Area Defense surface-to-air missile systems, will have to evaluate the risk and manage any integration of those systems with non-NATO surface-to-air missile systems.
- Turkish cooperation with the Russian Navy, as well as the fact that Turkey's navy is not a top priority of the Turkish political leadership, may have an adverse effect on cooperation with the United States and NATO in Black Sea maritime operations. However, U.S. and NATO forces' continued engagement with Turkish naval and marine forces can help counterbalance these influences. In addition to deepening engagement via the Sea Breeze exercises, the U.S. Marine Forces Europe command might strengthen crisis response capacity by exploring further engagement of Turkish maritime forces with the Black Sea Regional Force, the special-purpose Marine Air-Ground Task Force that conducts security cooperation and exercises in the region.

Other Force Planning and Regional Issues

The Turkish government will continue to seek to balance (1) concerns about Iran's expanding influence in the Middle East and improving military capabilities, including its nuclear breakout capability, with (2) Turkey's interests in deepening economic and energy cooperation and finding ways to defuse volatile elements of Sunni-Shi'a tensions. The Turkish government does not assess Iran's nuclear program and testing of long-range ballistic missiles to be an imminent threat. Erdoğan and other officials have repeatedly defended Iran's right to develop a nuclear-fuel cycle, accepted that the program is peaceful, and supported the 2015 Joint Comprehensive Plan of Action. That said, Iran's prospective acquisition of nuclear weapons is inimical to Turkey's security and is another reason that Turkey has continued to support NATO European Phased Adaptive Approach missile defense programs and efforts of the nuclear dimension of Alliance deterrent capabilities. An Iranian move to break out of the Joint Comprehensive Plan of Action could bring Turkey closer to the United States and NATO on countering this threat.

Although Turkey's political and military support to Qatar in the 2017–2018 crisis among the GCC states caused strains in its partnerships both with several GCC states and with the United States, Turkey's support may have deterred Saudi military action against Doha, which would have undermined U.S. efforts to bolster GCC cooperation to help contain Iran. The stakes of that GCC conflict are likely to further bind Qatar and Turkey, potentially inviting a situation in which the United States is forced to choose between competing constellations of Middle East partners. In a worst-case scenario, perceived U.S. favoritism toward one of those camps could lead to denial of U.S. military access in nations of the other camp, possibly complicating response to a military contingency in the U.S. Central Command area of responsibility, such as a naval escalation with Iran in the Persian Gulf. Given the U.S. Army's major role in the military's forward presence (and rapid reinforcement) in the Persian Gulf region south of Iraq (as a hedge against Iranian regional aggression and to assure Israel and other regional partners), Army planners will need to be cognizant of these tensions that could disrupt current contingency plans.

Given the volatility of relations with Turkey, U.S. defense planners need be prepared to deal with the loss of access to İncirlik Air Base and other U.S. and NATO facilities in Turkey. The implications of the loss of İncirlik to sustaining Operation Inherent Resolve and other operations in Southwest Asia, as well as NATO deterrence missions, would be enormous, and alternative facilities in the region have substantial limitations. Exploring alternative bases in the region not only would help assure continuity of operations but also could provide leverage with Ankara if it were to again threaten to restrict or deny U.S. or other NATO forces' access.[33]

With respect to military-to-military relations, further efforts should be taken to revitalize the U.S.-Turkish High-Level Defense Group, taking into account the increased importance of the Turkish minister of defense, and to deepen the dialogues between the Joint Staff and services and the TGS.[34] Finally, the U.S. Army and other services could assist Turkey with the development of curricula at its new National Defense University and could encourage the TSK to continue to send officers to schools in the United States. These steps would help improve civil-military relations in Turkey and influence the future course of the TSK in ways that could strengthen bilateral and NATO cooperation with Turkey over the long term.

---

[33] For an overview of possible alternatives to İncirlik Air Base, see Bipartisan Policy Center, "The Alternatives to Incirlik," webpage, undated.

[34] For background on the High-Level Defense Group and its past role in the management of bilateral defense relations, see Flanagan and Brannen, 2009, p. 92.

References

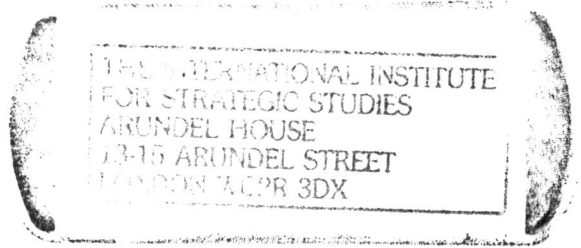

"A Change of Route for TurkStream Second Leg," *Oil & Gas Observer*, August 2, 2019.

"A New Generation of Kurdish Militants Takes Fight to Turkey's Cities," Reuters, September 15, 2016.

Abbasov, Shahin, "Azerbaijan-Turkey Military Pact Signals Impatience with Minsk Talks—Analysts," *Eurasianet*, January 2011.

Abdulrazaq, Tallah, "Iranian General Is Iraq's Kingmaker and Arbiter," *Arab Weekly*, April 30, 2017. As of March 21, 2018:
http://www.thearabweekly.com/Opinion/8338/
Iranian-general-is-Iraq%E2%80%99s-kingmaker-and-arbiter

Abrahamyan, Eduard, "Russia and Armenia Establish Joint Ground Forces," *Central Asia-Caucasus Analyst*, December 2016. As of March 21, 2018:
https://www.cacianalyst.org/publications/analytical-articles/item/
13416-russia-and-armenia-establish-joint-ground-forces.html

Abu Amer, Adnan, "Is Turkey Trying to Bypass Abbas in Gaza?" *Al-Monitor*, March 30, 2017.

Abu Zeed, Adnan, "Will Iraq Boycott Turkey?" *Al-Monitor*, October 19, 2016.

Ahren, Raphael, "In Battle for the Skies, Turkey Beats Israel 112:0," *Times of Israel*, October 31, 2013.

———, "Lapid Calls for More Aggressive Stance on Turkey," *Times of Israel*, July 27, 2017.

Akpınar, Pınar, *From Benign Donor to Self-Assured Security Provider: Turkey's Policy in Somalia*, Istanbul: Istanbul Policy Center, Sabanci University, December 2017. As of March 21, 2018:
http://ipc.sabanciuniv.edu/wp-content/uploads/2017/12/Turkeys_Policy_in_Somalia_Akpinar.pdf

Akşin, Sina, "The Nature of the Kemalist Revolution," *PAGES of the United Nations Association of Turkey*, Vol. 2, No. 2, October 1999. As of March 21, 2018:
http://www.unaturkey.org/dergiler-bulletins/38-say-02-number-02-october-1999-/
58-the-nature-of-the-kemalist-revolution-.html

Aktar, Cengiz, "The Positive Agenda and Beyond: A New Beginning for the EU-Turkey Relations?" *Insight Turkey*, Vol. 14, No. 3, 2012, pp. 35–43.

Aktürk, Şener, *Regimes of Ethnicity and Nationhood in Germany, Russia, and Turkey*, Cambridge, United Kingdom: Cambridge University Press, 2012.

———, "The Crisis in Russian-Turkish Relations, 2008–2015," *Russian Analytical Digest*, No. 179, Center for Security Studies, February 12, 2016, pp. 2–5.

Akyol, Mustafa, "Did Zbigniew Brzezinski Blame CIA for Turkey's Coup?" *Hürriyet Daily News*, September 7, 2016. As of October 27, 2017:
http://www.hurriyetdailynews.com/did-zbigniew-brzezinski-blame-cia-for-turkeys-coup.aspx?pageID=449&nID=103647&NewsCatID=411

Aliriza, Bulent, "Turkey and the Crisis in the Caucasus," Center for Strategic and International Studies, September 9, 2008. As of March 21, 2018:
https://www.csis.org/analysis/turkey-and-crisis-caucasus

———, "Turkey's Changing Dynamics," in Stephen J. Flanagan, Samuel J. Brannen, Bulent Aliriza, Edward C. Chow, Andrew C. Kuchins, Haim Malka, Julianne Smith, Ian Lesser, Eric Palomaa, and Alexandros Petersen, *Turkey's Evolving Dynamics: Strategic Choices for U.S.-Turkey Relations*, Washington, D.C.: Center for Strategic and International Studies, March 2009a, pp. 1–11.

———, "President Obama's Trip to Turkey: Building a 'Model Partnership,'" Center for Strategic and International Studies, April 8, 2009b. As of April 23, 2019:
https://csis-prod.s3.amazonaws.com/s3fs-public/legacy_files/files/media/csis/pubs/090408_turkey_update.pdf

———, "Erdogan Wins a Fresh Mandate in Turkey's New Presidential System," Commentary, Center for Strategic and International Studies, June 25, 2018. As of July 2, 2018:
https://www.csis.org/analysis/erdogan-wins-fresh-mandate-turkeys-new-presidential-system

"All You Need to Know About the Israel-Turkey Reconciliation," *Haaretz*, June 27, 2016.

"Al-Mu'alim: Fikra Idara Dhatiya fi Sharq Halab Marfuda Jamlatan wa Tafsilan" ["Muallem: The Idea of Self-Administration East of Aleppo Is Rejected Part and Parcel"], *ChamTimes*, November 20, 2016.

Alon, Amir, "Turkish Ambassador to Israel Trying to Coax Israelis Back to Antalya," *Ynet News*, May 25, 2017. As of October 31, 2017:
https://www.ynetnews.com/articles/0,7340,L-4967500,00.html

Altunısık, Meliha, "The Turkish-Israeli Rapprochement in the Post-Cold War Era," *Middle Eastern Studies*, Vol. 36, No. 2, 2000, pp. 172–191.

Amnesty International, *Gezi Park Protests: Brutal Denial of the Right to Peaceful Assembly in Turkey*, London, October 2, 2013. As of March 21, 2018:
https://www.amnesty.org/en/documents/EUR44/022/2013/en/

"Ankara's Oil Business with ISIS," *RT*, November 25, 2016.

Arango, Tim, and Eric Schmitt, "A Path to ISIS, Through a Porous Turkish Border," *New York Times*, March 9, 2015.

Arbell, Dan, *The U.S.-Turkey-Israel Triangle*, Washington, D.C.: Brookings Institution, Analysis Paper No. 34, October 2014. As of March 14, 2019:
https://www.brookings.edu/wp-content/uploads/2016/06/USTurkeyIsrael-TriangleFINAL.pdf

"Armenia and Russia: Stuck with Each Other," *The Economist*, March 20, 2015. As of March 21, 2018:
https://www.economist.com/news/europe/21646947-russian-ally-rues-its-dependence-upon-moscow-stuck-each-other

"Army, Navy, Air Force Commanders Reshuffled in Turkey's Supreme Military Council," *Daily Sabah*, August 2, 2017.

Ataman, Muhittin, "Özal Leadership and Restructuring of Turkish Ethnic Policy in the 1980s," *Middle Eastern Studies*, Vol. 38, No. 4, October 2002, pp. 123–142.

Aydıntaşbaş, Asli, *With Friends Like These: Turkey, Russia, and the End of an Unlikely Alliance*, London: European Council on Foreign Relations, policy brief, June 2016.

Aykan, Mahmut Bali, "The Turkey-U.S.-Israel Triangle: Continuity, Change, and Implications for Turkey's Post-Cold War Middle East Policy," *Journal of South Asian and Middle Eastern Studies*, Vol. 22, No. 4, Summer 1999, pp. 1–31.

Aytürk, İlker, "The Coming of an Ice Age? Turkish–Israeli Relations Since 2002," *Turkish Studies*, Vol. 12, No. 4, 2011, pp. 675–687.

Azulay, Yuval, "Machon Ha'Yetzu: Ha'Piyus Im Turkkya Yiten 'Boost' Nosaf Le'Kishrey Ha'Sachar," *Globes*, June 27, 2016.

Bachner, Michael, "Turkey, Israel Humiliate Each Others' Envoys in Escalating Diplomatic Tiff," *Times of Israel*, May 16, 2018.

Baconi, Tareq, *A Flammable Peace: Why Gas Deals Won't End Conflict in the Middle East*, London: European Council on Foreign Relations, policy brief, December 2017.

Baev, Pavel K., and Kemal Kirişci, *An Ambiguous Partnership: The Serpentine Trajectory of Turkish-Russian Relations in the Era of Erdoğan and Putin*, Washington, D.C.: Brookings Institution, Turkey Project Policy Paper No. 13, September 2017. As of December 6, 2017: https://www.brookings.edu/wp-content/uploads/2017/09/pavel-and-kirisci-turkey-and-russia.pdf

"Baghdad 'Reaches Deal' on Turkish Forces in Northern Iraq," *Middle East Eye*, January 7, 2017.

"Baku-Tbilisi-Kars Railway Line Officially Launched," Radio Free Europe/Radio Liberty, October 30, 2017.

Balci, Bayram, "What Are the Consequences of the Split Between Erdoğan and Gülen on Turkey's Foreign Policy?" *Foreign Policy Journal*, January 17, 2014.

Bardakçi, Mehmet, "Coup Plots and the Transformation of Civil–Military Relations in Turkey Under AKP Rule," *Turkish Studies*, Vol. 14, No. 3, 2013, pp. 411–428.

Barigazzi, Jacopo, "EU Ministers Reject Austria's Call to Freeze Turkey Membership Talks," *Politico*, December 13, 2016.

Barkey, Henri J., *Turkey's New Engagement in Iraq: Embracing Iraqi Kurdistan*, Washington, D.C.: United States Institute of Peace, 2010a.

———, "Turkey's Moment of Inflection," *Survival*, Vol. 52, No. 3, June–July 2010b, pp. 39–50.

———, "One Year Later, the Turkish Coup Attempt Remains Shrouded in Mystery," *Washington Post*, July 14, 2017.

———, "For Erdogan and His Cronies, Losing Was Never an Option," *The National*, June 26, 2018.

Barnes, Julian E., and Emre Peker, "Disputes Between Germany and Turkey Threaten to Affect NATO Mission," *Wall Street Journal*, July 24, 2017.

Başaran, Ezgi, *Frontline Turkey: The Conflict at the Heart of the Middle East*, London: I.B. Tauris, 2017.

Baugh, Peter, "Turkey Vetoes NATO-Austria Partnership," *Politico*, May 23, 2017.

Bayaliyev, Alim, "The Turkic Council: Will the Turks Finally Unite?" *Central Asia-Caucasus Analyst*, February 19, 2014. As of March 21, 2018: https://www.cacianalyst.org/publications/analytical-articles/item/ 12916-the-turkic-council-will-the-turks-finally-unite?.html

Baydar, Yavuz, "Questions and Bitter Truths in a Hazy Post-Election Landscape," *Ahval News*, June 28, 2018. As of July 3, 2018:
https://ahvalnews.com/2018-elections/questions-and-bitter-truths-hazy-post-election-landscape

Baysal, Nurcan, "Why Turkey Is Posting Paramilitary Forces to Its Own Cities," *Ahval News*, November 13, 2017. As of March 21, 2018:
https://ahvalnews.com/pkk/why-turkey-posting-paramilitary-forces-its-own-cities

Beaumont, Peter, "Far-Right Israeli Minister Plans Bill to Annex One of Biggest Settlements," *The Guardian*, January 3, 2017.

Bechev, Dimitar, "Erdoğan and Putin: Unalike Likeness," *Open Democracy*, November 28, 2015.

———, *Rival Power: Russia in Southeast Europe*, New Haven, Conn.: Yale University Press, 2017.

Beiser, Elana, "Record Number of Journalists Jailed as Turkey, China, Egypt Pay Scant Price for Repression," Committee to Protect Journalists, December 13, 2017. As of October 16, 2017:
https://cpj.org/reports/2017/12/journalists-prison-jail-record-number-turkey-china-egypt.php

Bekdil, Burak, "Erdogan Raising 'Devout Generations,'" Gatestone Institute, April 1, 2015a. As of January 16, 2011:
https://www.gatestoneinstitute.org/5416/turkey-devout-generations

———, "Germany Pulls Patriot Systems from Turkey," *Defense News*, December 23, 2015b. As of November 14, 2017:
https://www.defensenews.com/home/2015/12/23/germany-pulls-patriot-systems-from-turkey

Belgium, Germany, France, Italy, Luxembourg, the Netherlands, the Council of the European Communities, and Turkey, "Additional Protocol and Financial Protocol Signed on 23 November 1970, Annexed to the Agreement Establishing the Association Between the European Economic Community and Turkey and on Measures to Be Taken for Their Entry into Force—Final Act—Declarations," Brussels, November 23, 1970. As of November 21, 2017:
http://eur-lex.europa.eu/legal-content/EN/TXT/?uri=CELEX:21970A1123(01)

Bengio, Ofra, *Turkish-Israeli Relationship: Changing Ties of the Middle Eastern Outsiders*, London: Palgrave Macmillan, 2004.

Benmeleh, Yaacov, and David Wainer, "Israel and Turkey Seek to Shield Natural Gas Ties from Politics," *Bloomberg*, December 12, 2016.

———, "Fraying Israel-Turkey Ties Threaten Planned Natural Gas Venture," *Bloomberg*, February 5, 2018.

Bennhold, Katrin, "Leaders of Turkey and Israel Clash at Davos Panel," *New York Times*, January 29, 2009.

Bershidsky, Leonid, "Turkey's Troubled NATO Status," *Bloomberg*, March 14, 2017.

Bertrand, Natasha, "ISIS Is Exploiting a Crucial Weakness in Turkey That Lets Them Walk 'Free,'" *Business Insider*, August 1, 2015.

Bilgic-Alpaslan, Idil, Bojan Markovic, Peter Tabak, and Emir Zildzovic, "Economic Implications of Russia's Sanctions Against Turkey," European Bank for Reconstruction and Development, December 7, 2015. As of November 14, 2017:
http://www.ebrd.com/news/2015/economic-implications-of-russias-sanctions-against-turkey.html

Binnie, Jeremy, "Turkey Deploys Artillery to Qatar," *Jane's Defense Weekly*, July 19, 2017.

Bipartisan Policy Center, "The Alternatives to Incirlik," webpage, undated. As of January 15, 2018:
https://bipartisanpolicy.org/incirlik-alternative-airbase/

"Black Sea Economic Cooperation Organization: Turkey's Third Option," *Daily Sabah*, December 15, 2016.

Blockmans, Steven, "Participation of Turkey in the EU's Common Security and Defence Policy: Kingmaker or Trojan Horse?" Leuven Centre for Global Governance Studies, Working Paper No. 41, March 2010.

Bob, Yonah Jeremy, "Israel Arrests Head of Turkish Humanitarian Group in Gaza for Financing Hamas," *Jerusalem Post*, March 21, 2017.

Bode, Kim, and Alessandria Masi, "Expert View: The YPG, PKK and Turkey's Options in Syria," *Syria Deeply*, May 15, 2017. As of January 20, 2018:
https://www.newsdeeply.com/syria/community/2017/05/15/
expert-view-the-ypg-pkk-and-turkeys-options-in-syria

Borger, Julian, "Turkey Confirms It Barred Israel from Military Exercise Because of Gaza War," *The Guardian*, October 12, 2009.

Bozinovski, Igor, "Cyprus Boosts Maritime Capabilities with First Offshore Patrol Vessel," *Jane's Navy International*, January 16, 2018.

Bozkurt, Abdullah, "Turkey's Foreign Ministry Labels 394 Turkish Diplomats as Terrorists," Stockholm Center for Freedom, May 22, 2017. As of January 15, 2018:
https://stockholmcf.org/turkeys-foreign-ministry-labels-394-turkish-diplomats-as-terrorists

Brown, Carl L., *Imperial Legacy: The Ottoman Imprint on the Balkans and the Middle East,* New York: Columbia University Press, 1996.

Buchan, R., "II. The Palmer Report and the Legality of Israel's Naval Blockade of Gaza," *International and Comparative Law Quarterly*, Vol. 61, No. 1, January 2012, pp. 264–273.

Butler, Daren, "Turks Believe Cleric Gülen Was Behind Coup Attempt: Survey," Reuters, July 26, 2016.

———, "Pro-Kurdish Opposition Leader's Trial Opens in Turkey," Reuters, December 7, 2017.

Byman, Daniel, and Jeremy Shapiro, *Be Afraid. Be a Little Afraid: The Threat of Terrorism from Western Foreign Fighters in Syria and Iraq,* Washington, D.C.: Brookings Institution, Policy Paper No. 34, November 2014. As of January 15, 2018:
https://www.brookings.edu/wp-content/uploads/2016/06/Be-Afraid-web.pdf

Cagaptay, Soner, *The New Sultan: Erdoğan and the Crisis of Modern Turkey*, London: I.B. Tauris, 2017.

Carlstrom, Gregg, "Why Egypt Hates Al Jazeera," *Foreign Policy*, February 19, 2014.

Caliskan, Koray, "Explaining the End of Military Tutelary Regime and the July 15 Coup Attempt in Turkey," *Journal of Cultural Economy*, Vol. 10, No. 1, 2017, pp. 97–111.

Çandar, Cengiz, "Turkey: The Self-Fulfilling Prophecy of the Hakan Fidan Story," *Al-Monitor*, October 21, 2013.

———, "A Generational Change Is Looming in Turkish Politics," *Al-Monitor*, September 13, 2019.

Cantürk, Safure, "Students Educated by Maarif Foundation Exceed 10,000," *Daily Sabah*, November 6, 2017.

Capezza, David, "Turkey's Military Is a Catalyst for Reform: The Military in Politics," *Middle East Quarterly*, Vol. 16, No. 3, Summer 2009, pp. 13–23.

Cascais, Antonio, "Turkey Seeks Greater Role in Africa,"" *Deutsche Welle*, June 2, 2016.

Çayhan, Esra, "Towards a European Security and Defense Policy: With or Without Turkey?" in Ali Çarkoglu and Barry Rubin, eds., *Turkey and the European Union: Domestic Politics, Economic Integration and International Dynamics*, London: Frank Cass, 2003, pp. 32–51.

Cecire, Michael Hikari, "Georgia-Turkey-Azerbaijan Cooperation: Pragmatism Proves Durable Formula," *Eurasianet*, June 1, 2017.

Çelikkol, Oğuz, *Turkish-Israeli Relations: Crises and Cooperation*, Istanbul: Global Political Trends Center and Mitvim Institute, November 2016.

Center for Army Lessons Learned, *Strategic Landpower in Europe: Special Study*, Washington, D.C.: U.S. Army, No. 18-05, December 2017.

Cetingulec, Mehmet, "Can Turkey Break Its Russian Gas Habit?" *Al-Monitor*, April 7, 2016.

Cevikoz, Unal, *Turkey in a Reconnecting Eurasia: Foreign Economic and Security Interests*, Washington, D.C.: Center for Strategic and International Studies, April 2016.

Champion, Marc, "Conspiracy or Not, Turkey's Ties to West Are at Risk," *Bloomberg*, December 5, 2017.

China Internet Information Center, "The Silk Road Economic Belt," webpage, undated. As of March 18, 2019:
http://china.org.cn/business/node_7207419.htm

Chorev, Shaul, Mary Landrieu, Ami Ayalon, Seth Cropsey, Charles D. Davidson, Douglas J. Feith, Arthur Herman, Ron Prosor, Gary Roughead, and Eytan Sheshinski, *Report of the Commission on the Eastern Mediterranean*, Washington, D.C.: University of Haifa and the Hudson Institute, September 2016.

"CHP Presidential Candidate İnce Vows to Be 'Everyone's President,'" *Hürriyet Daily News*, May 4, 2018.

Çil, Uğur, "Turkey Slams German Daily over NATO Summit Accusations," Anadolu Agency, May 2, 2017.

Cohen, Gili, "Turkey Holds Naval Drill off Cyprus in Heated Response to Israeli Commando Exercise on Its Doorstep," *Haaretz*, June 15, 2017.

Cohen, Tova, and Ari Rabinovitch, "Leviathan Gas Field Developers Approve $3.75 Billion Investment," Reuters, February 23, 2017.

Commission on the Black Sea, *A 2020 Vision for the Black Sea Region*, Gütersloh, Germany: Bertelsmann Stiftung, May 2010.

Cook, Steven A., "Tarnished Brass," *Foreign Policy*, August 2, 2011.

Cornell, Svante E., "Erdoğan's Looming Downfall," *Middle East Quarterly*, Vol. 21, No. 2, Spring 2014.

Cornell, Svante E., and Fariz Ismailzade, "The Baku-Tbilisi-Ceyhan Pipeline: Implications for Azerbaijan," in S. Frederick Starr and Svante E. Cornell, eds., *The Baku-Tbilisi-Ceyhan Pipeline: Oil Window to the West*, Washington, D.C.: Central Asia-Caucasus Institute and Silk Road Studies Program, 2005, pp. 61–84.

Coskun, Orhan, "Update 1—Russia Halts Turkey Nuclear Work, Ankara Looks Elsewhere," Reuters, December 9, 2015.

Costello, Katherine, *Russia's Use of Media and Information Operations in Turkey: Implications for the United States*, Santa Monica, Calif.: RAND Corporation, PE-278-A, 2018. As of March 19, 2019:
https://www.rand.org/pubs/perspectives/PE278.html

Council of the European Union, "Council Common Position 2006/1011/CFSP of December 21, 2006," *Official Journal of the European Union*, L 379/129, December 28, 2006. As of January 15, 2018:
http://eur-lex.europa.eu/LexUriServ/LexUriServ.do?uri=OJ:L:2006:379:0129:0130:EN:PDF

Crowley, Stephen, "Why Protests Keep Putin Up at Night," *Foreign Affairs*, April 19, 2017.

Curtis, Michael, "The European Union vs. Turkey," *American Thinker*, June 24, 2013. As of January 15, 2018:
http://www.americanthinker.com/articles/2013/06/the_european_union_vs_turkey.html

Dahl, Brock, and Danielle Slutzky, "Timeline of Turkish-Israeli Relations, 1949–2006," Washington Institute for Near East Policy, 2006. As of May 19, 2018:
https://web.archive.org/web/20090319134207/http://www.washingtoninstitute.org/documents/44edf1a5d337f.pdf

Daloğlu, Tülin, "Syrian Downing of Turkish Plane Adds to Strain on Both Regimes," *Al-Monitor*, June 25, 2012.

Danforth, Nicholas, "Turkey's New Maps Are Reclaiming the Ottoman Empire," *Foreign Policy*, October 23, 2016.

———, "The New Turkey: One Nation, Indivisible, Under God," *War on the Rocks*, June 24, 2017.

Dargham, Raghia, "At-Ta'awun Al-Istratiji bayn As-Sa'udiya wa Turkiya fi Wajh At-Tahidiyat" ["Strategic Cooperation Between Saudi Arabia and Turkey in the Face of Challenges"], *Al Hayat*, January 1, 2016.

Davtyan, Erik, "Armenia Recalls the Zurich Protocols," *Eurasia Daily Monitor*, Vol. 12, No. 40, March 4, 2015.

Davutoğlu, Ahmet, "Turkey's Foreign Policy Vision: An Assessment of 2007," *Insight Turkey*, Vol. 10, No. 1, Winter 2008.

———, "Turkey's Mediation: Critical Reflections from the Field," *Middle East Policy*, Vol. 20, No. 1, Spring 2013.

Dawisha, Adweed, *Iraq: A Political History from Independence to Occupation*, Princeton, N.J.: Princeton University Press, 2009.

De La Baume, Maïa, and Guilia Paravicini, "'Sleepless Nights' for Gülen's Supports in Europe," *Politico*, August 24, 2016.

Dehghanpisheh, Babak, Tulay Karadeniz, Tuvan Gumrukcu, and Parisa Hafezi, "Iran Summons Turkish Envoy over Comments by President, Foreign Minister," Reuters, February 20, 2017.

Demir, Sertif, "Turkey's Contribution to the European Common Security and Defense Policy," *Turkish Public Administration Annual*, Vol. 38, 2012, pp. 1–22.

Demirtaş, Serkan, "Is Only President Erdoğan Immune to 'Metal Fatigue'?" *Hürriyet Daily News*, October 25, 2017.

"Deutschland ist ein wichtiger Hafen für Terroristen," *Zeit Online*, November 3, 2016. As of February 15, 2018:
http://www.zeit.de/politik/ausland/2016-11/recep-tayyip-erdogan-deutschland-terrorismus

Devitt, Polina, Dmitry Solovyov, and Jack Stubbs, "Factbox: Impact of Russian Sanctions on Trade Ties with Turkey" Reuters, June 27, 2016.

DeYoung, Karen, "U.S. and Turkey Negotiate Plan for Their Troops to Jointly Patrol Safe Zone in Syria," *Washington Post*, April 25, 2019.

Doğan, Zülfikar, "Iraq, Turkey Strengthen Energy Relationship." *Al-Monitor*, January 23, 2015.

———, "First the Middle East, Now Central Asia Slipping Away from Turkey," *Al-Monitor*, January 6, 2016a.

———, "Erdogan Expected to Put Anti-Gulen Movement in High Gear," *Al-Monitor*, June 17, 2016b.

———, "Turkey Poised to Open a Military Front in Iraq," *Al-Monitor*, March 12, 2018.

Dombey, Daniel, and Funja Guler, "Turkey Emerges as True Iraq War Victor," *Financial Times*, March 12, 2013.

Duran, Burhanettin, "Turkey's New Security Concept," *Daily Sabah*, October 26, 2016.

Dursun-Özkanca, Oya, "Turkish Soft Balancing Against the EU? An Analysis of the Prospects for Improved Transatlantic Security Relations," *Foreign Policy Analysis*, Vol. 13, No. 4, October 1, 2017, pp. 894–912.

Edelman, Eric, and Aykan Erdemir, "Turkey's President Is Holding Americans Hostage. Why Aren't We Doing Anything About It?" *Washington Post*, April 15, 2018.

Edelman, Eric, and Merve Tahiroglu, "It's Time for NATO to Call Turkey's Bluff," *Weekly Standard*, May 25, 2017.

Eder, Florian, "Austria to the EU: We Need to Talk About Turkey," *Politico*, December 12, 2016.

Efron, Shira, *The Future of Israeli-Turkish Relations*, Santa Monica, Calif.: RAND Corporation, RR-2445-RC, 2018. As of March 28, 2019:
https://www.rand.org/pubs/research_reports/RR2445.html

Eisenbud, Daniel K., "Turkey Remains Popular Tourist Destination for Israeli Arabs," *Jerusalem Post*, January 1, 2017.

Eissenstat, Howard, *Uneasy Rests the Crown: Erdoğan and "Revolutionary Security" in Turkey*, Washington, D.C.: Project on Middle East Democracy, December 2017. As of February 10, 2018:
http://pomed.org/pomed-publications/
pomed-snapshot-uneasy-rests-the-crown-erdogan-and-revolutionary-security-in-turkey

Eldem, Tuba, *Guardians Entrapped: The Demise of the Turkish Armed Forces as a Veto-Player*, doctoral thesis, Toronto: University of Toronto, 2013. As of January 11, 2018:
https://tspace.library.utoronto.ca/bitstream/1807/70076/8/Eldem_Tuba_201311_PhD_thesis.pdf

Eligür, Banu, *The Mobilization of Political Islam in Turkey*, Cambridge, United Kingdom: Cambridge University Press, 2010.

Elitok, Seçil Paçacı, *A Step Backward for Turkey? The Readmission Agreement and the Hope of Visa-Free Europe*, Istanbul: Istanbul Policy Center, Sabanci University, December 2015. As of November 25, 2017:
http://ipc.sabanciuniv.edu/wp-content/uploads/2015/12/A-Step-Backward-for-Turkey_
The-Readmission-Agreement-and-the-Hope-of-Visa-Free-Europe.pdf

Elyan, Tamim, and Abdel Latif Wahba, "Egypt to Freeze Israeli Gas Import Talks After Court Ruling," *Bloomberg*, December 6, 2015.

Engdahl, F. William, "Top USA National Security Officials Admit Turkey Coup," *New Eastern Outlook*, August 31, 2016. As of October 27, 2017:
https://journal-neo.org/2016/08/31/top-usa-national-security-officials-admit-turkey-coup

Entous, Adam, and Joe Parkinson, "Turkey's Spymaster Plots Own Course on Syria," *Wall Street Journal*, October 10, 2013.

"EP's President Schulz Opposes Liberalisation of Visa Regime with Turkey," *News for Turkey*, December 28, 2016.

Erdemir, Aykan, and Oren Kessler, "A Turkish TV Blockbuster Reveals Erdogan's Conspiratorial, Anti-Semitic Worldview," *Washington Post*, May 15, 2017.

"Erdoğan, Bahçeli Agree Not to Extend State of Emergency in First Meeting After Elections," *Daily Sabah*, June 27, 2018.

Erdoğan, Emre, and Pınar Uyan Semerci, "Attitudes Towards Syrians in Turkey—2017," presentation slides, Ankara, March 12, 2018. As of May 10, 2018:
https://goc.bilgi.edu.tr/media/uploads/2018/03/12/
turkish-perceptions-of-syrian-refugees-20180312.pdf

"Erdoğan: Listu Radian 'an At-Tawasu' Al-Farasi" ["Erdoğan: I Am Not Content with Persian Expansionism"], *Asharq al-Awsat*, June 17, 2017.

"Erdoğan Marks Armenian Dead from 1915 Events in Message," *Daily Sabah*, April 25, 2017.

"Erdoğan Not Backing Down on Turkish Role in Mosul," *Al-Monitor*, October 16, 2016.

"Erdogan Offers Citizenship to Syrian and Iraqi Refugees," *Al Jazeera*, January 7, 2017. As of January 12, 2018:
http://www.aljazeera.com/news/2017/01/
erdogan-offers-citizenship-syrian-iraqi-refugees-170106195134961.html

"Erdoğan Won't Restore Egyptian Ties 'Until Morsi Freed,'" *Al Jazeera*, April 9, 2015.

Ereli, Adam, "Putin's Newest Satellite State," *Forbes*, February 24, 2016.

Erkul, Nuran, "SOCAR's Investments in Turkey to Exceed $18 Billion," Anadolu Agency, December 2016. As of January 10, 2018:
http://aa.com.tr/en/economy/socars-investments-in-turkey-to-exceed-18-billion/706843

Escobar, Pepe, "Who Profits from Turkey's Sarajevo Moment?" *RT*, December 20, 2016.

Escritt, Thomas, and Daren Butler, "Merkel Attacks Turkey's 'Misuse' of Interpol Warrants," Reuters, August 20, 2017.

Esen, Berk, and Şebnem Gümüşçü, "A Small Yes for Presidentialism: The Turkish Constitutional Referendum of April 2017," *South European Society and Politics*, Vol. 22, No. 3, October 2017, pp. 303–326.

"EU Commission President Warns Europe Not to Lecture Turkey over Migration," *Euronews*, November 25, 2016. As of November 21, 2017:
http://www.euronews.com/2016/11/25/
on-migration-i-d-like-europe-to-refrain-from-giving-lessons-to-turkey-says-jean

"EU: Don't Send Syrians Back to Turkey," Human Rights Watch, June 20, 2016. As of March 21, 2018:
https://www.hrw.org/news/2016/06/20/eu-dont-send-syrians-back-turkey

"EU Loses Ankara's Trust," *AzerNews*, October 16, 2017. As of January 21, 2018:
https://www.azernews.az/region/120590.html

"EU Warns Turkey to Step Up Reforms to Avoid 'Train Crash,'" *Deutsche Welle*, March 10, 2006.

European Border and Coast Guard Agency, "Migratory Map," webpage, November 6, 2018. As of November 21, 2018:
https://frontex.europa.eu/along-eu-borders/migratory-map

European Commission, "EU-Turkey Joint Action Plan," fact sheet, October 15, 2015a. As of November 21, 2017:
http://europa.eu/rapid/press-release_MEMO-15-5860_en.htm

———, *Turkey 2015 Report*, Brussels, November 10, 2015b. As of November 21, 2017:
https://ec.europa.eu/neighbourhood-enlargement/sites/near/files/pdf/
key_documents/2015/20151110_report_turkey.pdf

———, *Turkey 2016 Report*, Brussels, September 11, 2016a. As of November 21, 2017:
https://ec.europa.eu/neighbourhood-enlargement/sites/near/files/pdf/
key_documents/2016/20161109_report_turkey.pdf

———, *Fourth Report on the Progress Made in the Implementation of the EU-Turkey Statement*, Brussels, December 8, 2016b. As of March 28, 2019:
https://www.refworld.org/docid/584ad1fb4.html

———, *Seventh Report on the Progress Made in the Implementation of the EU-Turkey Statement*, Brussels, September 6, 2017. As of March 28, 2019:
https://ec.europa.eu/neighbourhood-enlargement/sites/near/files/20170906_seventh_report_on_the_
progress_in_the_implementation_of_the_eu-turkey_statement_en.pdf

———, *Turkey 2018 Report*, Strasbourg, April 17, 2018a. As of June 30, 2018:
https://ec.europa.eu/neighbourhood-enlargement/sites/near/files/20180417-turkey-report.pdf

———, "The EU Facility for Refugees in Turkey," fact sheet, December 2018b. As of January 15, 2019:
https://www.avrupa.info.tr/sites/default/files/2019-01/frit_factsheet.pdf

———, "Turkey," webpage, February 15, 2019a. As of March 21, 2019:
http://ec.europa.eu/trade/policy/countries-and-regions/countries/turkey

———, "Key Findings of the 2019 Report on Turkey," press release, Brussels, May 29, 2019b. As of June 5, 2019:
http://europa.eu/rapid/press-release_COUNTRY-19-2781_en.htm

European Commission, Directorate-General for Trade, "European Union, Trade in Goods with Turkey," June 11, 2018. As of March 18, 2019:
https://webgate.ec.europa.eu/isdb_results/factsheets/country/details_turkey_en.pdf

European Council, "EU-Turkey Statement," press release, March 18, 2016. As of January 15, 2018:
http://www.consilium.europa.eu/en/press/press-releases/2016/03/18/eu-turkey-statement

European Parliament, "European Parliament Resolution on the 2004 Regular Report and the Recommendation of the European Commission on Turkey's Progress Towards Accession," September 15, 2005.

———, "Parliament Wants to Suspend EU Accession Negotiations with Turkey," press release, March 13, 2019. As of June 5, 2019:
http://www.europarl.europa.eu/news/en/press-room/20190307IPR30746/
parliament-wants-to-suspend-eu-accession-negotiations-with-turkey

European Union and Republic of Turkey, "Agreement Between the European Union and the Republic of Turkey Establishing a Framework for the Participation of the Republic of Turkey in the European Union Crisis Management Operations, of December 21, 2006," *Official Journal of the EU*, Brussels, L 189/17, June 29, 2006.

European Union External Action, "Turkey-EU Counter Terrorism Dialogue," press release, June 8, 2016. As of January 11, 2018:
http://eeas.europa.eu/statements-eeas/2016/160608_06_en.htm

———, "Military and Civilian Missions and Operations," webpage, May 3, 2019. As of July 2, 2019: https://eeas.europa.eu/headquarters/headquarters-homepage/430/military-and-civilian-missions-and-operations_en

Europol, *European Union Terrorism Situation and Trend Report 2016*, The Hague, Netherlands: European Police Office, 2016a.

———, "Turkey and Europol Sign Liaison Agreement," press release, March 21, 2016b. As of March 21, 2018: https://www.europol.europa.eu/latest_news/turkey-and-europol-sign-liaison-agreement

"Excerpts of Turkish Army Statement," BBC News, April 28, 2007. As of May 19, 2018: http://news.bbc.co.uk/2/hi/6602775.stm

Fabbe, Kristin, Chad Hazlett, and Tolga Sinmazdemir, "What Do Syrians Want Their Future to Be?" *Foreign Affairs*, May 1, 2017.

Fache, Wilson, "What Is Turkish Army Really Doing In Iraq?" *Al-Monitor*, September 6, 2016.

Fantini, Giacomo, "The Coup and the Referendum: Ascent and Decline of Military Influence on Turkish Constitutionalism," Lista Dei Working Paper, March 2017.

"FDI into Turkey Upward Despite Political Rift with EU," *Daily Sabah*, August 7, 2017.

"Fight Against Terror Number One Foreign Policy Issue in Turkey, Says Poll," *Hürriyet Daily News*, July 21, 2017.

Finn, Tom, "Turkish Troops Hold Exercises in Qatar," Reuters, August 7, 2017.

Fırat, Hande, "New Military Base in Qatar to Inaugurate in Autumn," *Hürriyet Daily News*, August 14, 2019.

Flanagan, Stephen J., "The Turkey-Russia-Iran Nexus: Eurasian Power Dynamics," *Washington Quarterly*, Vol. 36, No. 1, 2013, pp. 163–178.

Flanagan, Stephen J., and Samuel J. Brannen, "Implications for U.S.-Turkey Relations," in Stephen J. Flanagan, Samuel J. Brannen, Bulent Aliriza, Edward C. Chow, Andrew C. Kuchins, Haim Malka, Julianne Smith, Ian Lesser, Eric Palomaa, and Alexandros Petersen, *Turkey's Evolving Dynamics: Strategic Choices for U.S.-Turkey Relations*, Washington, D.C.: Center for Strategic and International Studies, March 2009, pp. 81–96.

Flanagan, Stephen J., Samuel J. Brannen, Bulent Aliriza, Edward C. Chow, Andrew C. Kuchins, Haim Malka, Julianne Smith, Ian Lesser, Eric Palomaa, and Alexandros Petersen, *Turkey's Evolving Dynamics: Strategic Choices for U.S.-Turkey Relations*, Washington, D.C.: Center for Strategic and International Studies, March 2009.

Flower, Kevin, and Shira Medding, "Israel-Turkey Tensions High over TV Series," CNN, January 12, 2010.

"Four-Party Opposition Bloc Set Up for Turkey's Snap Parliamentary Election," *Hürriyet Daily News*, May 2, 2018.

Fraser, Susan, "Erdogan Catches Turkey Off Guard by Calling Early Elections," PBS NewsHour, April 18, 2018.

Freedom House, "Freedom of the Press 2014: Turkey," webpage, 2014. As of January 15, 2018: https://freedomhouse.org/report/freedom-press/2014/turkey

———, "Freedom in the World 2017: Turkey," webpage, 2017. As of January 15, 2018: https://freedomhouse.org/report/freedom-world/2017/turkey

Gabai, Ramzi, "Lenatzel et Hamomentum Hachiyuvi," *Marker Magazine*, trans. by Shira Efron, March 1, 2017.

Galeotti, Mark, "What Turkey Can Learn from Russia About Coup-Proofing the Military," *War on the Rocks*, August 2, 2016.

Gall, Carlotta, "'March for Justice' Ends in Istanbul with a Pointed Challenge to Erdogan," *New York Times*, July 9, 2017a.

———, "Erdogan Trains His Broom on a Sweep of Turkey's Governing Party," *New York Times*, December 23, 2017b.

———, "Istanbul's New Mayor Quickly Emerges as a Rival to Erdogan," *New York Times*, July 3, 2019.

Ganioglu, Ayla, "How Long Can Erdogan's Alliance Survive?" *Al-Monitor*, July 2, 2018.

Garamone, Jim, "Dunford Visit to Turkey Is First by Senior U.S. Official Since Coup Attempt," DoD News, August 1, 2016.

Gazprom Export, "Delivery Statistics," webpage, undated-a. As of March 28, 2019:
http://www.gazpromexport.ru/en/statistics

———, "Foreign Partners: Turkey," webpage, undated-b. As of October 16, 2017:
http://www.gazpromexport.ru/en/partners/turkey

Gebauer, Matthias, "Türkei untersagt Besuch von deutschem Staatssekretär," *Spiegel Online*, June 6, 2016. As of November 21, 2017:
https://www.spiegel.de/forum/politik/
bundeswehr-incirlik-tuerkei-untersagt-besuch-von-deutschem-staatssekretaer-thread-476785-11.html

———, "Türkei blockiert Abgeordneten-Besuch auf Nato-Basis," *Spiegel Online*, July 14, 2017. As of November 21, 2017:
http://www.spiegel.de/politik/deutschland/
tuerkei-blockiert-erneut-abgeordneten-besuch-a-1157827.html

"Georgia, Azerbaijan and Turkey Signed an Agreement on Military Cooperation," *Front News International*, October 18, 2017.

German Marshall Fund of the United States, *Transatlantic Trends 2008*, Washington, D.C., September 20, 2008.

"Germany Becomes Magnet for FETO Suspects," Anadolu Agency, September 11, 2017.

"Germany Sees No FETÖ Presence Despite Hundreds of Schools and Fugitives," *Daily Sabah*, November 2, 2016.

"Germany to Invest €58 Million in Turkish Airbase: Report," *The Local*, September 6, 2016.

Ghiasy, Richard, and Jiayi Zhou, *The Silk Road Economic Belt: Considering Security Implications and EU–China Cooperation Prospects*, Stockholm: Stockholm International Peace Research Institute, 2017.

Girit, Selin, "Syria Conflict: Kilis, the Turkish Town Enduring IS Bombardment," BBC News, May 9, 2016.

Glenewinkel, Klaas, "Kurds Condemn Security Agreement Between Turkey and Iraq," *Niqash*, October 1, 2007. As of January 20, 2018:
http://www.niqash.org/en/articles/politics/2016

Göksel, Nigar, "Turkey's Siege Mentality," International Crisis Group, March 23, 2018. As of May 19, 2018:
https://www.crisisgroup.org/europe-central-asia/western-europemediterranean/turkey/turkeys-siege-mentality

Gonzales, Richard, "Feds Drop Prosecution of 7 Turkish Bodyguards Involved in Assault of Protesters," National Public Radio, March 22, 2018.

Gordon, Philip H., and Ömer Taşpınar, *Winning Turkey: How America, Europe, and Turkey Can Revive a Fading Partnership*, Washington, D.C.: Brookings Institution Press, 2008.

Gorenburg, Dimitry, "Russia's New and Unrealistic Naval Doctrine," *War on the Rocks*, July 26, 2017.

"Greece Says Court Decision Not to Extradite Turkish Soldiers Must Be Respected," *VOA News*, June 19, 2017. As of April 18, 2018:
https://www.voanews.com/a/greece-turkey-soldiers-extradition/3906403.html

"Greek Court Overturns Extradition Decision Against Two More Turkish Coup-Plotting Soldiers," *Hürriyet Daily News*, December 8, 2016.

Gross, Judah Ari, "In First, U.S. Establishes Permanent Military Base in Israel," *Times of Israel*, September 18, 2017.

Groves, David G., and Robert J. Lempert, "A New Analytic Method for Finding Policy-Relevant Scenarios," *Global Environmental Change*, Vol. 17, No. 1, 2007, pp. 78–85.

Gurbanov, Ilgar, "Armenia Seeks to Boost Its Role in the Iran-Georgia Gas Talks," *Central Asia-Caucasus Analyst*, October 17, 2016. As of January 22, 2018:
https://www.cacianalyst.org/publications/analytical-articles/item/13404-armenia-seeks-to-boost-its-role-in-the-iran-georgia-gas-talks.html

Gurcan, Metin, "Splitting Gendarmerie from Turkish Army: Reform or Bad Timing?" *Al-Monitor*, November 3, 2014.

———, "What Turkey Can Learn from Coup Plot Case Dismissal," *Al-Monitor*, April 25, 2016a.

———, "Why Turkey's Coup Didn't Stand a Chance," *Al-Monitor,* July 17, 2016b.

———, "Power Struggle Erupts in Turkey's Security Structure," *Al-Monitor*, October 12, 2016c.

———, "Why U.S.-Educated Turkish Officers Could Soon Be out of Their Jobs," *Al-Monitor*, October 18, 2016d.

———, "Turkey's New 'Erdogan Doctrine,'" *Al-Monitor*, November 4, 2016e.

———, "Turkish Government Outsources Urban Security," *Al-Monitor*, March 6, 2017a.

———, "Turkey Seeks to Replenish Severely Depleted Military," *Al-Monitor*, May 10, 2017b.

———, "The Rise of the Eurasianist Vision in Turkey," *Al-Monitor*, May 17, 2017c.

———, "Turkey, Iran Could Unite to Overcome Their Kurdish Worries," *Al-Monitor*, October 10, 2017d.

———, "Russia's Winning the War for Turkish Public's Trust," *Al-Monitor*, November 20, 2017e.

———, "Turkish Military Purges Decimate Career Officer, Pilot Ranks," *Al-Monitor*, May 29, 2018.

Gurcan, Metin, and Megan Gisclon, "Turkey's Security Sector After July 15: Democratizing Security or Securitizing the State?" *Turkish Policy Quarterly*, Winter 2017.

Gürel, Ayla, and Harry Tzimitras, "Beyond Energy: Remarks About the Direction of Turkish-Russian Relations and Their Implications for the Cyprus Problem," *Euxeinos: Governance and Culture in the Black Sea Region*, Vol. 18, 2015, pp. 28–38.

Gurses, Ercan, "Turkey Stands by Azerbaijan in Nagorno-Karabakh Conflict: Davutoglu," Reuters, April 5, 2016.

Hacaoglu, Selcan, and Onur Ant, "Turkey Core Inflation Hits Its Highest Level in 13 Years," *Bloomberg*, November 3, 2017. As of May 10, 2018:
https://www.bloomberg.com/news/articles/2017-11-03/
turkish-core-inflation-hits-highest-level-in-more-than-13-years

"Hadhahi Matalib al-Duwal al-Muqati'a li Qatar wa Mahla 10 Ayam li Tanfidhiha" ["These Are the Demands of the Boycotting States and the 10 Day Deadline to Implement Them"], al-Arabiya, June 23, 2017.

Halpin, John, Michael Werz, Alan Makovsky, and Max Hoffman, "Is Turkey Experiencing a New Nationalism? An Examination of Public Attitudes on Turkish Self-Perception," Center for American Progress, February 11, 2018.

Hamid, Mohamed Talib, *Al-Siyasa Al-Kharijiya Al-Turkiya wa Athriha 'ala Al-Amn Al-'Arabi* [*Turkish Foreign Policy and Its Impact on Arab Security*], Cairo: Al-Arabi Publishing, 2016.

Harel, Amos, "Gaza Power Crisis Explained: Why Israel and Hamas Are Heading for a Face-Off Neither Side Wants," *Haaretz*, June 12, 2017.

———, "Israel's India Missile Deal Will Be Partially Implemented After Netanyahu's Attempts at Persuasion," *Haaretz*, January 21, 2018.

Hasanov, Bakhtiyar, "Caucasus Eagle 2017 Military Drills Underway," CBC News Azerbaijan, June 10, 2017.

Hauge, Hanna-Lisa, Atila Eralp, Wolfgang Wessels, and Nurdan Selay Bedir, "Mapping Milestones and Periods of Past EU-Turkey Relations," Future of EU-Turkey Relations Working Paper, September 2016. As of October 25, 2018:
http://www.iai.it/sites/default/files/feuture_2.pdf

Hearst, David, "Can Turkey and Russia Push Back Iran in Syria?" *Middle East Eye*, January 3, 2017.

Heine, Hannes, "De Maiziere will mit der Türkei kooperieren," *Der Tagesspiegel*, November 16, 2016. As of October 16, 2017:
http://www.tagesspiegel.de/politik/
verfolgung-der-pkk-in-deutschland-de-maiziere-will-mit-der-tuerkei-kooperieren/14852582.html

Heinrich, Daniel, "Turkey and Israel: Animosity Ends When It Comes to Money," *Deutsche Welle*, December 12, 2017.

Heller, Jeffrey, "Israel Endorses Independent Kurdish State," Reuters, September 13, 2017.

Henze, Paul B., *Georgia and Armenia—Troubled Independence*, Santa Monica, Calif.: RAND Corporation, P-7924, 1995. As of May 18, 2018:
https://www.rand.org/pubs/papers/P7924.html

Herszenhorn, David M., and Jacopo Barigazzi, "Snubbing Turkish Offer, NATO Plans Next Summit in Brussels," *Politico*, June 29, 2017.

Hill, Fiona, and Ömer Taşpınar, *Russia and Turkey in the Caucasus: Moving Together to Preserve the Status Quo?* Paris: Institut Français des Relations Internationales, Russie.Nei.Visions No. 8, January 2006a. As of January 22, 2018:
https://www.ifri.org/sites/default/files/atoms/files/hilltaspinaranglais.pdf

———, "Turkey and Russia: Axis of the Excluded?" *Survival*, Vol. 48, No. 1, Spring 2006b, pp. 81–92.

Hill, Fiona, Kemal Kirişci, and Andrew Moffatt, "Armenia and Turkey: From Normalization to Reconciliation," *Turkish Policy Quarterly*, Vol. 13, No. 4, Winter 2015, pp. 127–138.

Hiltermann, Joost, "Syria: The Hidden Power of Iran," *New York Review of Books*, April 13, 2017. As of May 10, 2018:
http://www.nybooks.com/daily/2017/04/13/syria-hidden-power-of-iran

Holehouse, Matthew, "Turkey to Get Visa-Free Travel Despite Failing to Meet EU Targets," *The Telegraph*, May 4, 2016.

Hubbard, Ben, "Saudis Cut Off Funding for Military Aid to Lebanon," *New York Times*, February 19, 2016.

Hubbard, Ben, and David E. Sanger, "Russia, Iran and Turkey Meet for Syria Talks, Excluding U.S.," *New York Times*, December 20, 2016.

"'I Do Not Recognize Erdoğan as President,' MHP Head Says," *Hürriyet Daily News*, May 22, 2015.

Iddon, Paul, "Coordinated Iraqi-Turkish Action Against PKK Unlikely," *Rudaw*, March 11, 2018.

Idiz, Semih, "Erdogan Blames International Conspiracy for Protests," *Al-Monitor*, June 14, 2013.

———, "Turks Blame US, Iran for Encouraging Baghdad Against Ankara," *Al-Monitor*, October 11, 2016a.

———, "Why KRG Will Remain Turkey's Main Ally in Iraq," *Al-Monitor*, October 25, 2016b.

———, "NATO Blunder Ignites Turkish Calls to Leave Alliance," *Al-Monitor*, November 21, 2017.

———, "After Erdogan's Win, What's Next for Turkey's Foreign Policy?" *Al-Monitor*, July 3, 2018.

Inbari, Pinhas, "Why Did the PA's Mahmoud Abbas Avoid the UN Secretary-General When He Toured the Region?" Jerusalem Center for Public Affairs, September 4, 2017. As of October 16, 2017:
http://jcpa.org/pas-mahmoud-abbas-avoid-un-secretary-general-toured-region

International Centre for the Study of Radicalisation, "Up to 11,000 Foreign Fighters in Syria; Steep Rise Among Western Europeans," London, December 12, 2013.

International Crisis Group, *Nagorno-Karabakh's Gathering War Clouds*, Brussels, Report No. 244, June 1, 2017a.

———, *Central Asia's Silk Road Rivalries*, Brussels, Report No. 245, July 2017b.

———, "Turkey's PKK Conflict: A Visual Explainer," as updated April 5, 2019. As of April 9, 2019:
https://www.crisisgroup.org/content/turkeys-pkk-conflict-visual-explainer

International Election Observation Mission, *Republic of Turkey—Early Presidential and Parliamentary Elections—24 June 2018: Statement of Preliminary Findings and Conclusions*, Ankara: Organization for Security and Co-operation in Europe, June 25, 2018. As of June 30, 2018:
https://www.osce.org/odihr/elections/turkey/385671?download=true

"Iran-Erbil Agree on Energy Deals and Boosting Trade," *Rudaw*, April 24, 2014.

"Iran, Iraq Agree to Build Kirkuk Pipeline," *Iraq Business News*, July 31, 2017.

"Iran, Iraq Initialize Plans for Oil Sector Cooperation," Radio Free Europe/Radio Liberty, February 20, 2017.

"Iraq to Stop Kirkuk Oil Exports to Iran, Deal in Works to Use KRG Pipeline: Report," *Rudaw*, October 26, 2018.

"Israeli Tourists Flock to Turkey as Relations Normalize, Number of Tourists Rise 80 Percent," *Daily Sabah*, February 5, 2017.

"Israel-Turkey Gas Pipeline Could Be Ready in Four Years—Company," Reuters, March 2, 2017.

Issacharoff, Avi, "Hamas Says Turkey to Send Fuel to End Gaza Electricity Crisis," *Times of Israel*, January 14, 2017a.

———, "Arrest of Gaza Manager Exposes Hamas's Turkish Connection," *Times of Israel*, March 21, 2017b.

"Istanbul Stadium Attacks: Kurdish TAK Group Claim Attacks," BBC News, December 11, 2017.

Jacinto, Leela, "Turkey's Post-Coup Purge and Erdogan's Private Army," *Foreign Policy*, July 13, 2017.

Jardine, Bradley, "Armenia and Azerbaijan Compete to Attract Iranian Cargo," *Eurasianet*, April 9, 2018.

Jeffrey, James F., and David Pollack, "How to Stop the War Between Turkey and the Syrian Kurds," *Foreign Policy*, January 25, 2018.

Jenkins, Gareth, "Continuity and Change: Prospects for Civil–Military Relations in Turkey," *International Affairs*, Vol. 83, No. 2, 2007, pp. 339–355.

———, "Erdoğan's Volatile Authoritarianism: Tactical Ploy or Strategic Vision?" *Turkey Analyst*, Vol. 5, No. 23, December 5, 2012.

John, Tara, "Is Turkey Really Benefiting from Oil Trade with ISIS?" *Time*, December 2, 2015.

Johnson, Keith, "Striking Pipeline, Kurdish Militants Deal Blow to Fellow Kurds," *Foreign Policy*, July 30, 2015.

———, "A Mysterious Pipeline Closure Is Bankrupting Iraqi Kurds," *Foreign Policy*, March 2, 2016.

Johnston, Chris, "Isis Militants Release 49 Hostages Taken at Turkish Consulate in Mosul," *The Guardian*, September 20, 2014.

Jones, Clive, and Yoel Guzansky, "Israel's Relations with the Gulf States: Toward the Emergence of a Tacit Security Regime?" *Contemporary Security Policy*, Vol. 38, No. 3, 2017, pp. 398–419.

Jones, Dorian, "Turkey Hosts Iranian, Russian FMs as Ankara-NATO Dispute Festers," Voice of America, November 19, 2017.

Jones, Sam, and Kathrin Hille, "Russia's Military Ambitions Make Waves in the Black Sea," *Financial Times*, May 13, 2016.

Jongerden, Joost, "Dams and Politics in Turkey: Utilizing Water, Developing Conflict," *Middle East Policy Council Journal*, Vol. 17, No. 1, Spring 2010.

Joudeh, Safa, "Why Turkey and Egypt Won't Reconcile Anytime Soon," *Al-Monitor*, August 2, 2016.

Kader, Mohammad Abdel, "Turkey's Relationship with the Muslim Brotherhood," Al Arabiya Institute for Studies, October 14, 2013. As of November 14, 2017:
http://english.alarabiya.net/en/perspective/alarabiya-studies/2013/10/14/
Turkey-s-relationship-with-the-Muslim-Brotherhood.html

Kadercan, Burak, "Turkey's Anti-Americanism Isn't New," *National Interest*, August 23, 2016.

Kadir Has University, Center for Turkish Studies, "Public Perceptions on Turkish Foreign Policy," Istanbul, July 20, 2017. As of March 28, 2019:
http://ctrs.khas.edu.tr/sources/TDP-2017(EN)_vfinal.pdf

Kambas, Michele, "Cyprus Blocks Israel-Turkey Gas Pipeline Until Ankara Mends Ties," *Haaretz*, July 6, 2016.

Kanat, Kilic Bugra, "Turkish-Israeli Reset: Business As Usual?" *Middle East Policy Council*, Vol. 20, No. 2, Summer 2013. As of October 16, 2017: http://www.mepc.org/journal/middle-east-policy-archives/turkish-israeli-reset-business-usual?print

Karaveli, Halil, "Referendum Victory Opens the Way for Erdogan's Presidency," *Turkey Analyst*, September 15, 2010.

Kardas, Saban, "Turkish Civilian-Military Relations Overhauled," *Eurasia Daily Monitor*, Vol. 7, No. 156, August 12, 2010.

Kart, Emine, "Ankara, Berlin in Joint Anti-Terror Mechanism," *Hürriyet Daily News*, January 27, 2016.

Katz, Mark N., "Russia's Middle East Policy and the Trump Administration," Arab Gulf States Institute in Washington, January 13, 2017. As of November 14, 2017: http://www.agsiw.org/russias-middle-east-policy-trump-administration/

Kaya, Karen, "The Turkish-American Crisis: An Analysis of 1 March 2003," *Military Review*, July–August 2011, pp. 69–75.

Kaya, M. K., "The 'Eastern Dimension' in Turkish Foreign Policy Grows," *Turkey Analyst*, Vol. 2, No. 18, October 2009.

———, "Candidate Lists for the Election to Parliament Display Worrying Fault Lines," *Turkey Analyst*, Vol. 8, No. 8, April 22, 2015.

Kaya, M. Kemal, and Svante E. Cornell, "The Big Split: The Differences That Led Erdogan and the Gulen Movement to Part Ways," *Turkey Analyst*, Vol. 5, No. 5, March 5, 2012.

Keinon, Herb, "Netanyahu Apologizes to Turkey over Gaza Flotilla," *Jerusalem Post*, March 22, 2013.

———, "Israeli, Turkish Generals Meet for First Time in Years," *Jerusalem Post*, January 19, 2017.

Kelly-Clarke, Victoria, "Why Is Central Asia Dumping Russia for China?" Global Risks Insights, May 23, 2016. As of January 21, 2018: http://globalriskinsights.com/2016/05/why-central-asia-is-dumping-russia-for-china/

Kershner, Isabel, "Israel Agrees to Remove Metal Detectors at Entrances to Aqsa Mosque Compound," *New York Times*, July 24, 2017.

Kestler-D'Amours, Jillian, "Analysis: Dissecting Turkey's Gulen-Erdogan Relationship," *Middle East Eye*, July 21, 2016.

Khan, Bilal, "Kazakhstan Aselsan Engineering Begins Posting Exports," *Quwa Defence News and Analysis Group*, February 1, 2017. As of January 21, 2018: http://quwa.org/2017/02/01/kazakhstan-aselsan-engineering-begins-posting-exports/

Khattak, Inamullah, "Pak-Turk Schools to Be Taken Over by Turkey's Maarif Foundation," *Dawn*, February 14, 2017. As of October 16, 2017: https://www.dawn.com/news/1314766

Kingsley, Patrick, "Turkey Detains 6,000 over Coup Attempt as Erdoğan Vows to 'Clean State of Virus,'" *The Guardian*, July 17, 2016.

———, "Turkey in Turmoil and Chaos Since Purge Aimed at Dissenters," *New York Times*, April 12, 2017a.

———, "Videos Fuel Charges of Fraud in Erdogan's Win in Turkey Referendum," *New York Times*, April 18, 2017b.

Kingsley, Patrick, and Alissa J. Rubin, "Turkey's Relations with Europe Sink Amid Quarrel with Netherlands," *New York Times*, March 12, 2017.

Kiniklioglu, Suat, *The Anatomy of Turkish-Russian Relations*, Washington, D.C.: Brookings Institution and Sabanci University, 2006. As of December 15, 2017: https://www.brookings.edu/wp-content/uploads/2012/04/20060523sabanci_3a.pdf

Kirchner, Magdalena, *Why States Rebel: Understanding State Sponsorship of Terrorism*, Opladen, Germany: Barbara Budrich, 2016.

———, "'Out-Cirlik': After Months of Tensions, Domestic Pressure Drives German Cabinet to Vacate Turkey's Incirlik Airbase Diminishing Support for the Assault on Raqqa," American Institute for Contemporary German Studies, June 14, 2017a. As of January 15, 2018: http://www.aicgs.org/issue/out-cirlik/

———, "Will the German Election Outcome Change Berlin's Turkey Policy?" German Marshall Fund of the United States, September 26, 2017b. As of November 21, 2017: http://www.gmfus.org/publications/will-german-election-outcome-change-berlins-turkey-policy

Kirişci, Kemal, "The Transformation of Turkish Foreign Policy: The Rise of the Trading State," *New Perspectives on Turkey*, No. 40, 2009, pp. 29–57.

———, "Will the Readmission Agreement Bring the EU and Turkey Together or Pull Them Apart?" Centre for European Policy Studies, February 4, 2014.

Kirişci, Kemal, and Onur Bülbül, "The EU and Turkey Need Each Other. Could Upgrading the Customs Union Be the Key?" Washington, D.C.: Brookings Institution, August 29, 2017.

Kirişci, Kemal, and Andrew Moffatt, "Turkey and the South Caucasus: An Opportunity for Soft Regionalism?" *Regional Security Issues: 2015*, April 25, 2016, pp. 67–88.

Kızıltan, İhsan, "Improving the NATO-EU Partnership: A Turkish Perspective," *Turkish Policy Quarterly*, Vol. 7, No. 3, Summer 2008, pp. 33–46.

Kohen, Sami, "NATO Stands Behind Turkey, Condemns Syria for Downing Jet," *Al-Monitor*, June 26, 2012.

Körkemeier, Tom, and Shadia Nasralla, "Turkey Blocks Some Cooperation with NATO Partners as EU Row Escalates," Reuters, March 15, 2017.

Kosereisoglu, Zeynep, "Turkey and Iraq: How Identity and Interests Mix in Foreign Policy," *Muftah*, January 23, 2014.

Kosolapova, Elena, "Some in Europe Still Interested in Trans-Caspian Gas Pipeline—Expert," *Trend News Agency*, May 19, 2017. As of January 21, 2018: https://en.trend.az/other/commentary/2756769.html

Kroet, Cynthia, "Austrian Minister: EU Doesn't Need Turkey," *Politico*, August 16, 2016a.

———, "Wolfgang Schäuble: EU Needs Turkey for Migration Crisis," *Politico*, August 17, 2016b.

———, "Resistance Against Turkish EU Membership Highest in Germany: Poll," *Politico*, May 19, 2017.

Kucera, Joshua, "Azerbaijan Has Advantage over Armenia in U.S. Military Aid," *Eurasianet*, May 17, 2016a.

———, "Russia Claims 'Mastery' over Turkey in Black Sea," *Eurasianet*, September 25, 2016b.

———, "As Russian Military Exercises in Armenia, Is Syria on Its Mind?" *Eurasianet*, October 10, 2017.

Kuchins, Andrew C., Jeffrey Mankoff, and Oliver Backes, *Azerbaijan in a Reconnecting Eurasia: Foreign Economic and Security Interests*, Washington, D.C.: Center for Strategic and International Studies, June 2016.

Kuchins, Andrew C., and Alexandros Petersen, "Turkey, Russia, the Black Sea, the Caucasus, and Central Asia," in Stephen J. Flanagan, Samuel J. Brannen, Bulent Aliriza, Edward C. Chow, Andrew C. Kuchins, Haim Malka, Julianne Smith, Ian Lesser, Eric Palomaa, and Alexandros Petersen, *Turkey's Evolving Dynamics: Strategic Choices for U.S.-Turkey Relations*, Washington, D.C.: Center for Strategic and International Studies, March 2009, pp. 61–72.

Kucuksahin, Sukru, "This Woman May Be the Biggest Opposition to Erdoğan," *Al-Monitor*, May 26, 2016.

Kulaoglu, Huseyin, and Burcu Arik, "Turkish Court Remands 44 in Nightclub Attack Trial," Anadolu Agency, December 16, 2017.

Kurban, Vefa, *Russian-Turkish Relations from the First World War to the Present*, Newcastle, United Kingdom: Cambridge Scholars Publishing, 2017.

Kutay, Acar, "From Guardianship to Civilian Control: How Did the Turkish Military Get Here?" *Outlines of Global Transformations*, Vol. 10, No. 3, 2017, pp. 68–82.

Landau, Noa, and Jonathan Lis, "Turkey and Israel Expel Envoys Over Gaza Deaths," *Haaretz*, May 16, 2018.

Larrabee, F. Stephen, *Turkey as a U.S. Security Partner*, Santa Monica, Calif.: RAND Corporation, MG-694-AF, 2008. As of March 28, 2019:
https://www.rand.org/pubs/monographs/MG694.html

———, *Troubled Partnership: U.S.-Turkish Relations in an Era of Global Geopolitical Change*, Santa Monica, Calif.: RAND Corporation, MG-899-AF, 2010. As of January 21, 2018:
https://www.rand.org/pubs/monographs/MG899.html

———, "Turkey and the Changing Dynamics of the Kurdish Issue," *Survival*, Vol. 58, No. 2, April–May 2016, pp. 67–73.

Larrabee, F. Stephen, and Stephen J. Flanagan, "Making Waves on the Black Sea," *U.S. News and World Report*, July 7, 2016. As of January 21, 2018:
https://www.usnews.com/opinion/articles/2016-07-07/
nato-summit-should-prioritize-the-growing-importance-of-black-sea-security

Larrabee, F. Stephen, and Ian O. Lesser, *Turkish Foreign Policy in an Age of Uncertainty*, Santa Monica, Calif.: RAND Corporation, MR-1612-CMEPP, 2003. As of January 19, 2018:
https://www.rand.org/pubs/monograph_reports/MR1612.html

Larrabee, F. Stephen, and Gönül Tol, "Turkey's Kurdish Challenge," *Survival*, Vol. 53, No. 4, August/September 2011, pp. 143–152.

"The Latest: Turkey Releases Official Referendum Results," *U.S. News and World Report*, April 27, 2017.

Lavrov, Sergey, "The Present and the Future of Global Politics," *Russia in Global Affairs*, May 13, 2007. As of March 28, 2019:
https://eng.globalaffairs.ru/number/n_8554

Lehman, Eyal, and Roi Kais, "Erdoğan Rebukes Israel over Muezzin Bill and Calls on Muslims to Go en Masse to Al-Aqsa," *Ynet News*, May 8, 2017. As of May 10, 2018: https://www.ynetnews.com/articles/0,7340,L-4959239,00.html

Letsch, Constanze, "A Year After the Protests, Gezi Park Nurtures the Seeds of a New Turkey," *The Guardian*, May 29, 2014.

———, "Ankara Bombing: Kurdish Militants Claim Responsibility," *The Guardian*, March 17, 2016.

Letsch, Constanze, Kareem Shaheen, and Spencer Ackerman, "Turkey Carries Out First Ever Strikes Against Isis in Syria," *The Guardian*, July 24, 2015.

Levinson, Charles, "Leadership Rifts Hobble Syrian Rebels," *Wall Street Journal*, September 10, 2012.

Liel, Alon, *Turkey and Israel: A Chronicle of Bilateral Relations*, Ramat Gan, Israel: Mitvim Institute and Friedrich-Ebert-Stiftung, February 2017. As of October 16, 2017: http://mitvim.org.il/images/ Alon_Liel_-_Turkey_and_Israel_-_A_Chronicle_of_Bilateral_Relations_-_February_2017.pdf

Lindenstrauss, Gallia, and Süfyan Kadir Kıvam, "Turkish-Hamas Relations: Between Strategic Calculations and Ideological Affinity," *Strategic Assessment*, Vol. 17, No. 2, July 2014.

Litovkin, Nikolai, "Russia and Armenia to Create Joint Defense Force in Caucasus," *UPI*, November 16, 2016.

Lowen, Mark, "Turkey's Erdogan Battles 'Parallel State,'" BBC News, December 17, 2014.

Majumdar, Dave, "Why Are Russia and Turkey Holding Joint Naval Exercises in the Black Sea?" *National Interest*, April 5, 2017.

Makortoff, Kalyeena, "Major Russian Pipeline Faces Revival After Rapprochement with Turkey," CNBC, August 11, 2016.

Makovsky, Alan, "Turkey's Growing Energy Ties with Moscow," Center for American Progress, May 6, 2015.

———, "Erdoğan's Proposal for an Empowered Presidency," Center for American Progress, March 22, 2017.

Malik, Hamdi, "Can Iran Stop Iraqi Kurdistan Independence?" *Al-Monitor*, April 20, 2017.

Malka, Haim, "Turkey and the Middle East: Rebalancing Interests," in Stephen J. Flanagan, Samuel J. Brannen, Bulent Aliriza, Edward C. Chow, Andrew C. Kuchins, Haim Malka, Julianne Smith, Ian Lesser, Eric Palomaa, and Alexandros Petersen, *Turkey's Evolving Dynamics: Strategic Choices for U.S.-Turkey Relations*, Washington, D.C.: Center for Strategic and International Studies, March 2009, pp. 37–59.

Mamouri, Ali, "Iraqi Kurdistan Oil a Slippery Issue," *Al-Monitor*, January 6, 2017.

Mandıracı, Berkay, "Turkey's PKK Conflict Kills Almost 3,000 in Two Years," International Crisis Group, July 20, 2017a.

———, "Turkey's PKK Conflict: The Death Toll," International Crisis Group, July 20, 2017b.

Mankoff, Jeffrey, "Why Russia and Turkey Fight: A History of Antagonism," *Foreign Affairs*, February 24, 2016a.

———, "Russia and Turkey's Rapprochement: Don't Expect an Equal Partnership," *Foreign Affairs*, July 20, 2016b.

———, "A Friend in Need? Russia and Turkey After the Coup," Center for Strategic and International Studies, July 29, 2016c.

Markedonov, Sergey, and Natalya Ulchenko, "Turkey and Russia: An Evolving Relationship," Carnegie Endowment for International Peace, August 19, 2011.

Martini, Jeffrey, Becca Wasser, Dalia Dassa Kaye, Daniel Egel, and Cordaye Ogletree, *The Outlook for Arab Gulf Cooperation*, Santa Monica, Calif.: RAND Corporation, RR-1429-RC, 2016. As of January 10, 2018:
https://www.rand.org/pubs/research_reports/RR1429.html

"Matter of National Security? The Turkish-Kurdish 'Secret Agreement,'" *Niqash*, April 23, 2015. As of January 20, 2018:
http://www.niqash.org/en/articles/politics/3641

Maurice, Eric, "Turkey Holds Key at Last-Ditch Cyprus Talks," *EUobserver*, January 9, 2017.

"Mavi Marmara: Why Did Israel Stop the Gaza Flotilla?" BBC News, June 27, 2016.

Media and Law Studies Association, "845 People in Turkey Detained for Criticizing Military Campaign in Syria," February 27, 2018.

Mejdini, Fatjona, "Albania Weighs Turkey's Claim to Be Gulenist Hub," *Balkan Insight*, November 3, 2016.

Michalopoulos, Sarantis, "EU Tells Ankara to Stay Calm, Respect UN Framework for Cyprus," *EURACTIV*, October 17, 2017. As of May 22, 2018:
https://www.euractiv.com/section/global-europe/news/
eu-tells-ankara-to-stay-calm-respect-un-framework-for-cyprus

"The Middle-Income Trap Has Little Evidence Going for It," *The Economist*, Special Report: Emerging Markets, October 7, 2017.

Milburn, Franc, "Iranian Kurdish Militias: Terrorist-Insurgents, Ethno Freedom Fighters, or Knights on the Regional Chessboard?" *CTC Sentinel*, Vol. 10, No. 5, May 2017, pp. 29–35.

"Millions Stand for Democracy in Turkey," *Hürriyet Daily News*, August 5, 2016.

Misztal, Blaise, Nicholas Danforth, and Jessica Michek, *What's Next for Turkey: Authoritarian Stability or Chaos?* Washington, D.C.: Bipartisan Policy Center, May 2017.

Mitchell, Gabriel, *The Risks and Rewards of Israeli-Turkish Energy Cooperation*, Ramat Gan, Israel: Global Political Trends Center, Mitvim Institute, and Friedrich-Ebert-Stiftung, January 2017.

Mkrtchyan, Hasmik, and Margarita Antidze, "Armenia Ratifies Agreement on Joint Air-Defense System with Russia," Reuters, June 2016.

Moubayed, Sami, "Israel and Turkey Are Drifting Apart," *Gulf News*, January 19, 2010.

Nabsi, Turkiye'nin, "Is Turkey Turning Its Stern on the West in the Black Sea?" *Al-Monitor*, December 2016.

Nader, Alireza, *Iran's Role in Iraq: Room for U.S.-Iran Cooperation?* Santa Monica, Calif.: RAND Corporation, PE-151-OSD, 2015. As of January 20, 2018:
https://www.rand.org/pubs/perspectives/PE151.html

Nader, Alireza, Larry Hanauer, Brenna Allen, and Ali G. Scotten, *Regional Implications of an Independent Kurdistan,* Santa Monica, Calif.: RAND Corporation, RR-1452-RC, 2016. As of January 20, 2018:
https://www.rand.org/pubs/research_reports/RR1452.html

Nasi, Selin, *Turkey-Israel Deal: A Key to Long-Term Reconciliation?* Ramat Gan, Israel: Global Political Trends Center, Mitvim Institute, and Friedrich-Ebert-Stiftung, January 2017.

National Consortium for the Study of Terrorism and Responses to Terrorism, Global Terrorism Database, undated. As of March 28, 2019:
https://www.start.umd.edu/gtd

Nationalist Movement Party, *Ülkenin Gelecegi* [*Future of the Country*], Ankara, November 2015. As of October 16, 2017:
http://www.mhp.org.tr/usr_img/mhpweb/1kasimsecimleri/beyanname_1kasim2015.pdf

NATO—*See* North Atlantic Treaty Organization.

"NATO Apologises to Turkey for War Games Blunders," *Al Jazeera*, November 17, 2017.

"NATO Ends Partnership Deadlock over Turkey-Austria Dispute," *New Arab*, May 24, 2017. As of October 16, 2017:
https://www.alaraby.co.uk/english/news/2017/5/24/
nato-ends-partnership-deadlock-over-turkey-austria-dispute

"NATO's Aegean Patrols to Continue," *Ekathimerini,* February 16, 2017. As of November 21, 2017:
http://www.ekathimerini.com/216266/article/ekathimerini/news/natos-aegean-patrols-to-continue

Neumann, Peter R., "Foreign Fighter Total in Syria/Iraq Now Exceeds 20,000; Surpasses Afghanistan Conflict in the 1980s," London: International Centre for the Study of Radicalisation, January 25, 2015.

Nichols, Michelle, "Egypt Blocks U.N. Call to Respect 'Democratically Elected' Government in Turkey," Reuters, July 16, 2016.

North Atlantic Treaty Organization, North Atlantic Treaty, Washington, D.C., April 4, 1949.

———, "NATO Support to Turkey: Background and Timeline," Brussels, February 19, 2013. As of November 22, 2017:
https://www.nato.int/cps/en/natohq/topics_92555.htm

———, "NATO-EU Relations," Brussels, fact sheet, July 2016a. As of November 21, 2017:
http://www.nato.int/nato_static_fl2014/assets/
pdf/pdf_2016_07/20160630_1607-factsheet-nato-eu-en.pdf

———, "Press Conference by NATO Secretary General Jens Stoltenberg Following the Meeting of the North Atlantic Council at the Level of NATO Defence Ministers," Brussels, transcript, October 27, 2016b. As of January 21, 2018:
http://www.nato.int/cps/en/natohq/opinions_136581.htm

———, "Augmentation of Turkey's Air Defence," Brussels, fact sheet, January 2017a. As of November 14, 2017:
https://www.nato.int/nato_static_fl2014/assets/pdf/
pdf_2017_01/20170113_1701-factsheet-patriot_en.pdf

———, "Joint Press Statements by NATO Secretary General Jens Stoltenberg and the President of Montenegro, Filip Vujanović—Secretary General's Remarks," Brussels, press statement, June 7, 2017b. As of November 21, 2017:
https://www.nato.int/cps/en/natohq/opinions_144734.htm?selectedLocale=uk

———, "NATO Deputy Secretary General Leads Parliamentary Delegation to Konya," Brussels, September 8, 2017c. As of November 16, 2017:
https://www.nato.int/cps/en/natohq/news_146773.htm

———, "Kosovo Force (KFOR): Key Facts and Figures," Brussels, November 19, 2017d. As of March 28, 2019:
https://www.nato.int/nato_static_fl2014/assets/pdf/
pdf_2018_07/20180706_2018-07-KFOR_Placemat.pdf

———, "Resolute Support Mission (RSM): Key Facts and Figures," Brussels, November 19, 2017e. As of January 15, 2018:
https://www.nato.int/nato_static_fl2014/assets/pdf/pdf_2017_05/
20170523_2017-05-RSM-Placemat.pdf

O'Connor, Tom, "Turkey Tries to Scare Voters with Warning About Jews Ahead of Kurdish Referendum," *Newsweek*, September 15, 2017.

Öğütcü, Özge Nur, "The Current State of Relations Between Kazakhstan-Turkey," Avrasya İncelemeleri Merkezi, Analysis No. 2017/29, September 13, 2017. As of January 21, 2018:
http://avim.org.tr/en/Analiz/the-current-state-of-relations-between-kazakhstan-turkey

Onis, Ziya, and Şuhnaz Yılmaz, "Turkey and Russia in a Shifting Global Order: Cooperation, Conflict, and Asymmetric Interdependence in a Turbulent Region," *Third World Quarterly*, Vol. 37, No. 1, 2015, pp. 71–95.

Organisation for Economic Co-operation and Development, "Turkey," *OECD Economic Outlook*, Vol. 2017, No. 2, November 2017. As of January 21, 2018:
https://www.oecd-ilibrary.org/sites/eco_outlook-v2017-2-en/1/2/4/44/index.html?itemId=/content/
publication/eco_outlook-v2017-2-en&_csp_=dee5cfb1e126ccdb34abe871d842a8ba&itemIGO=
oecd&itemContentType=book#IDf011c369-f0ea-47e6-bbe7-254c0cea60eb

———, "Turkey," *OECD Economic Outlook*, Vol. 2018, No. 2, December 2018. As of January 18, 2019:
https://www.oecd-ilibrary.org/sites/eco_outlook-v2018-2-47-en/index.html?itemId=/content/
component/eco_outlook-v2018-2-47-en

Organization for Security and Co-operation in Europe, *Turkey, Constitutional Referendum, 16 April 2017: Final Report*, Warsaw, June 22, 2017. As of January 18, 2018:
https://www.osce.org/odihr/elections/turkey/324816?download=true

Organization of the Black Sea Economic Cooperation Permanent International Secretariat, "Press Release on the 34th Meeting of the BSEC Council of Ministers of Foreign Affairs," Sochi, July 1, 2016. As of March 28, 2019:
http://www.bsec-organization.org/UploadedDocuments/PressReleases/
20160701%2034th%20CMFA%20Sochi%20(01.07.2016).pdf

Osborne, Simon, "EU Torn in Two over Turkey—Austria Calls for End to Talks as Juncker Seeks Accession," *Sunday Express*, April 3, 2018.

Ose, Hoshnag, "Relationship Issues: Feud Between Turkey and Iraq Is All Syria's Fault," *Niqash*, February 9, 2012. As of January 10, 2018:
http://www.niqash.org/en/articles/politics/2989

Oskay, Çınar, "Government Supported 'Ergenekon' Case, Says Turkey's Former Military Chief," *Hürriyet Daily News*, April 24, 2016.

Özbay, Fatih, "The Relations Between Turkey and Russia in the 2000s," *Perceptions*, Vol. 16, No. 3, Autumn 2011, pp. 69–92.

Ozdemir, Cagri, "Analysis: Turkey's Former Generals Walk Free on 'Coup' Verdict," *Middle East Eye*, April 5, 2015.

Ozkan, Behlül, "Turkey, Davutoglu and the Idea of Pan-Islamism," *Survival*, Vol. 56, No. 4, August–September 2014, pp. 119–140.

Paksoy, Yunus, "Germany Insists It Does Not Support PKK Despite Own Intelligence Reports," *Daily Sabah*, November 17, 2016.

Palmer, Geoffrey, Alvaro Uribe, Joseph Ciechanover Itzhar, and Süleyman Özdem Sanberk, *Report of the Secretary-General's Panel of Inquiry on the 31 May 2010 Flotilla Incident*, New York: United Nations, September 2011.

Pangalos, Philip, "European Parliament Calls for Suspension of Turkey EU Accession Talks," *Euronews*, September 30, 2019.

Pannier, Bruce, "Russia Flexes Muscles in Turkmenistan," Radio Free Europe/Radio Liberty, June 13, 2016.

———, "The End of the (Gas Pipe-) Line for Turkmenistan," Radio Free Europe/Radio Liberty, March 6, 2017.

Papuashvili, Tamaz, "The Future of Azerbaijani-Turkish Military Cooperation," Meydan TV, May 22, 2017. As of January 21, 2018:
https://www.meydan.tv/en/article/the-future-of-azerbaijani-turkish-military-cooperation

Paraskova, Tsvetana, "Iran, Iraq Plan Pipeline to Export Kirkuk Crude Oil," *OilPrice*, July 31, 2017. As of January 19, 2018:
https://oilprice.com/Latest-Energy-News/World-News/
Iran-Iraq-Plan-Pipeline-To-Export-Kirkuk-Crude-Oil.html

Paul, Christopher, and Miriam Matthews, *The Russian "Firehose of Falsehood" Propaganda Model: Why It Might Work and Options to Counter It,* Santa Monica, Calif.: RAND Corporation, PE-198-OSD, 2016. As of January 15, 2018:
https://www.rand.org/pubs/perspectives/PE198.html

Peker, Emre, "Russia, Turkey Complete Initial Turk Stream Gas Pipeline Talks," *Wall Street Journal*, December 11, 2014.

Peretz, Sami, "An Angry Erdogan Stands to Harm Israel-Turkey Economic Ties," *Haaretz*, May 17, 2018.

Perry, Tom, and Humeyra Pamuk, "Turkey-Backed Syrian Rebels Clash with Army in North," Reuters, February 27, 2017.

Peuch, Jean-Christophe, "Turkey: Prime Minister's Criticism of Israel Does Not Mark Shift in Policy," Radio Free Europe/Radio Liberty, June 10, 2004.

Pfeffer, Anshel, "Israel Supplies Turkey with Military Equipment for First Time Since Gaza Flotilla," *Haaretz*, February 18, 2013.

Phillips, David L., "Research Paper: ISIS-Turkey Links," *Huffington Post*, November 9, 2014. As of October 27, 2017:
https://www.huffingtonpost.com/david-l-phillips/research-paper-isisturke_b_6128950.html

———, "Research Paper: Turkey-ISIS Oil Trade," *Huffington Post*, December 14, 2016. As of March 28, 2019:
https://www.huffpost.com/entry/research-paper-turkey-isi_b_8808024

"PM Netanyahu Thanks Turkey for Plane to Fight Israel's Wildfires," *Daily Sabah*, November 24, 2016.

Pollock, David, "To Kurdistan and Back: Iran's Forgotten Front," Fikra Forum, Washington Institute for Near East Policy, March 3, 2017. As of January 20, 2018:
http://www.washingtoninstitute.org/fikraforum/view/to-kurdistan-and-back-irans-forgotten-front

Popp, Maximilian, "Turkish Power Struggle: Brotherly Love Begins to Fray in Ankara," *Spiegel Online*, June 25, 2013.

President of Russia, "High-Level Russian-Turkish Cooperation Council," press release, March 10, 2017a. As of October 16, 2017:
http://en.kremlin.ru/events/president/news/54022

———, "Joint News Conference with President of Turkey Recep Tayyip Erdoğan," transcript, March 10, 2017b. As of January 15, 2018:
http://en.kremlin.ru/events/president/news/54023

"Profile: Fethullah Gulen's Hizmet Movement," BBC News, December 18, 2013. As of March 18, 2019:
http://www.bbc.com/news/world-13503361

"Profile: Free Gaza Movement," BBC News, June 1, 2010. As of October 16, 2017:
http://www.bbc.com/news/10202678

"Prosecutor Seeks Life Sentence for HDP Co-Chair," *Rudaw*, December 1, 2017.

"Public Trust in Military Plunges After Turkey's Failed Coup: Poll," *Hürriyet Daily News*, January 19, 2017.

al-Qaher, Sara, "Iran, Iraq Seek to Send a Message with Joint Naval Exercises," *Al-Monitor*, January 9, 2017a.

———, "Iraq and Iran Agree to Resolve Dispute on Joint Oil Fields," *Al-Monitor*, March 5, 2017b.

Radin, Andrew, and Clint Reach, *Russian Views of the International Order*, Santa Monica, Calif.: RAND Corporation, RR-1826-OSD, 2017. As of July 2, 2019:
https://www.rand.org/pubs/research_reports/RR1826.html

Ramani, Samuel, "Why the Russia-Azerbaijan Alliance Is Weaker Than It Looks," *Huffington Post*, August 23, 2017.

Ravid, Barak, "Livni, Turkish FM Hold Reconciliation Talks in Brussels," *Haaretz*, March 6, 2009.

———, "Peres: Humiliation of Turkey Envoy Does Not Reflect Israel's Diplomacy," *Haaretz*, January 13, 2010.

———, "NATO Okays Israel Office in Its Brussels Headquarters After Turkey Lifts Veto," *Haaretz*, May 4, 2016.

———, "Israel Responds to Erdogan: Temple Mount Statements 'Unfounded and Distorted,'" *Haaretz*, July 25, 2017.

Religious Literacy Project, "Alevism," Harvard Divinity School, webpage, undated. As of January 19, 2018:
https://rlp.hds.harvard.edu/faq/alevism

Republic of Turkey Ministry of Foreign Affairs, "IV. Turkey's International Security Initiatives and Contributions to NATO and EU Operations," webpage, undated-a. As of January 10, 2018:
http://www.mfa.gov.tr/iv_-european-security-and-defence-identity_policy-_esdi_p_.en.mfa

———, "PKK," webpage, undated-b. As of June 1, 2019:
http://www.mfa.gov.tr/pkk.en.mfa

————, "Relations Between Turkey and Armenia," webpage, undated-c. As of January 21, 2018: http://www.mfa.gov.tr/relations-between-turkey-and-armenia.en.mfa

————, "Turkey's Relations with NATO," webpage, undated-d. As of January 10, 2018: http://www.mfa.gov.tr/nato.en.mfa

————, "Turkey's Relations with Southern Caucasus Countries," webpage, undated-e. As of January 21, 2018: http://www.mfa.gov.tr/turkey_s-relations-with-southern-caucasus.en.mfa

Republic of Turkey, Supreme Election Council, "C) Parliamentarian Election Results Including Domestic, Overseas and Customs," election notice, July 5, 2015a. As of June 2, 2019: http://www.ysk.gov.tr/doc/dosyalar/Ingilizce/ElectionResults/2018MV-96C_en.pdf

————, "D) Presidency Election Results Including Domestic, Overseas and Customs Ballot Boxes," election notice, July 5, 2018b. As of June 2, 2019: http://www.ysk.gov.tr/doc/dosyalar/Ingilizce/ElectionResults/2018CB-416D_en.pdf

Republic of Turkey and Republic of Armenia, "Protocol on Development of Relations Between the Republic of Armenia and the Republic of Turkey," October 10, 2009a. As of April 23, 2019: http://www.mfa.gov.tr/protocol-on-development-of-relations-between-the-republic-of-turkey-and-the-republic-of-armenia.en.mfa

————, "Protocol on the Establishment of Diplomatic Relations Between the Republic of Turkey and the Republic of Armenia," October 10, 2009b. As of January 21, 2018: http://www.mfa.gov.tr/site_media/html/zurih-protokolleri-en.pdf

Rettman, Andrew, and Eric Maurice, "Merkel: EU to Cut Turkey Pre-Accession Funds," *EUobserver*, October 20, 2017.

Reynolds, Michael A., "Vladimir Putin, Godfather of Kurdistan?" *National Interest*, March 1, 2016.

"Reza Zarrab Case: Gold Trader Implicates Turkish President Erdogan," BBC News, December 1, 2017.

Riegert, Bernd, "Opinion: An Absurd Threat from Ankara," *Deutsche Welle*, August 1, 2016.

"Rojava Peshmerga Deployed to Syrian Border, No Plans to Enter Rojava," *Rudaw*, March 2 2017.

Rubin, Michael, "The Showdown for Control of Turkey's Military," American Enterprise Institute, November 29, 2016. As of October 20, 2017: http://www.aei.org/publication/the-showdown-for-control-of-turkeys-military

Rukhadze, Vasili, "Defying Georgia, Turkey Gradually Cultivates Its Influence in Separatist Abkhazia," *Eurasia Daily Monitor*, Vol. 12, No. 177, October 1, 2015.

————, "Completion of Baku–Tbilisi–Kars Railway Project Postponed Again," *Eurasia Daily Monitor*, Vol. 13, No. 42, March 2, 2016.

"Russia Discussing Turkish Stream Entry Point with European Countries, Russian PM Says," *Daily Sabah*, May 22, 2017.

"Russia Drops South Stream Gas Pipeline Plan," BBC News, December 1, 2014.

"Russia Halts Turkish Stream Project over Downed Jet," *RT*, December 3, 2015.

"Russia Keeps a Wary Eye on the Trans-Caspian Pipeline," *Stratfor*, November 19, 2014. As of January 21, 2018: https://worldview.stratfor.com/article/russia-keeps-wary-eye-trans-caspian-pipeline

"Russia, Turkey Sign Gas Pipeline Deal," Radio Free Europe/Radio Liberty, October 10, 2016.

"Russia Warned Turkey of Imminent Army Coup, Says Iran's FNA," TASS, July 21, 2016.

"Russian Gas Flows to Europe, Turkey Break New Records in 2017: Gazprom," *S&P Global Platts*, January 9, 2017.

"Russian Tourist Numbers to Turkey Skyrocket in January but Foreign Arrivals Keep Declining," *Hürriyet Daily News*, February 28, 2017.

"Russia's Gazprom Starts Building TurkStream Gas Pipeline Under Black Sea," *Deutsche Welle*, May 7, 2017.

"Russia's TASS Signs Cooperation Deal with Turkey's Anadolu News Agency," Radio Free Europe/Radio Liberty, March 11, 2017.

"Rusya: Erdoğan ve Ailesi, IŞİD'in Suriye'deki Yasadışı Petrol Sevkıyatıyla Doğrudan İlişki" ["Russia: Erdoğan and His Family Directly Involved in ISIS's Illegal Oil Shipment in Syria"], *Sputnik*, December 2, 2015.

Saadoun, Mustafa, "Iran, Turkey Fight over Tal Afar," *Al-Monitor*, November 18, 2016.

Saeed, Saim, "EU Countries Move to Block Turkey from Hosting NATO Summit: Report," *Politico*, May 31, 2017. As of November 21, 2017:
https://www.politico.eu/article/eu-countries-move-to-block-turkey-from-hosting-nato-summit-report

Sanamyan, Emil, "Russia Details USD200 Million Arms Sale to Armenia," *Jane's Defence Weekly*, February 19, 2016a.

———, "Armenian Parade Reveals Iskander Ballistic Missiles," *Jane's Defence Weekly*, September 23, 2016b.

———, "The Armenian Diaspora and Armenia: A New Relationship?" *Eurasianet*, November 14, 2016c.

Sanderson, Sertan, "European PKK Ban Could Undermine Turkish Democracy," *Deutsche Welle*, November 25, 2016.

———, "Germany Grants Asylum to Turkish Military Personnel," *Deutsche Welle*, May 8, 2017.

Sassounian, Harut, "Israel May Retaliate Against Turkey by Recognizing the Armenian Genocide," *Huffington Post*, May 25, 2011.

Satke, Ryskeldi, Casey Michel, and Sertaç Korkmaz, "Turkey in Central Asia: Turkic Togetherness?" *The Diplomat*, November 28, 2014.

Savranskaya, Svetlana, and Vladislav Zubok, "Cold War in the Caucasus: Notes and Documents from a Conference," *Cold War International History Project Bulletin*, No. 14/15, Winter 2013–Spring 2014.

Schanzer, Jonathan, "An Unhelpful Ally: ISIS and Other Violent Factions Have Benefited from Turkey's Loose Border Policies," *Wall Street Journal*, June 25, 2015.

Schmitt, Eric, "After Delicate Negotiations, U.S. Says It Will Pull Patriot Missiles From Turkey," *New York Times*, August 16, 2015.

Schulz, Ludwig, and Colin Dürkop, "The Organization of the Black Sea Economic Cooperation (BSEC)—A Mechanism for Integration in a Geopolitically Sensitive Area," Konrad-Adenauer-Stiftung, Country Report, November 10, 2014. As of November 30, 2017:
http://www.kas.de/wf/doc/kas_39457-1522-2-30.pdf?141121133850

Schwartz, Paul, "Amphibious Plans and Posture in Support of NATO," presentation at a RAND Corporation workshop related to the Amphibious Leaders Expeditionary Symposium, Arlington, Va., January 19, 2008.

Seufert, Günter, *Is the Fethullah Gülen Movement Overstretching Itself? A Turkish Religious Community as a National and International Player*, Berlin: German Institute for International and Security Affairs, January 2014. As of January 15, 2018:
https://www.swp-berlin.org/fileadmin/contents/products/research_papers/2014_RP02_srt.pdf

Shahbazov, Fuad, "Azerbaijan-Turkey-Georgia: A Geopolitical Axis or an Accidental Alliance?" *Eurasia Daily Monitor*, Vol. 14, No. 75, June 7, 2017.

Shaheen, Kareem, "Turkish Officials: Europe Wanted to Export Extremists to Syria," *The Guardian*, March 25, 2016.

Shalal, Andrea, "NATO Nearing Solution to Continue Aegean Migrant Mission: UK General," Reuters, November 30, 2016.

Shargai, Nadav, "Ha'Pe Shel Erdoğan, Ha'Milim Shel Hamas," *Israel Hayom*, December 28, 2017. As of December 28, 2017:
http://www.israelhayom.co.il/article/524425

"She-Wolf v Sultan: A Challenge to Turkey's Erdogan," *The Economist*, November 17, 2017.

Shiriyev, Zaur, "Will the North–South Transport Corridor Overshadow the Baku–Tbilisi–Kars Railway?" *Eurasia Daily Monitor*, Vol. 14, No. 53, April 24, 2017.

Siboni, Gabi, and Gal Perl Finkel, "The IDF Exercises in Cyprus and Crete," Tel Aviv: Institute for National Security Studies, Insight No. 945, June 28, 2017. As of April 18, 2018:
http://www.inss.org.il/publication/idf-exercises-cyprus-crete/

Simsek, Ayhan, "Confusion over Turkey's Request for Patriots," *Deutsche Welle*, November 23, 2012.

Simsek, Mehmet, "Proposal—Escaping the Middle-Income Trap: Turkey's Strategy," Global Economic Symposium, 2014.

Sladden, James, Becca Wasser, Ben Connable, and Sarah Grand-Clement, *Russian Strategy in the Middle East*, Santa Monica, Calif.: RAND Corporation, PE-236-RC, 2017. As of May 15, 2018:
https://www.rand.org/pubs/perspectives/PE236.html

Slav, Irina, "Iran Starts Exporting Nat Gas to Iraq," *OilPrice*, Jun 22, 2017. As of November 14, 2017:
https://oilprice.com/Latest-Energy-News/World-News/Iran-Starts-Exporting-Nat-Gas-To-Iraq.html

Smith, Helena, "Cyprus Reunification Talks Collapse amid Angry Scenes," *The Guardian*, July 7, 2017.

Smith, Julianne, "Turkey and Europe: A Widening Gap," in Stephen J. Flanagan, Samuel J. Brannen, Bulent Aliriza, Edward C. Chow, Andrew C. Kuchins, Haim Malka, Julianne Smith, Ian Lesser, Eric Palomaa, and Alexandros Petersen, *Turkey's Evolving Dynamics: Strategic Choices for U.S.-Turkey Relations*, Washington, D.C.: Center for Strategic and International Studies, March 2009, pp. 19–31.

Sokollu, Senada, "European Jihadists Use Turkey as Transit Country," *Deutsche Welle*, May 14, 2014.

Solaker, Gulsen, Daren Butler, and Ali Kucukgocmen, "Turkish Parliament Passes Security Law to Replace Emergency Rule," Reuters, July 25, 2018.

Sonne, Paul, "Russian Media Takes Aim at Turkey," *Wall Street Journal*, November 30, 2015.

Sowell, Kirk H., "The Regional and Domestic Political Context of the Mosul Offensive," *Sada*, October 18, 2016. As of January 20, 2018:
http://carnegieendowment.org/sada/64885

Srivastava, Mehul, "Erdogan Moves in on Executive Presidency After Crackdown on Kurds," *Financial Times*, November 7, 2016.

————, "Assets Worth $11bn Seized in Turkey Crackdown," *Financial Times*, July 7, 2017.

Srivastava, Mehul, and Henry Mance, "Turkish TV Station Aims to Switch Western Views," *Financial Times*, March 11, 2016.

Srivastava, Mehul, and Stefan Wagstyl, "Turkey's Parliament Votes to Strip Immunity from a Third of MPs," *Financial Times*, May 20, 2016.

Stefanini, Sarah, "Erdoğan Shadow over Cyprus Peace Bid," *Politico*, February 2, 2016a.

————, "Cyprus Reunification Talks Break Down in Switzerland," *Politico*, November 22, 2016b.

————, "Cyprus Fears Russia Could Wreck Reunification," *Politico*, January 12, 2017.

Stein, Aaron, "A Collapsing Regional Order: Turkey's Troubles in Iraq and Syria," *War on the Rocks*, March 12, 2015.

————, "Inside a Failed Coup and Turkey's Fragmented Military," *War on the Rocks*, July 20, 2016.

Steinberg, Guido, *Leading the Counter-Revolution: Saudi Arabia and the Arab Spring*, Berlin: German Institute for International and Security Affairs, June 2014.

Stelzenmueller, Constanze, and Joshua Raisher, *Transatlantic Trends 2013: Key Findings*, Washington, D.C.: German Marshall Fund of the United States, September 18, 2013.

————, *Transatlantic Trends 2014*, Washington, D.C.: German Marshall Fund of the United States, September 10, 2014.

Stocker, Joanne, "Coalition Retraining 15,000 Veteran SDF Fighters to Serve as Syrian Border Force," *Defense Post*, January 13, 2018.

Stronski, Paul, "Armenia at Twenty-Five: A Rough Ride," Carnegie Endowment for International Peace, December 7, 2016. As of April 23, 2019:
http://carnegieendowment.org/2016/12/07/armenia-at-twenty-five-rough-ride-pub-66351

————, "Turkmenistan at Twenty-Five: The High Price of Authoritarianism," Carnegie Endowment for International Peace, January 30, 2017. As of May 19, 2018:
http://carnegieendowment.org/2017/01/30/
turkmenistan-at-twenty-five-high-price-of-authoritarianism-pub-67839

Stubbs, Jack, and Dmitry Solovyov, "Kremlin Says Turkey Apologized for Shooting Down Russian Jet," Reuters, June 27, 2016.

Tabler, Andrew, Soner Cagaptay, David Pollock, and James F. Jeffrey, "The Syrian Kurds: Whose Ally?" remarks to a policy forum at the Washington Institute for Near East Policy, PolicyWatch 2597, March 29, 2016. As of March 21, 2018:
http://www.washingtoninstitute.org/policy-analysis/view/the-syrian-kurds-whose-ally

Tagliapietra, Simone, "Is the EastMed Gas Pipeline Just Another EU Pipe Dream?" *Bruegel*, May 10, 2017.

Tahhan, Zena, "Egypt-Israel Relations 'at Highest Level' in History," *Al Jazeera*, September 20, 2017.

Tanrısever, Oktay F., *Turkey and Russia in the Black Sea Region: Dynamics of Cooperation and Conflict*, Washington, D.C.: German Marshall Fund of the United States, Edam Black Sea Discussion Paper Series 2012/1, 2012. As of January 30, 2018:
http://gpf-europe.com/images/bsdp3.pdf

Tardy, Thierry, "CSDP: Getting Third States on Board," Paris: European Union Institute for Security Studies, issue brief, March 2014. As of March 28, 2019:
https://www.iss.europa.eu/sites/default/files/EUISSFiles/Brief_6_CSDP_and_third_states.pdf

Taştekin, Fehim, "Turkish Military Says MİT Shipped Weapons to al-Qaeda," *Al-Monitor*, January 15, 2015.

———, "Turkey's Brash Behavior Riles Iraq," *Al-Monitor*, October 7, 2016.

Tattersall, Nick, and Alexander Winning, "As Turkey's Coup Strains Ties with West, Detente with Russia Gathers Pace," Reuters, August 6, 2016.

Tattersall, Nick, and Ayla Jean Yackley, "Suicide Bomber Kills Four, Wounds 36 in Istanbul Shopping District," Reuters, March 16, 2016.

TİKA—*See* Turkish Cooperation and Coordination Agency.

Tillerson, Rex W., "Remarks on the Way Forward for the United States Regarding Syria," Hoover Institute at Stanford University, January 17, 2018. As of January 23, 2018: https://sy.usembassy.gov/remarks-way-forward-united-states-regarding-syria/

"Timeline of Gezi Park Protests," *Hürriyet Daily News*, June 6, 2013.

"Timeline: The Worst Airport Shootings in the Last 15 Years," Fox News, January 6, 2017.

Timur, Şafak, and Rod Nordland, "Erdogan Threatens to Let Migrant Flood into Europe Resume," *New York Times*, November 25, 2016.

Tocci, Nathalie, *Turkey and the European Union: A Journey in the Unknown*, Washington, D.C.: Brookings Institution, Turkey Project Policy Paper No. 5, November 2014. As of January 19, 2018: https://www.brookings.edu/wp-content/uploads/2016/06/Turkey-and-the-European-Union.pdf

———, "Turkey and the European Union: Scenarios for 2023," Future of EU-Turkey Relations Background Paper, September 2016.

Toksabay, Ece, Tuvan Gumrukcu, and Nick Tattersall, "Turkey Could Put EU Talks to a Referendum Next Year: Erdogan," Reuters, November 14, 2016.

Tol, Gönül, "Turkey's Kurds Split by AKP Policies," *Cairo Review of Global Affairs*, December 10, 2015. As of May 10, 2018: https://www.thecairoreview.com/tahrir-forum/turkeys-kurds-split-by-akp-policies/

Tol, Gönül, and Ömer Taşpınar, "Erdogan's Turn to the Kemalists: How It Will Shape Turkish Foreign Policy," *Foreign Affairs*, October 27, 2016.

Torbakov, Igor, "Turkey-Russia: Competition and Cooperation," *Eurasianet*, December 27, 2002.

———, "The Turkish Factor in the Geopolitics of the Post-Soviet Space," Foreign Policy Research Institute, E-Notes, January 1, 2003.

———, *The Georgia Crisis and Russia-Turkey Relations*, Washington, D.C.: Jamestown Foundation, 2008. As of January 21, 2018: https://jamestown.org/wp-content/uploads/2008/11/GeorgiaCrisisTorbakov.pdf

———, "Royal Role Models: Historical Revisionism in Russia and Turkey," *Eurasianet*, January 16, 2018.

Tremblay, Pinar, "Post-Coup Shake-Up at Turkey's Intelligence Agency," *Al-Monitor*, November 6, 2016a.

———, "Iranian-Turkish Tug-of-War over Kurds," *Al-Monitor*, December 13, 2016b.

———, "Erdogan's 'Pious Generation' Curriculum Gets Failing Grade," *Al-Monitor*, November 17, 2017. As of December 9, 2019: https://www.al-monitor.com/pulse/originals/2017/11/ turkey-erdogan-pious-generation-dream-fails.html

Trenin, Dmitri, "Russia in the Middle East: Moscow's Objectives, Priorities, and Policy Drivers," Carnegie Endowment for International Peace and Chicago Council on Global Affairs, 2016.

"Trump Adviser Seeks Political Deal to Settle Iran Sanctions Case," Radio Free Europe/Radio Liberty, April 21, 2017.

Tsiboukis, George, "Cyprus Buys 1+3 Offshore Patrol Vessels," Dartmouth Center for Seapower and Strategy News, Plymouth University, United Kingdom, November 4, 2015: As of May 3, 2018: http://blogs.plymouth.ac.uk/dcss/2015/11/04/cyprus-buys-13-offshore-patrol-vessels

Turhan, Ebru, "Europe's Crises, Germany's Leadership and Turkey's EU Accession Process," *Focus*, Vol. 17, No. 2, Summer 2016a, pp. 25–29.

———, "The Struggle for the German-Turkish Partnership: Preventing the 'Train Crash,'" E-International Relations, December 4, 2016b. As of May 19, 2018: https://www.e-ir.info/2016/12/04/ the-struggle-for-the-german-turkish-partnership-preventing-the-train-crash

"Türkei verlangte seit Putschversuch 81 Auslieferungen" ["Turkey Has Demanded 81 Extraditions Since Coup Attempt"], *Welt*, October 23, 2017. As of November 14, 2017: https://www.welt.de/politik/ausland/article169932321/ Tuerkei-verlangte-seit-Putschversuch-81-Auslieferungen.html

"Turkey, Azerbaijan, Georgia Unity Help Regional Stability: Experts," *Daily Sabah*, June 6, 2017.

"Turkey Banned 53,000 Foreign Fighters So Far: Erdoğan," *Hürriyet Daily News*, July 6, 2017.

"Turkey Calls on NATO to 'Not Cover Up' Scandal," *Hürriyet Daily News*, November 20 2017.

"Turkey Confirms German MPs Will Visit Troops in Konya Under NATO Flag," *Hürriyet Daily News*, August 10, 2017.

"Turkey Disapproves of Iran's 'Persian Expansionism': Erdoğan," *Hürriyet Daily News*, June 16, 2017.

"Turkey Discusses Joint Weapons Development with Russia," *Middle East Monitor*, May 3, 2017.

"Turkey Does a U-Turn, Imposes Entry Visas on Syrians," *New Arab*, December 29, 2015. As of October 14, 2017: https://www.alaraby.co.uk/english/news/2015/12/29/ turkey-does-a-u-turn-imposes-entry-visas-on-syrians

"Turkey, France Work Closely in Deporting Foreign Fighters," *Daily Sabah*, August 23, 2017.

"Turkey Grants Germany Access to İncirlik After Meeting 'Expectations,'" *Rudaw*, September 8, 2016.

"Turkey Has Shelved Turkish Stream Gas Pipeline Project, Says President Erdoğan," *Hürriyet Daily News*, December 5, 2015.

"Turkey 'Neutralized' over 2,000 Terrorists in One Year," *Yeni Şafak*, December 27, 2017. As of January 14, 2018: https://www.yenisafak.com/en/news/turkey-neutralized-over-2000-terrorists-in-one-year-2911471

"Turkey Not 'Lonely' but Dares to Do So for Its Values and Principles, Says PM Adviser," *Hürriyet Daily News*, August 26, 2013.

"Turkey out of Migrant Deal If EU Fails on Visa-Free Travel: Cavusoglu," *Deutsche Welle*, July 31, 2016.

"Turkey Processing Citizenship for 50,000 Syrians," *Daily Sabah*, September 23, 2017.

Turkey Purge, homepage, undated. As of July 1, 2018:
https://turkeypurge.com

"Turkey Referendum: The Numbers That Tell the Story," BBC News, April 17, 2017. As of March 28, 2019:
http://www.bbc.com/news/world-europe-39619354

"Turkey Remands in Custody 118 Soldiers over Suspected FETÖ Links," *Hürriyet Daily News*, December 18, 2018.

"Turkey, Russia Steps 'May Influence Middle East,'" *Hürriyet Daily News*, May 3, 2017.

"Turkey Seeks Advanced S-400 Anti-Air Missiles from Russia," Military.com, May 22, 2017. As of October 22, 2017:
https://www.military.com/defensetech/2017/05/11/
turkey-seeks-advanced-s-400-anti-air-missiles-russia

"Turkey Takes Pragmatic Approach to International Peacekeeping," *World Politics Review*, January 20, 2015.

"Turkey's Defence Sector to Boost Exports as It Transitions from Arms Procurement to Manufacture and Sale," in Oxford Business Group, *The Report: Turkey 2015*, London, 2016. As of January 15, 2018:
https://www.oxfordbusinessgroup.com/analysis/
turkeys-defence-sector-boost-exports-it-transitions-arms-procurement-manufacture-and-sale

"Turkey's Economy Is One of the World's Fastest Growing; But for How Long?" *The Economist*, January 4, 2018.

"Turkey's Elections Explained in 100 and 500 Words," BBC News, June 25, 2018. As of March 28, 2019:
https://www.bbc.com/news/world-europe-44562011

"Turkey's First Nuclear Power Plant Akkuyu to Be Operational by 2023," *Daily Sabah*, February 3, 2017.

"Turkey's Mediation in Nagorno-Karabakh Peace Process Ruled Out—Armenian MP," *Tert*, November 8, 2016. As of January 21, 2018:
http://www.tert.am/en/news/2016/08/11/bekaryan/2102602

"Turkey's New Top Soldier Appointed by First Presidential Decree," *Hürriyet Daily News*, July 10, 2018.

"Turkey's Spy Agency Has Captured 80 FETÖ-Linked Suspects from 18 Countries: Bozdağ," *Hürriyet Daily News*, April 5, 2018.

"Turkey's Supreme Election Board Announces Final Results in June 24 Elections," *Daily Sabah*, July 4, 2018.

"Turkish Businesspeople Seek Trade Boost with Israel," *Hürriyet Daily News*, November 27, 2017.

"Turkish Contractors Hopeful as Russia Relaxes Sanctions," *Hürriyet Daily News*, June 2, 2017.

Turkish Cooperation and Coordination Agency, "About Us," webpage, undated. As of March 21, 2018:
http://www.tika.gov.tr/en/page/about_us-14650

———, *Turkish Development Assistance Report 2015*, Ankara, 2015. As of December 19, 2017:
http://www.tika.gov.tr/upload/2017/YAYINLAR/TKYR%202015%20ENG/KALKINMA%20.pdf

"Turkish FM: No Danger to Israel-Turkey Relations," *Arutz Sheva*, January 7, 2018.

"Turkish Foreign Ministry Voices Solidarity with TIKA Worker Arrested by Israel," *Hürriyet Daily News*, March 22, 2017.

"Turkish General Staff to Recruit over 40,000 Personnel as Compensation for Post-Coup Attempt Dismissals," *Hürriyet Daily News*, January 2, 2018.

"Turkish Gov't Introduces New Decree Law to Overhaul Army," *Hürriyet Daily News*, July 31, 2016.

"Turkish-Israeli Economic, Trade Ties Expected to Soar After Deal," *Hürriyet Daily News*, June 27, 2016.

"Turkish-Israeli Relations: An Axial Shift?" *Stratfor*, March 25, 2004. As of May 3, 2018: https://www.stratfor.com/analysis/turkish-israeli-relations-axial-shift

"Turkish Military Dismissed 16,540 Personnel Since Coup Attempt," *Hürriyet Daily News*, April 29, 2019.

"Turkish Min. Criticizes EU 'Double Standards' on PKK," *World Bulletin*, November 7, 2016. As of November 24, 2017: http://www.worldbulletin.net/turkey/179757/turkish-min-criticizes-eu-double-standards-on-pkk

"Turkish Parliament Debates Controversial New Constitution," *The Guardian*, January 9, 2017.

"Turkish Parliament Passes Controversial Law on Election Alliances amid Brawl," *Hürriyet Daily News*, March 13, 2018.

Tusk, Donald, Jean-Claude Juncker, and Jens Stoltenberg, "Joint Declaration by the President of the European Council, the President of the European Commission, and the Secretary General of the North Atlantic Treaty Organization," press release, North Atlantic Treaty Organization, July 8, 2016. As of November 21, 2017: http://www.nato.int/cps/en/natohq/official_texts_133163.htm

Tuysuz, Gul, and Sabrina Tavernise, "Top Generals Quit in Group, Stunning Turks," *New York Times*, July 29, 2011.

Tüzün, Sezgin, *Lost and Regained AKP Votes and the Ways for Plebiscite Constructed Through the State of Emergency*, London: Research Turkey, 2017.

Udasin, Sharon, "Turkish Industrial Leaders Call for Trade Increase with Israel," *Jerusalem Post*, May 16, 2017.

Uğurlu, Sibel, "Turkey's Opposition MHP Unveils Election Manifesto," Anadolu Agency, May 5, 2018.

Ulgen, Sinan, "Get Ready for a More Aggressive Turkey," *Foreign Policy*, July 2, 2018.

Ulutaş, Ufuk, *Turkey-Israel: A Fluctuating Alliance*, Ankara: Foundation for Political, Economic and Social Research, Policy Brief No. 42, January 4, 2010. As of October 22, 2017: http://setadc.org/wp-content/uploads/2015/05/SETA_Policy_Brief_No_42_Turkey_Israel_Fluctuating_Ufuk_Ulutas.pdf

Ünal, Ali, "Turkey Ends Tutelage by Military with Gendarmerie Reform," *Daily Sabah*, March 10, 2015.

———, "TRT World Ceo Ibrahim Eren: We Will Tell the Truth, Even If It Is Inconvenient or Disturbing," *Daily Sabah*, November 20, 2016.

United Nations High Commissioner for Refugees, "Refugees & Migrants Sea Arrivals in Europe," monthly data update, Regional Bureau Europe, August 2016. As of January 15, 2018: https://reliefweb.int/sites/reliefweb.int/files/resources/20160928_Monthly_Arrivals_to_Greece_Italy_Spain_Jan_Aug_2016.pdf

————, "Returns from Greece to Turkey," Greece, October 6, 2017a. As of March 21, 2018: https://data2.unhcr.org/fr/documents/download/60306

————, "Operational Portal, Refugee Situations: Mediterranean Situation," web tool, October 29, 2017b. As of January 15, 2018: https://data2.unhcr.org/en/situations/mediterranean/location/5179

"Update—Turkey: Opposition Leader Slams NATO Dig at Defense Buy," *Haberler*, October 31, 2017. As of January 21, 2018: https://en.haberler.com/update-turkey-opposition-leader-slams-nato-dig-at-1124421/

"Update 1—Turkey's 2017 Tourism Revenues Jump as Russians Return," Reuters, January 31, 2018.

Uras, Umut, "Ex-Turkish Minister Meral Aksener Launches New Party," *Al Jazeera*, October 26, 2017.

U.S. Energy Information Administration, *Country Analysis Brief: Turkey*, Washington, D.C., February 2, 2017. As of November 22, 2017: https://www.eia.gov/beta/international/analysis_includes/countries_long/Turkey/turkey.pdf

"US to Stop Arming Anti-IS Syrian Kurdish YPG Militia—Turkey," BBC News, November 25, 2017.

Vaez, Ali, "Turkey and Iran's Dangerous Collision Course," *New York Times*, December 18, 2016.

Vladimirov, Victor, and Taras Burnos, "Poll: Russians See US, Ukraine, Turkey as Top 3 Enemies," Voice of America, June 3, 2016.

von Schwerin, Ulrich, "Is Turkey's AKP Showing Goodwill Towards Gulen Sympathizers Within the Party?" *Deutsche Welle*, June 16, 2017.

Weiss, Andrew S., F. Stephen Larrabee, James T. Bartis, and Camille A. Sawak, *Promoting International Energy Security*, Vol. 2: *Turkey and the Caspian*, Santa Monica, Calif.: RAND Corporation, TR-1144/2-AF, 2012. As of November 22, 2017: https://www.rand.org/pubs/technical_reports/TR1144z2.html

Weiss, Michael, "Turkish TV Depicts IDF as Bloodthirsty," *Tablet*, October 15, 2009. As of November 14, 2017: http://www.tabletmag.com/scroll/18437/turkish-tv-depicts-idf-as-bloodthirsty

Whitaker, Joel, and Anand Varghese, "The Tigris-Euphrates River Basin: A Science Diplomacy Opportunity," Washington, D.C.: United States Institute of Peace, Peace Brief 20, April 22, 2010.

White House, *National Security Strategy of the United States of America*, Washington, D.C., December 2017.

Williams, Lauren, "Turkey's AKP Power Struggle Comes to a Boil," *Al Jazeera*, August 26, 2014.

Wintour, Patrick, "Erdogan Says US Is Creating 'Terrorist Army' in Syria," *Irish Times*, January 15, 2018.

World Integrated Trade Solution, "Turkey Exports, Imports and Trade Balance by Country and Region 2012," web tool, undated. As of January 20, 2018: https://wits.worldbank.org/CountryProfile/en/Country/TUR/Year/2012/TradeFlow/EXPIMP

Yackley, Ayla Jean, "One Year into Crackdown, Turkey's Pro-Kurdish Opposition Battered but Defiant," *Al-Monitor*, November 6, 2017a.

————, "Trial of Turkey's Opposition Leader Starts Without Him in Court," *Al-Monitor*, December 8, 2017b.

————, "Former Turkish President Rules Himself Out of Election," *Financial Times*, April 28, 2018.

Yashar, Ari, "Turkey Wants Normalization to Buy Israeli Weapons," *Arutz Sheva*, December 24, 2015.

Yavuz, M. Hakan, *Islamic Political Identity in Turkey*, Oxford, United Kingdom: Oxford University Press, 2003.

Yeğen, Mesut, *The Kurdish Peace Process in Turkey: Genesis, Evolution and Prospects*, Istanbul: Stiftung Mercator, Istituto Affari Internazionali, and Istanbul Policy Center, Global Turkey in Europe Working Paper 11, May 2015. As of January 21, 2018: http://www.iai.it/sites/default/files/gte_wp_11.pdf

Yetkin, Murat, "İnce Brings a New Style to Turkish Politics," *Hürriyet Daily News*, June 30, 2018.

Yinanç, Barçın, "Turkey's New Foreign Policy Item: FETÖ Diaspora," *Hürriyet Daily News*, August 11, 2016.

———, "What Will Happen to Syrian Refugees After Turkey's Election?" *Hürriyet Daily News*, June 21, 2018.

Zaman, Amberin, "The Iraqi Kurds' Waning Love Affair with Turkey," *Al-Monitor*, September 1, 2015.

———, "Iraqi Kurds Step into Ankara-Baghdad Row," *Al-Monitor*, October 6, 2016a.

———, "KRG PM: Talk of Iraqi Kurdish Independence Red Line for Iran, but Not Turkey," *Al-Monitor*, December 23, 2016b.

———, "Are Hit Squads About to Take Aim at Turkey's Dissidents Abroad?" *Al-Monitor*, December 20, 2017.

Zanotti, Jim, and Clayton Thomas, *Turkey: Background and U.S. Relations*, Washington, D.C.: Congressional Research Service, R41368, August 26, 2016.

Zeybekci, Nihat, "Turkey Deserves a Better EU Trade Deal," *Bloomberg*, April 12, 2017.

Zucchino, David, "Iraqi Forces Retake All Oil Fields in Disputed Areas as Kurds Retreat," *New York Times*, October 17, 2017.